CRAFTING DEMOCRACY

CRAFTING DEMOCRACY

HOW NOVGOROD HAS COPED WITH RAPID SOCIAL CHANGE

NICOLAI N. PETRO

CORNELL UNIVERSITY PRESS
ITHACA AND LONDON

First published 2004 by Cornell University Press

Library of Congress Cataloging-in-Publication Data

Petro, Nicolai N.
   Crafting democracy : how Novgorod has coped with rapid social change / Nicolai N. Petro.
      p.   cm.
   Includes bibliographical references and index.
   ISBN 0-8014-4294-X (cloth : alk. paper)
      1. Local government–Russia (Federation)–Novgorod.
2. Democracy–Russia (Federation)–Novgorod.   3. Social change–Russia (Federation)–Novgorod.   I. Title.

   JS6117.9.N675P48   2004
   320.947'22–dc22

                                    2004007164

Printed in the United States of America

Design by Scott Levine

Cornell University Press strives to use environmentally responsible suppliers and materials to the fullest extent possible in the publishing of its books. Such materials include vegetable-based, low-VOC inks and acid-free papers that are recycled, totally chlorine-free, or partly composed of nonwood fibers. For further information, visit our website at www.cornellpress.cornell.edu.

Cloth printing   10 9 8 7 6 5 4 3 2 1

Спокойной и уверенной любови
Не превозмочь мне к этой стороне.
Ведь капелька новгородской крови
Во мне, как льдинка в пенистом вине

A calm and confident love for this land
I will never overcome.
A tiny drop of Novgorod blood
Is in me, like a shard of ice in frothy wine.

ANNA AKHMATOVA
an untitled poem from her collection *Belaya staya* (1917)

CONTENTS

List of Figures and Tables   ix

Acknowledgments   xi

Note on Style   xiii

Introduction   1

PART I. SHIFTING THE FOCUS

1. Defining Democracy   7

   The Many Meanings of Democracy   7

   From Authoritarianism to Democratic Transition   9

   From Transition to Democratic Consolidation   11

   From Consolidation to Mature Democracy   13

   The Case for Regional Democratic Development   16

   Democratization Theory in Disarray   20

2. Democratic Development in Russia: The Novgorod Model   22

   A New Constitutional Order   24

   Economic Success   34

   Voluntary Associations   45

3. How We Missed Novgorod's Democratic Consolidation   57

   Criticisms of Novgorod as a Democratic Model   57

   The Most Common Failures of Democratization Theories   67

   Explaining Away the Differences between Novgorod and Pskov   81

   How Current Democratic Theory Overlooks Democracy   90

CONTENTS

PART II. CULTURE, MYTH, AND SYMBOLS

4. Three Keys to Understanding Rapid Social Change   95

    What Works and What Doesn't When Studying Transition   96

    Why Cultural Analysis Is Best for the Study of Transition   98

    What is Missing from Cultural Analysis?   105

    Should There Be a Metafield of Symbolic Politics?   122

5. Novgorod in Russia's Memory   126

    The Republic of St. Sophia   129

    Novgorod's Enduring Message of Freedom   134

    The Image of Novgorod in the Twentieth Century   138

6. Symbols at Work   146

    Activating the Novgorod Myth   146

    How Symbols Promoted Democratic Consolidation in Novgorod   159

    Symbols and Myths as Political Resources Elsewhere in Russia 164

    How Different Is Russia?   176

    The Variety and Power of Symbols   179

7. Crafting Democracy   181

    The Russian Idea versus Regional Myths   184

    What Symbols Can Do for Democratic Development   187

    The Cultural Audit   189

    Training for a New Type of Development   193

    Opportunities and Pitfalls   197

Notes   203

Index   245

FIGURES AND TABLES

FIGURES

2.1. Growth of territorial housing fellowships in Novgorod the   27
Great, 1997–2002

2.2. Trust in public institutions in the Novgorod Region, 1995–1999   33

2.3. Annual foreign direct investment in the Novgorod Region,
1993–2003   36

2.4. Annual donations to the "Christmas Marathon," 1993–2003   39

2.5. Poverty trends in the Novgorod Region, 1995–2002   44

2.6. Civic and voluntary associations registered in the Novgorod   52
Region, 1991–2002

2.7. Registered political parties and associations in the Novgorod   55
Region, 1994–2001

3.1. Monetary income per capita for the Novgorod and Pskov   83
Regions, 1985–2000

3.2. Percentage living below poverty level in the Novgorod and   84
Pskov Regions, 1997–2002

3.3. Industrial production in the Novgorod and Pskov Regions,   85
1990–2000

3.4. Percentage of Novgorod and Pskov regional budgets provided   88
by federal subsidies, 1994–2001

3.5. FDI in the Novgorod and Pskov Regions, 1995–2000   89

6.1. Elite values compared to popular values in the Novgorod   161
Region, July 1999

6.2. Increased popular interest in Novgorodica, 1980–2000   163

TABLES

2.1. Matrix for measuring progress toward democratization in Novgorod   24

2.2. Anticipated election participation in Novgorod, 1995–1999   34

2.3. FDI inflows among transition economies of Central and Eastern Europe, 1996–2000   37

2.4. Most numerous types of voluntary associations in the Novgorod Region, 1997 and 2001   50

2.5. Most rapidly growing types of voluntary associations in the Novgorod Region, 1997 through 2001   53

3.1. Selected sayings of Governor Prusak   63

3.2. Comparative indicators for the Novgorod and Pskov Regions   82

3.3. Percentage division of basic factory assets in the Novgorod and Pskov Regions   87

7.1. Two development paradigms   196

ACKNOWLEDGMENTS

It would take an entire volume to properly thank the scores of people who have so enriched my life and that of my family in Novgorod. I relied heavily on the wonderful staff of the municipal research center Dialog, the hub of the city's political and economic life. Its director, Alexander V. Zhukovsky, proved to be an indispensable guide to the intricacies of the region's politics and arranged for me to serve as adviser to the mayor on civic affairs in 2001. In the regional administration, I am equally indebted to Igor V. Verkhodanov, a key adviser to both the first deputy governor and the speaker of the Novgorod Regional Duma. He proved an invaluable source of contacts, information, and historical knowledge about the Novgorod Region.

My first contact with the city came in 1996, thanks to a Fulbright award to lecture for a year at Novgorod State University. Those ties were subsequently deepened thanks to two university affiliations agreements between the University of Rhode Island and Novgorod State University funded by the United States Information Agency, and a research grant from the National Council for Eurasian and East European Research.

Among the many memorable university colleagues, I owe a special debt of gratitude to Anatoly P. Donchenko, the dean of the university's Humanities Institute; Valery N. Zelenin, the university's vice president for international relations and an extraordinary ambassador for the region; Valery P. Bolshakov, the founding director of the Novgorod Interregional Institute for the Social Sciences; and his successor Sergei V. Devyatkin. Elizabeth N. Kustova, head of the Novgorodica department of the

Novgorod Regional Library and history professors Svetlana Kovarskaya and Vasily F. Andreyev provided valuable clues to local history and legends while the late Vladimir A. Tsalpan helped to unlock the secrets of the State Archives of the Contemporary Political History of the Novgorod Region for me. Without their guidance, I might never have fully appreciated the importance of the key symbols of Novgorod's past.

Over the years I have had the fortune to befriend many people who were active participants in the heady days of the first post-Soviet city and regional administrations, including journalists, human rights activists, and former political officials. Space precludes me from naming them all, but our lengthy discussions formed the basis for chapter 6.

As this project evolved, many Western scholars have shared with me the benefits of their criticism. I was able to present preliminary findings at two important conferences on Russian regions, one organized by Cameron Ross at the University of Dundee in Scotland, and another by Stephanie Harter at the Federal Institute for East European and International Studies in Germany. A yearlong workshop on Russian regions, organized by the Kennan Institute for Advanced Russian Studies, proved especially fruitful, as every few months participants gathered to compare notes about a wide variety of regions. Subsequent invitations to speak at St. Antony's College, Oxford, Cornell University, Rutgers University, the Watson Institute at Brown University, and the Davis Center at Harvard University, allowed me to work out the kinks in the manuscript.

I also wish to acknowledge my intellectual debt to the late Harry Eckstein, who invited me to give my first talk about Novgorod at the University of California at Irvine's Center for the Study of Democracy shortly after I arrived back from Russia in 1997. He strongly encouraged me to pursue the idea that Novgorod could indeed be a distinctive model of democratic development, pointed out the cultural significance of the city's historical ties to the Hanseatic League, and suggested that new "national ideas" often originate not in the capital but at the periphery. Though his untimely death deprived me of the benefits of his critique, I was infected by his excitement about the region's potential as a test case of democratic theory and hope that my efforts serve as a small testament to his enduring intellectual legacy.

Finally, I dedicate this book to my wife Allison, without whom nothing is possible, and to our many friends in Novgorod who, by sharing their lives and their stories, helped us to appreciate its magic.

NOTE ON STYLE

I have followed the transliteration system of the Library of Congress, with some minor exceptions. Both hard and soft signs have been omitted. When a soft sign appears in the middle of a word preceded by a vowel, however, it has been replaced by a *y*. The letters ю and я are transliterated as *yu* and *ya*. Otherwise, established English usage has taken precedence in the spelling of common Russian words and proper names. When citing translations and quoting from them, I have preserved the original transliteration. All other translations are my own.

CRAFTING DEMOCRACY

INTRODUCTION

In 1996 the J. William Fulbright Scholarship Board afforded me an opportunity to teach comparative politics in Russia. My family and I chose to spend our Fulbright year in Novgorod the Great (Veliky Novgorod), the capital city of a sparsely populated region about the size of West Virginia, best known for its folklore and medieval churches.[1] Two-thirds of the way from Moscow to St. Petersburg, this ancient town in Russia's heartland seemed like the ideal place to immerse ourselves in the country's culture and history. Although I specialize in contemporary Russian politics, like most scholars I actually knew very little about life outside of Moscow or St. Petersburg. We researched the area as best we could, but found that most information about the region was decades out of date, so we hardened ourselves to the prospect of facing numerous difficulties adjusting to daily life there.

After reading scores of apocalyptic press accounts about Russia's imminent collapse, however, the last thing we expected to find was an oasis of social and economic tranquility. Even in 1996 there were almost none of the chronic delays in government pension and salary payments that plagued other regions, and the local elite seemed to have a common agenda that the national elite clearly still lacked.

By the end of our stay, I had gathered enough statistical evidence to confirm that something very unusual was indeed going on. Between 1995 and 1998, while Russia's Gross Domestic Product was declining by 2.7 percent annually, Novgorod's regional domestic product grew by 3.8 percent annually.[2] Since then industrial production in the region has continued to grow at twice the Russian average, and official unemployment hovers at 1 percent.[3] Average monthly wages in the region have risen spectacularly (17.8 percent in 2001 and 19 percent in 2002 *after* inflation), while the number of families living below the poverty line has dropped to its lowest level in a decade.[4] During the latter half of the 1990s, foreign investors, who generally shunned the Russian countryside, poured money into this region at a per capita rate second only to Moscow, creating almost twenty thousand new local jobs in the process. Today, more than a quarter of the region's factory workers are employed by foreign companies, and are paid, on average, three times more than their domestic counterparts.[5]

Novgorod has been a political trailblazer as well. While local self-government has been a dead letter in the rest of Russia, Novgorod enacted its own legislation on local self-government in 1994 and became the first region in Russia to hold elections for every level of government, from village elder to governor. Whereas the growth of nongovernmental organizations in Russia peaked in the late 1990s, the Novgorod region has continued to register scores of new civic organizations annually, reaching a level of per capita civic activism and private entrepreneurship that rivals areas of Western Europe.[6]

By the end of the 1990s a few journalists and scholars had begun to notice that peculiar things were happening in Novgorod. While lavish in their praise of the "Novgorod model," however, none could venture any explanation for such an unexpected transformation in a region that *Ekspert* magazine rated sixty-third out of Russia's eighty-nine regions in investment potential.[7] Analysts seemed to be missing something crucial about the very earliest stages of democratic development, something that set Novgorod apart from its neighbors.

This book is my attempt to identify that difference and explain its significance for democratic development. It is divided into two parts. The first part identifies the weaknesses of current approaches to democratization and explains how analysts easily overlooked evidence of democratic development in Novgorod. In chapter 1 I sift through the many conflicting definitions of democratic development, settling on "democratic consolidation" as the standard to apply to Novgorod because it is the most demanding. I argue that shifting the focus of democratization from the nation-state to the regional level improves the reliability of evidence gathered in support of democratic consolidation.

I present this evidence in chapter 2, where I measure Novgorod's success across three well-established categories of democratic development: the construction of a new constitutional order, the level of economic development, and the quality and quantity of voluntary associations. To minimize the problem of subjective judgment, I apply three additional measures of progress within each of these categories: (a) behavioral changes within the elite; (b) structural changes in government; and (c) attitudinal changes among the populace. Presenting the evidence in this way allows the reader to track the region's progress along multiple measures and shows that, by any measure chosen, democratic consolidation is well under way in Novgorod.

In chapter 3 I look at several popular explanations for regional differences in Russia and find that none of them explains Novgorod's success or, for that matter, the equally dramatic political and economic stagnation of Novgorod's neighbor, Pskov. This conceptual failure is rooted in the reluctance of development analysts to take regional cultural identity seriously and suggests that we need an approach that values regional identity on its own terms, rather than simply as a fraction of national identity.

In the second part of my book I suggest that culturally based approaches do just that and, therefore, provide a better explanation of democratic development. I end by looking at how the Novgorod elite used local myths and symbols to manage rapid social change in the region.

In chapter 4 I explain why cultural analysis is ideally suited to understanding both the emergence of regional identity and the roots of social change. During periods of social turmoil, when institutions collapse and calculations of benefit lose their predictive value, people's core beliefs are undermined. Seeking to restore stability, people turn to what is most familiar to them—local cultural traditions. These traditions are generally overlooked as resources for political transition because their impact on politics is hard to measure. The study of key cultural symbols, however, allows us to trace the impact of culture during social and political transitions. After reviewing the rich tradition of symbolic studies in the social sciences, I suggest that it can be even further refined to provide the basis of a theory that explains rapid social and political changes. In chapter 5 I identify Novgorod's key cultural symbols and their political meaning, and then trace their influence on the policies and attitudes of the past decade.

In chapter 6 I show how Novgorod's elite used the key symbols of Novgorod's past to create an environment receptive to economic and political reforms. By systematically contrasting Novgorod's heritage as a medieval trade center and cradle of Russian democracy to Moscow's heritage of political and economic centralization, they redefined reform as a return to the values of a better and more prosperous Russian past. Embracing a positive political myth rooted in Russia's past eased the shock of cultural discontinuity, broadened the social constituency in favor of reforms, and contributed to much higher levels of confidence in local government. The result is the remarkable level of economic and democratic development the region displays today.

Such a finding has obvious implications for democratic assistance (and not only in Russia). In the concluding chapter, therefore, I discuss the need for a new, culturally based approach to democratic assistance. Novgorod is an excellent test case because it is a poor region in a country widely considered to be totally lacking in democratic traditions. Its unexpected success suggests that democratic assistance programs that graft key cultural symbols onto reform initiatives are likely to yield results faster than programs that give priority to exclusively Western-style institutions and training programs. Although the latter are indispensable for long-term democratic stability, too early an emphasis on such cultural "imports" typically results in new democratic institutions being labeled as foreign, thus heightening public animosity to reform.

To avoid any misunderstanding, let me say at the outset that I do not regard Novgorod as a mature democracy. Its significant accomplishments, however, have received far too little recognition, in part because current democratization strategies focus too much on structural change and not enough on the conditions needed to make these changes stick. For the rule of law, free markets, and fair elections to gain broad public support, they must *first* make sense within the local cultural tradition. The conscious use of symbols in crafting and implementing reforms helps people make that connection.

It is my hope that the inspiring story of Novgorod's regional democratic development will encourage scholars and practitioners to look more carefully at the very earliest stages of democratic transition so as to appreciate both the potential for democracy that is inherent in every culture and the tools that can unlock it.

PART I

SHIFTING THE FOCUS

CHAPTER 1

DEFINING DEMOCRACY

THE MANY MEANINGS OF DEMOCRACY

As one of the oldest forms of government, democracy has often been defined as much by what it is not as by what it is. Authors of antiquity often contrasted democracy—the authority of the "common people"—to tyranny—the illegitimate rule of a single individual. For Aristotle, however, a democracy was more than simply the mathematical expression of the majority. It was where the free-born and poor could share in the control of government.[1] A certain equity was presumed essential to democratic governance. Thus, early on two distinct strands emerge in democratic discourse. One stresses the opportunity for broad popular participation in political life, while the other argues that a true democracy must create not only the opportunity of a political life but also greater social equality. These two strands lead to very different ways of measuring democracy.

One of the first modern writers to attempt to find a way through this theoretical thicket was Joseph Schumpeter. Schumpeter defined democracy as "that institutional arrangement for arriving at political decisions in which individuals acquire the power to decide by means of a competitive struggle for the people's votes."[2] This simple formula, which equates democracy with electoral competition, has the great advantage of being based on an unequivocal act—voting.

Schumpeter influenced many subsequent democratic theorists including, most notably, Seymour Martin Lipset, who modified Schumpeter's

7

definition slightly to underscore the importance of stable political institutions. Democracy for Lipset is "a political system which supplies regular constitutional opportunities for changing the governing of officials and a social mechanism which permits the largest possible part of the population to influence major decisions by choosing among contenders for political office."[3] Lipset is probably best known for arguing that there is a strong correlation between democracy and economic development.[4] The intensity of distributional conflicts within a society, he surmised, was bound to lessen with higher levels of income. This postulate has since become widely accepted, though debate still rages over whether it is democracy that leads to economic development, or vice versa.[5]

Another widely cited democratic theorist of modern times, Robert Dahl, identified three distinct types of democratic regimes: Madisonian, populist, and polyarchal. Madisonian democracies merely constrain the rights of majorities, populist democracies stress popular sovereignty and equality, while polyarchies focus on the social prerequisites of democratic order. Because polyarchies exhibit a higher degree of political contestation and inclusiveness, Dahl argued that they represent a more advanced form of democracy.[6]

These three authors are among the most widely cited representatives of what I call the "minimalist approach" to defining democracy. Beyond regular voting, minimalists tend to regard only economic success as important to democracy, arguing that popular support for government rests largely on the effective delivery of state services. The minimalist approach has the advantage of drawing a clear line between old and new regimes by applying a few simple criteria.

The minimalist approach remained popular throughout the 1980s, but as the number of democracies began to swell, the very simplicity that had once made it so appealing became suspect. For one thing, it seemed ill-advised to simply equate democracy with democratic procedures. This placed advanced democracies with extensive traditions of civic control over government on an equal footing with countries that had only fledgling institutions and tenuous electoral procedures. Surely, critics argued, the qualitative differences between such regimes meant more than their procedural similarities.

Minimalist definitions had made it relatively easy to quantify democratic progress, and this, in turn, had led to an intoxicating optimism about the prospects of democracy worldwide, indelibly associated with Francis Fukuyama's article "The End of History."[7] But as the Latin American democracies that epitomized the "Third Wave" continued to display many authoritarian characteristics, despite having regular elections, that optimism slowly began to fade. Minimalists, it turned out, had no language with which to describe stable, but still incomplete, democracies.

As more and more nations struggled to make the transition to democracy, democratic theorists tried to come up with definitions that distinguished between incipient and more mature democracies. One study identified more than 550 definitional subtypes of democracy![8] This blizzard of definitions has forever buried the comfortable notion that democracy can be characterized as a specific set of conditions and has, instead, taught analysts to think of democracy as a process that moves through phases: first, from the end of authoritarian rule to democratic transition; second, from transition to democratic consolidation; and finally, from democratic consolidation to mature democracy.

In describing the first phase scholars often continue to rely on minimal definitions. This allows them to draw a clear distinction between the previous regime and its successor. During the second and third phases, however, scholars now look for more exacting measures by which to measure democratic development. In theory, distinguishing democratic transition from democratic consolidation should allow analysts to isolate the factors that are common to democratic development in all societies, without setting the standard so high that it excludes all but a handful of nations. As we shall see, however, these efforts have been only partly successful.

FROM AUTHORITARIANISM TO DEMOCRATIC TRANSITION

The first and most unambiguous phase of democratization is the end of authoritarian rule. It is the easiest to define because it begins with the end of a particular dictator's reign. In Chile this date is the election in 1989 of Patricio Aylwin to the presidency, formally ending the dictatorship of General Augusto Pinochet. In Poland it is the election in 1990 of Solidarity leader Lech Walesa to the presidency. In Spain democratic transition began in 1975, after the death of General Francisco Franco. And in Russia it began after the resignation of Mikhail Gorbachev on December 25, 1991.

Dating the end of an authoritarian regime generally arouses little controversy. Far more ink has been spilled trying to identify precisely what is meant by "democratic transition." Some scholars use it to describe the full sweep of transition from authoritarian rule to mature democracy, while others use it only to refer to the period from the end of the preceding regime to the onset of democratic consolidation. Because the former is simply synonymous with democratization, we shall be referring here only to the second usage.

The first thing to clarify is where transition ends and how we can distinguish it from consolidation. For some, transition involves the creation of new democratic institutions, while consolidation involves the legitimization of those institutions and the internalization of democratic behavioral norms.[9] The key characteristic of transition then becomes the breakdown of old institutions and their replacement with new ones. As Doh Chull Shin puts it, "Transition . . . is considered to have ended when a new democracy has promulgated a new constitution and held free elections for political leaders with little barrier to mass participation."[10]

Others, however, argue that it is uncertainty about the prospects of democratic continuity that distinguishes transitional from consolidated democracies.[11] This approach suggests that a certain social consensus in favor of new institutions must exist as a prerequisite to consolidation. As Giuseppe Di Palma writes, "When agreement on democratic rules is successfully reached, the transition is essentially over."[12] Attempting to bridge this gap, Juan Linz and Alfred Stepan argue:

> A democratic transition is complete when sufficient agreement has been reached about political procedures to produce an elected government, when a government comes to power that is the direct result of a free and popular vote, when this government de facto has the authority to generate new policies, and when the executive, legislative and judicial power generated by the new democracy does have to share power with other bodies *de jure*.[13]

It is also often argued that regimes in transition must progress fairly rapidly from authoritarianism to consolidation or risk "deconsolidating." This is because, as social tensions rise so does the temptation to revert to past practices.[14] Many analysts therefore argue that rapid movement forward in the creation of new institutions is imperative for both social stability and democracy. As Guillermo O'Donnell has persuasively demonstrated, however, this has often not been the case in Latin America. Having thrown off previous dictators and adopted the basic characteristics of Dahl's polyarchies, many Latin American regimes have stubbornly refused to evolve into fully representative, institutionalized democratic regimes.[15] They are, in essence, stuck in democratic transition.

Some theorists insist that such "delegative democracies" are unstable because they never develop a strict distinction between the public and private spheres. The fact that they survive for decades, however, suggests otherwise. To O'Donnell this stability indicates that democratic equilibrium can result not only from the creation of new, formal democratic institutions but also from a proliferation of informal institutions. When we say that such societies lack democratic institutions, he suggests, what we really should be saying is that their institutions are not necessarily the same ones we find in Western democracies.[16]

This concept becomes important as we try to understand what democratization means in Novgorod, for it suggests a wide array of possible definitions for democratic consolidation. Second, O'Donnell's analysis calls into question the unique role accorded to formal institutions and challenges the guiding assumption of many development practitioners that the creation of democratic institutions and procedures can, in and of itself, promote the social consensus needed for stable democracy. Finally, as if this weren't enough, he challenges one of the most important unspoken assumptions of modern democratization theory—the idea that all democracies exhibit certain universal characteristics that can be objectively measured. Our image of democracy, he suggests, is really a mental construct rooted in the culture and history of Western Europe and North America. It can therefore easily overlook alternate patterns of democratic development.

O'Donnell seems to suggest that the best theorists can hope for is a minimal definition of democracy. Attempts at further refinement run the risk of imposing inappropriate values and institutions on other cultures. These risks become apparent when we examine definitions of democratic consolidation.

FROM TRANSITION TO DEMOCRATIC CONSOLIDATION

This "second transition," as O'Donnell calls it, reflects society's movement from a democratically elected government to an institutionalized democratic regime.[17] At this point, in Linz's widely cited definition, "none of the major political actors, parties, or organized interests, forces, or institutions consider that there is any alternative to democratic processes to gain power. . . . To put it simply, democracy must be seen as 'the only game in town' "[18] This definition makes democratic consolidation dependent on the emergence of a new social consensus in which democracy becomes "routinized and deeply internalized in social, institutional, and even psychological life."[19]

Other definitions of consolidation emphasize the absence of antisystem actors and the loyalty of major political forces to the regime.[20] But while many scholars argue that profound social and cultural changes need to take place before democratic consolidation can occur, Philippe Schmitter views such changes as the result, rather than the cause, of specific structural changes in government.[21] Richard Gunther and his colleagues even go so far as to say that the absence of fundamental disputes among significant political groups is more important to democratic consolidation than support for abstract democratic values.[22]

In sum, the desire to define democratic consolidation in a way that encompasses political culture, political structure, and political behavior has led to another alarming proliferation of criteria. Mark Gasiorowski and Timothy Power identify consolidated democracies as ones that hold a second national election for chief executive, survive an "unambiguous change in the partisan character of the executive branch," and "simply survive for an appropriate period of time"—twelve years, to be precise, which conveniently coincides with three legislative sessions.[23]

For Larry Diamond the designation "liberal democracy" should be bestowed only on regimes that add to minimalist features the absence of "reserved domains" of power, horizontal accountability that constrains the power of the executive, and extensive provisions for political and civic pluralism.[24] For David Becker, however, it must also include the governing institutions that constitute a "moderate state," including constraints forged by the legal system, and a civil society that enjoys rights to free expression and association on all issues of political import.[25] Richard Gunther lists the following five "tests" to help us distinguish between transitional and consolidated democracy: (1) "alternation in power between former rivals"; (2) "continued widespread support and stability during times of extreme economic hardships"; (3) "successful defeat and punishment of a handful of strategically placed rebels"; (4) "regime stability in the face of a radical restructuring of the party system"; and (5) "the absence of a politically significant antisystem party or social movement."[26]

By contrast, Arturo Valenzuela seeks to shift the emphasis away from what needs to be established to what impediments need to be removed following a democratic transition. For Valenzuela only four impediments really stand in the way of democratic consolidation: nondemocratic "tutelary powers" that oversee the decisions of elected governments; "reserved domains" of policy; electoral systems with egregious biases that minimize the influence of specific sectors of opinion; and the sense among actors and informed publics that the electoral process may not be the only means to renew governments.[27]

In short, while some analysts see democratic transition as a rare window of opportunity that will close all too rapidly unless steps are taken to ensure consolidation, others regard it as the beginning of a natural evolution that will invariably lead society to find its own particular form of democratic consolidation. In the latter view, once transition begins, "countries are doomed to remain democratic almost by default."[28]

For the first group, it is imperative to set up new Western-style institutions as quickly as possible. The second group, on the other hand, takes a more relaxed view of democratization and tends to regard Western assistance as being of only marginal significance. One could almost say that this group insists on new institutions being introduced as *slowly* as possible, so that they have time to adjust to the elements of tradition culture that are needed to ensure popular support. The debate, in a nutshell, is about whether democratic consolidation is best achieved by revolution or by evolution.

This split has enormous implications for how the West assists democratic assistance programs and training, yet democratization theorists have often tried to skirt these by embracing contradictory views. Thus, in a highly regarded volume on democratic consolidation, one group of authors refers to Spain, Greece, Italy, and Portugal as consolidated democracies that "stand in sharp contrast with the great majority" of recently democratized countries, while a few pages later these same countries are described by another group as exhibiting "pervasive feelings of political alienation and cynicism, an intense distrust of elites, and limited legitimacy of parties. . . ."[29] Troubling inconsistencies also arise when trying to reconcile the widely held view that "democracy . . . is about displacing entrenched elites, undermining the powerful, and empowering the powerless," with the view that an elite consensus is "the essential precondition of consolidated democracy."[30]

Serious definitional problems, however, also arise for the proponents of evolutionary democratic development. Here there is a tendency to identify democratic consolidation with longevity, which raises questions about what is specifically democratic about regimes that have simply been around a long time.[31] In much the same vein, identifying the behavioral dimension of democratic consolidation as merely the absence of significant antisystem actors and labeling as "democratic" forces that "do not engage in semiloyal politics" sets the bar very low indeed.[32] The unwillingness of an opposition to challenge the political system might, after all, just as easily stem from a decision to await a better opportunity to challenge the system.

Such contradictions have led some to label the term democratic consolidation "a garbage-can concept, a catch-all concept," so hopelessly compromised that it would be best to abandon it entirely.[33] Yet, those scholars who have done so have not gotten very far. Still nobly striving to distinguish between fledgling and mature democracies, they wind up devising new terminology that mimics the same distinction, whether it be Becker's "moderate state," Diamond's "liberal state," or Gunther's "middle range" criteria.

FROM CONSOLIDATION TO MATURE DEMOCRACY

Some analysts have sought a definition of democratic consolidation by working backward from what a "mature democracy" looks like. One might assume that at least this, the final stage of democratic development, would be easy to define. Here too, however, we find so many contradictory characteristics cited for democratic maturity that the distinction between it and consolidated democracy is hard to pinpoint. The following is a brief review of several features commonly associated with mature democracy.

Formal separation of powers and coherence among government institutions. Most Western European parliamentary democracies have no formal separation of powers, leading John Mueller to conclude that "a government with an overwhelmingly strong executive or legislature is not undemocratic because of that."[34] Giuseppe Di Palma has even argued that a certain degree of "fuzziness and incoherence" among institutions "may give democratic institutions a peculiar value in the eyes of opposing players."[35]

Lack of corruption. Although undesirable, corruption is certainly not incompatible with mature democracy; indeed there are some who suggest that "creative corruption" may play a role in democratic development.[36] Interestingly, the most commonly cited indicator of transnational corruption, by the watchdog group Transparency International, does not measure corruption, but only the perception of corruption, which is largely driven by press coverage. Scholars who have looked at the issue in depth have found no significant correlation between political openness and lack of corruption within the postcommunist region.[37]

Public support for democracy and tolerance of diversity. Although some studies have found dramatic differences in belief systems and support for democratic values among mature and fledgling democracies, others have not.[38] One famous study that compared the attitudes of New Yorkers and Muscovites in the early 1990s unexpectedly found New Yorkers less tolerant of economic inequality, more distrustful of "speculators," and less appreciative of the importance of material incentives.[39]

Despite political and economic instability, many observers have noted that attachment to basic democratic values in Russian society has been remarkably consistent and that the populace is routinely willing to assimilate democratic values faster than the elite is willing to build democratic institutions.[40] Political tolerance also seems to vary widely among mature democracies. When asked, for example, if the government should ban all public protests, 49 percent of Swiss, 52 percent of West Germans, and 60 percent of Austrians agreed that it should.[41] Some surveys in Russia show a higher tolerance for public protest.[42]

Confidence in public officials. Russian governments are both popularly elected and widely distrusted, just as they are in most mature democracies. A 1994 poll showed that only 10 percent of Americans rated the honesty and ethical standards of congressmen as "very high" or "high." A British poll found that 73 percent of Britons thought of their ruling party as "very sleazy and disreputable."[43] Since 1970, indicators of political trust in every Western democracy except Germany have been well below 50 percent.[44]

Private property, a market economy, and the rule of law. Robert Dahl has argued that an advanced market economy is neither "strictly necessary nor sufficient to create a robust democratic culture," and Max Weber dismissed as "completely ridiculous" any attempt to attribute any affinity of advanced capitalism to democracy or freedom ("in *any* meaning of the word").[45]

Finding the relationship between socioeconomic development and democratization to be weak, M. Steven Fish modifies this argument to say that it is not GDP growth but marketization of the economy that correlates positively to democratization.[46] This makes sense because the creation of markets requires a consensus on new rules and reaching agreements, whereas GDP growth may be very unevenly distributed across regions or segments of the population and, hence, lead to increased social tension. Fish's argument is similar to Seymour Martin Lipset's, that it is not wealth per se but the distribution of wealth that is key to political stability.[47] Still, some Western countries display income inequalities rivaling or exceeding those of Russia, yet this does not seem to disqualify them from being considered mature democracies.[48]

This review is not meant to suggest that these features are not desirable but rather to note that their absence in so many countries widely held to be mature democracies makes it difficult to view any of them as essential to democracy. Moreover, the fact that many of these characteristics are Western in origin lends a certain credence to O'Donnell's contention that they may be simply by-products of a particular historical experience. Critics can point to Linz and Stepan's assertion that democratic consolidation requires not just any set of rules but rules that reflect "the major accomplishments of nineteenth century liberalism."[49] Andreas Schedler has even called on analysts to discard the pretense of scientific objectivity and admit that what scholars look for and define as democratic consolidation is purely subjective.[50]

The temptation to define democracy by what it lacks compared to the West has indeed significantly narrowed our appreciation of democracy and the diverse ways in which it can develop. The confident assumption that Western assistance is both a benevolent and a necessary instrument of social change has made two seemingly unconnected themes of democratization mutually reinforcing: the lack of concern for cultural and regional differences; and the inability to explain the longevity of "delegative," or incomplete, democracies. International development agencies' penchant for ignoring local governments is the logical outcome of the view that regional cultural differences are irrelevant to *both* democratic and economic development.[51]

So where does all this leave democratization theory? Some see no way to avoid the trap of turning democratization into "neomodernization," with its accompanying misapplication of Western models of economic and political development. The search for a universal model of democratization, they say, is both fatuous and destructive. Only by abandoning such ethnocentric notions can we learn to appreciate our differences, instead of obliterating them in the name of progress.[52] Others urge a return to minimalism, or at least to definitions broad enough to embrace both transitions and "very long lasting transitions."[53] Yet a third group is firmly convinced of the supremacy of the Western model of cultural and economic development and hopes to export it throughout the globe.[54]

It is too early, however, to give up on the term democratic consolidation. We can overcome many of the difficulties that plague current definitions by taking two bold steps. The first is to shift the focus of attention from national to regional political life. The second step, to which we will devote the second half of this book, is to renew our focus on cultural symbols and the practical uses to which political elites put them.

THE CASE FOR REGIONAL DEMOCRATIC DEVELOPMENT

In many respects Russia epitomizes the dilemmas facing analysts of democratization. By minimalist standards the country is clearly in democratic transition and, depending on the criteria one might wish to apply, might even be said to have made progress toward democratic consolidation. The mass media, and most academics, however, still describe Russia as very far from democratic transition and perpetually at risk of backsliding.[55] While popular and historical stereotypes certainly play a prominent role in this perception gap, another key factor is our long-standing neglect of regional life.

Sprawling over eleven time zones, Russia is one of the most ethnically and culturally diverse countries on earth. In Soviet times scholars dismissed this diversity as politically irrelevant since all critical decisions were made in Moscow. With the collapse of the USSR and the ensuing weakening of political authority, however, regional governments have been forced to assume many new responsibilities, particularly in the area of social welfare. As a result, in post-Soviet Russia regions have become the level of society where the impact of political and economic reforms is most readily felt. With regional disparities in rates of economic growth that range from negative 3 percent to over 25 percent, and average per capita incomes that differ as much as tenfold, an individual's quality of life can vary substantially depending on which region of Russia they live in.[56] Moreover, as people's identities become increasingly linked to their region, the differences in regional social and economic policy are beginning to reflect distinct cultural preferences.

But even if regions have become vital to understanding Russian politics, is it meaningful to speak of democratization occurring purely in a regional context? Most social scientists would probably say no, in that political subunits are by definition subordinate to the center, both politically and financially. Indeed, for a long time scholars even treated such subordination as a blessing.[57] Talcott Parsons saw regionalism as a manifestation of entrenched social conservatism standing athwart civilization's progress toward "cultural universalism."[58] Hans Kohn and Charles Tilly both argued that by clinging stubbornly to archaic local customs, regions impeded economic and social progress. Michael Keating simply put it more bluntly than most when he referred to regionalism as a "hangover from the past."[59] The sooner societies sobered up and centralized the sooner they would be able reap the inestimable benefits of the modern bureaucratic state. The view that regionalism is a "premodern phenomenon" is so deeply entrenched in Anglo-American thought that in the volumes of literature on democratization the subject of subnational democratic development rarely even appears.[60] Regional studies have come to be defined as dealing with ethnic or national, but not democratic, identity. Even studies of regional government tend to dismiss the possibility of democratic development resulting from purely local efforts.[61]

This pattern of political and economic centralization (and ensuing modernization) certainly dominated Soviet history. Many would-be reformers, however, have seen the collapse of the USSR as proof of the failure of that developmental model and seized on the erosion of party control as an opportunity to alter this historical pattern once and for all, encouraging local governments at all levels to take "all the sovereignty they could swallow."[62]

By the late 1990s, however, these same people began to worry that decentralization had gone too far and was now eroding the central government's ability to impose reforms. Growing regional inequality convinced them that a strong center was still the best way to guarantee social progress. This more traditional theme has since been embraced wholeheartedly by Boris Yeltsin's successor as Russian president, Vladimir Putin.

Still, the renewal of efforts to recentralize political authority, whose outcome is still uncertain, should not lead us to forget that for the better part of the past decade the traditional pattern of relations between local and national government in Russia was turned upside down. Many of the political and economic reforms of that period, consequently, were not ones the center was imposing but ones that the center was incapable of preventing.

These developments did not escape the attention of Russian area specialists.[63] Still, among the dozens of books and articles written about Russian regions, there has been remarkably little discussion of distinctive regional paths of development or of regional political and economic development strategies, even though the decentralization of political control, fragmentation of the economy, and resurgence of local cultural identify all point in this direction. Today, more than a decade after the fall of communism, the consensus view can still be summed up as follows: (1) regional political debates don't really matter much compared to national politics; (2) regional economic policies have little impact on regional political development; (3) regional elites oppose reforms, while elites at the center promote them; and (4) regional politics is all about who controls the local natural resources. All other motives—ideological, cultural, ethnic, or religious—can be safely ignored.[64] There is also a stubborn tendency to view regions that are overwhelmingly Russian by ethnicity as fundamentally incapable of autonomous political choices, which stems partly from the view that they have no real power and partly from the belief that they have no distinct cultural, and hence no political, identity.

Both of these assumptions are wrong. Just as regions in Russia have become singularly important politically, with the collapse of national political institutions, they have become singularly important culturally, with the collapse of ideological controls. Rather than being praised as evidence of incipient diversity, however, regional diversity in things such as income distribution and application of the laws is often cited as evidence of the failure of democracy.[65] This is odd because, as we have just seen, uneven levels of democratic development are very much the norm among mature democracies, and for good reason. It is precisely the absence of homogeneity that provides balance and encourages the development of stabilizing institutions. Regional diversity within mature democracies is indeed so commonplace that it raises an intriguing question. If, in countries such as Great Britain and Spain, democracy can be considered consolidated at the national level while still being unconsolidated at the regional level, could the reverse occur as well? Could democracy be consolidated in a particular region, while being as yet unconsolidated at the national level?

On the face of it, the disparity of power between regions and the center makes this seem unlikely. But suppose we factor in the erosion of central state power and approach the issue from a slightly different angle by asking, is it possible for regions to preserve their autonomy from the encroachment of the center? Obviously, the answer would depend on the resources available to the center and the relative cost of enforcement. In the Russia of the 1990s, the resources available to the center were so limited, and the costs of imposing the center's will so high, that significant opportunities existed for regions to pursue local policies independently of the center. Once we recognize the center's limitations, we must also acknowledge the possibility of democratic development progressing further regionally than at the center. Shifting the focus of our analysis from the national to the regional level is therefore essential if we wish to understand local patterns of democratization.

Some may ask: Why stop at regions? Why not shift the focus to municipalities, or even families? Because regions are where community and national concerns intersect. Regions, moreover, tend to serve as focal points for identity in ways that most municipalities cannot. Lower levels of society may exhibit greater civic involvement, but they do so only in clearly circumscribed neighborhood matters that generally do not involve broader issues of identity. The region is thus the optimal level of analysis when trying to understand rapid social change, because it is the juncture at which individuals can most conveniently express their cultural identity through civic involvement, conveniently isolating what Aaron Wildavksy identified as the most important unit of analysis—"the individual in cultural context."[66]

Another reason for shifting our analysis to the regional level is that most primary socialization occurs at this level. While it is often argued that values tend to resist change, Harry Eckstein has drawn attention to the flip side of this process. Alongside "intact parochial structures," there can also emerge "particular segments that have traits especially conducive or susceptible to reorientation . . . , structural or dispositional traits readily accommodated to new cultural patterns or, indeed, anticipations of them."[67] At the regional level these create what Eckstein called "islands of achievement in a sea of ascription."[68] A research strategy that seeks to explain the appearance of such islands obviously demands a detailed case study of both the region and its culture.

Some comparativists question the value of case studies for theory building, but in his classic essay "Case Study and Theory in Political Science," Harry Eckstein argued that they are uniquely valuable because, unlike wide-ranging comparative studies, they permit an intensive analysis of multiple variables, increasing the likelihood that critical variables and relations will be found.[69]

Other scholars have suggested that case studies are particularly well suited to the study of regime change because they make it possible to more precisely match analytical intent with empirical observation.[70] Large-scale comparisons perforce tend to treat structural constraints as given, and although this may not be significant in countries where institutions have been stable for decades, it seems a questionable assumption to make about newly formed democracies.[71]

To get around the bias in favor of existing institutions, Dietrich Rueschemeyer prefers a case study method rooted in sophisticated historical explanation.[72] Interestingly, it closely resembles the historically based approach to rational choice advocated by Margaret Levi.[73] Judging from their critiques, the conceptual advantages of case studies seem greatest when maximum attention is paid to the specifics of local history and culture. As Laurence Whitehead puts it:

> Convincing accounts of democratization in a specific country require good knowledge of the context (including relevant history, the cultural idiom, and the appropriate collective symbols or reference points). Abstracting from this is likely to lead to little more than empty theorems about abstract cause and effect that carry little conviction with the population in question; for however solid they may seem to a disembodied social scientist, they do not correspond with the people's own understanding of their predicament.[74]

In explaining Novgorod's distinctive evolution we will therefore try to build on the strengths and learn from the weaknesses of current theories of democratization. First, we will shift our focus from the national to the regional level. Such a shift seems particularly appropriate for Russia because of the weakness of the central government and the dramatic rise in local cultural identity during the period in question. Second, we will privilege the case study approach over a broad comparison among regions because it allows for a more meaningful comparison of multiple variables and avoids the pitfalls that ensue from excessive focus on stable institutions, which, by definition, fledgling democracies cannot have. Third, by focusing intensely, but not exclusively, on the Novgorod region, we will be able to test the theory that regional myths and symbols play a decisive role in speeding up democratic development. The fact that Novgorod has been so successful in an environment seen by many as particularly hostile to democracy makes it, in Eckstein's words, just the kind of "crucial case study" that can provide valuable theoretical insight.[75]

DEMOCRATIZATION THEORY IN DISARRAY

Democratization theory is in disarray. The minimalist consensus on the definition of democracy, established by Schumpeter and codified by Dahl more than thirty years ago, has given way to a bewildering hodgepodge of standards, some of which seem to apply to some areas of the world some of the time. The proliferation of definitions is a clear sign that efforts to find one universal standard of democratization have reached a dead end. The most valuable thing analysts can do now is to narrow and deepen the focus of democratization by shifting their attention to the regional level and reconnecting the amorphous definitions of democracy to the practices and values of people's daily lives.

The collapse of communism has added a new twist to the puzzle of democratic development—the reemergence of regional life during a period of critical weakness of the central government. Although we do not know how far the balance between center and periphery will ultimately shift in Russia, we can already see two important results.

The first is that the new national and subnational institutions that are emerging in Russia are competing for popular credibility. While the former has recent Soviet history and patterns of socialization on its side, the latter has a far more ancient history and the new power to forge local allegiances. As a result, in Russia the political and administrative tensions that would exist in any case are interlaced with issues of cultural and historical identity.

The second is the disintegration of the once all-encompassing ideology of Marxism-Leninism. Too often this is treated simply as a liberation from intellectual constraint. It has been that, of course, but for many it has also been the demise of a comforting sense of personal identity and social mission. Its abrupt end therefore left many people feeling like cultural exiles in their own country. Increasingly, regions have filled in this gap and provided cultural continuity. Regional cultural identity has thus come to play a crucial role in postcommunist democratization, and we must adjust our theories to reflect the ways that such reconstituted local identities affect democratic development.

Having set out the theoretical rationale for my approach to democratization, I can now provide a definition of democratic consolidation. I see it as the station between democratic transition and mature democracy that is characterized by levels of economic development, civic participation, and social consensus around new values and institutions that are high enough to make a regression to the past unlikely. This definition accepts the minimal definitions of democratic transition that characterize polyarchies and adds two that are characteristic of democratic consolidation, which, for very different reasons, advocates of radical and evolutionary change both agree on—longevity and stability. Such regimes ought to be considered consolidated democracies, because the only thing they require to mature is time.

CHAPTER 2

DEMOCRATIC DEVELOPMENT IN RUSSIA

THE NOVGOROD MODEL

At times entire revolutions can occur in Russia,
though these remain completely unknown abroad.

ALEXANDER HERZEN

The most serious problem facing any assessment of Russian democracy, as Harry Eckstein has aptly noted, is that "the abundance of hypotheses about the determinants of the performance of democracies is not matched by an abundance of information about Russia pertinent to them."[1] In this chapter I will try to correct this situation, at least with respect to one region of Russia.

In *Can Democracy Take Root in Post-Soviet Russia*, Eckstein provides a valuable summary of the characteristics that most commonly correlate with mature democracies. The closer a society is to these "ideal conditions," he suggests, the better it will perform as a democracy.[2] Although not all democracies score well in each category, three hypotheses regarding democracy, he says, are supported by extensive research: the establishment of a new constitutional order, a high level of economic development, and numerous and active voluntary associations.[3]

The establishment of a new constitutional order includes "formal-legal (explicit) rules governing elections, executive and legislative structures, powers and relations, policy-making processes, civil rights and liberties." In the decade after the Second World War it was widely assumed that democracy relied on the proper functioning of specific mechanisms of government, and that these mechanisms derived their legitimacy from an effective constitutional framework. Although the subsequent failure of many Third World regimes patterned on this "Westminster model" has undermined faith in a strict linkage between constitutional design and democratic governance, elements of this approach have been revived by "new institutionalists."[4] Today, the importance of supporting institutions for government effectiveness is widely understood, and the establishment of a new constitutional order has emerged as a key indicator of democratic consolidation.

The second relationship, between economic development and democracy, is one of the most thoroughly researched. Despite broad agreement that a correlation does exist between high levels of economic development and mature democracy, however, there is still uncertainty about whether this is more accurately portrayed by levels of economic growth or by measures of quality of life.[5] Still, it remains one of the best-known and widely accepted empirical measures of democratic consolidation.

Almost as popular, thanks to the seminal writings of Robert Putnam, is the proposition that successful democracy is associated with the existence of a large number of voluntary associations and active participation in them.[6] "As with the economic development hypothesis," says Eckstein, this proposition "approaches certainty about as closely as possible."[7]

High performance on any one of these criteria, Eckstein suggests, would support the argument that a regime has made the transition to consolidated democracy; yet even if we accept that all are valid indicators of democratic maturity, they remain highly subjective. The case for democratic consolidation would be more compelling if one could establish measures of progress and achievement within each indicator. As a regime progressed toward maturity, one would expect to find greater consistency both within and among indicators, while the reverse would be true of regimes still in democratic transition.

There is a scholarly consensus on three characteristics that distinguish transitional from consolidated democratic regimes. They are:

1. *Structural changes* in government. These refer to institutionalized democratic procedures and the removal of any significant reserve domains of power;
2. *Behavioral changes* within the elites. These include the absence of antisystem actors and loyal behavior toward the new system by major political actors;
3. *Attitudinal changes* among the populace. These reflect widespread acceptance by the populace of the legitimacy of new institutions.[8]

In this assessment I will be looking not only at Novgorod's progress in each of the three categories by which mature democracies are commonly measured—constitutional order, economic success, and associational life—but also at whether these have been accompanied by the type of

TABLE 2.1
Matrix for measuring progress toward democratization in Novgorod

Characteristics of mature democracies	Structural changes	Behavioral changes	Attitudinal changes
New constitutional order	Local self-government	Greater elite self-reliance	Support for new institutions
Economic success	Foreign direct investment	Economic innovation	Support for new economic policies
Voluntary association	"Open Doors"	Social partnership	Increased social activism

behavioral, structural, and attitudinal changes one would expect to find in consolidated democracies. Supplementing discussion of how Novgorod measures up on indicators of democratic maturity with a discussion of the patterns of change within each indictors will thus provide an unusually comprehensive assessment of Novgorod's progress toward democratic development.

A NEW CONSTITUTIONAL ORDER

Constructing "Our Own System of Government"

The reason typically given for Novgorod's remarkable turnaround is the impact of foreign direct investment.[9] The region's ability to attract more than $800 million over the past ten years, however, was the culmination of a larger strategy aimed at ending the region's financial dependence on Moscow.

Like the other regions, Novgorod was forced to "swallow" as much sovereignty as it could after 1990, but while most regions did so resentfully, Novgorod did so purposefully and with the stated intention of freeing itself from dependence on federal subsidies. This has led to a major reorganization of government structures and an unprecedented emphasis on local self-government—the heart of Novgorod's reform strategy.

The priority accorded to local self-government is specified in Novgorod's new constitution, adopted in 1994. It gives organs of local self-government the exclusive right to use local resources and property and obliges the region to distribute financial resources, with the specified objective of "creating the necessary financial foundation for self-government."[10]

The two intellectual pillars of the Novgorod constitution are functionality and subsidiarity.[11] As the former deputy head of the regional duma, Lyubov Andreyeva, explains:

> Our region's laws were devised so that the executive and legislative branches function together, that is, this or that subject or institution is given only as much power and authority as it needs to accomplish the task it was designed by law to accomplish. That is why our legislative process is developing so much faster than in other regions.[12]

The speed with which the regional duma has tackled the creation of new legislation is indeed impressive. In its first three years it passed 120 new laws (15 on local self-government) and 656 normative acts (49 on local self-government). To put this in perspective, in roughly the same period of time more than a quarter of Russia's regions had not adopted a single law on local self-government.[13]

In July 1995 the chairman of the regional duma, Anatoly Boitsev, even remarked that Novgorod's laws on local self-government were better than those adopted in Moscow.[14] One might consider this an empty boast but for the fact that the Novgorod Regional Duma had sent more than three hundred recommendations on federal legislation to the Russian State Duma between 1994 and 1998, and Anatoly Lukyanov, then head of the state duma committee on legislation, has acknowledged that these proposals laid the foundation for much of the early legislative authority that granted local self-government in Russia.[15] Not surprisingly, Novgorod was one of only three Russian regions ready to conduct direct gubernatorial elections in 1996, and it was the first region to hold elections for every level of government, from village elder to governor.[16]

A key local innovation is the designation of elected municipal and district heads as simultaneously the heads of local self-government. This allows the chair of the district or city council to run as a candidate for the regional legislature. The twenty-two district heads in the Novgorod Region supervise both the legislative and executive branches, and typically they constitute 30–40 percent of the Novgorod Regional Duma.

This intentional violation of separation of powers was hotly debated in the press and opposed by several members of the first session of the regional duma. They feared that the legislators would be beholden to the governor and unable to exercise any supervisory function.[17] Others worried that having the heads of districts in the regional legislature would increase the likelihood of pork barrel politics by the districts. The region's governor, Mikhail Prusak, countered that this was the best way to give heads of districts the power they need to carry out their mandate. Moreover, he argued, many other countries combine executive and legislative functions at the subnational level.[18]

The question that concerns us, however, is not efficiency but whether such an arrangement constitutes a reserved domain of power. I would argue it does not. Given the constitutionally enshrined separation of local self-government from the rest of the country's administrative system, the Novgorod practice of treating local municipal heads as the head of local self-government gives them an unprecedented degree of autonomy. The ability to elect independent heads of local municipalities to the regional legislature strengthens rather than weakens the legislature's independence from the governor, hence the fear that they would be tempted to advance the interests of their own districts at the expense of the region. To counteract this temptation electoral districts have been redrawn in such a way that they overlap with several administrative districts.

This design has two advantages. First, overlapping constituencies broaden the electoral base to which officials must appeal. Unable to promote one district without adversely affecting another, district heads who also serve in the duma are forced to consider the needs of two (in one instance, three) distinct electoral constituencies.[19] Second, because serving in the regional duma is a part-time occupation for all but the chairman and his deputy, heads of districts rely heavily on their district staffs. District staffs thus have substantial control over the content and direction of legislative initiatives. This encourages fiscal responsibility, because these officials are the same ones who will be implementing the budget in their districts.[20]

At its most basic level, local self-government in the region is embodied in neighborhood associations known as TOS (*territorialno obshchestevennoe samoupravlenie*), or "territorially based public self-government." Reasoning that few areas are more likely to elicit civic involvement than the condition of one's backyard, back in 1997 the administration encouraged the formation of such neighborhood associations and granted them the right to raise funds, represent their interests before the city council, and even sue in local courts.[21]

Typically, the first step in the creation of a TOS is the establishment of a "fellowship of home owners" (*tovarishchestvo sobstvennikov zhilya* or TSZh) in a particular housing block. Such fellowships are usually set up to save residents money, but as they begin to solve their own problems, as one Novgorod City Duma deputy remarked, "a chain of public self-government is formed: from the stairwell elder to the housing committee to the TOS (which includes several housing committees) and on to the local organ of self-government, in this case the city administration."[22]

The growth of these fellowships has been dramatic (fig. 2.1). At their present rate of growth, Novgorod city officials estimate that in a few years

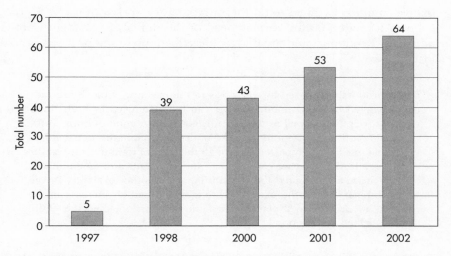

Source: Vladimir Shaikovsky, "Okhrana doma svoego . . .," *Novgorod* (November 4, 1998); Viktor Troyanovsky, "Reforma ZhKKh po-Novgorodsky," *Itar-Tass* (July 12, 2001); Kira Vasilyeva, "Put ternistyi, no vernyi," *Novgorod* (September 6, 2001) 5; Vasily Dubovsky, "Zhilye so znakom kachestva," *Novgorod* (March 14, 2002), 3.

FIGURE 2.1 Growth of territorial housing fellowships in Novgorod the Great, 1997–2002

they will account for nearly a third of the municipal housing fund.[23] The city eventually plans to have the TSZh and TOS combine and form the basis for electoral districts. To encourage this process, the Novgorod City Duma and the mayor have set up public advisory councils linked to the TSZh/TOS. Together, they have already adopted procedures that require a formal public hearing on all major issues affecting these neighborhoods.[24]

Even critics concede that Novgorod's constitutional innovations have improved coordination among different levels of "local government" (a term I use to refer to regional, municipal, and village administration). The emergency midyear supplemental district funding requests, so routine in other regions, do not occur in Novgorod.[25] Such predictability, rooted in a carefully crafted constitutional framework, has mitigated one of the most serious shortcomings of the post-Soviet era—the lack of integration between local and regional levels of administration.[26]

This does not mean that there is no conflict in the Novgorod government. One internal review of the regional duma's work between 1994 to 1997 reveals that sessions could be highly contentious, particularly if legislative committees failed to do their preparatory work with care.[27] Here is how Alexander Yashin, former head of the duma's Permanent Committee for Economics and the Budget, described the review process to the local press:

> Often proposals prepared by specialists in the executive branch are radically changed by the committee. They can be introduced by both "independent" deputies as well as the executive branch. A good example is the regional constitution. Deputies worked on it for two months, debated it at two duma sessions, then passed it through the filter of town meetings at the district level. After that we gathered all the comments and amendments, refined them, and adopted the constitution. . . . Another example: Driven by the budget deficit, the executive branch proposed an increase in the property tax from 1 to 2 percent. First the commission, then the entire duma, rejected this proposal.[28]

One can glean something of the intensity of these debates from the number of times committees refused to approve legislative proposals for review by the full duma. Between April 1994 and October 1997 permanent legislative committees reviewed 1,018 submissions, but they passed only 558 on for further consideration.[29]

In sum, the Novgorod system of government was specifically designed to increase communication among different branches of government and to resolve issues of contention *before* they reach the level of institutional confrontation. Despite its success, however, Novgorod's constitutional distinctiveness came to an end in 2002 when, under pressure to bring local laws into conformity with the Russian constitution, the regional duma adopted legislation specifically prohibiting the heads of municipalities from also being members of legislative assemblies.[30]

The second key principle of the Novgorod model of local government is adequate local financing. As then Deputy Governor Sergei Fabrichny put it back in 1995, "True independence is determined by two interwoven factors: the existence of a legislative basis and a developed economic foundation for local self-government. Of the two, the economic foundation must be established first."[31]

The system of dual appointments described above, with its strong district heads, has encouraged the transfer of a major portion of revenues from the regional to the district level. Even as federal subsidies to the regional budget have shrunk, the average amount shifted from the region's consolidated budget to districts and cities has averaged more than two-thirds, the reverse of the rest of Russia.[32] So strong is the commitment to political and fiscal autonomy that in years when the region has received significantly less from federal authorities than it was owed, the regional administration has transferred to districts and cities as much as 80 percent of its revenues to make up the difference.[33]

The key mechanism for preserving this commitment has been an innovative stabilization fund.[34] Each district transfers at least 15 percent of its local income to the fund, with the two richest districts, the city of Novgorod the Great and Chudovo, contributing 33 percent and 28 percent respectively. District authorities can use this fund only to pay for mandatory items in their budget. The funding of additional items depends entirely on revenues that the district can attract on its own.[35]

Shifting financial decision making to the district and municipal level has put pressure on local administrators to become effective managers. It has also allowed the region to fund reforms in such areas as small business administration, communal housing reforms, taxation, and land ownership, while simultaneously reducing the overall dependence of the regional budget on federal subsidies from 60 percent in 1994 to 6 percent in 2004.[36] Last but not least, it has allowed for a degree of stability in social payments that is the envy of other regions of Russia.

How Constitutional Reform Changed Elite Behavior

After Boris Yeltsin abolished all local Soviets in October 1993, the Novgorod elite worked quickly to reestablish local self-government. By late 1994, long before any federal laws on local self-government were adopted, Novgorod had already elected nearly 1,300 *starosty*, or village elders. Following a practice begun in 1993 by the head of the Kresttsy District, Nikolai Renkas, regional officials were sent out to 188 villages to brief local elders on the contents of the regional budget.[37] This proved so popular that regionwide "information days" have become a fixture of Novgorod government.

Every two to three months working groups made up of deputy governors, heads of committees, and their professional staffs descend on villages and cities throughout the region to answer questions and listen to people's complaints. About two hundred such town meetings are held each year.[38] The budget process then culminates with the governor's public presentation of the budget before the regional duma in December. This event, which is open to the public, is also broadcast live over local television and radio. At the end of his presentation the governor answers questions from the floor about the budget and the socioeconomic projections on which it is based.[39] This annual practice, begun in 1996, is still so unusual for Russia that when people from Novgorod describe it to visitors, they are often met with disbelief.

A more subtle example of changing elite attitudes can be seen in the ease of access to government buildings. There is no document check at the city administration building. People simply walk in and ask for the official they wish to see. At the regional administration people are generally stopped and asked whom they wish to see, but in my more than three dozen visits over seven years, I have never seen anyone asked to present identification. As anyone who has ever tried to enter a government office building elsewhere in Russia can attest, such accessibility is highly unusual.

The process of working on regional constitutional reforms has also taught local elites to respect the legislative process. One sees this in the exceptionally high participation rate (85.4 percent) of deputies in duma sessions.[40] By encouraging legislative coordination and the devolution of economic and political authority, Novgorod's system of government seems to have taught local elites the value of political compromise. A number of observers have remarked on the exceptional degree of consensus displayed by the Novgorod elites, and linked it to early mutual consultation and a clear delineation of functions and responsibilities. "The end goal," says Novgorod Regional Duma Chairman Boitsev, "is the adoption of a real budget without any, if you'll pardon the expression, fluff or guesswork. This is accomplished by long and often boring preparatory work among all groups."[41] Novgorod's much-vaunted political stability is thus largely the result of institutional procedures that force competing constituencies to reach a consensus.

A good example of how the process manufactures consensus is the regional Trilateral Commission. The commission, set up in October 1995, serves as the "permanently acting organ of the system of social partnership in the Novgorod Region."[42] It is composed of the governor, the chairman of the regional branch of the Federation of Trade Unions, and the head of the Union of Industrialists and Employers of the Novgorod Region.

Commission members have the right to review all regional legislation that concerns socioeconomic policy and labor relations. No less important, any member can review all information relevant to the formulation of policy decisions for any level of government. Commission regulations also stipulate that the principals must meet at least once every three months and that such meetings will be chaired alternately, with each new chair determining the agenda for the meeting. The commission is assisted by a permanent secretariat, and its decisions must be published in the leading local newspaper, *Novgorodskie vedomosti*.[43]

The commission's work culminates in the annual signing of a detailed agreement on the economic and social targets for the coming year, which then becomes the foundation for the region's budget. The public signing ceremony likewise sends a message of unity to the region's inhabitants and to potential investors. The social benefits of such public pacts and rituals have been widely discussed in the literature on social transitions.[44] What is unusual about Novgorod, however, is that the *negotiations*, as well as the rituals, are widely publicized.

The parties meet every two to three months with the press to discuss progress on the next year's accord and to air their disagreements. Thus, Novgorodians know that factory owners are complaining about the inordinate zeal of tax inspectors, that the governor is accusing the trade unions of making unrealistic demands, and that the trade unions are calling for higher wages and more social guarantees. At the same time, however, they also learn that each side has suggested compromises to be discussed further at the next meeting.[45] If, as Laura Edles suggests, the very process of drafting social pacts teaches elites to redefine their interests and the means by which it is appropriate to attain them, then in Novgorod this process has become second nature to the elites.[46]

Some might counter that such public rituals are merely for show, but the fact that the annual agreement becomes the basis for budget planning and that trade union officials and industrialists have access to government planning documents clearly suggests otherwise. The trilateral approach, moreover, has proved so successful at the regional level that it has been adopted by the city of Novgorod the Great as the basis for its own budgetary planning cycle. One telling indication of its importance is that before the Novgorod city pact could be signed in 2000 the sides had to reach agreement on the hot button issue of putting up public services for competitive bidding. The city got the trade unions to agree to this, but in turn it had to concede that bidding commissions would include a trade union representative and that local Novgorod service providers would receive preference in the awarding of city contracts.[47]

Finally, Novgorod's government institutions have also taught the elite to be more self-reliant and to value horizontal ties more than vertical ones.[48] An example has been the initiative shown in creating alternative infrastructures of political support. To this end, both the Novgorod City Duma and administration have been staunch supporters of the Union of Russian Cities of Northwest and Central Russia. Originally formed in 1990 by twelve northwestern Russian cities that wanted to learn from one another's experience in self-government, by 2002 it encompassed twenty-three cities throughout central and northwestern Russia.[49]

From the organization's inception Novgorod has been its official headquarters.[50] Each year the union conducts twenty to thirty seminars at which city officials and local activists gather to compare notes on the problems facing small businesses, historic preservation, drug addiction, housing reform, and local self-government. As the former deputy mayor of Novgorod, Aleksandr Vasilyev, remarked, "While the center was establishing its vertical integration of authority, we have been actively developing cooperation horizontally."[51]

Although my review of behavioral changes has emphasized the Novgorod elite's acceptance of new political actors and values, the region also displays another characteristic of consolidated democracies—weak antisystem actors.

Although opinion surveys generally show the Communist Party placing second or third among major parties in the region, behind the pro-Putin Edinaya Rossiya and liberal Yabloko parties, its candidates have never been able to translate this into success at the polls.[52] The main problem seems to be the enormous personal popularity of the governor and his policies. Thus, despite a turnover rate of more than 60 percent in regional duma elections, only once has the head of the region's Communist Party organization managed to win a seat on it, and he beat out his rival by a scant four percentage points. This has been the only electoral success the CPRF has been able to boast of in the region during the past decade.[53]

The maverick Liberal-Democratic Party of Russia (LDPR), which has the most official members, also opposes the local leadership and hoped to capitalize on the election of one if its members as governor of the neighboring region of Pskov by launching a grassroots voter registration drive in the Novgorod region. Yet despite officially being the region's largest party, it has no prominent local sponsors and has been unable to elect a single candidate to political office at any level.

Popular Support for the New Constitutional Order

Local surveys consistently show a high level of public support for local political figures and local institutions. Since late 1998, Governor Prusak's approval rating has hovered between 62 and 81 percent, considerably higher than the average approval rating for governors in Russia, which hovers between 47 and 56 percent.[54] Even more striking is the contrast between levels of trust in local political elites compared to national ones (see fig. 2.2). A survey of forty Russian regions completed in 2002 confirms that Novgorodians in general display the lowest level of trust in federal authorities of any region, while Novgorod businessmen showed the highest disparity between trust in local and federal officials of any region.[55]

Novgorodians also have an unusually positive view of post-Soviet institutions. In addition to a positive assessment of the work of the regional duma, more than half of Novgorodians have a "positive" or "mostly positive" view of the Russian Constitution. Several institutions that are rated negatively in nationwide surveys, such as non-Orthodox religious

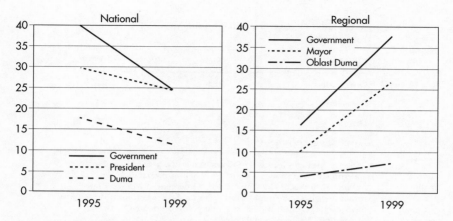

Source: "Analiticheskaya zapiska ob itogakh sotsiologicheskogo issledovaniya sotsialno-ekonomicheskoi situatsii v Novgorodskoi oblasti v avguste-sentyabre 1998 goda" (Veliky Novgorod: MNOU Dialog), personal copy. For the 1995 survey there were 100 participants from the city of Novgorod-the-Great and 50 from each of the region's 22 districts. For the 1999 survey, commissioned by Sberbank of Novgorod, 2,586 participants responded from all 22 districts of Novgorod and the city of Novgorod-the-Great, "Monitoring—Novgorodskaya oblast, July 1999" (Veliky Novgorod: MNOU Dialog), personal copy.

FIGURE 2.2 Trust in public institutions in the Novgorod Region, 1995–1999 (Percentage responding as follows to the question "Who do you pin your hopes on for an improvement in conditions?")

institutions, the judicial system, current social guarantees, and the system of law enforcement all hold preponderantly positive associations for Novgorodians.[56]

As the percentage of people who are homeowners has grown so has the perception that local self-government is the proper venue for addressing many of the region's problems. Surveys of Novgorod homeowners reveal them to be significantly more likely to pay their taxes and to view local self-government as the best means of defending their property and rights. More than two-thirds believe that local authorities, not federal authorities, should set taxes. Summing up these survey results, analysts conclude: "They [homeowners] have completely different sociopolitical orientations from the majority of the population: They focus primary attention on themselves and their immediate surroundings, are less politicized, and tend to receive fewer [social] benefits. They show a higher willingness to pay taxes and have more trust in government, but not in the bureaucracy."[57]

Another indicator of changing popular attitudes is the strikingly liberal voting pattern of the Novgorod Region in the 1990s. Less obvious in dis-

TABLE 2.2
Anticipated election participation in Novgorod,
1995–1999

Election	1995	1998	1999
Governor	40%	86%	81.6%
President	51	80	74.1
Duma	35	50	40.9
Local self-government	33	58	55.1

Source: Averages for head of districts, mayors, heads of local self-government, and *starosty* omitted. In 2000, in preparation for the mayoral elections of October 8, 2000, 74 percent of Novgorodians responded that they would participate in those elections. "Monitoring—Novgorodsdkaya oblast" (Veliky Novgorod: MNOU Dialog, June-August 2000), personal copy.

trict elections, it becomes quite pronounced during gubernatorial and presidential elections. The popularity of the liberal Yabloko Party in the 2000 presidential election seems particularly out of character for a region with Novgorod's economic and demographic profile.[58] This has been accompanied by an increased willingness to participate in elections at all levels (see table 2.2).

In sum, the creation of a new constitutional order emphasizing local self-government and collective elite accountability has dramatically enhanced trust in the local political system and its leaders. Fiscal devolution, initiated largely as a cost-cutting measure, has had the unanticipated benefit of enhancing the legitimacy of new institutions. Constant public interaction with these new political structures has forged a culture of compromise that has encouraged political stability, civic engagement, and, as we are about to see, economic dynamism.

ECONOMIC SUCCESS

The Structural Impact of Novgorod's "NEP"

Novgorod's distinctive strategy for regional economic development has affected government institutions, elite behavior, and public attitudes. By embracing a radical strategy of attracting foreign direct investment, the local government embarked on a path that has had long-term social, as well as economic, consequences.

To put Novgorod's economic achievements in context, we must begin with a bit of basic data about the region. The Novgorod Region is situated in the northwestern economic area of Russia, three hours southeast of St. Petersburg, along the main highway to Moscow. The region has a population of approximately 700,000 and covers an area approximately the size of West Virginia or Ireland. The largest city and capital, Novgorod the Great, has about 230,000 inhabitants; it is followed by Borovichi, with 60,000, and Staraya Russa with 40,000. The urban population constitutes about 71 percent of the region's inhabitants, 96 percent of whom are ethnic Russians. The region's main natural resources are peat and timber.

Many years of lagging government investment had left the region with a woefully outdated manufacturing base and a heavy dependence on defense-related electronics and machine manufacturing. Unable to compete with the better-quality imported goods after 1991, factory output plummeted and tens of thousands fled to nearby St. Petersburg in search of employment. "We were about to lose another third of our population" just when the federal government, citing fiscal constraints, was reneging on its social transfer payments, recalls current Deputy Governor Mikhail Skibar.[59]

The one ray of hope in this bleak landscape was the joint Russo-Finish plywood factory, Chudovo–RWS, that had begun operations in 1990. Despite initial controversy, the factory quickly turned a profit and began to contribute to the local budget and to support schools and fix roads, eventually even donating funds for the reconstruction of a local monastery.[60]

Convinced that the federal government would not bail out the region and that Russian businessmen were unlikely to invest in such a small region, the Novgorod administration decided on the high-risk strategy of trying to attract foreign investors. Any foreign investor willing to set up a factory in the region would be exempt from all local taxes until their investment turned a profit.[61] To sweeten the deal, the local administration instituted a "one window" policy under which a senior official, usually a deputy governor, was assigned to shepherd the project through any bureaucratic obstacles it might encounter, either locally or at the federal level. Finally, all agreements signed between foreign investors and the administration were made legally binding on the region. To allay the fears of foreign investors, the administration asked the international accounting firms of Arthur Andersen, Siar Bossard, and Price Waterhouse Coopers to help them write the region's investment laws in such a way that investors would be protected from any losses they might incur as a result of changes in legislation, including federal legislation![62]

This combination of tax deferments, help in cutting through red tape, and legal guarantees proved successful beyond the administration's fondest hopes. By the end of the decade, nearly two hundred foreign companies had invested over half a billion dollars in the region's factories (fig. 2.3). They currently employ nearly twenty-thousand workers, account for

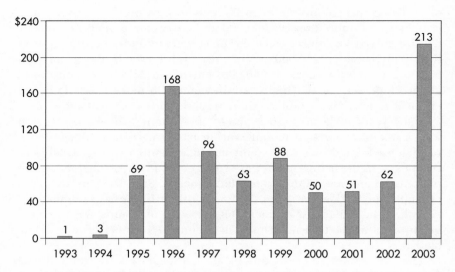

Source: V. N. Podoprigora et al., *Lider s severa—tekhnologiya uspekha* (Veliki Novgorod: MNOU Dialog, 2000), 9; Semyon Khoroshukhin, "Novgorodskaya oblast: geograficheskoe polozhenie," in *Promyshlennost Novgorodskoi oblasti, 2002* (Veliky Novgorod: "Kompass Nord-West," 2002), 47–53; Andrei Lazarev, "Novgorodtsev zastavlyayut zhit po moskovskim pravilam," *Ekonomika i vremya*, St. Petersburg (July 15, 2002); Tomas Tommingas, "Biznesmeny volnuyutsya, TsB negoduet," *Novgorodskie vedomosti* (June 27, 2003), 3; Soobshechnie press-tsentra Novgorodskoi administratsii za 19.02.2004 v 14:33."

FIGURE 2.3 Annual foreign direct investment in the Novgorod Region, 1993–2003 (in millions of US$)

two-thirds of local industrial production, and provide over 40 percent of regional budget revenues.[63] By the end of 1997 foreign direct investment per capita in the Novgorod region was ten times the per capita average for Russia, higher than many countries in Eastern Europe.

Thanks to foreign direct investment (or FDI), administration officials estimate the region preserved twenty-four thousand jobs and added nearly seven thousand new ones.[64] Most important, unlike the rest of Russia, where two-thirds of the money invested by foreign companies was short-term speculative investment, Novgorod offered tax incentives *only* to companies that were willing to invest in production up front.[65]

As a result, FDI has fundamentally altered the region's revenue base. Even though investors are freed from local taxes, their contributions to the pension fund, medical insurance fund, and employment fund make up as much as half of total receipts in the region and allow payment of

TABLE 2.3

FDI inflows among transition economies of Central and Eastern Europe, 1996–2000 (US$ millions, annual averages)

Country	Annual average	$ per capita
1. Czech Rep.	3,463	337
2. Estonia	310	214
3. Hungary	2,029	201
4. Croatia	882	196
5. Poland	6,528	169
6. Latvia	403	164
7. Slovakia	699	129
Novgorod	92	128
8. Slovenia	236	119
9. Azerbaijan	681	86
Kazakhstan	1,289	86
10. Bulgaria	594	74
...		
18. Russia	3,246	22

Source: "Foreign Investment Boom in Transition Economies Will Withstand Global Slowdown: A New Report by the Economist Intelligence Unit," *Transition Newsletter* (April 24, 2002), http://www.worldbank.org/transitionnewsletter/octnovdec01/pgs52–54.htm; V. N. Podoprigora et al., *Lider s severa—Tkhnologiia uspekh* (Veliki Novgorod: MNOU Dialog, 2000), 9; Semyon Khoroshukhin, "Novgorodskaya oblast: Geograficheskoe polozhenie," in *Promyshlennost Novgorodskoi oblasti,* 2002 (Veliky Novgorod: "Kompass Nord-West," 2002), 47–53.

pensions and other social payments without delays.[66] Regional officials estimate that for every dollar the regional budget has lost in tax deferments for foreign direct investments three were gained.[67]

Foreign companies, moreover, often invest additional resources. In the city of Chudovo, for example, where Cadbury Schweppes built its first local factory, the company has invested more than three million dollars in improving the city's sewage and water filtering systems and in building a new fire station.[68] This combination of real money (rather than barter) paid into local budgets and higher wages (from which taxes can be collected) has led to an unusually high degree of monetization of the regional economy that stands in sharp contrast to the "virtual economy" that characterized the rest of Russia in the late 1990s. While most regions at the time received local taxes in barter or money surrogates, three-quarters of Novgorod's tax revenues were paid in cash.[69]

FDI and local self-government initiatives evolved in tandem. Because foreign investors were looking for legal guarantees, it became imperative for the duma to adopt proinvestor legislation. This created a strong incentive for regional authorities to specify the competencies of each level of local government. The need for better business legislation thus spurred a more concerted effort to pass local laws on self-government, to increase district accountability, and to build greater transparency into the budget process.[70]

The administration's bold strategy has produced the rather remarkable result of steadily reducing the region's dependence on subsidies from Moscow, while simultaneously allowing it to invest in local industries, pursue decentralization, and provide for greater social welfare. It has even given the region a bit of leeway in setting budgetary priorities, allowing it to support the construction of a regional cancer care center, assist in the restoration of regional churches and monasteries, and even sponsor its own "offshore investment zones"—four depressed districts within the Novgorod region.[71] Its remarkable success has also made the case rather convincingly to local elites that pursuing fiscal autonomy from Moscow is not only desirable but feasible.[72]

Novgorod, Inc.

From its inception the local administration aimed at creating a climate favorable to entrepreneurship in the region in the belief that without such a climate even the most favorable legislation would have little impact. As the former deputy chair of the city duma of Novgorod the Great, Irina Kibina, put it, success would only be assured when Novgorod officials understood the need for government not merely to work *with* business but to work *as* a business.[73]

Many local government officials echo this sentiment. The late mayor of Novgorod, Alexander Korsunov, commented that "factories that are not capable of increasing wages at a consistent rate have no right to exist. . . . Let's not wait around; let's have the courage to begin bankruptcy proceedings so that with whatever is left [we can] create viable enterprises."[74] Deputy Governor Skibar tells his subordinates that foreign investors should not have to learn to speak the local language; it is local officials who should learn to speak their language.[75] Governor Prusak has even suggested that the region's new economic policy is, first and foremost, an effort to teach local bureaucrats to deal with Westerners on a commercial basis.[76]

This unusual attitude has its roots in the prominent role played by businessmen in local politics. Businessmen in politics are certainly not uncommon in Russia, but what makes Novgorod different is that they play a prominent role not just behind the scenes but as publicly accountable legislators.[77] In the 2001 session of the regional duma, businessmen out-

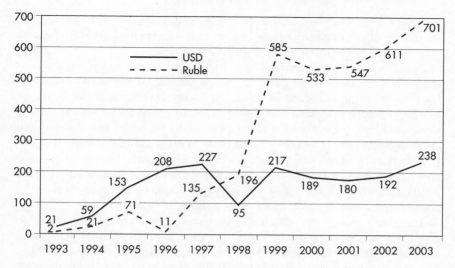

Source: Correspondence from A. V. Dubonosov, chairman of the Committee for Labor and Social Assistance of the Novgorod Oblast, to Alexander I. Zhukovsky, May 30, 2002 (Correspondence No. 01-717/05), Novgorod administration "Soobshchenie press-tsentra" for January 23, 2003 and January 28, 2004. The ruble/dollar exchange rate is taken from the web site: "Main Macroeconomic Indicators, Central Bank of the Russian Federation": http://www.cbr.ru/eng/statistics/credit_statistics/.

FIGURE 2.4 Annual donations to the "Christmas Marathon" charity drive, 1993–2003 (in thousands of US$ and tens of thousands of rubles; tens of millions before 1998)

numbered heads of districts. The close intertwining of political and economic interests suggests the emergence of an elite consensus that I call "Novgorod, Inc."

In addition to a strong desire for regional autonomy, Novgorod, Inc. is characterized by a high level of corporate philanthropy. In an unusual display of social solidarity, the region has, since 1992, held an annual television Christmas fund drives for the needy (fig. 2.4). Although in recent years almost twenty thousand individuals have donated to this fund drive, the bulk of the funding is provided by some twelve hundred Novgorod companies, who also distribute an additional $2 million annually throughout the region.[78]

Public-private partnerships of this sort are regarded as models by local leaders. The administration estimates that nearly two-thirds of all support for the poor is private, with the rest divided more or less evenly between district and regional budgets.[79] Getting things done at the neighborhood level with neighborhood resources, the governor likes to point out, results in greater efficiency in the distribution of resources and greater community ownership of public programs.[80]

Another way local elites have manifested their social concern is through the expansion of microcredit. At the suggestion of local business leaders, the regional administration has set up the Regional Credit Cooperative [Gubernskoe Kreditnoe Sodruzhestvo], a not-for-profit association that provides regional government guarantees for some half-dozen local credit associations. The cooperative makes credit available to small entrepreneurs at 10 percent below commercial lending rates and also conducts special membership drives to attract pensioners and low-income households. In 2002 the number of private participants enrolled in such credit cooperatives increased by more than a third.[81]

Like any good corporation, Novgorod Inc. places considerable emphasis on innovation. In 1998, for example, the city of Novgorod shocked federal authorities in Moscow by requesting that it be allowed to pay for the training of its civil servants out of its own budget. Such training, the city argued, could be done better and more cheaply in Novgorod.[82] Although the sale of land to foreigners remains a contentious issue in much of Russia, in Novgorod the sale of land to greenfield investors has been commonplace for years, thanks to the early completion of a regional land cadastre.[83] In 2000 and the first half of 2001 over six hundred thousand square meters were sold to investors.[84] It seems to critics that no money-making idea is too outlandish for the regional administration, as when the governor proposed the creation of a toll highway connecting Moscow, Novgorod the Great, and St. Petersburg.[85]

One innovation very much in keeping with the legislature's view that the business of government is to help business has been the administration's support for small businesses.[86] There has been a dramatic growth in the number of individuals involved in small businesses in the past decade, from 1,000 businesses employing 13,000 people in 1992 to 12,627 small businesses in 2000 that employ 25,000 people. Such businesses currently employ over 20 percent of the workforce and provide nearly a quarter of the regional budget.[87]

While the rest of the country acrimoniously debates the extent of housing reforms, Novgorod has gone ahead on its own and reorganized the housing management system so that administrators now serve as intermediaries between owners and service providers, who are hired on the basis of competitive bidding. This, along with a five-tiered tariff system based on residence size, has yielded a reduction in administrative costs of 13 percent, and an additional 2–3.5 percent annual saving in costs for repairs.[88] From 1995 to 2001 the cost of providing communal housing services fell by two-thirds, and the burden on local budgets decreased threefold.

These savings have been targeted to families whose per capita income falls below the official poverty level and to subsidize families whose costs for housing and services exceeds 17 percent of household income. They have also allowed the region to conduct a number of interesting experiments. In 2001, for example, Novgorod the Great approved a plan whereby people over sixty-five could transfer ownership of their apartment to the city in exchange for a lifelong monthly payment. That year the city also began offering ten-year housing loans at 8 percent annually for up to 20 percent of the cost of a new home.[89] So far, Novgorod authorities have been able to keep the total cost of housing services at 50 percent of actual cost, the lowest in the Northwest Federal District of Russia. They intend to keep them from exceeding 70 percent until after 2004, making up the difference with the 90 percent federal standard from the district budget.[90]

It should come as no surprise that the Novgorod Region has been chosen as the site for many federal and international initiatives. In the past four years, such programs have included a pilot program to address child homelessness by supporting foster families; an "anticrisis management" program funded by the European Union; a Russo-Danish program to recycle industrial waste; a program to support ecologically clean modernization of the communal housing system; a Finnish program for better waste utilization; and Russia's first regional seminar for young political leaders, sponsored by the Dutch Alfred Moser Foundation.[91]

From 1998 until 2000 the region also served as a pilot for USAID's Regional Investment Initiative. Although the program achieved only modest success in attracting American investors to the region, the internal assessment highlights some notable differences between Novgorod and the three other pilot regions—Samara, Khabarovsk, and Sakhalin:

> One U.S. government observer described the success of Novgorod in terms of their attitude about the future and about getting "rich." Their growth strategy for the Oblast is focused not on today's spoils or the current size of the "pie," but rather how quickly the "pie" is growing. They are willing to be patient and wait for longer range, future benefits. Other regions . . . are still concentrating on dividing up the pie as it exists today. . . . Novgorod has been a clear success story—particularly relevant because it is a story about what a region without natural resources, strategic location, or important manufacturing assets *can* accomplish through sheer will, competence and self-promotion.[92]

The "FDI effect" seems to have changed behavior patterns on a number of different levels. A recent survey found that workers in Novgorod factories with foreign investment were *seven times* more productive than those in their purely domestic counterparts.[93] Senior civil servants in the region speak not of being willing to work with foreigners but of anticipating their needs.[94] Foreign companies in Novgorod even have their own chamber of commerce, which can review and comment on all legislation pending before the regional duma and which is a member of the Social Chamber [obshchestvennaya palata] where every month representatives of registered social organizations can review legislation pending before the duma and suggest amendments and offer alternatives. In sum, a decade of meeting the needs of foreign business investors has taught Novgorod elites to be confident of their ability to compete in a global marketplace, a confidence reflected in Mayor Korsunov's comment that, as far as Novgorod was concerned, Russian membership in the European Union and the World Trade Organization couldn't happen quickly enough.[95]

Popular Adaptation to FDI and Economic Reform

When the proposal to let FDI into Novgorod first arose in the press in 1989 it was met with strong public resistance.[96] As this innovative strategy began to perceptibly improve the local quality of life, however, initial opposition gave way to strong support. Foreign investment has eliminated pension and wage arrears for government employees and, more recently, even in the payment of government subsidies to families with children.

One of the most striking things about Novgorod is the size of its middle class. Typically, for regions of this type in Russia, less than a quarter of the populace qualifies as middle class.[97] Officially, in Novgorod the Great alone, in 2001 there were 18,600 employees earning roughly 9,000 rubles (or over $300) per month. When considering actual family incomes, however, this must be considered the lowest possible figure, because it includes no domestic companies (at one of the largest, Akron, which employs more than five thousand people, the *average* reported wage was then over $250); it omits second wage earners in the family; and does not include under-the-table salary supplements from employers, which most estimates place at 40 percent of actual earnings.[98] Still, these official figures, which are no doubt understated, already indicate a solid middle-class income is provided to a quarter of all families in Novgorod the Great.

Indirect indications that there is an even larger group of people with considerable discretionary income can be gleaned from the fact that more than fifty thousand debit/credit cards (Visa and MasterCard) have been issued in the city of Novgorod the Great, one for every four inhabitants; and that whereas roughly 40 percent of Russian families have cars, in the city this figure is close to 100 percent.[99] It is interesting to note, in passing, that Russia's first used Mercedes-Benz car dealership opened in the city of Novgorod the Great.[100]

But while it seems safe to assume that the middle class and wealthy together constitute at least a third of the region's urban population, at the other end of the spectrum are the chronically poor, which officials say constitute 35 percent of the population. That percentage, however, seems inflated (see fig. 2.5). For one thing, it does not take into account that nearly two-thirds of Novgorodians grow their own food and thus save considerably on grocery costs. Nor does it take into account that many pensioners supplement their income by taking odd jobs, the income from which they do not report. Finally, it does not include the vast number of subsidies that people benefit from in everyday life, including transportation, housing, school, and vacations. It has been estimated that adding in all non-wage incomes from social transfers, earnings from private plots, and interests on bank deposits would add 50–60 percent to regional household incomes.[101]

Recent research on consumer spending patterns in Russia also suggests there is good reason to doubt the official poverty statistics. When American Express analyzed cash savings nationwide at the end of 2002, it came to the startling conclusion that the average Russian family kept about $230 stashed at home, while every second family had foreign currency savings of $860. The lesser figure, if true, would mean that the average Russian household has disposable cash income amounting to nearly 20 percent of official wages.[102] As Peter Odland, IKEA project manager, remarked when confronted with the evidence that the average Moscow customer spends about the same amount as the average customer in Sweden while officially earning five to six times less, "We have given up on statistics; we are relying on reality."[103]

Indeed, one must conclude that there is far more economic activity occurring below the surface than is reflected in official statistics. The mayor of Novgorod the Great has pointed out that while 47 percent of the working population reports an income of less than 1,500 rubles per month, for the two largest sectors of the economy—local industry and government employees—the average wage exceeds 4,000 and 3,500 rubles respectively. The only explanation for this gap, he concludes, is that people grossly understate their true earnings.[104] This helps to explain the following paradox: at the same time as official statistics showed the ranks of the poor swelling the number of citizens turning for assistance to Centers for Social Adaptation fell by nearly 60 percent.[105]

Another explanation, however, lies in the perverse incentives created by the federal government that punish regions that reveal they are doing

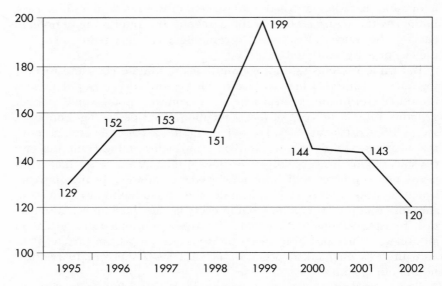

Source: Information obtained from the chairman of the Committee for Labor and Social Assistance of the Novgorod Oblast, A. V. Dubonosov, in a letter to Alexander I. Zhukovsky, May 30, 2002 (Correspondence No. 01-717/05). Note: The letter actually states the following:

2000	298,677
2001	264,266
May 2002	253,827

Subsequent discussions with Vera T. Dmitrieva, who prepared these figures at Dubonosov's request revealed that the methodology for determining poverty level had changed in 2000 from the number of people who applied for assistance to the number who would potentially qualify for assistance. Through the assistance of Galina Ruzhentseva (correspondence of November 6, 2003), the committee was able to provide me with the number of people who had applied:

2000	144,289
2001	143,464
2002	119,540

FIGURE 2.5 Poverty trends in the Novgorod Region, 1995–2002 (in thousands of people)

well. Novgorod officials point out that in 1994 both Pskov and Novgorod received 1.5 billion rubles in federal subsidies. In 2001, however, Pskov continued to receive 1.6 billion, while Novgorod was "rewarded" for its economic progress by having its subsidy slashed to 318 million rubles.[106] Given the payoff, increasing the local poverty level on paper can be an attractive survival strategy for local officials.[107]

Although one would be hard pressed to call Novgorodians prosperous, the region clearly seems to have done better than its neighbors at preventing the growth of poverty, while slashing federal subsidies. Most regions have done one or the other. Novgorod is remarkable for having done both. The populace, as a result, has developed considerable confidence in the administration's ability to shelter the local economy from the storms that buffet other regions. This has spilled over into public support for initiatives that are highly controversial in other regions, and suggests that popular attitudes are increasingly being shaped by the economic stability and predictability that have resulted from foreign direct investment.

Interestingly, local officials like to point out that the region's focus on constructing a strong middle class without extremes of either wealth and poverty is actually a Novgorod tradition that goes back to the Middle Ages.[108] Foreign direct investment, they say, merely allowed them to act on that tradition.

VOLUNTARY ASSOCIATIONS

The Policy of "Open Doors"

Increasingly, mature democracy has been associated with the existence of a large number of voluntary associations and active participation in them. Voluntarism has been linked to "civil society," a term that can include local self-government, worker's self-management, homeowner's associations, and "a great variety of clubs and leagues."[109] In my assessment of Novgorod's civil society I will consider the institutionalization of new relations between the government and civic associations, elite attitudes toward this new phenomenon, and the number and character of local voluntary associations.

Novgorod's unusual social consensus originated in the early 1990s. During this time of tremendous social and economic turmoil political, business, and labor leaders in the region were faced with the problem of how to combat the further erosion of institutional authority and effectiveness. At one extreme of the political spectrum lay the leadership of the local Communist Party, staunchly opposed to change. At the other extreme were several new political associations, many staunchly anticommunist, who viewed any working relationship with communist officials as unacceptable. Prusak's new administration needed a way to identify those individuals in both camps who were willing to look beyond ideological differences and use their talents on behalf of the new regional government. Thus was born the policy of "open doors."

"Open doors" simply reflects the government's willingness to work with any group or interested citizen for the common welfare. By continually and publicly inviting such participation, the administration hoped to elicit new ideas for ways out of the economic crisis. Second, it provided government a mechanism for gauging the depth of popular sentiment for or against new initiatives, by testing them initially with these groups. Finally, by involving social and business activists in the formulation of policy, it allowed the administration to co-opt important constituencies. As former First Deputy Governor Valery Trofimov, one of the chief architects of the "open doors" policy, puts it, "It would be strange indeed to hear some Novgorod entrepreneur complain about the region's economic laws, since they designed them."[110]

The open doors policy is most tangibly felt in the work of the regional Social Chamber. Regional officials set up the regional Social Chamber on August 29, 1994, to serve as a public forum to bring together "all social forces interested in noncrisis development, in search of mutually acceptable decisions and in their timely correction."[111] Novgorod thus became one of the first regions in Russia to heed Boris Yeltsin's call to establish regional versions of his own presidential Social Chamber, established in February 1994. Unlike other regions, however, in Novgorod the Social Chamber was sponsored by the executive *and* legislative branches, giving members equal access to both.

Unlike social chambers in other regions, which are largely ceremonial, the Novgorod Social Chamber quickly became an integral part of the deliberative process. Before being considered by the full duma, legislation *must* be reviewed by the Social Chamber, which thus serves unofficially as a lower house. While its recommendations are nonbinding, it is extremely important to the administration that the Social Chamber be seen as influential, hence meetings are always chaired by either the governor or the speaker of the regional duma. Once a month they respond publicly to the criticisms of various social organizations, a practice unheard of in other regions of Russia.[112]

Any registered social organization may join the Social Chamber and send delegates to its monthly meetings. Legislative bills on the agenda of the regional duma are distributed to all participants no less than five working days before the session. Although the chairman sets the preliminary agenda, members may change it by simple majority vote. To encourage the airing of minority opinions, regulations require that any opinion supported by at least one-fifth of the members present be noted in the records and that all items discussed and decisions reached be conveyed to the media.[113] Meetings are typically attended by thirty-five to forty-five individuals representing as many social organizations. In the meetings I have attended, roughly one-quarter of the participants were under thirty-five, one third were pensioners, and four-fifths were men. Meetings usually last three to four hours, although meetings lasting more than six hours are not unknown.

The Social Chamber is designed as much to vent public frustrations as it is to have an impact on policy. During the 1999 elections, for example, the regional Electoral Commission received several complaints that Governor Prusak was exerting undue influence on the media to promote his candidate for the Federation Council, Gennady Burbulis. These were duly raised during a meeting of the Social Chamber, where the governor retorted that anyone who thought electoral procedures had been violated should feel free to pursue the matter in court. His response failed to satisfy the majority, however, so the chamber asked the chairman of the Regional Electoral Commission, Lyubov Fyodorova, to further investigate the allegations. After her formal report and a lengthy question and answer period, the chamber was mollified, but it admonished the Electoral Commission head to be more attentive to potential violations in the future.[114] In fact, it is rather common for the governor, who likes to give interviews to the national media, to be asked to explain this or that comment before the Social Chamber. Nor is all criticism focused on the government. During deliberations over the adoption of a regional law on party financing, opinion among NGOs was sharply divided.[115]

The administration's strategy of initiating consultations with social organizations has proved successful on a number of levels. First, because the administration has given it the important task of reviewing legislation, civic organizations take the Social Chamber seriously. Even critics concede that it is "the connecting link between the ruling elite and Novgorod social organizations."[116] Second, the open door policy has frustrated the efforts of antisystem actors such as the communists far more effectively than overt suppression, with concomitant economic as well as political benefits. Deputy Governor Skibar recalls that some foreign investors initially worried about possible opposition by the local Communist Party but were greatly reassured after visiting the Social Chamber.[117]

The success of the Social Chamber has led to similar initiatives at the district level. The result has been a proliferation of "social councils" attached to various municipal and district governments. According to local civic activists, such councils have become important facets of two-way contact between the government and key social groups.[118] Along with the TOS described earlier, officials treat these organizations as a training ground for the citizenry. In 1999, for example, the Novgorod mayor's office sponsored two conferences on contemporary issues facing young people and also decided to set up a Youth Parliament. To encourage young people to better understand their rights, this parliament was even given the right to place items on the agenda of the Novgorod City Duma.[119]

Social Partnership and the Third Sector

As we have seen, the concept of social partnership is central to the thinking of the Novgorod elite. It appears in the original accord establishing the Trilateral Commission, which the local press refers to simply as "the social partnership agreement," which has since been codified into law.[120] This legislation also reveals, however, that the social partnership concept was designed to harmonize the interests of government, trade unions, and employers, while ignoring voluntary civic organizations. At the time this reflected the reality that there were only a handful of such groups and that most of them had little interest in politics.

This situation changed dramatically at the end of 1997 when, as one leading local activist puts it, "a torrential shower of investments and grants fell upon the Novgorod Region in the form of the Russian-American program, Partnership for Peace."[121] The following year sixty projects received some $2 million from the Eurasia Foundation, another thirty projects received $800,000 from the Open Society Institute and seven more projects were funded by IREX (the International Research & Exchanges Board) for $60,000 to 150,000 each.[122] Thanks to a fifteen-fold increase in funding, almost overnight, Novgorod nongovernmental organizations (NGOs) became a force to be reckoned with. Tatyana Tikhomirova, a consultant for the Novgorod Center for NGO Support, estimated that one in three members of the Novgorod intelligentsia received Western grant money.[123]

This sudden surge of funding clearly caught the administration by surprise and led to initial suspicions. Tatyana Shchipanova, a local journalist with close ties to the city administration, wrote a scathing article accusing foreign aid programs of promoting a drug-like sense of dependency and of creating a community of people different from "ordinary Russians"—people who think of social service as a business and who are not willing to sacrifice for the common good the way their parents had. She wondered about what political ambitions such people might have. Alas, she concluded, it may already be too late to do anything about it. In Novgorod the Great, she wrote, such people were already "a new political force" who could, if need be, summon tens of thousands to their aid.[124]

The economic and political potential of this new constituency ultimately forced the administration to reevaluate its original social partnership model. To qualify for aid, NGOs had to show that they had local government support. Given that the Partnership for Peace was part of an even larger $10 million Regional Investment Initiative designed to attract U.S. investors to Novgorod, the administration could not afford to simply brush it aside. Marriages of convenience were thus entered into between the government and NGOs for the sake of attracting these funds to the region. With money, however, came the first hints of financial independence for NGOs. As one local NGO leader puts it, "Western cash demagnetized people. People became more aggressive in pursuing their goals. . . . The authorities no longer bark at us, they receive us with politesse."[125]

As with FDI, the influx of NGO funding obliged local elites to respond creatively. Governor Prusak has proposed that local government officials do more to involve NGOs in the distribution of scarce resources and services. In remarks to a national conference on local self-government in April 2002, he argued that closer linkages between local self-government and civil society were an "irreversible" trend, and pointed out that civic organizations in the region already provide many social support services more effectively than local governments.[126]

Under pressure from the governor and local constituencies, some municipalities have adopted a utilitarian approach to NGOs, working with them to see if they really can, as they claim, improve the delivery of government services. Many prominent Novgorod voluntary associations, particularly those forming the "third" or noncommercial sector of society, seem quite content with this role. The "third sector" refers to a specific subsection of the universe of nongovernmental organizations that "works toward the resolution of problems of diverse groups of the population (children, the disabled, women, and the like)."[127] Such groups have no political, trade union, or religious affiliation and define themselves merely as conduits between society and the "first sector"— government.[128]

The third sector regards close cooperation with government as the natural state of affairs. If the government can help NGOs fulfill their mandate then NGOs in turn should help the government implement its social agenda. The main demand of third sector organizations is therefore not independence but getting the government to share its "social mandate" [*sotsialnyi zakaz*] with NGOs, preferably through a process of competitive bidding for social services that are paid for with government funds but carried out by the third sector.[129]

This ability to identify a common social agenda may explain the high ratings that Novgorod NGO leaders give to local government and business elites. In two surveys, one conducted in Chelyabinsk, Volgograd, St. Petersburg, and Novgorod and another in Novosibirsk, NGO leaders were asked to evaluate their relations with government, commercial organizations, and the media in eleven different categories. Novgorod NGOs rated their relations with the regional administration, the media, commercial organizations, and municipal administrations more positively than any city in this group.[130] As one Novgorod NGO leader put it,

TABLE 2.4

Most numerous types of voluntary associations in the
Novgorod Region, 1997 and 2001

1997		2001	
Professional	60	Professional	103
Various	54	Political	77
Philanthropic	44	Philanthropic	68
Youth	40	Sports	66
Sports	38	Youth	61

Source: Compiled from "Perechen obshchestvennykh obedinenii
i politicheskikh partii," a computer-generated list received from
Dmitry G. Zavidovsky, head of the Novgrood regional administration's committee on relations with social organizations (November
3, 1998); Kira Kononovich and E. Yu. Naumova, *Informatsionnyi
spravochnik NKO, obshchestvennye obedineniya, i nekommercheskie organizatsii: Veliky Novgorod i Novgorodskaya oblast* (Veliky Novgorod:
Severo-zapadnyi tsentr obshchestvennogo razvitiya, 2001); Vasily
Dubovsky, "Propolka politicheskogo polya . . . ," Novgorod (November 29, 2001).

"Novgorod officials know how to listen. They do not always follow our sug-
gestions, and we may have disagreements. But it would be sinful to complain. When I tell my NGO colleagues from other cities that I can just
come to the mayor or the governor and say what I intend to say, they roll
their eyes in amazement."[131]

Just as local self-government has changed elite attitudes by shifting
decision making to lower levels, and FDI has encouraged elites to be
responsive to the demands of foreign investors, so Western democratic
assistance has altered the model of social partnership, forcing the
Novgorod elite to accept this new social constituency. Unlike the typical
Eastern European NGO that rarely survives beyond the initial grant
period, a recent review of USAID programs found that since 2001 in
Novgorod the majority of financial support has come from local sources
rather than Western sponsors. Novgorod NGOs now employ nearly three
hundred people full time, and pay eleven thousand dollars in local
taxes.[132]

The expansion of the social partnership model has thus provided the
elite with another opportunity to discover the value of compromise and
social consensus. The next step in the evolution of the Novgorod social
partnership model seems clear—to incorporate third sector organizations
in the annual social partnership agreements, formalizing their role as an
essential component of Novgorod's social consensus.[133]

Novgorod elites are beginning to understand that while social tensions
can be managed by a close working relationship between government,

business, and trade unions, a civil society requires the creation of mechanisms for regular feedback and political involvement from organized civic constituencies. Although the administration may initially have been interested only in co-opting potential political opponents, its strategy has wound up encouraging civic organizations to more readily support existing political institutions.

Popular Involvement in Voluntary Associations

External funding may have created new opportunities for civic activism since 1998, but the steady growth and variety of voluntary associations throughout the past decade testifies to the a priori existence of a remarkable level of civic consciousness in the region. At the beginning of 1989, there were already some four hundred clubs and discussion groups of various kinds in the region—though only ten were classified as independent sociopolitical organizations at the time.[134] The heyday of local political activism came with the formation of the electoral coalition Veche, which successfully led a slate of candidates in the elections to local Soviets in 1989.

Efforts to forge a more lasting political coalition, however, proved unsuccessful. This failure of party political activism stands in sharp contrast to the *sixteen-fold* increase in the number of local voluntary associations between 1991 and 1996.[135] Commenting on civic activism in the region *before* the Partnership for Peace initiative, Eurasia Foundation observers took special note of the "energy and enthusiasm of the NGO sector in Novgorod and in some of the smaller towns of the Novgorod Oblast. Many citizens' groups, especially in Novgorod city, are already implementing successful programs in areas as diverse as children's health, human rights issues, and homeowners' associations."[136] Even more remarkably, while growth in new civic associations had essentially ceased in Russia as a whole by 1998, in Novgorod it has continued rather spectacularly.[137]

Many of these organizations pursue agendas quite apart from those of the administration (table 2.5). One of the most important is the Women's Parliament, which was set up in 1995 as a place where women could turn for help in getting into business for themselves. Gradually its agenda has expanded to include the organization of seminars and conventions on issues like women in business, gender education in schools, and domestic abuse. Its annual conferences are attended by some 150 to 200 women.[138]

Dissatisfied with the pace of social change, the Women's Parliament has turned to grooming women candidates for political office. In this task it can rely on a number of prominent women in political office, includ-

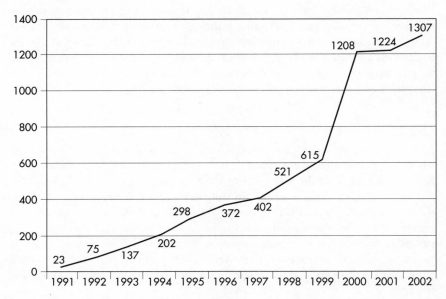

Source: Compiled from "Perechen obshchestvennykh obedinenii i politicheskikh partii," a computer-generated list received from Dmitry G. Zavidovsky, chairman of the Novgorod regional administration's committee on relations with social organ-izations, (November 3, 1998); S. Petrova, "Tendentsii razvitiya 'tretyego sektora' v regione (na primere Novgorodskoi oblasti)," *Upravlencheskoe konsultirovanie* (Veliky Novgorod: MNOU Dialog, vol. 3 (1999), pp. 18–29; Kira Kononovich and E. Yu. Naumova, *Informatsionnyi spravochnik NKO, obshchestvennye obedineniya, i nekommercheskie organizatsii: Veliky Novgorod i Novgorodskaya oblast* (Veliky Novgorod: Severo-zapadnyi tsentr obshchestvennogo razvitiya, 2001); "Soobshchenie press-tsentra za 20.02.2002 v 16:13."

FIGURE 2.6 Civic and voluntary associations registered in the Novgorod Region, 1991–2002

ing Lyubov Andreyeva, former deputy head of the Novgorod Regional Duma and currently regional representative of the Federal Inspector for the Northwest Federal District; Elena Soldatova, chair of the regional duma's budget committee; and three former deputy mayors of Novgorod the Great: Galina Matveeva, Irina Kibina, and Ekaterina Krasnovidova. The Women's Parliament notes that in recent years forty-two women have held political office in the region.[139]

Another focal point of regional civic activism is the Northwest Center for Social Development, also known as the Novgorod NGO support center. Established in 1997 with a $40,000 seed grant from the Eurasia Foundation, it now serves as a clearinghouse for NGOs in the region. It organizes competitive grants, distributes local funding, offers consulta-

TABLE 2.5
Most rapidly growing types of voluntary associations in
the Novgorod Region, 1997 through 2001

Type	1997	2001	Average annual growth rate
Women's	4	22	110%
Political	20	77	77
Human/Civil Rights	9	34	76
Disabled	15	43	56
Ecological	8	22	55

Source: Compiled from "Perechen obshchestvennykh obedinenii
i politicheskikh partii," a computer-generated list received from
Dmitry G. Zavidovsky, head of the Novgorod regional administration's committee on relations with social organizations (November
3, 1998); Kira Kononovich and E. Yu. Naumova, *Informatsionnyi
spravochnik NKO, obshchestvennye obedineniya, i nekommercheskie organizatsii: Veliky Novgorod i Novgorodskaya oblast* (Veliky Novgorod:
Severo-zapadnyi tsentr obshchestvennogo razvitiya, 2001); Vasily
Dubovsky, "Propolka politicheskogo polya . . . ," *Novgorod* (November 29, 2001).

tion to individuals wishing to apply for grants or to set up an NGO,
and initiates meetings between NGO leaders and representatives of
the regional administration. Through its participation in the regional
Social Chamber, it serves as the NGO community's primary voice on local
legislation.[140]

Not all NGOs, however, are pleased with being forced to choose
between joining the apolitical third sector or being left outside the administration's "social partnership" tent entirely. They are highly critical of the
governor for having created "cardboard social organizations."[141] Some
complain that the administration's effort to portray the region as
politically stable to attract foreign investment has created "ideological
pressure" that prevents challenges to the status quo.[142] The head of the
Women's Parliament, Irina Urtayeva, even contends that there is no
meaningful interaction between NGOs and the government, only "silent
opposition" to the regime by both citizens and NGOs. Paradoxically, to
remedy this she urges passage of a law guaranteeing that municipal grants
are awarded to local NGOs.[143] Displeasure with the current state of affairs
has led some twenty civic associations to form a coalition that openly calls
for breaking up the political monopoly held by the current political and
business elite. In June 2001 it issued a public appeal to the regional duma,
calling on its current members not to seek reelection.[144]

Although some NGO leaders blame the governor for social apathy,
others suggest that the problem has deeper roots. For one thing, they say,
NGOs must learn how to lobby more effectively. They may see themselves

53

as representing the interests of constituents, but all too often that constituency has not heard about their efforts. The reluctance of many NGOs to sully themselves in the political arena has led to an artificial distinction between organizations that "do real work that is useful and good" and those that are "merely political."[145]

Another problem is that activists often define success exclusively in terms of large-scale social engagement. Anything short of "raising the masses" is dismissed as political apathy. This unfortunate legacy of the Soviet era unjustly belittles the impact that small, grassroots organizations can have on people's lives. Finally, for older generations, fear of the consequences that unsanctioned public activism can have is still deeply ingrained and no doubt contributes to social apathy. This apathy is compounded by the younger generation's lack of ability—or desire—to speak to the older generation in political terms the latter can understand.

Even with all these caveats, it is hard to ignore the impact that volunteer organizations are having in Novgorod. Although federal laws have made registration notably more cumbersome in recent years and organizations inactive for three years must now reregister, the number of voluntary associations in the region continues to rise at an impressive rate. It seems unlikely that people would go through all the effort and expense if they did not consider it worthwhile. Indeed, the speed of the socioeconomic changes Novgorod society has undergone has created quite another dilemma for civic activists. While the more established civic associations of the third sector strive to join the social partnership proffered by the administration, others reject such a partnership in principle.

A development that may ultimately tip the scales in favor of the latter is the steadily growing number of registered political parties (fig. 2.7). Prompted by new federal legislation that requires the election of no less than half of the members of regional legislatures on the basis of party lists, more national parties are now focusing on district-level political party building.[146] This development poses a fundamental challenge to the region's traditionally apolitical concept of social partnership.

It remains to be seen whether these two very different types of NGOs, those in the third sector and those that are overtly political, will find a way to work together. If the third sector can learn to overcome its disdain for politics and overtly political associations can strive to be more relevant to people's daily lives, they could conceivably forge a formidable coalition that would raise local civic activism to an entirely new level. The essential components of such a broad-based civil society are all in place.

Novgorod not only demonstrates impressive progress on essential aspects of democracy, such as the creation of a new constitutional order, eco-

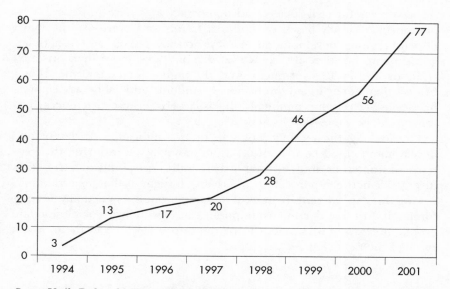

Source: Vasily Dubovsky, "Propolka politicheskogo polya. . .," *Novgorod* (November 29, 2001); Darya Ivanova, "Spisok politicheskikh obshchestvennykh obedinenii, zaregistrirovannykh Upravleniem Ministerstva Iustitsii RF po Novgorodskoi oblasti," *Regions.ru*(February 6, 2001), http://www.regions.ru/article/comments/id/418041.html.

FIGURE 2.7 Registered political parties and associations in the Novgorod Region, 1994–2001

nomic development, and civic activism, but a more detailed look reveals a remarkable depth and consistency to the structural patterns, elite behavioral consensus, and popular acceptance of new values. Taken together they point inescapably to the conclusion that Novgorod has moved well beyond democratic transition and into democratic consolidation.

But there is an even greater significance to these mutually reinforcing indicators of democratic consolidation. In several innovative case studies, Harry Eckstein found that as democracies mature they exhibit patterns of increasing congruence among authority patterns and institutions at all levels of society. When such congruence is found, he says, it makes a further, stronger case for long-term democratic stability.[147] Novgorod may have developed so rapidly, precisely because the different components shaping its democratic development—local self-government, fiscal autonomy, and civic volunteerism—all interacted with and complemented one another.

It would be difficult, however, to find many analysts of Russia who have reached the same conclusion. Most remain profoundly pessimistic about the prospects for civil society and democracy anywhere in Russia. This pessimism is largely based on national trends and overlooks the many hopeful regional developments. Surveys do show falling trust in national government, but they also show that this has been more than offset by rising trust in local government. And although it is true that the "broad fronts" that once united professional, student, and labor associations have failed to regroup nationally, this is largely because civic energy has refocused elsewhere—on local needs.[148]

Overlooking the existence of one or two indicators of democratic development could be written off as an anomaly. Overlooking the existence of numerous, mutually reinforcing indicators points to a troubling divergence between perception and reality. It suggests that instead of narrowing this gap, current theories of democratization may actually be reinforcing it. Just how current assumptions cause us to overlook democratic development, and what needs to be done to break free of them, is the focus of the next chapter.

CHAPTER 3

HOW WE MISSED NOVGOROD'S DEMOCRATIC CONSOLIDATION

By the end of the 1990s, Novgorod's phenomenal success in attracting foreign investment had begun to draw the attention of both journalists and scholars. As a rule, however, their writings focused on the region's friendly tax regime and charismatic governor, overlooking the crucial role played by local self-government and social partnership. Typically, the region was depicted as benefiting from an unusually benign, but still highly authoritarian and clientelistic, local leadership.[1]

Skeptics usually focus on three shortcomings of democracy in Novgorod: the lack of political parties; rampant political clientelism and the weakness of political institutions; and the absence of a free press. A closer look, however, reveals that these "failures" reflect a conscious effort by the local elite to reconcile Novgorod's traditions (as they interpreted them) with modern European democratic practices.

CRITICISMS OF NOVGOROD AS A DEMOCRATIC MODEL

Democracy without Parties?

Along with the rest of Russia, Novgorod has been widely criticized for not having a party system. Regional polls conducted over the last decade show that voters consistently avoid party politics. Because political parties play a key role in mature democratic societies, it is simply assumed that they should play a similar role in postcommunist societies. Few bother to ask whether strong political parties are as essential to developing democracies as they are to mature democracies.

Most of the literature on political parties draws a clear distinction between parties and other social organizations.[2] Larry Diamond, for example, argues that interest groups cannot substitute for parties, because they cannot aggregate interests as broadly across social groups and political issues and do not provide the discipline needed to form governments and pass legislation.[3] Jack Bielasiak argues that only parties can teach competing interests to accommodate, permit the selection of alternative policy programs, and ensure effective public monitoring of government.[4] Political parties, one influential study concludes, play a "crucial role as mediators in both the installation and consolidation of democracy," and Leonardo Morlino has even characterized Southern Europe's two decades-long process of democratization as a "consolidation through parties."[5]

Yet, alongside this impressive list of benefits, one also finds widespread cynicism about political parties.[6] Parties are seen as self-serving constructs that fragment interest articulation along ideological lines and lead to gridlock in government. Hungarian sociologist Gabor Toka argues that voting patterns in Eastern Europe show that parties have done a remarkably poor job of aggregating interests across social groups.[7] In Russia, according to Suzanna Pshizova, the very factors that make the Communist Party of the Russian Federation a good "traditional" party (having a clearly defined political message and meaningful party discipline) led to its electoral defeat in 1995 and 1999. Like many Western Europeans, she concludes, Russians find the old model of long-term attachment to a single party outdated.[8]

There is a good deal of research, much of it emanating from earlier democratic transitions, that suggests that alternative models of social participation can take the place of political parties.[9] In South Africa, for example, researchers have found that political activism is more a function of participation in NGOs than in political parties.[10] In Chile, the reemergence of parties following the collapse of the regime of Augusto Pinochet did not, as many had predicted, lead individuals to shift their primary political allegiance away from other interest associations.[11]

The widespread popular disillusionment with political parties, stemming from self-aggrandizing political behavior, has led some to question the conventional wisdom that parties are essential to democracy. Philippe Schmitter contrasts the behavior of political parties to that of "monopolistic, hierarchically coordinated and nationally focused interest associations," which are better able to "link . . . directly with one another or to state agencies in bargaining over economic and social policies."[12] In countries where parties have historically played a minor role, Schmitter suggests, the preferred form of democratic interest articulation may be "formalized and centralized intermediation, primarily (but not exclusively) through associations representing class, sectoral, and professional interests."[13] Examples might include the foundational pacts that played such a crucial role in the democratic transitions of Columbia and Venezuela in the late 1950s, the Moncloa Accords in Spain in 1970, the social partnership agreements in Ghana and Botswana in the 1980s, and, of course, the Trilateral Accords signed annually in Novgorod.[14]

Critics, however, often dismiss such accords as nothing more than sophisticated instruments of political control. Moreover, they say that the use of the term "pacts" in Russia is highly misleading because it implies an agreement among relatively autonomous entities, which do not exist there.[15] Not everyone, however, agrees that the success of pacts reflects the independence of key actors. Some stress the mutual dependence of key actors. It is the recognition of mutual dependence, says John Higley, that sets the stage for a "restrained partisanship" or "elite settlement" among key groups. "By virtue of their breadth and procedural guarantees of security they give to all important elites," such pacts, he says, directly foster consolidated as opposed to limited democracy.[16]

This aptly describes what happened in the Novgorod Region in the 1990s. Under Governor Prusak's leadership, Novgorod's government reached out to the local business elite for support; in return for supporting the governor's course toward financial autonomy from Moscow, they received a prominent voice in the formulation of local legislation. The government also reached out to local civic organizations to defuse social tensions and expand trust in government. The resulting web of dependencies has fostered a commingling of corporate and civic identity and led to the creation of several innovative institutions for mediating the conflicts that inevitably arise among key constituencies. Novgorod thus illustrates that rare type of democracy that develops around organized constituencies which function so much like political parties that former Czech President Vaclav Havel has aptly called them "nonpolitical parties."[17]

Novgorod's active civic infrastructure allows us to view the region's lack of party development in a different light—not as a symptom of inadequate democratization but as an alternative type of democratic development. Those who argue that party politics are the sine qua non of any democratic system insist that parties are the only effective vehicles for interest articulation and aggregation.[18] The problem is that because parties have no history of effective interest articulation in Novgorod (and in much of Eastern Europe), people there do not view them as either effective or representative. They therefore turn to the more familiar voluntary associations.

Faced with an urgent need to establish legitimacy in government, it is hardly surprising that Novgorod elites avoided unpopular political parties and turned instead to civic associations for support. What is surprising, and unusual, is that they recognized the value of giving such groups an institutional forum—the Social Chamber—within which to exercise and develop many party-like functions. Still, critics might counter that the prolonged absence of an institutionalized party system ultimately prevents democratic consolidation from ever taking place.

After reviewing the impact of parties in the four most advanced Eastern European democracies (Poland, the Czech Republic, Slovakia, and Hungary), Toka has determined that it need not do so, so long as there are alternative forms of political representation. He points out that even as parties in these four countries have become more institutionalized, the level of public satisfaction with parties has not increased (indeed, a reverse correlation emerges for the Czech Republic between 1992 and 1996). Very modest levels of party institutionalization may suffice to make democracy "the only game in town" if other favorable conditions are also present. He cites the proximity to the European Union, a tradition of civilian control of the military, the shock of the loss of monopoly status by the former leading party, and the integration of remnants of the old regime into new political structures.[19]

Democratic consolidation in Novgorod seems to have profited from similar factors. The Novgorod Region has been the special focus of attention by several Nordic countries, special initiatives of TACIS, the European Union program designed to assist postcommunist states, as well as the United States–sponsored Regional Investment Initiative. As the national Communist Party of the Soviet Union collapsed, the regional political administration simply resigned and the local CPSU apparatus never recovered. Finally, both the city and regional administrations have pursued policies of retaining and using members of the old regime who were capable of making the transition to a market economy.

A key flaw in the assumption that democratic development requires an institutionalized party system is that it simply disregards constituent opinion. Why should Novgorodians believe that "developed parties would increase the accountability of elected officials," when their own experience has shown them that this is not so? Although the low level of party identification might be the result of elite collusion in favor of the status quo, a botched or "partial reform equilibrium," it seems simpler to argue that local candidates avoid party identification because voters dislike parties.[20]

Yet, just because voters dislike parties does not mean they are not politically active. One might just as easily assume that when citizens eschew ineffective civic organizations (that happen to call themselves "parties") in favor of other more effective civic organizations, this reflects a choice in favor of more meaningful civic and political engagement.

Although there is ample reason to question the simplistic linkage of democracy to institutionalized political parties, I am not suggesting that parties are never important to democracy. I am, however, suggesting that they are a mixed blessing, whose value to society grows as democracy consolidates. At the outset of democratic transition, people do not prize the ability of civic associations to aggregate and articulate interests as highly as they do their ability to serve the common good. Promoting regional party development seems especially questionable at the outset of democratic transition because, although at the national level a party's ideology can serve as a convenient shorthand for voters who know little else about a candidate, at the local level we know that people are put off by candidates who emphasize political partisanship and thus accentuate social cleavages.[21] In any case, it is at least worth asking whether it really makes sense for Western aid agencies to invest in party institutionalization when 83 percent of people polled say they have no interest in parties.[22]

Parties may be indispensable for mature democracies, where they reflect long-standing class and social differences, but they are a poor measure of democratic development in countries that are emerging from decades of forced participation in political activity. The real test of democratic consolidation should not be how closely the party system in Novgorod resembles that in the West but whether the essential democratic functions of interest aggregation and articulation are being carried out, albeit by other means. An excessive devotion by scholars to the importance of parties has largely obscured this line of inquiry.

Clientelism, Corporatism, or Concertation?

A second common criticism of Novgorod involves the weakness of its legislature. Neil Melvin suggests that such weakness can be measured by looking at the degree to which local charters enshrine a separation of powers between the local legislature and the executive. The absence of a formal agreement on the separation of powers suggests to him a lack of legislative influence, and in a careful survey of thirty-one regions of Russia, Melvin finds Novgorod's legislature to be one of the weakest.[23] Such weakness, he says, is a characteristic sign of political clientelism.

In fact, a separation of powers is explicitly enshrined in Article 4, paragraph 2 of the Novgorod constitution: "All three branches of government are independent within the framework of their responsibilities, as established by the Constitution of the Russian Federation, federal laws, and the Constitution of the Novgorod Region, and carry out their activities on the basis of a separation of powers."[24] To prevent institutional logjams, however, the Novgorod system of government has subordinated the principle of separation of powers to the principle of social partnership, variously codified and legislatively enshrined. Although some might interpret this as legislative weakness, it might just as well be seen as enhancing the influence of the legislature. The former deputy chair of the Novgorod Regional Duma, Lyubov Andreyeva, for example, suggests that the Novgorod legislature has been much more efficient than the perpetually conflict-ridden legislatures of St. Petersburg and Sverdlovsk precisely because it has avoided direct institutional conflicts by resolving problems earlier in the deliberative process.[25]

Nor is it accurate to describe Novgorod politics as clientelistic, if by clientelism one means privileged access to state resources in exchange for votes. The classic example of clientelism, well known to students of urban politics in the United States, is the populist politician who establishes an urban political machine that provides special access to city goods and services in exchange for "getting out the vote."[26] Although the similarity between such "political machines" and Governor Prusak's administration seem compelling at first glance, the devolution of governmental functions to municipalities, and the strict guidelines that districts must adhere to within the regional budget, make it difficult for politicians to "bribe" local citizens for their vote. It is therefore not uncommon for the governor's "political machine" to stumble, sometimes quite badly.[27]

A key facet of such clientelism is populism, typically expressed in extravagant promises made by officials during election campaigns. If anything, though, Governor Prusak has been disconcertingly frank with the electorate (table 3.1). In contravention of populist logic, he has embraced the country's most unpopular politicians (Gennady Burbulis, Yegor Gaidar, Boris Yeltsin), criticized the popular President Putin, and spoken out in favor of hot-button items such as Russian involvement in NATO and foreign direct investment. He promises people opportunities for hard work but warns that if they don't want to work, there is not much anyone can do for them. Saying openly that he represents the interests of "people who have money and power," he warns voters to "beware of politicians who tell you they serve the people."[28]

This absence of populist rhetoric is significant because it points to an important psychological milestone in the evolution of regimes away from electoral clientelism. Simona Piattoni, who has studied regional clientelist regimes in Italy, shows that once elite consensus is reached some elected officials will opt for a strategy that attracts new clients rather than continuing to compete for the same fixed pool. Instead of promoting themselves to a narrowly targeted constituency, they begin to portray

TABLE 3.1
Selected sayings of Governor Prusak

"It's time to get used to the notion that, aside from the disabled and those who can not work, there should not be any other socially protected social groups."
— *Novgorodskii universitet*, 27, no. 297 (August 30, 1996)

"I belong to the class of people who have money and power, so my goal is to offer that class a program. The authorities have one last chance to survive, but not by telling the people about how poor and backward Russia is. They must answer the question 'what needs to be done.' Here's what needs to be done: demand that power and money play by the rules."
— Elena Ogorodnikova, " 'Pravee pravykh: Chem Prusak luchshe Nemtsova," *Izvestiya.ru* (January 24, 2002)

"Do you remember professor Preobrazhensky [from Mikhail Bulgakov's *Heart of a Dog*] who was told 'You don't like the proletariat,' and replied, 'No, I do not.' Well . . . I agree with him completely."
— Dmitrii Travin, "Mikhail Prusak: Ya opirayus na neopartkhozaktiv," *Delo* (December 3, 2001)

"Let us not be embarrassed to learn from capitalists, instead of trying to prove that the world is flat."
— Remarks made at the opening of his second campaign for governor, June 28, 1999, at Novgorod State University, personal notes

"I want there to be rules that will force anyone succeeding me to follow the rules and not their own ambitions or their own spirit."
— Interviewed on Moscow radio station Mayak for the program *Politicheskii olimp* (December 23, 1998)

"On behalf of the government, my task as head of the administration is to create conditions where anyone can make money and work for themselves . . . but if people don't want to work (which we see all too often), then there is not a thing I can do."
— Viktor Krutikov, "Zasuchim rukava, Novgorodtsy!" *Novgorodskie vedomosti* (December 24, 1991)

"In a market economy there are no insoluble problems. The good thing about markets is that they give everyone a chance to thrive, get rich, and [they] force people to work."
— Yuri Krasavin, "Rynok vsem daet shans," *Zemlya novgorodskaya* (June 12, 1992)

"Introducing the elements of civil society into everyday Russian life is my number one task . . . Furthermore, I am convinced that a civil society can be constructed even at the regional level, if desired."
— Stanislav Stremidlovsky, "Gubernator Novgorodskoi oblasti Mikhail Prusak: 'Odin raz pokrivish dushoi—bolshe nikto ne poverit,' " *Vek* (August 9, 2002)

"I don't fight with anyone. In our country [people] are always fighting with someone. Fighting against capitalism, fighting for BAM [the Baikal-Amur Railway]. I'd much rather write sensible laws and look for compromises."
— Barbara Kerneck, "Von Steuern und Offizierspastete," *taz, die tageszeitung* (July 25, 2000).

themselves as guardians of the public welfare. The result is a more pragmatic political environment that transforms government from a "spoil of
war" into a "virtuous patron."[29]

The similarities with Novgorod are hard to miss. The elite's commitment to transcending ideological conflict (evident, among other things,
in its blatant disinterest in party politics) and the region's devotion to
administrative efficiency have already been noted. Another key aspect of
this daring strategy noted by Piattoni—the creation of rules that bind the
behavior of future authorities—has also been a central component of the
agenda in Novgorod. When it is successful, Piattoni says, former patrons
gradually free themselves from their dependence on a narrow client base
and build a broader social constituency.[30] The emphasis on making
reforms in Novgorod a task that involves "all of civil society," as former
First Deputy Governor Valery Trofimov put it, is meant to achieve the
same result.[31]

Politics in Novgorod today, therefore, resembles not clientelism, with
an elite narrowly focused on extracting wealth, but what Philippe
Schmitter calls a "concertation regime." An important characteristic of
such regimes is "class governance . . . the capacity to commit an entire
comprehensive social category—for example, owners of productive property, workers in all industries, self-employed people in all sectors—to a
common and long-term course of action as well as to ensure that those
bound by such a policy indeed comply with it."[32] This succinctly describes
the tripartite agreements that are so carefully forged by the administration, employers, and labor unions each year.

Although Schmitter boldly contends that such "pacted transitions" may
be the most favorable environment for democratic transitions, other analysts are skeptical that anything smacking of corporatism can be compatible with democratic development.[33] They suggest that elite settlements
merely provide a reserved domain for the wealthy and powerful. This
view, however, has been criticized by scholars who regard the legacy of
socialist corporatism as a potential asset for democratization.[34] In their
view, elites that show a modicum of respect for the socialist values that are
retained by a large segment of society are better able to implement
reforms. Bulgarian political scientist Elena Iankova calls this process
"transformative corporatism."[35]

At the heart of transformative corporatism lies a "bargained exchange
between conflicting interests that makes it quite different from clientelism."[36] In such an exchange "integrated interest organizations" (not
parties) gain a certain consultative and decision-making influence over
government.[37] This, says Iankova, is the model that best describes most
Eastern European democracies—Poland, Hungary, the Czech Republic,
Slovakia, and, one might add, Novgorod.

To be sure, all these regimes still display much higher levels of state control and elite self-interest than the more established corporatist societies of Western Europe, but Iankova is confident that these differences will be tempered by the passage of time: the philosophical similarities between Western and Eastern European corporatism are simply too great and the pressure of global integration too strong to resist. Thus, while scholars are right to point out the potential dangers that corporatism poses for democratic development, we need hardly view failure as set in stone. In much of Eastern Europe, including Novgorod, corporatism has so far taken a rather benign path.

Media Freedom in Novgorod

The final criticism of note is the alleged absence of a free press. Many Russians place access to the media in the same category as pension, education, and medical care—a public right, rather than a commodity one should have to pay for. From a Western (and particularly a U.S.) perspective, it is more common to assert that information should be paid for by private sponsors, rather than the government.

A related cultural nuance is the distress that many Russian journalists (particularly those in television) feel over having to find sponsors for their programming. Though this is slowly changing, it is still common to hear journalists complain about how commercialism limits press freedom even more than government censorship once used to. There is also a tendency among some older journalists and editors to regard the press as a vehicle for educating the populace on how to think "properly" about an issue. This group complains in private that they are no longer able to indoctrinate the populace as they once did. For them the press is indeed less "free" today than it was in Soviet times.

These differences make it problematic to evaluate media freedom in Russia. A case in point is the *Index of Mass Media Freedom in Russia* prepared by the Public Expertise Project and Russian Union of Journalists.[38] It purports to measure regional press freedom in Russian by looking at three criteria: access to information, production conditions, and ease of distribution. A closer look, however, reveals that the first category refers not to media availability but to how government officials responded to specific press inquiries (omitting what the reviewers term "deceitful" or "formal" responses). Novgorod does rather well in this category, ranking in the top ten.

The second category deals with the level of private support received by local media and the degree to which local laws governing the media correspond to federal law. The former presumably reflects the willingness of private entrepreneurs to finance the press. Although this may tell us something about whether the wealthy regard the media as a valuable resource, it tells us little about actual freedom of the press. Once again, though, Novgorod does well here, ranking eleventh out of the eighty regions sampled in 1999.

The third criterion is the most problematic. It measures press distribution, partly by the absence of government hurdles to registration but mostly by the number of tax credits that local authorities offer to the media. The more tax credits, the higher the rating. Such credits do indeed make the media more financially accessible to readers, but at the cost of greater dependence on the subsidizing authority.

Novgorod ranks close to the bottom in this category, and as a result the regional media is deemed "not free." The authors of the rating seem unaware that Novgorod authorities have for years pursued a policy of reducing subsidies to the media as the most sensible way to promote its independence.[39] Whereas in 1999 state-subsidized papers accounted for over half of Novgorod's newspaper circulation, by mid 2002 the percentage had fallen to 38 percent.[40] Even in the media that the local government continues to support—the daily paper *Novgorodskie vedomosti*, the local television station Slaviya, and the weekly Novgorod city paper, *Novgorod*—there has been conscious shift from direct government subsidy to buying advertising space.[41]

In sum, the administration has relied on the market to provide media diversity, and its strategy seems to be paying off. Since 2000 nearly a dozen new newspapers and journals have sprung up, along with several independent radio and television ventures. As advertising revenues have gone up, so has commercial interest in the independent media.[42] Banking on a steady rise in local advertising revenues (which rose 20 percent in 2002), Vladimir Romanishin, the head of Novgorod the Great's largest media consortium, says he plans to double the circulation of his publications. The newfound profitability of the local market has even begun to attract outsiders, like the family-oriented weekly newspaper *Volkhov*, owned by the northwest-based media consortium Provintsiya.[43]

It is also important, when discussing media freedom, to distinguish between the absence of alternative media and its suppression. By all accounts direct government censorship is virtually unheard of in Novgorod, though many journalists will tell you in private conversations that there were times when their antipathy to the communists led them to "clean up Prusak's act" and make him sound more polished. Today, however, the situation has reversed itself. The online review of the nation's regional press, *Regions.ru*, often ranks Prusak among the "losing" governors, those most often criticized by their local press. Indeed, in the weeks preceding the election of the new mayor of Novgorod the Great in December 2002, Prusak was consistently rated one of the top three "losers" nationwide, with negative local press coverage ranging from 17 to 50 percent in a given week.[44]

In addition, there are a number of local television programs, like the weekly *N-Buro*, which one would have to call confrontational. In the fall of 2002, when the regional health commissioner decided to close the field hospital in the village of Kulotino without first consulting the local population, as the law requires, an *N-Buro* reporter raised such a stink that the decision was reversed, the commissioner reprimanded, and the governor forced to issue a public pledge that not a single hospital, polyclinic, or social aid office anywhere in the region would be closed without the consent of municipal authorities.[45]

Finally, there is an influential group of journalists who are usually overlooked when discussing regional freedom of the press—the local stringers for major national newspapers such as *Nezavisimaya gazeta*, *Segodnya*, *Vremya-MN*, and *Rossiiskaya gazeta*. Each has published well over a hundred articles on the region, with *Itar-TASS*, *Ekonomika i zhizn*, *Argumenty i fakty*, *Ogonyok*, and radio *Rossiya* all having accredited local correspondents.[46] The most prolific local correspondent, Andrei Riskin, has published more than 250 articles in the St. Petersburg edition of *Nezavisimaya gazeta*, all unabashedly hostile to the governor and the mayor.

The greatest problem the Novgorod media has faced is thus not political control but the failure of business leaders to recognize its value, either financial or political. Since 2000, however, this has been changing. Business leaders are now coming to realize that owning a media outlet increases their social standing. It can be used to lobby the government and to promote political candidates as well as products. Now that, thanks to increased advertising revenues, such investments are beginning to make financial sense, more and more investors are jumping into the local media market.[47] Continued failure to distinguish between market constraints and political constraints can only lead, as it has in the case of Novgorod, to a misreading of the situation.

THE MOST COMMON FAILURES OF DEMOCRATIZATION THEORIES

This review of the most common criticisms of Novgorod is not meant to suggest that all is now smooth sailing. Promoting democracy effectively, however, requires an accurate assessment of the successes and failures to date, hence it is important to note that for Novgorod the challenges that remain more closely resemble those that societies encounter at the outset of democratic consolidation, rather than during democratic transition. Thus, one major problem that still looms is formalizing the role that political parties will play. I suspect that trying to integrate them into the existing corporatist structure will prove far more difficult than anyone anticipates, and that it will be accompanied by the emergence of fissures that further undermine the social consensus that characterized Novgorod in the 1990s.

A second problem is that Novgorod's comparative advantage as a magnet for foreign direct investment is rapidly evaporating. Many other regions have now adopted similar tax incentives, and, as the country attracts more large-scale foreign investment, Novgorod's low population, aging workforce, and distance from Moscow will become greater liabilities. If the region fails to attract new investors and improve its labor force both in quantity and quality, a vicious demographic cycle could ensue, reversing the progress toward fiscal autonomy and making the region more dependent on federal subsidies to provide for its aging population. Such dependence would make it extremely difficult to oppose Moscow's efforts at political and economic centralization.

Finally, there is the post-Prusak transition, which I see as the ultimate test of whether Novgorod has fully achieved democratic consolidation. If, after Governor Prusak leaves office in 2008, the social partnership he has helped forge perseveres, then it will have become a permanent fixture of the region's social consciousness. If, on the other hand, new political leaders succeed in personalizing the next regime to suit their needs, as occurred when another prominent young reformer, Boris Nemtsov, left the governor's post in Nizhny Novgorod, then Novgorod will still have some way to go to achieve democratic consolidation.

Some will, no doubt, argue that Novgorod cannot display the conditions of democratic consolidation simply because it is part a Russian political system that has strong authoritarian and centralizing tendencies. These may have temporarily receded under Yeltsin, but they have reemerged under Putin. But while the Novgorod Region is undoubtedly a part of Russia's evolving political system, it has also shown greater institutional stability and political resilience during the past decade than the country as a whole. From an institutional point of view, therefore, one would have to conclude that it is Novgorod's political model that has demonstrated better prospects for survival.

Such criticisms ultimately rest on dismal assumptions about Russian political culture that can be neither proved nor disproved. I believe, however, there is ample reason to be sanguine about the durability of Novgorod's reforms after Prusak leaves office, partly because they have been so well received by the local populace and partly because of the institutional constraints I identified in the previous chapter.

All the potential problems just cited, however, cannot detract from the remarkable progress the region has already made toward democratic consolidation. If anything, they underscore that Novgorod must now look beyond transition to the further institutionalization of its democratic patterns of governance. The evidence of Novgorod's democratic consolidation is serious enough that we must ask ourselves how it could have been so consistently overlooked. To answer this question, however, it is not enough to simply shift the level of analysis from the national to the regional level, for, as we are about to see, three of the most popular approaches to regional analysis in Russia—structuralist, elite, and charismatic—all failed to unravel the mystery of Novgorod's political and economic success.

The Limitations of Structuralism

One of the most popular approaches to explaining the widening differences among Russian regions focuses on inherited structural limitations. It asserts that physical, geographical, and institutional attributes severely limit a region's political and economic choices.[48] Bert van Selm, for example, argues that there is a clear relationship between the inherited economic infrastructure and economic success in the first years of transition in the Russian Federation. Regions that got a "winning" industry did far better than regions with a "losing" industry.[49]

While Van Selm highlights the importance of differences in natural resources, labor, and capital, other structuralists emphasize favorable geographic location, transportation, or industrial infrastructure.[50] But while certain regions are clearly endowed with natural advantages, it is equally apparent that some have been able to do more with less, and a rigid structuralist approach is one of the least effective at explaining why Novgorod, which was ranked among the bottom third of Russian regions in development potential, became one of the nation's fastest-growing regions so quickly.

A more sophisticated version of the structural limitations argument looks at how governors use the resources at their disposal. Peter Stavrakis suggests that "a careful analysis of who said what and supported whom during the events of October 1993 might be as good a predictor of regional success as any we might produce," while Philip Roeder makes the case that those "privileged" by the particular structural or power arrangements they inherited from the Soviet past tended to mobilize resources more effectively in response to political and economic challenges.[51] Both reflect a type of structuralist argument known as "resource mobilization," which argues that the different resources and organizational capacities of a region will affect a governor's bargaining strategy vis-à-vis the center.[52]

Although local elites in certain ethnic republics—such as Tatarstan, Yakutiya, and Bashkortostan—mobilized quickly to promote greater local autonomy from Moscow, no clear correlation has ever emerged between regional autonomy and democratization.[53] The two dozen Russian regions that negotiated treaties delimiting the powers of the federal government have not been noticeably more prosperous or democratic, particularly compared to Novgorod, whose governor explicitly rejected such a treaty, saying that what governors lack is not the power but the will to act.[54]

The structuralist approach has been applied specifically to Novgorod by Michael J. Bradshaw and Dimitri A. Zimine, who find no dramatic transformations in the region. Such modest economic success as Novgorod can boast of, they say, has been the result of two factors: Governor Prusak's success as a lobbyist for the region in Moscow, and an unusually high level of foreign direct investment. This high level of FDI, however, was the result not of reform but of the governor's ability to exert "direct control" over the regional duma and municipal authorities. His policies thus represent a Soviet-style mix of populism and paternalism purchased at the expense of true democratization.[55]

There are several problems with this analysis. The first is the inordinate weight it gives to social stability and the facile assumption that it can readily be imposed by fiat. If the link between paternalism, stability, and foreign investment were that obvious, Russian regions should be awash in foreign capital. While giving social stability its due, foreign investors more readily cite the Novgorod administration's solicitous attitude toward potential foreign investors, efforts to negotiate on their behalf with Moscow ministries, and, most especially, willingness to offer long-term lucrative tax credits as reasons for investing.

As for the implication that Governor Prusak's close relationship with former Prime Minister Viktor Chernomyrdin led to more federal funding, it is worth noting that Novgorod's decision to pursue fiscal independence from Moscow was also made during Chernomyrdin's tenure and that prior to 1998 Prusak is never mentioned as an effective lobbyist in any Moscow rating.[56] He achieved his highest ratings as a lobbyist only *after* Chernomyrdin left office and despite having tense relationships with Prime Ministers Evgeny Primakov and Mikhail Kasyanov. Novgorod did indeed receive its transfer payments from Moscow earlier than many other regions, but it also paid its taxes earlier.[57] It is telling that Zimine and Bradshaw make no mention of a key component of the Novgorod model—the effort to reduce the region's dependence on federal subsidies. To structuralists this makes no sense, because, by balancing its budget, Novgorod receives less transfer revenue from Moscow. It only begins to make sense when one appreciates that it was conducted not because Moscow approved but because Novgorod no longer believed that Moscow would fulfill its commitments. Caught between underfunded social mandates and a confiscatory tax policy, local officials reluctantly set fiscal autonomy from Moscow as their goal. That, not successful lobbying, is the reason FDI became the centerpiece of the region's economic strategy.

Zimine and Bradshaw also suggest that, in pursuit of the kind of regional stability that would attract foreign investors, Prusak has opposed the development of truly democratic institutions. They cite the deputy chair of the regional duma, Lyubov Andreyeva, as saying that "the purpose of deputies is not to create laws, but much simpler—to approve drafts presented by the Governor."[58] This quote, along with the appointment of the mayor of Novgorod to the position of deputy governor, suggests to Zimine and Bradshaw that the duma and municipal administration are just rubber stamps for the governor.

This is a serious misreading of the role of the legislative institutions in Novgorod. In her interview, Andreyeva does *not* say that the role of the regional duma is merely to approve legislation submitted to it by the governor. Rather, she notes that in other regions where, unlike Novgorod, deputies receive full-time salaries, they "feel obliged" to justify those salaries. This leads to an unnecessary proliferation of staff positions. She also says that she "absolutely does not understand" how paying for so many staff persons, whose main function is to promote the careers of legislators, can benefit a region. Novgorod's part-time legislature is a lot more effective, she argues, because instead of having large staffs that do a lot of "politicking," it concentrates on legislative work.[59]

Zimine and Bradshaw are also wrong when they say that the duma "has not rejected a single draft law proposed by the Governor."[60] It has never rejected *final* versions of legislation, but it returns three out of four draft laws to the administration for further revision.[61] In the same interview Andreyeva also insists that the branches of government must work independently, without intrusions or oversight by any other branch. Indeed, the duma initiates 20 to 30 percent of all legislation.[62]

Nor should the joint appointment of the mayor of Novgorod the Great as deputy governor necessarily be taken as a sign of subservience. The former deputy chair of the city duma of Novgorod the Great, Irina Kibina, describes their relationship this way:

> With a stable revenue base, municipalities can conduct policies that are relatively independent of the policies of the regional government. This erupts into the political arena in the form of numerous conflicts between the governor and the mayor. The fact of the matter is that even with all the economic, financial, and political crises, it is specifically municipal authorities that, in the majority of regions, have the greatest popular support. The governor cannot ignore this, particularly until he is himself elected. In addition, it is the

municipality that knows the daily life of the population best. Through systematic tax advantages offered to enterprises, budgetary institutions, and tailored social support, it can significantly influence public opinion. This in turn can be a valuable asset at election time, or it can simply affect how long this or that governor, mayor, or even bureaucrat holds office.[63]

The late mayor, Alexander Korsunov had considerable leverage in promoting the city's interests, because he had his own staff, his own electoral constituency, his own revenue stream—which goes directly to the city coffers, bypassing the regional administration—and because he was highly regarded both locally and nationally.

Explanations of regional democratic development that rely on inherited geographical, institutional, or economic limitations serve only to preclude the possibility of rapid social change. When such change does occur, structuralists either dismiss the evidence or explain it as a by-product of some external financial or political intervention that altered the previous structural boundaries. As a result, rapid social change motivated by indigenous factors that encourage a region to transcend its structural limitations simply goes unnoticed.

The Dismal Science of Elite Behavior

Whereas structuralists see local leaders as being unable to effect change due to circumstances beyond their control, elite theorists argue just the opposite—that collusion among key political and economic actors has allowed regional elites to overcome the limits and the collapse of Soviet era structures and retain political influence. As applied to Russian regions, theories of elite behavior typically share two basic assumptions. First, because "Moscow rules," the choices made by regional elites matter only at the margins. Second, regional elites in Russia are incorrigibly selfish. They would simply never consider voluntarily sharing power, the sine qua non of democratic consolidation. These assumptions again effectively preclude any possibility of rapid social change.

Joel Moses, for example, distinguishes between "monolithic" and "pluralist" regions of Russia. In the former, the political regime is basically unchanged from the Soviet era system, and no autonomous power centers are tolerated; in the latter, "subregional political clans" serve as surrogates for political parties and perform many of the same functions.[64] While acknowledging that such clans do promote a form of elite consensus, he says that the unbridled rivalry among them typically leads to bribery, physical intimidation, and criminal involvement. No Russian region, Moses says, should be given high marks for democratic development, because they all lack the basic underpinnings of democratic pluralism and civic activism.[65]

What Moses (and others) fail to see, however, is that the rivalry that they tout as being so beneficial to democracy when expressed through competing parties, is in fact exacerbated by party politics. Because parties presently have no stable electoral constituency, they do not constrain political behavior but merely legalize all-out political warfare. By looking at political conflict and party activism as his main measures of democratization, Moses falls into the trap of focusing on the two elements that most undermine democratic consolidation in Russia today.[66]

Another scholar who has applied elite theories to Russian regional development is Kathryn Stoner-Weiss. She has found that regions with a high concentration of particular industries tend to be more successful at mitigating internal dissension and at presenting a united front in negotiations with Moscow. The result was better governance and greater public satisfaction with government. The close connections between political and industrial elites fostered a mutual dependence reminiscent of "company towns" in the United States. The cooperation that arose from the concentration of the regional economy led regions to include economic interests in the policy process, and economic interests in turn gained material advantages from the state. Economic constituencies helped guarantee a broad consensus on key issues and used their resources to promote government efficiency and legitimacy. These convergent interests, she concludes, sustained consensus and higher government performance—at least in the short term.[67]

On the face of it this model sounds quite plausible. It is certainly not surprising to find that conflict between business and government lowers economic productivity, or that higher elite consensus leads to a more positive evaluation of government. It is problematical, however, to argue that such elite consensus is the direct result of higher regional economic concentration.

Stoner-Weiss argues that regional elites are so bound to local industry, which is in turn dependent on government investment, that pooling resources to maximize the effectiveness of their lobbying becomes an overwhelmingly attractive strategy for local elites. This is a variety of the rent-seeking explanations for elite behavior that assert that Russian elites can "capture greater rents" by bargaining for greater local control over resources. Elites in regions with greater economic resources do this better than elites in poorer regions because the federal government is more likely to pay attention to them. Although resource-rich regions have indeed attempted to coerce Moscow into redistributing tax revenues in their favor by threatening to assert control over local resources, because all foreign capital and access to international markets flows through

Moscow, they quickly learn that they had better cooperate with major Moscow banks or suffer financial starvation in the midst of abundant resources.

Rent-seeking explanations of regional differences also assume that elites can obtain meaningful rewards from negotiating with federal authorities in Moscow. Experience, however, has shown governors that such a strategy is unreliable. It therefore seems doubtful that higher industrial concentration per se would suffice to motivate elites to embrace such a dramatic behavioral shift as economic efficiency and political unity. Although it might temporarily rally local elites against Moscow, that unity would be severely undermined by the almost colonial dependence of regions on Moscow for revenues.

That is why regional leaders who counted on their lobbying efforts to salvage their decrepit industrial base often found their regions becoming poorer faster than regions that abandoned such lobbying. Nizhny Novgorod, a region noted for its high concentration of defense-related industries, is a case in point. Stoner-Weiss cites this concentration as the reason for Nizhny's economic success and political stability in the mid-1990s, and suggests that both will persist as long as economic benefits from the center continue to flow to the industrial elites there. In fact, however, the political consensus forged in Nizhny collapsed as soon as Governor Boris Nemtsov left the region to become deputy prime minister in Moscow, even though economically the regional elite stood to profit from Nemtsov's promotion.

By contrast, in Saratov, after Governor Dmitry Ayatskov sharply reduced government support for local industries, the region saw a burst of economic growth with no perceptible decline in political stability.[68] The contrast becomes even more pronounced in regions where elites chose to abandon unprofitable industries that could not be made globally competitive. In Novgorod the high level of sectoral concentration in electronics and machine building came to be seen as the root cause of the region's economic stagnation. Between 1990 and 1993 these industries were collapsing so fast that no reasonable effort by the government could have saved them. When this realization hit home, and the elite realized it was better to create new industries than to try to salvage old ones, Novgorod's distinctive "elite consensus around liberal values" was forged.[69]

Both examples highlight one of the most persistent flaws of theories of elite behavior—the failure to consider motives beyond the narrowest self-interest. Elite theories typically portray Russian elites as blinded by a desire to preserve their privileges and hostile to any change in the status quo. A high level of elite consensus in a region must, therefore, point to a self-serving oligarchy with a very narrow base of social support. Such an all-consuming desire to limit outsider access to power simply does not fit with what happened in Novgorod nor, I suspect, in many other regions. The motives behind elite behavior in Russia are far more complex.

One alternative possibility, noted earlier, is that elites may at some point see an advantage to broadening their base of social support. Another possibility is that members of the elite may genuinely believe that by satisfying their own interests they are also serving the broader public good. Either view would do a better job of explaining the apparently self-destructive behavior of both national and local elites between 1989 and 1991, when millions of people left the Communist Party and thereby willingly undermined their own privileged status. Finally, the attempt to create new rules and procedures at the regional level suggests that at least some regional elites recognize that to fully benefit from their positions they need to promote a new social consensus. This certainly seems to have been the case in Novgorod.[70]

Yet, the single most important factor restraining the greed of elites in Novgorod is what local civic activists and government officials call an "intuitive feeling for history." As one senior city official put it, "Our major goal is to develop Novgorod's identity. It is a unique city: it did not experience a Mongol-Tatar yoke; enemies seized Novgorod only twice during its long history. The city administration employs history to develop and maintain ideals."[71] Explaining the elite's concern with institutional stability, one local NGO leader remarked, "They [the elite] reside permanently in Novgorod and they intend to stay here forever. If they would steal, grab, exploit, or neglect things today, they would not have much to do tomorrow. By now, they have earned enough money and acquired plenty of property. It's time to pursue other goals, such as recognition from peers and society."[72] Another city official sees a fundamental difference between the mindsets of Novgorod and Moscow elites. The former have "made up their minds to live in Novgorod. Thus, they can't just steal and run. . . . There are well-defined rules of the game here. And they are enforced."[73]

Once such an outlook becomes widespread, institutional stability, public philanthropy, and social partnership all begin to make eminent sense. Still, it begs the question of why such a consensus emerged in Novgorod but not in most other regions. We will return to this question in chapter 6, but for now note only that the failure of elite theorists to take local history and cultural sentiments into account leaves them with a far too dismal view of elites and their willingness to support democratic consolidation.

Looking for Charisma; Finding Authoritarianism

Another popular approach to explaining the differences in Russian regional development privileges the role of the governor in shaping the political fortunes of the region. The continuing relevance of the "Great Man" in Russian politics seems confirmed by the dominant roles played by Boris Yeltsin and Vladimir Putin. It is not a big leap from there to ascribing similar local influence to regional governors.

One of the most prolific Russian analysts in this tradition is Vladimir Gelman. According to Gelman, all Russian regions follow one of four well-established patterns: (1) anarchy; (2) a "winner takes all" situation; (3) an "elite compact" to preserve the status quo; or (4) a "war of rules," that allows local elites to curb internecine strife.[74]

The first pattern, thankfully, has been limited to Chechnya. The second amounts to a reconcentration of power in the hands of the former communist elite. Such regimes, which include Kalmykia, Tatarstan, and the city of Moscow, systematically suppress opposition and blatantly control the local press.[75] The third pattern typically results from an agreement among members of the former communist elite to share influence with former factory directors. Such elite compacts are less stable than "winner takes all" regimes, says Gelman, because they tend to be informal. Sudden changes in the status of key players, particularly the governor, can lead to a new cycle of instability in the region, as in the cases of Nizhny Novgorod, Tomsk, and Omsk. In the final type of regime, the "war of rules," the actors competing for power are more evenly matched. Because they cannot win individually, they reluctantly agree on ground rules for political conflict. Examples, says Gelman, include Udmurtiya and Sverdlovsk.[76] The "war of rules" represents the best hope for local democratization, but even these regions, says Gelman, remain "hopelessly far from pluralistic democracy."[77]

The culprit in all four patterns is clearly the desire of local governors for absolute supremacy. Gelman classifies Novgorod as a typical "winner takes all" regime, dominated by a charismatic and highly authoritarian governor, whose 1999 electoral victory by 91 percent is seen as proof of his authoritarian tendencies. A closer look at the man and his political beliefs, however, reveals a far more nuanced picture.

Prusak was born in Ivano-Frankovsk, a region of Ukraine that, as he says in his political memoirs, "remembers its pre-Soviet past." Annexed to the USSR after World War II, collectivization there was not completed until the end of the 1940s. Both his grandparents were well-to-do private farmers and his relatives and neighbors retained vivid memories of private property and entrepreneurship. As a young man, Prusak's father was arrested for "anti-Soviet activities" and only released from prison in 1955.[78]

After finishing school Prusak worked briefly as a middle school instructor. During his compulsory tour of military service, however, he distinguished himself sufficiently to win a coveted entrance recommendation to the elite Higher School of the Communist Youth League in Moscow. There Prusak studied agricultural administration, and after completing his training, chose an assignment as second secretary of the communist youth league in Kholm, a rural district of the Novgorod Region. In his second year there he shrewdly asked if he could try his hand at administration and was appointed director of the local state farm. This latter position guaranteed him a berth in the 1989 Supreme Soviet of the USSR, under the quota reserved for members of the Communist Youth League.[79]

During his two-year stint in the Supreme Soviet he served on the committee for local self-government and joined the Interregional Deputies Group, where he met his future political protégés, Egor Gaidar, Gennady Burbulis, and Boris Yeltsin. His original choice of Novgorod proved quite fortuitous when Yeltsin became President and appointed his own regional administrators. The political leadership in Novgorod could not agree on a candidate, so the youthful, ambitious Prusak, who was familiar to Yeltsin's senior staff and had recently lived and worked in the region, emerged as the choice of the presidential administration.

Since his appointment as governor in 1991, Prusak has consistently argued that two things must occur for politics in Russia to change: government accountability must increase, and regions must become the focal point of political and economic life. Government accountability should be enhanced by the creation of a system of "popular self-government that combines the historical traditions of Russia with contemporary experience."[80] A rich variety of such traditions have survived to this day—Cossack circles in the Kuban, councils of elders in the Caucasus, tribal councils in Siberia and the far north, and the Novgorod *veche* (or popular assembly) tradition. These must all be encouraged to develop into regional counterweights to Moscow.[81]

In Prusak's scheme, the president and the national legislature should be responsible only for elaborating a common framework of rules applicable to the entire Russian Federation. Within that framework the responsibility for implementing policy rests with the governor, who should be appointed by the president and approved by the local legislature. Heads of districts should be accountable to the governor and the governor to the president. Their accountability, moreover, should be direct, not channeled through presidential intermediaries or government ministries. When you simplify lines of authority, Prusak says, you reduce the need for a large bureaucracy. Such a combination of state accountability and respect for local traditions would allow reforms to be conducted with the necessary "finesse."[82]

People instinctively have faith in their local institutions, says Prusak, but to command respect they must be invested with real political power and sufficient economic resources. No more than 4 percent of local property should be owned by the federal government.[83] Transferring resources to localities will prevent Moscow from dominating the regions, but what is to prevent local governors from abusing their power? First, because the position, as Prusak envisions it, is a presidential appointment there is the implicit threat of removal. Second, the governor would have to consult with a permanent "representative assembly" that Prusak envisions as a body of corporate civic representation and public sounding board for new initiatives. After due deliberation by the representative assembly, the best ideas would be enacted into law by the local legislature, a popularly elected body of professional lawmakers.[84]

Prusak argues that the addition of such representative assemblies would have several advantages over the current unicameral regional legislature organized around political parties. They would give an undiluted political voice to groups that are already active civically (such as veterans' groups, housing associations, and religious communities), rather than forcing them into artificial party structures that people do not respect. In such assemblies the political party elite would be forced to interact on a regular basis, rather than just at election time, with a large and diverse cross-section of interests. The result would be a sort of permanent civic forum—a school for responsible civic activism and a training ground for future politicians. Only such an assertive chorus of new political voices, he argues, can gain the attention of the self-absorbed elites in Moscow and St. Petersburg.[85]

Few took notice of Prusak's ideas until he published them in an open appeal timed to influence president-designate Putin's choice of prime minister.[86] In the ensuing media campaign, Prusak was accused absurdly of wanting to turn the country back into the USSR and of favoring an absolutist presidency. Adopting Prusak's proposals, Samara Governor Konstantin Titov warned, would lead to total Kremlin control over regional economies, the end of political parties, and "the loss of independent social-political activity among citizens."[87]

Prusak's opponents, however, need not have worried. His proposals were never seriously considered by Putin, and Prusak soon concluded that he and the president "seem to be on different wavelengths."[88] The problem, as Prusak sees it, is that Putin adopted the first half of his program—increasing state accountability—without shifting the necessary resources and authority to the regions. As a result, the country has drifted toward economic centralization and political sycophancy.[89] Seeing the momentum move away from regions back to the center, Prusak has sought to revive his political fortunes by reaching out to a new constituency—civil society.

Prusak defines civil society as an evolving social constituency, distinct from the state, that cannot be instigated from above. At the same time, however, the state has a vital role to play in establishing clear rules of the game for civil society. Although democracy and civil society frequently complement each other, at times they can be mutually disruptive. The important thing to remember, says Prusak, is that no single model works for all societies.

Prusak identifies four ways that government should assist civil society. First, government should shift political and economic decision making to lower levels. This would increase popular participation in both deliberation and voting. Second, government should make it easier for civic organization to receive private support. As Russia gets richer, he says, Western foundations will inevitably reduce their presence in the country. Before this happens, it is imperative that local philanthropists take their place. Third, there is an urgent need for local governments to pass laws that set up clear guidelines for the interaction of civil society, philanthropies, and state institutions. Finally, local governments should systematically include civic organizations in policy planning and implementation. They have become, he says, a resource for ideas and civic manpower that local officials can no longer afford to ignore.[90]

Although based on the experience of Novgorod, these prescriptions are obviously meant to serve as a prototype for all of Russia. To this end, in 2001 Prusak resurrected, and briefly led, the moribund Democratic Party of Russia (DPR) once headed by Yegor Gaidar. As leader of the DPR Prusak spread a simple message: Putin's centralization is taking Russia down the wrong path. Left to its own devices Moscow will never see this as a problem, so it must be forced to relinquish its stranglehold over the nation's wealth. The only power capable of accomplishing this is an alliance of local elites and local civil society. The two must unite forces to promote regional autonomy, or the country is doomed to repeat the mistakes of the past. To avoid this fate Russia urgently needs to reexamine its past and identify alternative paths of development that can serve as the basis for constructing a civil society with specifically Russian characteristics. The essential elements of Prusak's program—localism, political accountability, regional autonomy—can be summed up in the following agenda that local elites should begin implementing in their regions today: "Building civil society *is* the Russian national idea."[91]

Proponents of the view that regional differences depend largely on the will of the local governor typically overstate the governor's powers, and then compound this error by assuming that, however much power he has, he always wants more. This tendency to oversimplify the motives of the political elite is evident in the assumption that there can be only one "winner" who "takes all."

Prusak's view of what constitutes strong government, however, differs substantially from the typical pattern of regional authoritarianism that, as Gelman describes it, is characterized by the dominance of executive authority over legislative authority; a strong personal loyalty of the governor to Moscow; executive branch control over the mass media; neutralization or suppression of potential opposition in the region; and the patronage of nongovernmental organizations.[92] Indeed, Prusak insists that his proposals are the best way to create a true separation of powers between the executive and legislative branches and force the president to abide by specific rules.[93] One might disagree, but there is no question that Prusak is quite opposed to the "institutionalized arbitrariness" that Gelman claims all governors aspire to.[94]

As for loyalty to Moscow, although Prusak has avoided direct criticism of Putin, he has been fiercely critical of both Prime Minister Mikhail Kasyanov and his predecessor, Evgeny Primakov. The remaining points about the control of the press, absence of political opposition, and patronage of NGOs have already been discussed and simply misconstrue local government policies. Again, one may view these policies as misguided, but to suggest that Prusak is merely engaged in the suppression or neutralization of his potential opponents, in the face of such a long record of supporting civic involvement, seems very far off the mark.

Comparing Russia to Latin America, Andrei Tsygankov labels most Russian regions as typical "delegative democracies." Novgorod, however, seems much closer to Tsygankov's rival description of "representative democracy." Representative democracies, he says, are expected: "(1) to foster citizen's respect for independent parties and the legislature and, hence, stimulate their interest in the election of the legislature; (2) to take into consideration all of a society's organized interests and seek their accommodation via available legal institutions; and (3) to respect, or at least tolerate, the formal independence of liberal democratic institutions (media, legislature, courts, etc.)."[95]

How then can one best describe the governor's political role? If, as I believe, Novgorod politics is characterized by an elite consensus around local historical and cultural values, then the governor's pragmatic conservatism has played an important part in achieving it. Still, he could have done little without a receptive audience. Archbishop Lev of Novgorod and Staraya Russa neatly summed up the relationship by pointing out that, while Novgorod was fortunate to get Prusak, Prusak was also fortunate to get Novgorod.[96] A key task still facing democratization theorists is understanding what makes certain local audiences more receptive to innovative leaders and their ideas.

EXPLAINING AWAY THE DIFFERENCES BETWEEN NOVGOROD AND PSKOV

None of the three approaches examined here deals adequately with Novgorod's regional democratization. They fail, in large part, because the very task of fitting manifestly diverse regions into comparable categories forces analysts to set aside important cultural differences. How can we be sure that local culture is a crucial explanatory variable? In the case of Novgorod we have a nearly perfect control case—the adjacent region of Pskov. Not only are the two regions evenly matched in territory, population, demographic trends, climate, economic and social infrastructure, they even share similar histories—both were Hanseatic trading posts and both boast ancient traditions of local self-government. Yet, despite being all but twins, the two regions developed quite differently after 1991. Let us see how well the three approaches discussed in this chapter do in identifying and explaining these differences.

Structural approaches stress physical, social, and economic conditions as determinate of future development, and Pskov mirrored Novgorod in almost all basic economic and social indicators during the latter half of the 1980s and early 1990s. (see table 3.2) Nearly a decade later, however, Pskov's industrial output had fallen to half that of Novgorod's (despite receiving significantly more federal transfer payments than Novgorod) and observers began describing Novgorod as one of the country's most dynamically developing regions, while Pskov had become "stably depressed."[97]

The structuralist approaches does little to explain this divergence. It can be argued that, in Soviet times, production in Novgorod revolved around machine building and electronics for the military, while Pskov was more dependent on agriculture and light industry. If anything, however, this should have mitigated the decline of Pskov's gross regional product compared to Novgorod's. Instead, from 1991 to 1995 we see *both* agricultural and industrial production falling twice as fast in Pskov as in Novgorod.[98]

Some suggest that Novgorod profits from being on major transportation arteries. Although Novgorod is on the main highway between Moscow and St. Petersburg, Pskov has the advantage of being on the main highway connecting St. Petersburg with southern Russia and Kiev. Moreover, while railway lines connect the city of Pskov directly to St. Petersburg, Murmansk, Kaliningrad, Tallinn, and Riga (and a significant

TABLE 3.2

Comparative indicators for the Novgorod and Pskov Regions

	Novgorod	Pskov
Geography		
Territory sq. km.	55,300	55,400
Percent urban	70.6	66.4
Administrative districts	21	24
Cities	10	14
Villages	18	14
Rural administrations	272	248
Demography		
Population (1997)	720,900	790,600
Percent Great Russian	96	93
Age distribution	20.9/55.2/23.9	20.3/54.7/25
(percent below/working age/beyond)		
Life expectancy	62.14	62.21
Persons per sq. km.	13	14.3
Average age	38	38
Economy		
Apartments privatized	163,000	186,000
(1992–1995)		
Enterprises privatized	348	154
(1994–1997)		
Value of industrial production	2.5/4,655	2.4/2,695
in billions of rubles (1990/1997)		
Percent of economically active	5.3/13.5/7.8	5.1/14.3/12.8
population unemployed		
(1992/1997/2000)		
Number of small businesses	3,783/4,506	2,430/2,844
(1995/2001)		

Source: E. V. Vasilenko and I. A. Starodubtseva, *Sotsialno-ekonomicheskie pokazateli respublik i oblastei Severnogo i severo-Zapadnogo raionov, Kaliningradskoi i kirovskoi oblastei v 1990–2000 gg.* (Syktyvkar: Goskomstat Respubliki Komi, 2001), 6–10, 23, 62; Merja Tekoniemi and Laura Solanko, "Novgorod and Pskov—Examples of How Economic Policy Can Influence Economic Development," *Review of Economies in Transition* (June 1998): 65; Olga Kuznetsova, "Novgorodskaya i Pskovskaya oblasti: ekonomicheskoe polozhenie i faktory razvitiya," *Voprosy ekonomiki* 10 (1998): 154; V. I. Poleshchenko, et al., *Pskovskii statisticheskii ezhegodnik*, vol. 1 (Pskov: Pskovoblkomstat, 2001), 14; V. I. Galitskii, ed., *Regiony Rossii: Informatsionno-statisticheskii sbornik* (Moscow: Goskomstat Rossii, 1997), 405, 420, 453, 460.

portion of Russia's trade with the Baltic states and Western Europe), Novgorod the Great has no such direct links.

A variety of other geographically based explanations have been used to explain Pskov's stagnation. Journalist Alexei Zhuravlev suggests that Pskovians view their border with the Baltic states as a defensive barrier rather than as a bridge, and that this creates psychological obstacles to reform.[99] Pskov Governor Evgeny Mikhailov has suggested that voting

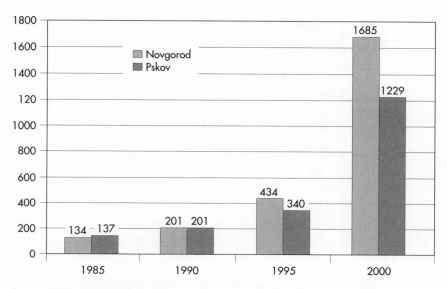

Source: E. V. Vasilenko and I. A. Starodubtseva, *Sotsialno-ekonomicheskie pokazateli respublik i oblastei Severnogo i severo-Zapadnogo raionov, Kaliningradskoi i kirovskoi oblastei v 1990-2000 gg.* (Goskomstat Respubliki Komi, Syktyrjar, 2001), p. 27; V. Galitskii, ed. *Regiony Rossii: Informatsionno-statisticheskii sbornik* (Moscow: Goskomstat Rossii, 1997), 454.

FIGURE 3.1 Monthly monetary income per capita for the Novgorod and Pskov Regions, 1985–2000 (up to 1995 in thousands of rubles)

patterns within the region reveal a deep historical and cultural split between the city of Pskov and the neighboring northern districts that were once part of the Novgorod Republic, and the city of Velikie Luki to the south, which has more in common with the politically conservative central Russian "Red Belt."[100] Ultimately, however, this type of subregional dissection is not very convincing. Although the residents of the northern Pechory District may have voted against joining neighboring Estonia in 1991, they voted in favor of liberal economic reform and self-government later on. Likewise, the distinctly prodemocratic voting pattern of the Pytalovsky District may have more to do with the fact that it was the site of one of the first private farming experiments in the USSR rather than with any deep historical affinity.[101]

Former Pskov Governor Vladislav Tumanov has suggested that the more than eighty thousand Russian speakers who fled Estonia and Latvia after 1991 are a significant source of regional conservatism. Disgruntled refugees can indeed provide fertile soil for nationalism, which makes it surprising that the migration, which peaked in 1995 and then fell sharply,

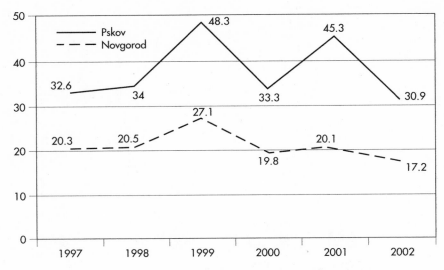

Source: General population data taken from *Regiony Rossii: Statisticheskii sbornik,* vol. 2 (Moscow: Goskomstat, 2000), 32–33, and from "2002 All-Russian Population Census" on the website of EastView Publication Services: http://www.eastview.com/docs/resident_population.xls (accessed November 25, 2003). Pskov poverty figures taken from V. I. Poleshchenko et al., *Otdelnye pokazateli urovnya zhizni naseleniya Pskovskoi oblasti: Statisticheskii sbornik* (Pskov: Pskovoblkomstat, 2001), 126. Data for 2001 and 2002 provided by Vladimir I. Kobyzhecha, deputy director of the Northwest Civil Service Academy in Pskov, in a meeting on June 5, 2002 and subsequent correspondence of November 25, 2003. Information on Novgorod obtained from the chairman of the Committee for Labor and Social Assistance of the Novgorod Oblast, A. V. Dubonosov, in a letter to Alexander I. Zhukovsky, May 30, 2002 (Correspondence No. 01-717/05). For more information, see figure 2.5.

FIGURE 3.2 Percentage living below poverty level in the Novgorod and Pskov Regions, 1997–2002

has had no perceptible impact on voting behavior. From 1991 to this day Pskov voters have been more or less evenly divided among centrist-democrats, communists, and nationalists.[102]

The striking difference between the voting patterns of Pskov and Novgorod, however, remains. As Bank of Finland analysts Merja Tekoniemi and Laura Solanko put it:

> Novgorod and Pskov appear to be opposites in their political behaviors. Novgorod voters choose pragmatic individuals to run the region; parties have little power . . . [it is] characterized by cooperation with various economic and political groups . . . Pskov are [*sic*] less stable. Political parties (mainly the Communists) are firmly established and conflict between the political and economic elite is more pronounced.[103]

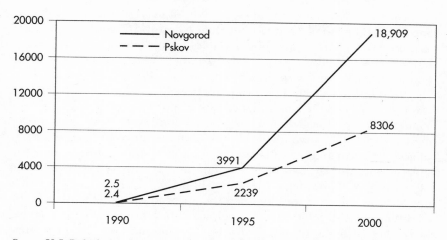

Source: V. I. Poleshchenko et al., *Pskovskii statisticheskii ezhegodnik*, vol. 1 (Pskov: Pskovoblkomstat, 2001), 14; Marja Tekoniemi and Laura Solanko, "Novgorod and Pskov—Examples of How Economic Policy Can Influence Economic Development," *Review of Economies in Transition* (June 1998): 68.

FIGURE 3.3 Industrial production in the Novgorod and Pskov Regions, 1990–2000 (in billions of rubles before 1998; in millions of rubles thereafter)

The crucial difference has been Novgorod's ability to forge an elite consensus around liberal values. In Novgorod that consensus encouraged structural reforms in local self-government and broad political support for economic reforms. In the absence of such a consensus, the same policies, halfheartedly begun by Pskov's former governor, Vladislav Tumanov, were quietly abandoned by his successor.

How can we explain such divergent elite behavior? *Elite theories* tell us that elites in Russian regions will collude in ways that are generally destructive of social capital. Although this appears to be true for Pskov, where elites seem to believe that the less effective local government is, the less of an obstacle it can be to them, in Novgorod elites colluded in ways that clearly benefited society as a whole. One would not have predicted such an outcome based on the track record of Yeltsin's early gubernatorial appointee to Pskov, Vladislav Tumanov. Like Novgorod, Pskov was one of the first regions to introduce local elections. Like Novgorod, Pskov sought to transfer regional budget revenues to towns and districts, and even received a federal grant to extend local self-government in two districts on the Estonian border.[104] Between 1994 and 1998 the Pskov Regional Duma enacted 160 laws and 578 decrees, not far off the 120 laws and 656 decrees enacted by the Novgorod Regional Duma.[105] The economic policies Tumanov pursued were basically liberal, and in one important respect they went even further than Novgorod. From 1993 to 1995 Pskov received more than a billion rubles from the federal government to promote small businesses. By July 1996 there were already some seven thousand small businesses operating in the Pskov region, a figure Novgorod did not reach until two years later.[106]

But one also sees a much higher rate of political infighting in Pskov. Conflict between local parties and the administration came out in the open in early 1992, when the local head of the Democratic Party of Russia called for the resignation of Governor Anatoly Dobrokhotov.[107] Tumanov replaced him in May, and in retaliation, the left gathered signatures for the removal of Pskov Mayor Alexander Prokofiev.[108] These tensions cast a long shadow over relations between the governor and the legislature; by 1998 they were so poor that the regional legislature refused to approve the budget until May of that fiscal year.[109] In the midst of this squabbling, a relative unknown, Evgeny Mikhailov, emerged as the figure least likely to upset the balance between competing factions of the elite. Mikhailov's ability to reconcile seemingly contradictory stances and to switch party affiliations entirely whenever it seems advantageous to do so has kept him afloat in Pskov's vicious political waters ever since.

Mikhailov's reelection campaign in November 2000 is a good example of how, in the absence a unifying consensus, Pskov's political elite has settled for thwarting change. Not only was Mikhailov elected with the lowest vote ever recorded in a Russian gubernatorial election—28 percent—but a postelection survey of those who did vote for Mikhailov revealed that a plurality did so because "change always leads to something worse," with the second most common answer being "everyone else is worse than E. Mikhailov."[110]

In Pskov a handful of people have accumulated great personal wealth at the expense of institutionalizing local rules of the game and a growing regional dependence on Moscow. Before 1995, Pskov had transferred more basic economic production capacity—buildings, equipment, machines, transportation equipment, instruments, and livestock—into private hands than almost any other region in Russia.[111] During this same period, by contrast, the leadership of Novgorod took the unprecedented step of asking Yeltsin to transfer ownership of all factories to the region rather than to private owners, so that reforms could be enacted "more quickly and flexibly."[112] As a result, in Novgorod less than 2 percent of local property remained in federal hands. The regional administration eventually transferred most of the rest from the regional administration to municipalities, and it was the sale and leasing of these assets that later helped fund local mandates.[113] The difference between the policies of elites in both regions can be seen graphically in table 3.3.

TABLE 3.3

Percentage division of basic factory assets in the Novgorod and Pskov Regions (as of January 1, 1996)

	Federal	Regional	Private	Mixed (w/out foreign)
Russia	20.7%	7.5%	18.2%	35.3%
Northwest	35.8	16.2	26.9	18.7
Novgorod Region	1.8	**74.4**	14.5	8.5
Pskov Region	23.5	0.5	**54.4**	19.6

Source: Vladimir V. Vagin, *"'Visokosnyi' politicheskii god v Pskovskoi oblasti: oktyabr' 1995-noyabr'" 1996 gg.* (Pskov: Izd. Tsentr "Vozrozhdenie," 1998).

In Novgorod, elite consensus has led to innovation and self-confidence. In Pskov, elite fragmentation has led to economic stagnation and dependence on Moscow. There are even those in Pskov who argue that the more dependent the region is on Moscow, the more leverage it has in negotiating budget transfers to the region, and they have a point (see fig. 3.4). With 70 percent of Pskov's budget supplied by Moscow, there is little incentive to enhance local revenues.[114]

In order to preserve the status quo Pskov's elite believes it needs only enough resources to maintain social tranquility. Significant new investments are actually unwelcome, because they introduce an element of uncertainty into the local political equation. This explains Pskov Governor Evgeny Mikhailov's seemingly irrational alienation of local businessmen. Broadening his own political base by courting them might destabilize the region's uneasy political balance and bring about his downfall. Not surprisingly, in a comparative measure of the responsiveness of regional governments to their constituents, Pskov ranked thirty-third while Novgorod ranked ninth.[115]

The final approach, focusing on *gubernatorial authoritarianism*, sees the governor's political dominance reflected in the absence of local civic activism and institutionalized parties. In Novgorod, as we have seen, this fails to explain the extent of local activism; while in Pskov no clear charismatic figure has emerged, despite an early attempt to develop a political party system in the region.

During the latter years of perestroika, Pskov's liberal intelligentsia was strongly influenced by the political activism of St. Petersburg, Moscow, and particularly the Baltic states. Indeed, during the first six months of its existence in 1988–89, the Pskov Popular Front was formally part of the Estonian Popular Front.[116] By the fall of 1989 the Pskov Popular Front had become the Union of Pskov Electors, Veche, which, although it could organize large rallies, was never able to elect a significant percentage of

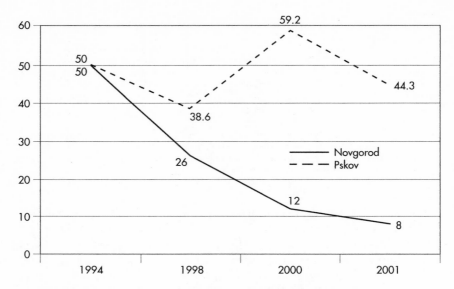

Source: Olga Kolotnecha, "Novgorodchina mozhet i budet sama sebya kormit," *Novgorodskie vedomosti* (June 14, 2000); Miles A. Pomper, "Economic Aid Goes Local," *Congressional Quarterly* (July 9, 1999); Ivan Generozov, "Novgorod ne khochet zaviset ot rossiiskogo budgeta," *Ekspert: Severo-Zapad* (October 1, 2001); "'Kto luchshe rabotaet, tot dolzhen luchshe zhit," *Novgorodskie vedomosti* (December 28, 2001).

FIGURE 3.4 Percentage of Novgorod and Pskov regional budgets provided by federal subsidies, 1994–2001

its candidates to public office.[117] The local communists, by contrast, were not only better organized but could count on the support of the troops in local military garrisons.[118] The local branch of the Democratic Party of Russia promoted a referendum on land reform and other radical initiatives, but it could not muster sufficient support among either elites or the populace (unlike Novgorod, Pskov has no state university). Yeltsin's abolition of all soviets in 1993 weakened his supporters in the region and effectively isolated his gubernatorial appointee Vladislav Tumanov.[119]

I believe the inability of democratic reformers in Pskov to capitalize on the anticommunist momentum of these early years stems from the premature politicization of local civic activism. Democratic activists radicalized the political atmosphere by aggressively promoting an interpretation of Soviet history that most residents of Pskov, with its large military population, were simply not willing to accept.[120] Unlike Novgorod, where civic groups and university officials actively promoted the region's medieval heritage as an alternative model, Pskov's intellectual elite looked away, to Moscow and Tallinn, for their models. The reliance on outside traditions,

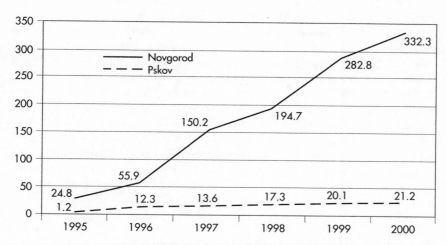

Source: E. V. Vasilenko and I. A. Starodubtseva, *Sotsialno-ekonomicheskie pokazateli respublik i oblastei Severnogo i Severo-zapadnogo raionov, Kaliningradskoi i Kirovskoi oblastei v 1990-2000 gg.* (Goskomstat Respubliki Komi, Syktyvkar, 2001), p. 70. The figures for Novgorod provided by Vasilenko and Starodubtseva are significantly lower than those provided by the Novgorod regional administration. For consistency, however, I have chosen to use this single source, even though it most likely understates total FDI in Novgorod.

FIGURE 3.5 FDI in the Novgorod and Pskov Regions, 1995–2000 (in millions of US$)

combined with the uncompromising course taken by local democratic activists, prevented them from establishing a broad base of social support for reforms.

Pskov illustrates the problems that can arise when party political activism has no social roots. Thanks to their overtly political beginnings, the Pskov elite always treated local NGOs as potential rivals rather than partners. And because, unlike Novgorod, there is so little engagement between civic activists and local government in Pskov, the region lurched from cliquish political radicalism at the beginning of the decade to widespread social and political apathy at its end.

Scholars rarely ask whether democratic development is affected by the way in which civic activism evolves. It is largely taken for granted that political parties represent the natural culmination of democracy, and the sooner they are established the better. Both Novgorod and Pskov belie that assumption. For the former, the proper sequencing of civic activism has been crucial to broadening the social base and teaching political activists the art of compromise. Pskov, by contrast, shows how premature attempts at party-based politicization can actually backfire.

Regional comparisons usually focus on the obvious similarities and differences among regions, leaving unanswered more important questions such as why, in defiance of nearly identical resources and geography, local elites in Novgorod and Pskov made such strikingly different political choices. That is because existing theories look to the economic, structural, and political choices made by elites, before they look at the cultural preferences that underlie them. As a result they fail to see that the Novgorod and Pskov elites made their choices based on different regional self-images, different "regional myths," that subsequently shaped local policies. I will explore the relationship between policies and elite myths in detail in chapter 6. For now, suffice it to say that because the status quo in Pskov so perfectly suits the region's current self-image, a turnaround in the region is unlikely without a prior change in its regional myth.

HOW CURRENT DEMOCRATIC THEORY OVERLOOKS DEMOCRACY

Current approaches to regional development fail to explain either the success of democratic development in Novgorod or its failure of Pskov. They remind us of what happened but provide little insight into what led regions that are so similar to develop so differently. Why did elites in Pskov fail to embrace a positive image of the region, as they did in Novgorod? Why do elites in Pskov seem to prefer the status quo over innovation? Finally, why did civic activism take hold in one region yet fail to do so in another, when their ethnic, cultural, and social characteristics (even historical traditions) match so closely? These are questions for which the current approaches to regional democratization have no convincing answers.

The persistent focus on national politics as the key to democratic development also cannot explain the variety of political regimes one finds in Russia today. That is because such approaches are not designed to understand regional developments on their own terms; they are designed only to search for comparable reference points among regions and, by aggregating these, to assess their impact on political decisionmaking in Moscow. Theories of democratization would be immeasurably strengthened if they were applied in a manner that allowed for meaningful cross-level comparison within a society as well as cross-national comparisons. To develop such criteria, however, we must do more than simply transfer existing analytical methods to a lower level. We must learn to truly value regional distinctions.

The failure to treat cultural differences within Russia seriously is made more acute by the fact that Russian studies experts have argued for a long time that attention to regions is hardly warranted in a country totally lacking democratic traditions. This has dimmed our awareness of the rich diversity of democratic myths and symbols that local leaders can evoke to build legitimacy for reforms. This is particularly true in today's Russia where, as historian Svetlana Mintz notes, "regional and cultural history provides a foundation for political consciousness . . . allowing each region to represent itself as an independent economic and cultural unity."[121] Diverse levels of democratic development still elicit surprise and skepticism, when it would be far more astonishing if they were absent.

In chapter 1 I argued that democratic theory can be improved by shifting its analysis to the regional level. Doing so in chapter 2 revealed an unexpectedly high level of democratic consolidation in Novgorod. The attempt to explain this evidence by using conventional theories of regional development in chapter 3 has proved unsuccessful. Theories of regional development, it seems, are as unprepared for democracy as theories of democratic development are for regional development. We need a theoretical framework that connects regional studies and democratic development, and the best vehicle for creating such a framework is cultural analysis. A focus on the culture of regions in the study of democracy would allow analysts to appreciate the distinctions among regions, while maintaining a perspective deep enough to see the significance of purely local changes in attitudes, structures, and behavior. This is precisely the focus we need to unlock the mysteries of the earliest stages of democratization.

PART II

CULTURE, MYTH, AND SYMBOLS

THREE KEYS TO UNDERSTANDING RAPID SOCIAL CHANGE

During the 1990s scholars concerned with democratic transition debated whether the newly minted Eastern European democracies were more likely to follow the path of Latin America or chart their own course. One group, promptly labeled transitologists, argued that because all nations embarking on political transition face similar constraints and choices, cultural and historical legacies should play only a minor role when assessing the prospects for democracy.[1] This provoked a sharp dissent from Valerie Bunce, who argued that cultural and historical differences lie at the very core of patterns of democratic development and that we should therefore anticipate divergences not only between Eastern Europe and Latin America but even between neighboring countries within each continent.[2]

Neither approach is entirely satisfying. If democratic development is strictly dependent on historical and cultural precedent, then simply replacing communist-era institutions will accomplish very little. Eastern Europe's only real hope for democracy would lie in rejecting its past, an unlikely prospect. If, on the other hand, the role of "a small but critical mass of pragmatic liberal politicians" is deemed key, then the fate of democracy rests on the equally implausible assumption that such a group could rise to prominence in defiance of a country's historical and cultural traditions.[3] Such an elite, even if it were able to come to power (as rabid Russian nationalists contend it already has in their country), would have so little public support that democratic consolidation around such a regime seems highly unlikely. Taken to its logical conclusion, neither approach leaves much hope for democratic consolidation.

One thing that both sides in this debate do agree on, however, is that for Russia the legacy of the past is an obstacle to reform. A radical and rapid break with that past should therefore be an essential part of any democratic transition.[4] Radical breaks with the past, however, also call into question the legitimacy of the state and, hence, undermine its capacity to implement the very changes that are needed. If that past is not replaced with a popularly accepted alternative, disorientation quickly spreads through society, leaving reformers with no intellectual or cultural vantage point from which to promote their policies.[5]

Pitting the past against the present is therefore no way to promote democracy. While transitologists dismiss Russian culture as unimportant, area studies specialists treat it as if it were a condition to be cured. Both fail to appreciate the degree to which a cultural environment receptive to change can be created and how much that creation relies on casting traditions in a new light.

WHAT WORKS AND WHAT DOESN'T WHEN STUDYING TRANSITION

The theories discussed in the previous chapter all have one thing in common—they take cultural continuity for granted. This may be a safe assumption for mature democracies, but it is a serious flaw when studying societies in transition. Although institutions and economic rationality serve admirably as guides to political behavior during periods of stability, they are quite useless when institutions are collapsing and core assumptions about values and proper behavior are being challenged. Simply put, the greater the degree of socioeconomic turmoil, the less people will believe that decisions should be made on the basis of what worked in the past. During periods of intense social upheaval, the disorientation can become so great that the reestablishment of commonly constructed social meanings takes center stage. People turn to culture for meaning; elites turn to it for legitimacy.

Culture, however, as Marc Howard Ross reminds us, "is not a concept with which most political scientists are comfortable."[6] It complicates the quest for causal explanations, it has unit-of-analysis problems; many deem it too vague to be of use in explaining political behavior, and even those who do use it, says Ross, do so "thinly" and fail to develop any sense of cultural dynamics.[7] As a result, for more than a generation now, most political scientists have preferred an analytical approach known as "rational choice theory," which assumes that even though people may inhabit irrational societies and suffer from incomplete knowledge, they are still bound by the universal human trait of rationality not to pursue conduct that makes them less well off. Because such "profit-maximizing" behavior is universal, cultural differences can be safely subordinated to individual utility maximization.[8]

Some have questioned whether it is safe to divorce interests from their cultural context in this way. The late Aaron Wildavsky has suggested that when the social context disintegrates so does the assumption that we know what individuals mean by self-interest.[9] For Wildavsky, the choices that individuals make take place on two distinct levels: decisional and cultural. Because it deals only with the first level, rational choice "robs its readers of the cultural dimension."[10] Moreover, Wildavsky suggests that rational choice theorists err when they assume that interests are given, because empirical studies reveal significant variations in interests across cultures.[11] For postcommunist societies such as Russia, however, the most serious drawback of rational choice is that it clings to inherited definitions of "reasonable behavior" long after the institutions that gave rise to such behavior have collapsed.[12] Without institutions to anchor them, interest-based analyses lose their moorings and are helpless as guides.

At least one distinguished group of rational choice scholars, led by Robert H. Bates, has acknowledged this potential weakness.[13] Although rational choice is well-suited to the study of politics in advanced Western democracies, where people can focus on the value of outcomes and evaluate alternatives, this group finds that it has been far less successful in explaining the choices made in unstable institutional settings, where people may "not know" where their interests lie, a situation they liken to "madness."[14]

Although Bates and his colleagues conclude that "the politics of culture" poses a challenge to the premises of rationality, culturalists can take scant comfort in this belated recognition. For one thing, Bates and his colleagues still relegate culture to the marginal, "theatrical" episodes in public life that are, for some reason, deemed more important in less stable, undeveloped countries.[15] Were we to follow their reasoning, we would soon have a discipline permanently divided between those who study the more "rational" West and those who study the "irrational" rest of the world, with little they could say to each other.

Bates and his colleagues want to reconcile cultural and rational choice approaches, but only on terms that subordinate the former to the latter. Wildavsky, however, suggests that it is rational choice theories that should be subordinated to culture because political strategies only make sense within a particular cultural context.[16] From this perspective, when the traditional cultural context is undermined, decision makers can rely less and less on "rationality" as society has traditionally defined it.[17]

Furthermore, because a rational act is one that supports cultural stability in times of turmoil, reestablishing the legitimacy of cultural norms in times of crisis becomes a task of paramount importance. Finally, if

97

rational political strategies depend on the predictability of institutions, then as one diminishes so does the other. As rational choice advocate Morris Fiorina puts it, if an individual does not feel that he or she can affect the outcome of the political process, or that the stakes are not significant, then the entire situation is simply not worth strategizing about.[18] Indifference to politics is exactly what one would expect, and indeed what one sees, in societies where institutions are in flux.

Although some rational choice scholars graciously concede that during times of intense social turmoil cultural analysis may perforce become the analytical tool of choice, I believe a strong case can be made that it should be the preferred approach for understanding political transitions.

WHY CULTURAL ANALYSIS IS BEST FOR THE STUDY OF TRANSITION

As applied to the study of politics, the most useful view of culture emphasizes its "public, shared meanings, behaviors, institutions, and social structures."[19] From this perspective, culture is a worldview that explains why and how individuals and groups behave as they do.[20] It does so by providing a system of meaning and a sense of identity to participants in a variety of discernible ways.

First, it orders society's political priorities. Second, it forces a political community to define itself. Third, it manages political conflict by defining what is worth fighting for and how that conflict should be undertaken and resolved. Fourth, it provides a common framework for interpreting the actions and motives of others. Finally, and most important for the purposes of this study, culture provides resources for political organization and mobilization. Political leaders will use cultural resources to achieve goals that they cannot pursue by other means. This can occur either consciously or unconsciously.[21] Cultural analysis is particularly sensitive to the rifts that arise between political beliefs and the institutions needed to carry them out. When this rift becomes too great, it can lead to "formlessness."

Harry Eckstein developed the notion of formlessness in response to the criticism that cultural analysis could not explain political upheaval. Change is part of the process by which cultures adapt and survive, but when changes occur too rapidly for a society to assimilate, he says, it leads not to the formation of a new culture but to formlessness, in which individuals and groups find their past experiential and cultural knowledge no longer useful for making sense of the world around them. This results in sharp inconsistencies between attitudes and behaviors, anarchy, and a general retreat into parochialism.[22] Formlessness heightens the political significance of culture because individuals instinctively respond to a loss of orientation by trying to reestablish propriety. Because the impact of culture as a political resource is most keenly felt at the regional level, the struggle against formlessness is usually joined first at that level, where it is often accompanied by an emphasis on regional identity.

Postcommunist societies certainly seem to fit this pattern, which suggests that scholars of transition in this region have good reason to prefer cultural analysis over rational choice.[23] In the specific case of Russia, each of the three most common cultural approaches taken—political culture, social capital, and congruence theory—has certain advantages. In the final analysis, however, they all fail to appreciate the speed of Russia's transformation, because they do not recognize the potential for rapid change that is inherent in culture.

Political Culture's Static View of Russia

According to Gabriel Almond, every political system is embedded within a "particular pattern of orientations to political action" that constrains its development.[24] By linking political culture to empirically observable behavior and measuring such behavior systematically over time, Almond suggests that it is possible to identify the specific attitudes, beliefs, or sentiments that give order and meaning to the political process. Eventually this should enable researchers to predict the evolution of political systems. Almond and his colleague Sidney Verba identified the political culture of democracy as the patterns of behavior observed in certain Western countries. When patterns of behavior in other countries matched those observed in Western democracies, they were said to have the type of political culture needed to support democracy—a civic culture.[25]

The civic culture model has been criticized for being conceptually fuzzy, for overlooking subcultures, for relying on mechanical methods of gathering information about culture, and for its tendency to deduce popular political values from those filtered through government sanctioned institutions.[26] In the case of mature democracies, it could reasonably be argued that some of these problems are mitigated by the existence of a wide variety of public and private institutions. In communist societies, however, the civic culture model tends to exaggerate public support for the political system and impede consideration of alternatives to it.

It thus became customary to explain Russia's inability to develop a civic culture as the product of a political culture rooted in centuries of autocratic values and institutions. Such a one-sided focus on a single aspect of any culture, however, is very much at odds with Gabriel Almond and Sidney Verba's finding that democratic stability rests not on homogeneous attitudes but on society's ability to manage conflicting elements within a culture. A civic culture is a mix of three disparate components in the general political culture and in the orientations of individuals—parochial, subject, and participant. Stable democracy results not from any one type of culture but from the proper blend of all three.[27] From a civic culture perspective, therefore, it is wrong to say that, so long as the cultural basis for democracy is mixed, "the prospect for democratic politics is not secure."[28]

Partly because of this confusion, students of political culture were strikingly late in recognizing the importance of the spontaneous systemic change that engulfed Russia in the late 1980s. To this day many cling to the view that any democratic initiatives in Russia can only be a short-lived respite from the inevitable reassertion of traditional authoritarian patterns. Political culture can, therefore, be of little use in understanding the type of rapid social and cultural change that has taken place in Novgorod because it rejects the very possibility of such changes occurring, except in response to cataclysmic events, and then only if reinforced by external pressure. Because students of political culture do not see culture itself as a resource for change, they generally remain oblivious to evidence of rapid social transformations until after the fact.

Social Capital and Socialist Networking

Like the civic culture approach, social capital theories seek to identify those individual and social attributes that are most important for democratic development. Social capital has been linked to the growth of trust in society, which has tangible economic and political benefits. At the same time, social capital is also a "moral resource" reflecting trust in social institutions.[29] Francis Fukuyama's writings have focused attention on how cultural differences in economic organization and kinship relations can lead to different levels of trust in different societies.[30] Along with other researchers, he has have concluded that the median level of trust in democracies is higher than in nondemocratic countries, a fact reflected in higher levels of social capital and better economic and government performance.[31]

As with civic culture, social capital theory was applied to the Soviet Union and other communist countries only to prove its absence.[32] According to Richard Rose, the absence of fundamental elements of trust in society made the Soviet Union "an ideal-typical anti-modern society." Even the social networks that emerged to cope with society's gross inefficiencies reflected "premodern" forms of social behavior. This premodern behavior continues in post-Soviet Russia, perpetuating low social involvement, cynicism, and economic inefficiency.[33]

When assessing the prospects for democratization in former communist countries, social capital theorists are thus left with one of two disappointing options: they either believe that the absence of cultural or historical traditions of building social networks precludes the emergence of civil society; or they believe that reliance on existing social networks will only promote cynicism and corruption. As proof, social capital theorists point to the collapse of social organizations throughout Eastern Europe at precisely the time when, thanks to the withdrawal of the state, they should be flourishing. Few have looked at a simpler explanation—that civil society and social capital have not disappeared but rather pursue functions different from the ones attributed to them in the West.

Studies of the social networks in Eastern Europe reveal that even the most repressive socialist regimes left some space for private social interaction. These networks promoted economic efficiency, built trust among independent actors, and provided a modest form of socialization outside official channels. Their interaction with the state created "assets, resources, and the basis for credible commitments and coordinated actions. . . . At the shop-floor level, shortages and supply bottlenecks led to bargaining between supervisors and informal groups; at the managerial level, the task of meeting plan targets required a dense network of informal ties that cut across enterprises and local organizations. . . ."[34] Some scholars have suggested that where the private sphere of friends and family overlapped with the sphere of state-mandated social intercourse, it led to a distinct, socialist brand of social capital.[35]

These informal networks have survived the collapse of the regime because they continue to provide practical solutions when formal institutions failed. Although Rose sees them as corrosive to trust in government, because they provide solutions outside of formal venues, Martin Aberg and Alyona Ledeneva suggest that such networks stand a good chance of evolving into "new path dependencies" that reflect the needs of a new society.[36]

The persistence of these old social networks may explain the puzzling collapse of associational activity in the former East Germany. This collapse surprised both those civil society theorists who argued that the state need only be constrained for civic associations to flourish and those who believed that the replacement of East German institutions with Western ones would automatically modernize social behavior and increase public trust. Just the opposite happened, and Joyce Mushaben has suggested this is because the West decided to undermine the cultural values and networks of the East. Had existing civic networks been used instead "like antique bricks to enlarge an older democratic house without disturbing the basic architectural style," there would be a much higher level of social capital and civic activism in eastern Germany today.[37]

Novgorod is an example of a region where the local government followed Mushaben's advice. The resulting dialogue between government and civic organizations encouraged attitudes and practices that diminished the rapaciousness of groups that might otherwise have engaged in destructive in-fighting or taken advantage of their position to enrich themselves at the expense of the community.

Yet, even if the positive role that social capital can play in postcommunist societies were more widely acknowledged, social capital theories still have no mechanism for explaining how transitions from low levels of social capital to high levels occur, or why civil society can emerge more rapidly in one region than in another. Despite being deeply rooted in cultural assumptions, social capital theorists do not turn to culture to explain rapid social change.

Congruence Theory and Russia

For most culturalists it is axiomatic that cultural attitudes change very, very slowly. It is this very immobility that allows analysts to identify which cultural values are translated into political preferences that sustain the political system. The failure of cultural theories to specify how this takes place, however, led Eckstein to formulate his theory of congruence.

Congruence exists if the authority patterns of all units in a society are similar. Authority patterns are the "structures and processes by which social units are directed . . . structures and processes of governance."[38] Simply put, they are the way in which all social units, including government, conduct business. They reflect, broadly, the authority culture—the "general orientations toward the polity shared by both government and other social actors."[39] Congruencies between governmental and other authority patterns should therefore be manifest throughout society, and this is precisely what Eckstein found in his landmark study of Norway and in subsequent multinational studies conducted with Ted Robert Gurr.[40]

Just as the absence of democratic institutions flows from the absence of democratic elements in a general authority culture, the existence of democratic institutions implies the existence of democratic elements within the authority culture.[41] For congruence theorists, the existence of democratic institutions Novgorod Region, therefore, implies the existence of democratic elements in the region's general authority culture.

A second valuable aspect of congruence theory is that, by linking cultural legitimacy directly to social institutions, it suggests how formlessness can be reversed. By their very nature, says Eckstein, societies abhor instability and the cognitive dissonance it entails.[42] Both can be reduced by promoting congruence between authority patterns and institutions. This is best accomplished by introducing institutional changes *only* when they are consonant with deeply seated norms of behavior—relying, in other words, on "antique bricks" to build the new democratic edifice.[43] In a formless era the search for cultural legitimacy, an inherently conservative act, becomes a vehicle for challenging the status quo (now disorder, form-lessness) and for creating a new political system.

At the same time that new structures must "fit" old patterns to dimin-ish resistance to change, Eckstein says they must also work to "democra-tize, as much as possible, social life in general." This requires the creation of institutions that "link and mediate between government and aspects of social life resistant to democratic traits."[44] Here Eckstein explains why social capital is such a valuable commodity—more voluntary associations increases social harmony because such associations build congruence among both their members and the government.

Congruence theory thus provides the first clear explanation of how democratization occurred in Novgorod. The local elite strengthened the similarity of authority patterns throughout the region, both by introduc-ing changes consonant with traditional norms and by encouraging the formation of intermediate social units. Still, congruence theory does not explain the unusual speed with which all this took place. Along with most culturalists, Eckstein believes that cultural continuity is at a premium in situations of upheaval. Consequently, new social patterns will emerge very slowly and only at a high cost to social stability.[45]

The cultural differences among regions, however, provides a clue to what makes rapid social change possible. Because "authority patterns are much the same in all social units, regardless of size or function," they can be traced through political institutions at every level of society.[46] Indeed, one could argue that a regional focus is preferable for testing congruence theory, precisely because it requires researchers to pay close attention to how local cultural values interact with local institutions to promote par-ticular authority patterns.[47]

As an approach for understanding democratic transitions, congruence theory is a notable advance over theories of social capital and political culture. It not only identifies the characteristics of stable democracies but specifies the mechanisms used to transmit democratic values. It provides a clear link between culture and democratization by matching general value orientations (authority culture) to measurable patterns of demo-cratic behavior (authority patterns). Ultimately, however, Eckstein's argu-ment that only cultural changes that are reflected in institutions can transform political culture does not bring us any closer to resolving a conundrum that has long plagued political analysts: Which comes first, the culture or the institutions? Both are vital to stable democracy, but insti-tutionalists answer this question very differently from culturalists. They see culture as little more than a construct of institutions, a derivative of economic and social choices that are made by individuals for entirely predictable (rational) reasons. Culture's impact on the political process is thereby reduced to a series of discreet decisions made by individuals for obvious reasons.

Culturalists, however, view culture as more than just the sum of individual choices. Precisely because it cannot be discretely segmented and compartmentalized, because it dissolves the rigid boundaries we create in our efforts to categorize political behavior, and subjects economic decisions to religious dogmas and political decisions to ethnic taboos, treating culture like any other variable risks fundamentally misunderstanding political behavior.

Culturalists look for the deeper, often hidden, long-term patterns that those who treat culture as a given often confuse with the frozen images offered by surveys. During periods of formlessness it is precisely to these deeper patterns that individuals turn.

Without a holistic understanding of culture, we are left with a conception of power that is too narrow and segregated to be of much use.[48] Taking advantage of culture to study political change, therefore, means bringing in as many cognate disciplines as possible. We need the historian's tools to understand the most significant landmarks in local history; we need the anthropologist's understanding of the political significance of rites, rituals, and customs; we need the social psychologist's awareness of patterns of collective action and the sociologist's explanations of the behavior of social movements. We need to be familiar with all these tools to understand culture's impact on social change.

Treating culture as simply another variable does not work because it is *the* variable constructed and chosen by key social actors to change political beliefs and behaviors. Wildavsky makes this linkage very clear:

> Cultural theory is based on the premise that preferences . . . emerge from social interaction in defending or opposing different ways of life. When individuals make important decisions, these choices are simultaneously choices of culture—shared values legitimating different patterns of social practice. Always, in cultural theory, shared values and social relations go together.[49]

Cultural preferences are, therefore, a choice—the application of selected values to the social reality in a way that makes it seem to conform better to one's value choices. Culture is constraining only in the common-sense definition of limiting unrealistic life choices, but beyond that, as Wildavsky says, "people decide for or against existing authority . . . [and] construct their culture in the process of decision making."[50] By regarding cultural preferences as a construct of choice, rather than as a limiting inheritance, we also open the door wide for rapid social change.

WHAT IS MISSING FROM CULTURAL ANALYSIS?

Widespread skepticism about culture's ability to change rapidly has hobbled our understanding of democratization. Francis Fukuyama merely sums up the current wisdom when he attributes the absence of civil society in Russia, Ukraine, and Belarus to longstanding "social and cultural pathologies" and suggests that, because cultural forces change "the most slowly of all," this places democracy "safely beyond the reach of institutional solutions and hence public policy."[51]

Every unexpected political transition, however, has renewed debate over how quickly individuals can adapt to cultural changes and how much the past constrains options for future development. Thus, after World War II, while culturalists argued that early learning provides such powerful conditioning that it made the reorientation of cultural assumptions later in life highly unlikely, Ronald Rogowski found that just one generation after World War II, Germans had developed high levels of civic culture *regardless of age group*.[52] Even skeptics like Charles Lockhart concede that "extraordinary events in later life may override aspects of earlier socialization."[53]

One scholar who argues that cultural reorientation can occur quite rapidly, even in peacetime, is Thomas Rochon. He has looked at how learning occurs and found that, while cultural change is typically slow, rapid change is different because it "relies uniquely on large-scale conversions to a new way of thinking about a subject."[54] Rochon finds evidence of such conversions in linguistic innovations that redefine our cultural and historical points of reference—for example, renaming the Supreme Soviet the State Duma—and thus allow us to define new realities.

Although Rochon's penchant for viewing cultural changes as highly innovative and decentralized underestimates the role of government, it usefully distinguishes three stages in the formation of values that lead to social change. The first, value conversion, replaces the existing ideas with new ones. The second, value creation, develops new ideas to apply to existing situations. The third, value connection, forges a conceptual link between phenomenon that were previously seen as unconnected or connected in a different way.[55] The last stage also provides opportunities for new values to extend across established political boundaries and forge new political alliances, thus broadening the base of support for social change.[56]

Rochon's approach is supported by the work of Richard Gunther and others, who find that democratic regimes can consolidate in relatively short periods of time, even in the absence of widespread democratic values. As long as "the active, organized sectors of a political system do not challenge the legitimacy of a new democracy's political institutions and consistently conform to its behavioral norms," says Gunther, the time frame for consolidation can be as short as five years![57]

Another area where opinions differ is how much the past constrains future development. Economists and political scientists often refer to this as "path dependency," and suggest that it precludes patterns of development not already well established in a nation's history.[58] Unfortunately, the criteria for identifying what is well established are highly subjective, and people tend to find exactly the type of path dependency they are looking for.[59] This can lead even distinguished scholars to make dismissive cultural judgments that are as superficial as they are insensitive.[60] Not surprisingly, path dependent analysis often finds that native "cultural pathologies" must be replaced with Western cultural and institutional models.

Not all analysts, however, view historical patterns as a *limiting* factor. John Mueller argues that a long time may not be needed for transition, because "one preexisting set of habits and perspectives may gradually (or perhaps suddenly) become eclipsed by the other preexisting set."[61] Wildavsky suggests that people do, in fact, "try out political cultures. They may adhere to a given culture until its contradictions become too blatant to be ignored; and then, if opportunities arise, they may shift their allegiance." This may occur gradually or as the result of "surprise and opportunity."[62]

Clifford Geertz suggests that rapid shifts in cultural identity may be far more common than we think, and that it indeed is cultural stability that defies explanation.[63] Even Eckstein concedes the possibility of rapid peacetime cultural adaptation under certain circumstances. Psychologists, he notes, have found that unfamiliar situations are interpreted as fitting into earlier, more familiar patterns. He cites the example of northern Nigeria where modern elections were reinterpreted as versions of the familiar elections to tribal chieftaincy.[64] Eckstein says such adaptations are "highly limited," but if we take to heart his point that the congruence of authority patterns serves to limit the scope of dramatic changes, then we cannot escape the conclusion that the sudden collapse of congruence will also diminish the ability of institutions to serve as constraints on the emergence of new authority patterns.

Advocates of path dependency, however, will likely counter that it is not just institutions but past history that constrains cultural development. If this were literally true, of course, no change would ever be possible, so while culture provides some boundaries, it must also provide some escape hatches. David Laitin finds it is useful to think of culture as having two faces. One face is made up of interpersonal ties and relational networks. People cannot escape their social networks, and during periods of formlessness they rely on them to preserve a semblance of continuity in a rapidly shifting world.

The other face of culture is made up of systems of meaning constructed by elites. These systems provide certain vocabularies, symbols, and value assumptions that offer people immediate help in dealing with formlessness. They set certain cultural boundaries that prevent preferences from being infinitely malleable and people from losing all social moorings. In stable societies, for example, only those combinations that are socially viable can be lived out and this knowledge is internalized through socialization.[65] Formlessness, however, seriously weakens the common framework of meaning that links people. At these times the variety of socially viable options temporarily becomes greater. This instability places pressure on elites to reassert a common framework of cultural preferences that will relegitimize elite policies and institutions. As we shall see in subsequent chapters, this cultural/political function of the elite is vital to the process of rapid social change.

Cultural analysis is ideally suited to the task of explaining the mechanisms by which cultural values are transformed into political choices, because it asks which cultural resources are being used to overcome formlessness and who controls those resources. State-supported institutions that inculcate values, such as schools, churches, and civic and community organizations, are obvious mechanisms, as are the common social experiences generated by ceremonies, rituals, festivals, and holidays. These promote an elite-approved way to make sense of new developments. Participation in these events forces individuals to update their cultural matrix, adjusting it to accept new institutions as part of the traditional value structure.

Popular interpretations of the past, and the symbols and images associated with them, are particularly potent vehicles for managing social change because they allow us to connect the two faces of culture. On the one hand, they serve to identify the core elements of culture that are embedded in established social networks—Geertz's definition of culture as "an historically transmitted pattern of meaning embodied in symbols, a system of inherited conceptions expressed in symbolic forms by means of which men communicate, perpetuate, and develop their knowledge about and attitudes toward life."[66] On the other hand, they are prominent actors in the political agenda of the elite, which, under the pressure of formlessness, is urgently seeking to shape a new set of cultural preferences. This unique connection provides analysts with both a baseline and a goal post, and makes cultural symbols the perfect yardstick by which to measure the progress of social change.

Wildavsky once quipped that both culture and theories about it seem equally resistant to change.[67] This may be why so few have addressed a glaring contradiction at the heart of the culturalist argument. On the one hand, it is argued that individual preferences change only slowly, and that this inertia lends stability to cultural assumptions and to the institutions that frame them. Yet, if cultural preferences were always stable, formlessness would never be a problem. The very fact that formlessness can engulf a society so abruptly suggests that, at least under certain conditions, cultural preferences are far from stable. This raises the intriguing possibility of reconstructing stable cultural preferences and, thus, more rapidly building a new social consensus.

As we have seen, cultural analysis provides a valuable framework for understanding rapid social transition but few analytical tools for appreciating how it occurs. There is a set of tools ideally suited to this task—myths and symbols. A brief review of their distinguished pedigree in the social sciences will reveal what makes them so well suited to the study of rapid political change.

Psychology: The Symbolic Life of the Mind

The first of the social sciences to recognize the importance of symbols was psychology. The two leading figures in twentieth century psychoanalysis, Sigmund Freud and Carl Jung, both regarded myths and symbols as central concerns. According to Freud, hidden meanings lie just beneath the surface of expression, but the complex layering of these meanings prevents us from understanding reality. Our hidden thoughts are given shape in myths, expressed in religious rituals and art, and their true nature is often revealed symbolically in dreams. Freud found certain universal patterns among myths that, he claimed, were the "distorted vestiges of the wish fantasies of whole nations—the age-long dreams of young humanity."[68] The study of such myths, he believed, might reveal the universal patterns that lie at the root of modern civilization's discontents.

Freud's view of myth as a disease of the psyche—a civilization's neurosis, to be revealed and treated—has had a profound impact on the social sciences. To this day it is common to describe myth as something that "must be taken seriously precisely in order that it may be gradually superseded in the interests of the advancement of truth and the growth of human intelligence."[69] Some political analysts have adopted the view that myths are "an illustration of the role of ideological delusions" typical of societies beset by discord, enmities, and problematic democratic traditions.[70] In such societies social malaise might very well take symbolic form and be translated into a dangerous political force, like nationalism. This is why "formlessness"—literally the lack of stable symbolic forms for government—is such a danger to society.[71]

Unlike Freud, Jung regarded myth more benignly. He posited the existence of a universal substratum of mythical images ("archetypes") that might provide clues for treating the patients in his care. Recurring images and symbols, he said, were representations of a universal set of values (the "collective unconscious" or "objective psyche") whose meaning could be recovered though a careful study of myths and legends. Such study could also uncover a deeper cultural wisdom that might eventually point the way toward the future psychological completeness of humanity—a prospect Jung described as fulfilling man's vocation.[72]

It was Freud's work, however, more than Jung's that identified social strategies for coping with cognitive dissonance.[73] The field of social psychology has evolved around the idea that the greater the level of dissonance, the stronger the pressure to reduce it—a notion that features prominently in the works of Eckstein. At the same time, however, Freud's negative interpretation of myths left analysts with two problematic assumptions for the further application of symbols in the social sciences.

The first is the view that myths are a deception that needs to be swept away in order to reveal the truth. The second is the idea that mythmaking (and, along with it, much of culture) takes place within the psyche and is buried deep under layers of accumulated cultural neuroses. As James Hillman aptly remarks, "A psychological approach means what it says: a way through the psyche into myth, a connection with myth that proceeds via the soul . . . only when myth is led back into the soul, only when myth has psychological significance does it become a living reality, necessary for life, rather than a literary, philosophical, or religious artifice."[74] This tendency to view myths and symbols as, first and foremost, mental constructs made it very difficult to show their causal impact on events. To be of any use to the study of political and social change, symbols would have to break free of these stereotypes.

One of the first to argue that myths could be studied in a rational and scientific manner was Ernst Cassirer. Cassirer described man as "the symbolic animal" and regarded the creation of meaning as one of the core function of human existence.[75] Although a great admirer of psychological insight, Cassirer did not see myths as a neurosis but as a natural aspect of human creative expression, the driving force behind culture. Ultimately, Cassirer found Freud too reductionist and, inspired by the unifying role that symbols had played in modern physics and math, he set out to develop a theory of symbolic forms that might encompass the entire sphere of human activity, including science, art, and poetry. "The facts of science," Cassirer wrote, "always imply a theoretical, which means a symbolic, element."[76]

Cassirer argued that all humanistic disciplines collaborated in the creation of a symbolic dimension of human existence, a conclusion that caused considerable excitement in its day and inspired literary critics and artists to popularize his work.[77] In his last book, *The Myth of the State*, he relied on anthropology, sociology, history, and psychology to analyze myths and mythmaking, and in a clear repudiation of Freud, counterposed the positive influence of mythical thought to an excessive reliance on rational thought, which he deemed a grave danger to mankind.[78]

Despite an enormous erudition that tapped into virtually every known field, however, Cassirer ultimately failed in his efforts to devise a "grammar of the symbolic function" that would provide a unified theory of culture.[79] The fact that symbols could be interpreted in so many various and partially overlapping ways seemed to make them inherently ambiguous—an insurmountable obstacle to any empirically based social science. To be seen as a causal agent for social change, symbols would have to provide a consistent range of meanings. Moreover, these meanings would have to be inherent in the symbol, rather than the mind of the observer.

Symbolic Anthropology: Moving Symbols from the Mind to the Social Arena

Anthropology responded to Freud's challenge with Clifford Geertz. Geertz argued that culture was embodied in public symbols and that members of society communicated their values through rituals associated with those symbols. There was no need to speculate about what was going on inside people's heads, for culture was manifest—"as public as marriage and as observable as agriculture."[80] Because symbols shape how social actors understand their world, social action can be understood by interpreting what symbols mean within the context of a particular cultural tradition.[81] Rituals, ceremonies, education, and the like provide "templates" or "blueprints" for the organization of social and psychological processes. They suggest how we ought to behave in certain circumstances, as well as what forms of government are "right" or "wrong."[82] The appropriate role of social science is therefore to interpret the significance of society's key symbols. Geertz called this "interpretive theory."[83]

For Geertz, the ideologies that drive men's passions are best understood as "ordered systems of cultural symbols."[84] Understanding the process of symbol formation is, therefore, the key to understanding all social processes. Like Eckstein, Geertz argues that such ideologies are most crucial in times of social upheaval, when the institutional constraints on behavior are weak or absent. At these times, elite control of political symbols becomes crucial, for it is through symbols that individuals are able to relate what is unfamiliar to them in the present to the familiar past, facilitating the transition. Paradoxically, the individual's need for a familiar past becomes stronger the more the new political system is able to free itself from received tradition.

While Talcott Parsons was urging social scientists to forge "the socio-logical equivalent of the Newtonian system," Geertz was calling on them, instead, to focus on the meaning rather than the measurement, on the specific rather than the universal.[85] For interpretivists, "those who still wait for a Newton are not only waiting for a train that won't arrive, they're in the wrong station altogether."[86] Because social scientists had lost sight of the meaning of social action, said Geertz, power had become discon-nected from the conditions of its generation or the immediacies of its application. It would remain so, he argued, so long as analysts are only concerned with where it lies and against whom it is directed, rather than with what brings it to life.[87] We can learn about meaning by focusing on "local knowledge"—the stories that convince people "that they belong, by fate and nature, politically together."[88]

Geertz's method for studying culture is rather conventional—observing, understanding, and interpreting modes of expression and what they mean to that society—but it requires a high degree of intuition about which "observable symbolic forms" are the most important.[89] To avoid falling into the trap of turning culture into a catch-all variable, Geertz insists that critical inquiry about culture must be about "mobilizing differ-ences [and] adjudicating contrasts . . . rather than overriding them or forcing them into some pallid, feel-good ecumenical whole."[90] Differences do not negate similarities, but comprise them, localize them, give them form. In "a world of restless identities and uncertain connections," ulti-mately, he says, "there is nothing for it but to get down to cases."[91]

Like Freud's, Geertz's impact on the social sciences is hard to overes-timate. By drawing attention to the importance of public symbols, he rede-fined the object of cultural analysis and helped to soften, just a bit, the separation within the social sciences between those who favor "hard" and those who favor "soft" approaches to the use of data.

By focusing on symbols as tangible artifacts, Geertz moved cultural studies beyond sterile debates over whether cultural attributes must be shared or consensual. Because the cultural context that illustrates the meaning of a symbol to analysts is the same one that provides its meaning to participants, symbols affect both individual behavior and public insti-tutions in ways that can be studied.[92] Power and political authority are always expressed in symbolic guise, and to understand how they are wielded, says Geertz, we need to understand how people select certain identities for themselves. Vesting culture in observable symbols allows us to search for what Geertz calls, in words strikingly reminiscent of Cassirer, "the underlying grammar of politics."[93]

Another leading anthropologist who focused on the mediating role of symbols was Victor Turner. Turner looked specifically at rituals—"a mechanism that periodically converts the obligatory into the desirable."[94] It was especially important to study rituals, said Turner, because they release social tensions. Turner showed how, during times of crisis, people turn to their most deeply held "root paradigms" for support, even as the crisis itself raises questions about why the traditional values and cultural patterns have failed.[95] While Geertz stressed how symbols shape the way social actors perceive the world, Turner saw symbols as active operators in the social process.[96] In certain ritual contexts they not only served as tools to resolve social contradictions but they could even "instigate social action."[97]

The practical political application of symbols was pursued even further by Abner Cohen, who illustrated Turner's notion that symbols are the primary social operators by showing how elites manipulate them. Social behavior, says Cohen, is an endless series of performances. Elite participants constantly intervene in those performances that are most critical, modifying symbols in ways that help promote their message.[98] The ability to mobilize old and new symbols in ways that "continuously transform the reality of differences into the appearance of similarity" is thus a key attribute of political leadership.[99] Those individuals who best create, mobilize, and articulate appropriate symbols are the ones who will emerge as leaders.[100]

Symbols also form a community's last line of defense against radical change. "Symbols of the 'past', mythically infused with timelessness . . . attain particular effectiveness during periods of intensive social change when communities have to drop their heaviest cultural anchors in order to resist the currents of transformation."[101] Because even the most dramatic political changes are marked by a considerable continuity in symbolic forms, analysts should pay particular attention to "dramatic performances" during periods of upheaval, for they determine the degree to which symbols are being used to change, or to preserve, the old order.[102]

Cohen identifies two ways that elites manage myths: "cultural extension," in which an idealized past is identified as a guide to the future; and "cultural substitution," in which the state imposes new institutions in order to generate new supportive values. Cultural revolutions, particularly communist ones, emphasize the latter approach. By contrast, both Novgorod and Cohen's own case study of Focaltown, Newfoundland, are examples of "cultural extension." In both Focaltown and Novgorod, elites sought to "reconcile the present with the past—ideologies of change which respect and evoke the past—by showing that the new is either not really new at all but has its essential roots in the past, or by arguing that the 'new' socioeconomic structures will be enhanced by traditional values which they preserve rather than deny."[103]

Symbolic anthropology thus suggests that social instability and malaise are as much the result of society's inability to aggregate symbols as they are of economic or institutional weakness. Formlessness is the direct result of the public's inability to link institutions to the customary symbolic repertoire. New institutions that can be so linked will be more readily accepted as legitimate, while those that cannot do so will have a difficult time and may never be accepted.

Despite the many new insights provided by symbolic anthropology, however, many analysts were uncomfortable with the notion that rapid social change might be accomplished through the manipulation of symbols. Although acknowledging that cultural adaptation to change is commonplace, symbolic anthropologists seem more comfortable with discussing cultural continuity than with identifying potential sources of cultural innovation. As a result, many do not take seriously enough the political implications of viewing men and women as the inventors of their own culture.

One who did is Roy Wagner. Unlike most anthropologists (even symbolic ones), Wagner saw cultural invention as a natural process that symbols help to mediate. As soon as society is comfortable with the changes that have occurred, the fact that they were established through invention is conveniently put out of awareness, so that the symbols of change can become part of hallowed tradition.[104] The door to change is always wide open because culture is constantly reinventing itself.[105] During periods of deep cultural turmoil, therefore, people literally invent a way out of their conventional orientations. In dire circumstances, rapid invention may be called for. Wagner reminds us that people are simultaneously the inventors and interpreters of culture, and that through their use of symbols, they act as both agents and objects of social change.

Forty years ago Geertz chastised his colleagues for not paying sufficient attention to "how symbols symbolize," that is, how they actually accomplish the mediation of meaning.[106] This problem remains. Understanding that symbols are as "public as marriage and as observable as agriculture" tells us nothing about whether any two people will eventually get married, or whether their marriage will be a successful one. The challenge of explaining precisely how symbols affect political behavior was taken up by sociologists, and specifically by social movement theorists.

Social Movement Theory: Tracing the Impact of Symbols

It was the pioneering work of Pierre Bourdieu and Harold Blumer that opened the door to tracing the political impact of symbols. As a young anthropologist Bourdieu felt dissatisfied with anthropology's lack of predictive power and set out to develop a social science in which actions were bound to "the generation and pursuit of strategies within an organizing framework of cultural dispositions."[107] He called this framework the habitus.[108]

The interconnectedness of all elements within the habitus allows analysts to treat symbolic and material interests as interchangeable. Social actors pursue investment strategies in cultural goods just as they would with economic goods and, under certain conditions, such goods are interchangeable.[109] A key task for sociology, therefore, is analyzing the production, circulation, consumption, and conversion of various forms of symbolic capital that serve as expressions of power. Because cultural symbols and practices embody interests and serve to enhance social distinctions, political struggle is the struggle for control over symbols, and victory is the ability to impose one's definition of the symbol on the social field. Good political administration is simply the efficient use of cultural symbols by the elite.[110]

Like Marx, Bourdieu believes that symbols are used to deflect attention away from the true, class-based nature of politics, masking them as noble or disinterested pursuits. Unlike Marx, however, he views the formation of the habitus as largely involuntary and constrained by inherited social hierarchies.[111] Thus, replacing one set of symbols with another will not change the fact of elite domination, for it is human nature to strive for power and to manipulate symbolic capital to achieve it.

Bourdieu desired a more predictive social science, yet his sociology leaves little room for meaningful social action, reducing it, as one analyst put it, to "a game of musical chairs and implicitly judged as both misguided and futile."[112] While Bourdieu describes the process of symbol formation as involuntary, he regards the creation of new ideological frameworks as an assertion of dominance by elites, and it thus appears that some aspects of cultural capital formation are unalterable, while others can be manipulated by elites. It is not always clear, in the fluid environment of the habitus, where Bourdieu draws the line.

He tries to resolves this contradiction by saying that the struggle for symbolic dominance is actually the purview of a small group of specialists who have a monopoly on interpretation and administration in their area of cultural expertise. He calls this area of expertise "the field." The field imposes on actors specific forms of struggle, as well as a tacit acceptance of the rules of the game. Contestants in the field might disagree as to the merits of a particular policy, but they all share an interest in preserving the field of political exchange, even as they disagree about who should dominate it.[113]

Bourdieu, however, does not address what happens if spoilers throw the rules out the window. Who picks up the pieces and establishes the new rules? The issue of agency is further complicated by Bourdieu's failure to discuss those individuals (like himself) who somehow manage to transcend their habitus and recognize it as a construct. As people who stand outside the stream of social manipulation, one would assume that, like Lenin's "vanguard of the proletariat," they could become autonomous agents of change.

Given its linguistic and theoretical idiosyncrasies, Bourdieu's work was not widely read in the United States until the 1990s. Long before Bourdieu became popular in the United States, however, Harold Blumer was faulting sociologists for focusing too heavily on social structure and for treating social action as merely an expression of these structures.[114]

Blumer argued that the analysis of social action ought to be divorced from the analysis of existing social organizations. Instead of treating individuals as surrounded by preexisting objects and patterns that condition their behavior, he believed it would be more accurate to envision human beings as constructing objects on the basis of on-going interactions with others. He calls this "acting on the basis of symbols," or "symbolic interactionism."[115]

By emphasizing the centrality of symbols in communicating shared meanings Bourdieu and Blumer both opened the door to what is commonly referred to as the "new cultural sociology."[116] One influential proponent of the new cultural sociology, Ann Swidler, showed that culture has a profound political impact during settled as well as unsettled periods.

It is traditionally assumed that culture affects action by supplying the ultimate ends, or values, toward which action is directed. This, however, does not tell us anything about the choices people make in a given social situation. Explanations that privilege interests and structural constraints tell us that people choose actions one at a time according to a deliberate calculation of interests. In fact, says Swidler, actions are always part of larger "strategies of action" that are shaped by culture in three ways.[117] First, culture offers a "tool kit" of symbols, stories, and rituals that people configure in various ways to solve their problems. Once the tools are in place, culture causes persistent ways of ordering action through time—"strategies of action."[118] Finally, culture provides the components used to implement these strategies of action.

By focusing on the organizing principles that form a chain of actions, Swidler bridges the gap between those who treat culture as the object of change and those who treat it as an agent of change, replacing the tra-ditional view of culture as a constraint on political action with one that suggests a wide variety of options for change. Earlier culturalists saw dem-ocratic consensus as being dependent on a preexistent "civic culture." The new cultural sociologists, however, envisioned the possibility of con-structing a political environment receptive to democratic values and insti-tutions by drawing on cultural symbols.

In settled societies, where there is a high level of comfort with estab-lished values, people rarely turn to the cultural symbols in their "tool kit" to challenge the status quo, but in unsettled societies these symbols are much more in demand.[119] Forced to develop new strategies within the framework of old cultural models, elites desperately recast old rituals into new ones and suffuse old patterns and practices with new meaning. Swidler, citing Michael Walzer, points to Calvin's Geneva as an example of how culture can be used "opportunistically" to create specific psycho-logical changes among the public, while at the same time appealing to elites who are "looking for new ways to exercise authority and a new ethos to regulate their own conduct."[120]

By viewing culture as a mechanism that people employ to solve their daily problems, Swidler makes it not only an independent influence on social change but the primary agent of change. The tools of social change are thus easy to identify and their function clear. What remains unclear, however, is why certain cultures use these tools more effectively than others. To answer that question, she suggests, scholars will need to pay attention to "historical junctures where new cultural com-plexes make possible new or reorganized strategies of action," as well as to how "the capacity of particular ideas, rituals, and symbols to organize given kinds of action affects the historical opportunities actors are able to seize."[121]

By separating social action from its dependence on social institutions, cultural sociologists remove two problems that have perplexed advocates of political culture: how to explain rapid social change when social insti-tutions lag, and, conversely, how to explain the lack of social change in the face of rapid institutional transformation. By linking the symbols that elites use to represent change to strategic policy choices, social change becomes something that activists can promote, even in opposition to their government.

The process by which social actors alter the status quo has been the concern of a group of sociologists known as social movement theorists. The study of social movements as agents of social change reveals that opportunities for political mobilization are often created by cultural breaks, which occur "when two or more cultural themes that are potentially contradictory are brought into active contradiction by the force of events, or when the realities of behavior are seen to be substantially different than the ideological justifications for the movement."[122]

Interpretive frameworks that "resonate with cultural narrations, that is, with the stories, myths, and folk tales that are part and parcel of one's cultural heritage," are key to social mobilization and, if that mobilization is successful, often get translated into public policy.[123] Because the impetus for change can be so easily overwhelmed by old mentalities and traditional political culture, however, successful social movements also draw on the values inherited from the society's tradition of collective action and opposition.[124] This seems to be a contradiction. Stephen Hart's fieldwork, however, suggests that social movements are commonly led by people with strong commitments to preexisting traditions. These traditions provide the symbolic repertoire of symbols used in the struggle for change.[125] A successful social movement is, therefore, generally the result of social construction that simultaneously co-opts old symbols and forges new ones.

According to Alberto Melucci, social movements often begin as submerged, small, distinct networks that serve as "cultural laboratories" within civil society.[126] They challenge the regime culturally for years, undermining the dominant symbols on which current social relationships are based and offering alternative ways of perceiving social reality.[127] When this effort reaches a critical mass within society, these hidden networks suddenly become visible and quickly coalesce in opposition to the state. Because the conventional definition of political culture is so slanted toward official institutions, and hence toward the status quo, Melucci prefers to view political culture as constantly in ferment, with the potential for change ever present. Although his research has focused on mature democracies, the process he describes also fits the role played by dissident groups in Eastern Europe and the USSR during the years preceding the collapse of communism.[128]

Both cultural sociology and social movement theory have done a great deal to validate the importance of culture (and symbols) in political change. But the causal link between the political outcomes sought and the cultural options preferred still seems tenuous. By focusing on social movement organizers as *Kulturtraeger*, social movement theorists can highlight the paths that change can take but not why certain changes succeed while others fail. Curiously, they have also shown little interest in bringing into this discussion the most obvious agent of rapid social change— the state—perhaps because it has traditionally been the purview of political scientists.

Symbols in Political Science: Irrelevant Spectacle or Motor of Social Change?

With the triumph of rational choice approaches, culture, as two noted political scientists put it, was pretty much relegated to "the professional dog house for a generation."[129] Few seemed interested in the role of myths and symbols, and even those few split between those who view them as critical variables and those who treat them as nothing more than part of "the political spectacle."[130] The most influential scholar in the latter group, Murray Edelman, argues that political action is not about satisfying popular demands, as most political scientists perceive it, but about manipulating popular expectations.[131]

According to Edelman, people look to social institutions, and especially to government, to provide them with social cues that will ease their anxieties.[132] The myths individuals create about their social institutions allow them to quell their fears. Government is in a unique position to shape cognition because it has the power to prevent the emergence of competing social cues. This power to shape perception is so strong that, even when challenged by clear counter-evidence, a high proportion of the population will believe the government.[133] Still, Edelman argues, governments are not omnipotent, because their actions must plausibly conform to widely accepted political myths.

Because of this constraint, social change can only occur when there is a link to alternative mythical and symbolic cues already in place.[134] In Edelman's view, governments do not identify and solve problems, but "construct problems to justify solutions."[135] By taking full advantage of its mythmaking capabilities, government transforms policy making into a political spectacle. Liberation from the political spectacle, says Edelman, cannot come from political action but only from the discourse of art, which transcends the government's manipulation of the present and affords a broader perspective on reality.[136]

Edelman's view that government is a necessary but self-serving manipulator of symbols and myths has influenced W. Lance Bennett, who argues that myths are not only a part of but totally dominate the political process.[137] No matter how ideologically diverse a society may seem, says Bennett, real political options are much more limited because people cannot truly imagine political solutions that are outside the myths they are familiar with.

In periods of turmoil, however, taboos erode and rituals lose their meaning. Established symbols no longer mean what they used to, heightening public uncertainty and social tension. In such conditions, says Bennett, focusing on practical solutions only exacerbates the problem because there is no agreed upon framework of meaning. The first task of the political elite should therefore be to "construct publics" by symbolically framing problems in a way that encourages targeted public acceptance of new solutions.[138] As the most powerful tool in the arsenal of the political elite, myths and symbols "underwrite the status quo in times of stability and they chart the course of change in times of stress."[139]

Whereas Edelman suggests that elites are at least somewhat constrained in how they use symbols, Bennett seems to suggest that elites can pretty much manipulate the public any way they wish to.[140] Edelman also argues that a political leadership can get taken in by its own rhetoric and be unaware of threats until it overthrown by the opposition. Before long, however, the opposition is co-opted into the elites, and the cycle begins anew. Real social transformation is thus best achieved by a spontaneous explosion that does not give elites a chance to regroup.[141]

Edelman's message that successful policies depend on the symbolic images that elites project challenges the view that democracy has anything at all to do with rational discourse. Public policy choices, he suggests, have little to do with the substantive issues and everything to do with whether the images associated with them make us feel emotionally secure. The practical implication is that people will always prefer the past they know to the future they don't. As a result, the use of symbols to sharpen confrontation with the past is likely to heighten resistance to new government policies, whereas the use of old symbols in ways that subtly link them to new policies will facilitate the acceptance of new values and institutions.

Political scientists such as Edelman and Bennett leave one with a sense of hopelessness about political action. Because politics is impervious to reason, political outcomes become arbitrary and political choices meaningless. Social activists trying to transform society are little more than dupes, parading their own ignorance through the political spectacle. Not surprisingly, critics, such as James Scott, find this "far too pessimistic for the social facts."[142]

Scott takes issue with the notion that elites can defuse social conflict by co-opting the opposition. "Large historical forms of domination," he writes, are still "unable to prevent the creation of an independent social space in which subordinates can talk about it [change] in comparative safety."[143] We do not see this space, he says, because official histories are written by the victors. To avoid repercussions, the losers seek to leave as few traces of themselves as possible, systematically concealing practices of resistance.

Pointing to "thousands of rebellions and violent protests," Scott finds it impossible to believe that oppressed groups would rebel so often if they did not believe the social order could be overturned.[144] Moreover, he says, such rebellions prove that elites are not very successful in co-opting oppressed groups and convincing them to accept their lot. What is rare, he says, is not rejection of the status quo but the ability to act openly on this rejection. What Edelman sees as successful co-optation, therefore, Scott views as an expedient disguise of popular sentiment that, given the violent nature of political struggle, is "both realistic and prudent."[145] Scott's view of the rebellious peasantry eventually overcoming all obstacles, however, seems far too sanguine. If, as he suggests, most acts of protest observe the rules so well that they are indistinguishable from compliance, then in what sense are they still a protest?

But while Edelman and Bennett reach the dispiriting conclusion that symbols can serve only to impede reforms and stifle social change, other culturalists disagree.[146] Political psychologist David Sears, for example, criticizes Edelman's conclusion that political action is meaningless and argues that political responses are predictable if one looks at the symbolic meaning associated with political action.[147] Because people transfer stable affective responses across comparable sets of symbols, researchers can easily identify which predispositions will be evoked by individual symbols. Sears calls the activation of political predispositions through the use of symbols "symbolic processing."[148] Symbolic processing tends to be most significant during times of political ambiguity, which is also when the public manipulation of symbols is most likely to occur.

Sears's theory of symbolic processing mirrors Swidler's finding that political agendas that reflect people's perceptions of what ought to occur are more likely to receive public support than agendas that offer sound policies; or, to put it more simply, emotions will always trump reason. Taken a step further, it also suggests that because symbols frame perceptions in emotionally satisfying and consistent ways, even unpopular policies that are framed in acceptable symbolic terms will be more successful than policies that aren't.

The search for a better way of predicting social change also led political scientist Lowell Dittmer to symbols. Dittmer begins by faulting Edelman's assertion that politics is a spectacle about symbols that are "empty."[149] This gives too much importance to elites and too little to the actual content of symbols. To correct this, Dittmer redefines political culture as a system of political symbols nested within a system of political communication. Because of this nesting, he says, political symbols can refer to actual events while at the same time relating those events to a broader category of meanings that evoke and convey emotions. Dittmer refers to this ability to tap directly into people's emotions as the "steering capabilities" of political symbols.[150]

The relationship between the symbol and the political reality is a loose one, but it is never arbitrary, because at the core of the symbol's conceptual meaning is the meaning of the original sign. Dittmer refers to symbols with "a clear plot structure; serving a practical argument and appearing to a perennial or historically recurring constituency" as political myths.[151] Such myths serve to legitimize power, build moral consensus, and establish a range of predictable social behavior. In times of crisis, the consensual nature and limited flexibility of political mythmaking serve as a natural defense mechanism, foreclosing improbable and immoral alternatives.

Like Sears, Dittmer argues that the role of elites in shaping public debate through symbols is not unconstrained, but while Sears sees early social conditioning as the key constraint, Dittmer argues that historical and cultural precedents impose the most consistent limits on acceptable varieties of political behavior. Dittmer, however, leaves open the possibility of rapid social change in situations in which existing political structures and historical precedents are themselves under attack and, therefore, can no longer guide political mythmaking. In such instances political symbols may develop autonomously, thus separating them from the prevailing political culture that reinforces the status quo.[152]

Ascribing to symbols a degree of autonomy allows them to be treated as an empirical variable rather than as an assumed constant. One way that researchers could then use symbols as an analytical variable, says Dittmer, is to identify the underlying value orientations, hierarchical patterns, and attitudes toward authority within a political system, and then search for the figure or image that best encapsulates these underlying sentiments. Another way might be to first identify objects of special attention in a political culture, then analyze their meaning. Either way, once the key symbols are identified, their impact on politics can be empirically evaluated.[153]

Whereas Dittmer turns to linguistics for guidance, political scientist Alison Brysk turns to the social challenges and symbols that emerge "from below." Prevailing models of collective action, says Brysk, cannot account for changing social preferences, changing identities, and changing responses to resources, because they view persuasion as a means of reinforcing the status quo.[154] A symbolic approach to politics allows us to treat collective action as a means of transforming the status quo. By drawing on the literature of "new social movements" analysts can document the use of symbols for social change and measure their effectiveness.

Agreeing with Edelman that collective action is "a kind of storytelling or political theater," Brysk argues that this gives it a power that can compensate for the lack of other resources. Under certain conditions, symbolic politics can produce a chain of events leading to social change by "shifting priorities, building collective identities, shaping social agendas, or challenging state legitimacy."[155] Such conditions emerge when rapid economic and political changes defy our expectations.

The political impact of alternative stories then depends on whether elites can persuade people to accept them. Along with social movement theorists, Brysk argues that tradition ("the canon") can be the source of both status quo and oppositional discourse. Counter-hegemonic discourse merely reverses the canon and attaches new characters to the narrative. Because the symbolic vocabulary of the canon is already well known, the new rhetoric of counter-hegemony can spread very quickly.

To be successful new stories must be (1) culturally appropriate; (2) have historical precedent; (3) be reinforced by other symbols; (4) signal a call for action.[156] To translate changes in consciousness into changes in political behavior, however, symbols must accomplish three more things. They must transform individuals by "rewriting and reframing elements of identity"; they must transform social identity by changing "roles, values, and collective identity"; and they must produce an "agenda change" in favor of social mobilization by challenging the legitimacy of old institutions and policies.[157]

Brysk's specific criteria for the study of what she calls "symbolic politics as a motor of social change" thus includes tracing the impact of symbols in five areas: collective identity, collective mobilization, the creation of new public agendas, changes in public policy, the establishment of new institutions, and challenges to authority relationships.[158]

To sum up, it is striking that, despite their different methods and conclusions, political scientists seeking to understand the causes of social change from a cultural perspective all regard symbols as being at the heart of that process. In retrospect, the advantages of using symbols to measure the speed of social change seem rather obvious. By their very nature, symbols link political action (as agents of political mobilization), political content (the specific political rhetoric and agendas), and political success (the degree to which changes in political institutions, alliances, and rhetoric are attached to symbols). As units of analysis symbols are easy to identify, their usage easy to trace, and their popularity easy to measure. To the extent that there is any consensus in the relevant social science literature on the issue of social change (rapid or otherwise), symbols have emerged as the one indispensable resource for understanding and measuring it.

SHOULD THERE BE A METAFIELD OF SYMBOLIC POLITICS?

Our brief review of the study of symbols has also revealed a sense among many social scientists that social change is a subject too broad for any one discipline to tackle successfully. A comprehensive analysis of how and why social changes occur can only be undertaken within a multidisciplinary framework. Psychology affords the insight that symbols reveal a hidden realm of social consciousness. Anthropology affords the insight that symbols act as observable indicators of public values. Sociology affords the insight that symbols are tools for change, while social movement theorists show how symbols mobilize people into political action. Finally, political science adds the insight that the state plays a key role in defining the meaning and impact of political symbols. This convergence of views is so striking that it has lead scholars such as Dittmer, Cohen, and Doty to call for the study of symbols to be treated as a distinct subdiscipline.

There is much to be said for a distinctive, symbolic approach to politics. It would encourage a holistic view of political change. It would lead researchers to select the tools most appropriate to the task and perhaps even encourage them to apply these tools in new ways.

The issue of rapid social change is a case in point. Our review shows that many analysts already suspect that, given the proper conditions, cultural resistance to even dramatic social changes can be overcome in much less than a generation. Among those who argue that such rapid social change is possible, many agree that these conditions arise when elites make the transition to new cultural patterns appear as if it were a natural evolution of previous patterns by, among other things, manipulating traditional symbols and myths.

A distinctive focus on symbols would transform our very understanding of how social change occurs by treating such change as a natural aspect of social adaptation, rather than a problem to be resolved. The proper issue for democratic development strategists would then be how to help societies remove the obstacles blocking their natural tendency to heal, rather than what new institutions must be introduced to overcome cultural resistance to change. Traditional culture might eventually come to be seen as a valuable asset for reformers.

Why then are so many analysts still reluctant to treat symbols as a meaningful unit of political analysis? Following in the footsteps of Freud, some see symbols as backward-looking, manipulative, and inherently misleading. This sort of criticism, however, confuses the message with the messenger. Although the manipulation of symbols was characteristic of great social tragedies, such as Nazism and communism, it has also spawned monumental efforts of sustained public sacrifice, such as space exploration and the civil rights movement, as well as the defeat of both Nazism and communism.

Others seem to think that a focus on symbols undermines efforts to produce an empirically based political science. Although culturalists are often skeptical of positivism, empiricism, and rational choice, political science is not served by ignoring the uncomfortable reality that emotions and subjective perceptions sway human behavior at least as much, if not more, than reason does. Indeed, by tackling this issue head-on, I would argue that culturalists do more to advance cross-disciplinary discourse than many proponents of positive social science.

Another common criticism is that symbols are more needed in primitive societies and play less of a role in modern, sophisticated societies.[159] Structural anthropologists, however, argue just the opposite—the more sophisticated the society, the more sophisticated the myths used to disguise the invention of tradition. And although it is probably true, as Eric Hobsbawm notes, that "in spite of much invention, new traditions have not filled more than a small part of the space left by the secular decline of both old tradition and custom," modern man has not evinced any less need for socially integrating structures and rituals.[160] Perhaps more than any other time in human history, the twentieth century has been one of compulsory traditions invented and propagated by the state.

There are also those who argue that myths should not be treated as true political agents but as epiphenomena, as Marx would have it. Even symbolists sometimes seem to treat their subject as less than real.[161] But if people believe a thing to be real, it can have real political consequences.[162] The creation of a history for the land of Israel, as Hobsbawm notes, "was in practice the negation of the actual history of the Jewish people for more than 2,000 years."[163] Swiss historians have shown that the founding acts of the Swiss Confederation were actually nineteenth-century literary inventions.[164]

Another criticism is that any approach rooted in symbols would be impossible to falsify because one would have to find an area of human existence where symbols are absent. Oddly enough, this view holds that symbols cannot be used for political analysis because they are so . . . pervasive! The key components of a theory of symbolic politics, however, would be quite easily falsifiable. For example, one could see whether the attempt to pursue "rational reforms" without reference to symbols has been as successful in a comparable setting, or whether in comparable regions where elites have relied on different symbols and myths the socioeconomic results have been different as well.

The most important reason for skepticism about using symbols to study social change, however, is not philosophical but practical—the absence of case studies that illustrate how such changes derive from the actual manipulation of a particular symbolic repertoire. Not enough has been done to identify such repertoires and to detail the causal linkages between them and political policies. As a result, the analytical power of symbolic studies has rarely been tested. Our next step must therefore be to test the hypothesis that an analysis of symbols can explain the rapid social change seen in Novgorod.

Such proof requires first that we identify the symbols that are associated with social and political change in Novgorod, and that we identify their meaning as framed for public consumption. Second, it requires that we trace the usage of those symbols by the elite, thus identifying the mechanisms by which symbols accomplish rapid social change. Finally, it requires that we identify the impact of symbols by linking symbols to specific government policies. A convergence of all three criteria—meaning, mechanism, and policy—would allow us to argue with a strong degree of confidence that democratic consolidation in the Novgorod Region is indeed the direct result of the effective manipulation of key symbols by Novgorod elites. The first step to identifying the meaning of Novgorod's key political symbols is examining the historical context in which they emerged.

CHAPTER 5

NOVGOROD IN RUSSIA'S MEMORY

No man can have in his mind a conception
of the future, for the future is not yet.
But of our conceptions of the past, we make a future.
THOMAS HOBBES

As the birthplace of Russian democracy, the cradle of its commerce and learning—"our own Russian Florence," as Prince Eugene Trubetskoi once dubbed it—Novgorod occupies a unique place in the nation's historical memory.[1] Today, when it is commonplace to dismiss Russia as "a nation with no history of democratic political culture in its 1,000–year existence," it is worth reviewing what made Novgorod so different from Moscow and why, centuries after its fall, it still serves as a beacon for Russian reformers.[2]

The origins of Novgorod can be traced back to the middle of the ninth century, when a multiethnic confederation of tribes living around Lake Ilmen invited the Norse clan headed by Ryurik to lead the army, collect taxes, and administer justice.[3] For these services Ryurik and his retinue would receive a salary and be allowed to settle at some distance from the city. The retinue and their descendants, however, would be precluded from ever owning land in the city proper or from collecting tribute for themselves.[4]

This contract forms the basis for Novgorod's renowned freedom to "choose among princes," a right recognized even before 1136, the first recorded instance of the city's removal of its prince.[5] From then until the fall of the republic in 1471, contracts with princely hirelings included a standard clause that allowed the city to fire them at will.[6] It rested on the assumption that supreme political authority resided with the community as a whole, a view underscored by the city's rather grandiose title, "Lord and Sovereign Novgorod the Great."[7] As a matter of custom, Novgorodians regarded the Grand Prince of Vladimir as primus inter pares among Russian princes but never regarded themselves as his subjects.[8]

Two early and distinctive features of what came to be known as the Novgorod republic were its ethnic diversity and its confederated system of administration.[9] The city's earliest records describe it as a mixed community of Slavic and Finno-Ugric peoples. The oldest surviving Finnish and Karelian texts come from these lands, and the names of several senior elected officials that have come down to us, as well as the names of two of the city's five borough's (known as *kontsy*), are of Finnish origin.[10]

Perhaps it was the need to satisfy these diverse constituencies that first led to decentralization emerging as the guiding principle of Novgorod's political life. In time, Novgorod established an intricate network of formal and informal institutions designed to preserve popular sovereignty and the republic's independence from covetous neighbors. These included the popular selection of princes, the election of magistrates (known as *posadniki*) as well as their counterweights (the people's tribunes known as *tysiatskie*), and neighborhood and district assemblies that sent delegates to the raucous citywide popular assembly known as the *veche*. The Novgorod political ideal can be summed up as one of local self-sufficiency, which modern-day Europeans would recognize as subsidiarity.[11]

Given the notable constraints imposed on princes, historians have wondered why Novgorod bothered having them at all. The city seemed to do just fine without them when it had to, and for a while citizens apparently considered doing away with the position (its easternmost settlement of Vyatka eventually did).[12] Getting rid of princes entirely, however, would have seriously destabilized the Novgorodian political system, which carefully balanced the interests of the heads of wealthy noble clans, the church, and the populace.[13] This system of checks and balances was deemed crucial to preserving the republic's tradition of civic involvement.

The ultimate repository of civic authority was the veche, a body similar in origin to parliament.[14] Anyone could call a meeting by ringing the veche bell, even resident German merchants, though they were not allowed to vote.[15] Formal rules for how these meetings were conducted have not come down to us, leading some historians to speculate that they resembled unruly brawls. Others, however, disagree, pointing out that the veche had a chancellery to draft formal treaties and record the innumerable elections to citywide and local offices. Most veche meetings, they conclude, must have been rather dull.[16]

There was, in fact, not one but many veches, organized in pyramid-like fashion. Each neighborhood had its own assembly, and the authority of the citywide veche was viewed as a direct extension of the authority of the neighborhoods, each with its own seal and its own treasury.[17] Several streets together formed a "hundred" [sotnya], and two hundreds a borough [konets].[18] The entire city was administratively divided into five boroughs that radiated like spokes from a wheel outward to the farthest reaches of the republic.

This administrative system was replicated in each of the republic's five outlying districts, known as prigorody, where the local magistrate, though appointed by Novgorod, had to be approved by the local veche.[19] Finally, there were the more distant and sparsely populated regions, colonies really, such as Perm, Yurga, and Vyatka, that Novgorod exploited economically. These were the least autonomous of all Novgorod territories, but they tended to be ruled with a light hand, so as not to endanger lucrative trade with indigenous peoples.[20]

As the republic's supreme legislative body, the citywide veche ratified its treaties, invited princes, declared war and peace, set taxes, conducted foreign relations, and served as the supreme court for public disputes. Much of its time, however, was apparently consumed by the election of the city's two executive officers—the city magistrate and the people's tribune.[21]

The city magistrate served as both chief executive officer and chief spokesman for the landed nobility. Initially a princely appointment, by the end of the thirteenth century the magistrate was popularly elected from among the elected representatives of the five boroughs.[22] The position of people's tribune was created to serve as a check on the magistrate and was, hence, reserved for someone who was not a member of the aristocracy. The two were elected simultaneously each year, and most civil acts required the seals of both. An additional constraint on power was provided by the custom of requiring that formal documents carry the archbishop's blessing, given in the presence of both the magistrate and people's tribune, and witnessed by the official representatives of all five boroughs.[23]

Although the nobility set the agenda of formal veche gatherings through the chancellery, it could not guarantee the outcome of deliberations in such an open forum. As a result, the purchase of popular votes was quite common. Medieval chroniclers describe, with obvious relish, the lavish parties that wealthy noble families held in key neighborhoods on the eve of important votes.[24] By playing off the interests of church, nobility, and princes against one another, Novgorod's complex system of government very effectively prevented the emergence of tyranny for more than four centuries.

THE REPUBLIC OF ST. SOPHIA

The Cathedral of St. Sophia served as the de facto state house of the republic, intertwining church and civil administration in accordance with the Byzantine view that good government was possible only through the consent of both the people and the Church.[25] The archbishop was custodian of the city coffers and official weights and measures.[26] After 1220 trade courts became part of the Church's court system, and in the fourteenth century the Church also gained the right to register property transactions.[27] The archbishop of Novgorod had his own military regiment and was also occasionally asked to administer particularly difficult border territories. The fact that his name always appears first on treaties is widely seen as an acknowledgment of his titular leadership over what Yale historian George P. Fedotov has aptly called "the Republic of St. Sophia."[28]

It is interesting to note that, although he chaired the Council of Lords, the body that set the veche's agenda, the archbishop was not allowed to take part in veche meetings unless specifically invited to do so. Nor did his political authority prevent the issue of the confiscation of Church lands from being publicly debated.[29] Yet, even during periods of intense confrontation between the Church and the landed nobility, the tradition that his blessing must appear on all official documents except for trade agreements held fast.

Another Novgorod tradition was the popular election of clergy. In medieval Novgorod it was common practice for the clergy and people to nominate candidates for senior church positions through their neighborhood veche. The names of the three most popular candidates would be placed in an urn, and the victor chosen by a blind man ("the finger of God"). In the case of bishops, the citywide veche would have to confirm this election, and only then would the candidate be presented to the metropolitan in Moscow for ordination.[30]

The Church in Novgorod took an unusually active role in commerce. Many priests and deacons were active entrepreneurs and traders.[31] Merchant guilds often formed around the city's stone churches, which made excellent warehouses. As one historian has remarked, the Church in Novgorod blessed the accumulation of wealth, participated in it, and helped to administer it for the republic.[32]

That wealth became the stuff of legends. One medieval chronicler writes that when the Prince of Kiev attempted to call the independent-minded nobles of Novgorod to heel, they laughed at him, saying, "What sort of fortress is Kiev? I, Stavr, a nobleman, have an estate no smaller than Kiev and guest houses with halls of white oak, covered with silver beaver's fur. Each has a ceiling of black sable, floors with inlays of pure silver, and gilded door frames and handles."[33]

The Burgundian traveler Gilbert de Lennoi, who visited the city in 1413, describes it as fabulously wealthy, and even a century later (after Ivan III had pillaged it), papal advisor Alberto Campense wrote that Novgorod was "the most famous and wealthy of all northern cities" and compared it favorably to Rome. His contemporary, Sigismund Herberstein, who made several trips to Russia between 1517 and 1526, described Novgorod as "the greatest trading center of all Russia ... Lithuania, Poland, Sweden, and even Germany itself would send enormous numbers of merchants, and from such a large gathering of different nationalities the citizens multiplied their wealth and well-being."[34]

At the height of the Hanseatic League, Novgorod was the League's fourth-largest trading port, with commercial ties reputed to be more extensive than those of even Venice and Genoa.[35] Archeological excavations in the city have revealed English and Persian coinage, and even African cowrie shells.[36]

During the fourteenth and fifteenth centuries there were two or three permanent foreign trade settlements in Novgorod, hosting as many as 150 to 200 foreign merchants annually (not including up to two assistants for each merchant).[37] These settlements were self-governing and could impose sanctions, including the death penalty, on members. Disputes between foreigners and the local population were settled by a conclave of the senior members of the settlement and the *tysyatski*, according to negotiated agreements known as *schra*.[38] Foreign merchants could live in Novgorod for only one year, though extensions were not hard to arrange. Although they were limited to bulk purchases and could only rarely engage in commerce outside their enclave, they were allowed to bring in goods worth up to 1,000 marks, a limit that in bad economic times was raised to 1,500 marks.[39] This suggests that the amount of wealth officially brought in by Hanseatic merchants alone could reach as much as 150,000 to 200,000 marks annually.

In return, Novgorod exported wax, honey, various leather artisanry, and, at its height, more than half a million fur pelts annually.[40] Trade thus had a perceptible impact on the quality of life in Novgorod (in the sixteenth century the city's main market reportedly hosted 1,500 shops, for a population that may have reached 35–40,000) and led to the early formation of a prosperous class of burghers, traders, and artisans.[41] In the latter days of the republic they controlled the office of people's tribune and thus significantly offset the influence of the landed noble families.

Although historians still disagree about just how much ancient Novgorod owed its unusual political structure to Western influences, the impact of Western trade on its commercial, legal, and intellectual life is easy to trace.[42] Early on Novgorod adopted a Western system of measuring weights that made its currency easily convertible with other European currencies.[43] There are also nearly three centuries of legal interaction reflected in the perennial renegotiation of the schras. The corporate arrangements of local government encouraged the early emergence in Novgorod of trading guilds similar to those of Western Europe. Eventually, some of these guilds become so powerful that they were given the administrative status of sotnya, or half a borough.[44]

Novgorod's intellectual life developed along Western lines as well. Philologist Yakov S. Lurye cites the proliferation of secular manuscripts during the late fifteenth century as proof of the existence of a "Renaissance spirit" in the city.[45] Novgorod was also the source of the Judaizer and Strigolnik heresies that, similar to the Reformation in Europe, promoted independent reading of the Bible and the right of laity to sermonize. Indeed, at one point even Catholic priests were allowed to preach in the city.[46] When newly appointed Archbishop Gennady Gonzov arrived in Novgorod in 1484 from the far more parochial Moscow, he was so shocked by the cultural differences that he wondered if the two churches were actually of the same faith![47] He eventually became an active proponent of reunification with the Catholic Church and surrounded himself with a circle of learned humanists and scientists comparable to those of Renaissance Italy.[48]

Having come into contact with European culture earlier than Moscow, Novgorod played a central role in the spread of Latin learning in Russia.[49] The first translation of the Bible into modern Russian and the first Russian encyclopedia both appeared in Novgorod.[50] Russia's first Greco-Slavonic academy was opened in Novgorod in 1706 by two graduates of the University of Padua. In addition to providing seminary training, it prepared teachers for the country's first fourteen grammar schools.[51] All these developments have led some historians to surmise that, had Novgorod somehow avoided annexation by Moscow, Russian culture would have opened up to the West two or three centuries earlier.[52]

As it was, by the end of the fifteenth century a fortunate location on the trade route from northern Europe to Constantinople, and a political culture that rewarded economic entrepreneurship and gave the lower classes some modest influence on government, had allowed Novgorod to amass a territory nearly half the size of European Russia—the largest state to emerge in Europe since Charlemagne's Empire. Just as important, despite repeated attacks from Mongols, Swedes, and Teutonic and Livonian crusaders, it preserved a republican form of government for more than four hundred years.

Yet, as often happens in history, misfortune and internecine conflict led to the republic's defeat in 1471 at the hands of Ivan III, Grand Prince of Muscovy. The nobility's attempts to thwart Muscovy's expansion by enlisting the Polish-Lithuanian Prince Casimir IV as an ally were cunningly portrayed by Ivan's supporters as a betrayal of Orthodoxy.[53] The city split into pro-Lithuanian and pro-Muscovite factions, and even though both envisioned the relationship with their favorites as an alliance among equals, after Casimir abandoned Novgorod and the archbishop's regiment refused to engage Ivan's armies, the city was left with no choice but to accept Ivan's terms of surrender.[54]

Although outrage at Moscow's surrender terms initially led the enraged crowd to lynch three magistrates, accession to Ivan's demands actually served a number of interests.[55] Ivan III got to claim Novgorod as his liege, the Novgorod nobility got Ivan to agree to preserve their rights and customs, and the Church received the promise of Moscow's support against Catholic encroachment. Given Novgorod's long history of independence, it is likely that contemporaries viewed this latest setback as akin to others the republic had survived in the past. In the thirteenth century, the rising principality of Suzdal had threatened Novgorod in a conflict that had also split the city and tested its institutions.[56] In the end, however, that conflict was just another colorful episode in Novgorod's history.

The coming decades at first seemed to support this confident view. Although Ivan III broke all his promises, and even tried to ensure the future loyalty of Novgorod by replacing seven thousand prominent Novgorod families with Muscovites, within two generations these newcomers had adopted Novgorod's traditions as their own.[57] As the city regained its former prosperity, it even felt strong enough to shelter the rebellious noblemen Vasily Shuisky and Andrey Kurbsky, prominent political opponents of Ivan III's successor, the notorious Tsar Ivan IV, "the Terrible."

Fearing that Novgorod might once again emerge as a rival to Moscow, in 1570 Ivan IV conducted a surprise raid on the city. Over the course of three days he murdered more than three thousand people, mostly noblemen and clergy, exiled forty prominent noble families to Moscow, and eliminated elected offices for merchant guilds.[58] To finally break the resistance of the Church, the mainstay of opposition, Ivan expropriated nearly all private and church lands, and offered peasants cash payments and credit to move from monastery lands to his own.[59] The resulting chaos disrupted trade throughout northern and central Russia for decades. Novgorod never recovered and, after the foundation of St. Petersburg in 1703, became little more than a provincial rest stop on the road from St. Petersburg to Moscow.

Remarkably, however, the deeply ingrained principles of local self-government survived even this last assault. In the seventeenth century street elections, the election of the city magistrate, and even town meetings (now called *zemskaya izba*) slowly reasserted themselves over the

Muscovite administrative system.[60] Zimin notes that Novgorod even retained its own exchequer and monetary system.[61]

Thanks to these institutions, the city's spirit of political activism extended well into the seventeenth century. Historian Pavel P. Smirnov describes the intense debates that took place in Novgorod in 1648 on the nomination of delegates to the national assembly, the *zemsky sobor*. Unlike the Muscovite nobles who regarded such nomination as a form of government service, the nobles of Novgorod, he says, viewed it as their right.[62] Nearly two centuries after being forced to submit to Moscow, historians noted that Novgorodians still displayed a keen dislike for Muscovite ways and complained that Muscovites "do not understand the customs of Novgorod."[63] Thus, it is not surprising that, at the first opportunity— the Swedish invasion of 1611—Novgorod opted to separate from Moscow and welcomed the invaders into their city.

Eager to reassert their independence, the Novgorod nobility reverted to their traditional strategy of playing one side off against the other. Hoping to promote a rivalry between Swedish King Gustavus Adolphus and Crown Prince Carl Philip, they appealed to the latter to become regent in Novgorod and promoted his candidacy for tsar in Moscow. In the end, however, the population feared a Swedish king would be no better than a Polish one. After that rejection, and again in keeping with custom, Novgorod Metropolitan Isidore informed the Swedish military commander that "with the rejection of the prince, we became free. Give us our freedom."[64]

Despite the ever-growing weight of the tsarist autocracy, echoes of popular resistance lingered even in the nineteenth century. When reformist Tsar Alexander II instituted the "Great Reforms" of 1864, which called for institutions of local self-government for cities and villages, Novgorod was one of the first regions to petition that self-rule be extended to the national level and that national officials be elected.[65] This may have something to do with the fact that many Novgorod farmers owned their land. Whereas only 23 percent of farmland was held privately in Russia at the turn of the twentieth century, in the Novgorod region peasants owned over 63 percent of arable land.[66] The Novgorod gubernatorial district led all others in the rate of land transfers from the nobility to private farmers.[67]

In looking back over Novgorod's history, although it was not a democracy in the modern sense of the word, in the Middle Ages it provided common people with an astonishing degree of input into government. Indirect confirmation of this high level of civic engagement can be gleaned from the almost one thousand medieval birch bark documents unearthed in the city.[68] The high percentage of commercial and corporate legal documents among them has led some modern Russian scholars to describe Novgorod's political system as a "social contract."[69] Constant participation in public affairs at so many levels amounted to a permanent referendum on government and helps explain why Novgorod's traditions proved so durable.

NOVGOROD'S ENDURING MESSAGE OF FREEDOM

As Muscovy waxed and Novgorod waned, the alternative path of development that Novgorod once stood for began to look like a distant mirage. Nearly all nineteenth-century historians treated Novgorod as a cautionary tale about the frailty of freedom. Even Nikolai Kostomarov, the famed historian of "northern Russian democracy," who could reputedly recite entire Novgorod epics by heart, reluctantly concluded that Russia's emergence as a modern state had demanded that freedom be sacrificed on the altar of national unity.[70]

Soviet historians too, for understandable ideological reasons, supported the historical "progressiveness" of centralizing political authority in Moscow, and it was not until the era of perestroika that contrary viewpoints could be voiced.[71] This overwhelming historical consensus makes the survival of the popular image of Novgorod as a prosperous, republican alternative to autocracy all the more striking.

After the fall of Novgorod, many peasants and traders fled north to preserve what they could of the sacred image of their own holy city. Legends arose that told of travelers to the far north finding Heaven there.[72] The descendants of this fifteenth-century exodus first settled on the banks of the White and Barents Seas and eventually began to refer to themselves as a distinct group—the Pomor—a distinctiveness that rests entirely on their cultural link with medieval Novgorod. The Pomor regard themselves as having a different mentality from Russians. Academician Vladimir Kotlyakov has even speculated that, had their traditions not been so fiercely suppressed by Moscow, "Northern Russians might today constitute a fourth branch of Slavdom, alongside Russians, Ukrainians, and Belorussians."[73]

One of the first legends to arise after the fall of Novgorod tells of the miraculous escape of the city's veche bell, the symbol of the republic. The bell refused to obey Tsar Ivan's will, and rather than suffer silence, it smashed itself on the hills of Valdai as it was being transported to Moscow. Its pieces gave birth to the famed miniature bells of Valdai, which are destined to be carried throughout Russia, ringing to arouse people's indignation and to comfort them, awaiting the time when they can return to Novgorod and be reunited in freedom.[74] Another version of this legend has itinerant carriage drivers picking up the pieces and fashioning tiny bells out of them that they put on their carriages to carry the message of freedom wherever they ride. Rather than fight this legend, Moscow chroniclers shrewdly adapted it to suit their own needs. Their version adds that carriages carry more than one bell as a lesson about unity and a warning that excessive pride leads to destruction.[75]

The main vehicle for preserving these and other Novgorod legends were the epic tales known as *byliny*, which were passed along through oral tradition until compiled by nineteenth-century ethnographers. Through the fantastic tales of legendary figures like Sadko and Vasily Buslayev, the byliny magnified Novgorod's wealth, power, and fierce love of freedom, preserving them for future generations. Writer Dmitry Mamin-Sibiryak, an early twentieth-century popularizer of Novgorod lore, noted in his journals the remarkable degree to which the "spirit of Novgorod" had survived in the Urals.[76]

The historical accuracy of such portrayals is, of course, beside the point. Their significance lies precisely in their ability to pass on to future generations a specific value orientation disguised as tradition and, where that tradition did not survive, to reinvent it as myth. Such myths can reemerge any time. After the collapse of the monarchy, amid the turmoil of 1917, the elected Novgorod city administration thought it was vital to send an official inquiry to Moscow city authorities about the fate of the veche bell that had been taken in 1478. If it could be found, they insisted that it be returned to Novgorod forthwith.[77]

After the mid-eighteenth century, national literature became the primary conduit for the Novgorod Myth. One could even say that the first works of modern Russian literature involved a debate over how to interpret Novgorod's subjugation to Moscow. The first modern Russian story is generally considered A. P. Sumarokov's "Sinav and Truvor" (1750), which is based on the Novgorod legend of two Varangian brothers who vie for the hand of the daughter of Novgorod nobleman Gostomysl. Sumarokov's tale is full of poignant references to Novgorod's suffering under Varangian tyranny, an indirect reference to the contemporary monarchy. A few years later the poet M. Chulkov picked up the same theme and compared ancient Novgorod to prerevolutionary eighteenth-century Paris. "At the time," he told his readers, "Novgorod was considered fashionable, like Paris is today in Europe."[78]

The popularity of this interpretation aroused the concern of Empress Catherine II, who in 1786 wrote a play in reply. Ponderously titled *Historical Images from the Life of Ryurik*, it argued that monarchy existed in Novgorod well before the arrival of the Varangians, and that the legendary rebel Vadim the Brave was not a native of Novgorod at all but a Varangian, Ryurik's cousin in fact! His rebellion was therefore nothing more than an attempt to seize the throne, and at the end of Catherine's play Vadim begs Ryurik's forgiveness which is magnanimously granted.[79]

In response, Yakov Knyazhnin, son of the vice-governor of Novgorod, wrote his own play, *Vadim of Novgorod* (1789), which was published posthumously. Knyazhnin portrays Vadim as a fearless military leader who organizes an uprising against the foreign tyrant Ryurik.[80] Calling Vadim "a citizen of Russia," he endows him with classic Roman civic virtues. Condemned to die, Vadim refuses to recant his ideals.

Although Catherine ordered all copies of Knyazhnin's play burned, Vadim the Brave became the first revolutionary portrayed in Russian literature, an inspiration to latter-day socialists such as Georgy Plekhanov.[81] At the same time, unbeknownst to Knyazhnin, Alexander Radishchev was putting the finishing touches on his essay "A Journey from St. Petersburg to Moscow," which takes him through Novgorod. Radishchev, too, compared Novgorod to ancient Rome and argued that the public veche, not the monarchy, was the original form of Slavic governance.[82]

In 1803, historian Nikolai Karamzin published *Martha the Magistrate, or the Subjugation of Novgorod.* Intended as a cautionary tale, his portrayal was considered so inflammatory that the chief censor of the empire initially rejected it.[83] Based on the historical figure of Martha Boretskaya, Martha quickly became the model female heroine, a metaphor for freedom in Russian literature and poetry.[84] In that same decade Vasily Zhukovsky wrote a poem about Vadim in which he imagines himself "a citizen of Novgorod the Great," and the poet Ivanov first popularized the image of the veche bell as the symbol of Novgorodian liberty.[85] The image of the Novgorod bell was soon picked up by scores of writers and poets, and it became a dominant symbol for Russia's first revolutionary movement—the Decembrists.

The Decembrists were the flower of Russian aristocracy, young noblemen who yearned to transform Russia from an autocracy to a republic. Their passionate interest in Russian history led them to exalt Novgorod, and their writings vastly expanded the literary and poetic tradition of using Novgorod symbols as metaphors for freedom. At his trial, Pavel Pestel remarked, "I compared the greatness and grandeur of Rome in the days of the republic to its pitiful fall under the rule of emperors. The history of Novgorod the Great likewise affirmed in me a republican way of thinking."[86]

The Decembrists saw Novgorod's ancient democratic heritage as proof that the court historians who asserted that democracy was alien to Russia were wrong. To the contrary, Novgorod clearly demonstrated that Russia's democratic roots were as old, if not older, than Europe's and that it was senseless to wait for democracy to be imported from abroad.[87] Their infatuation with Novgorod went so far that their meetings were called to order by the ringing of a miniature veche bell.[88] Indeed, Kondraty Ryleev once wrote to his fellow conspirator Gavril Batenkov that one need only strike the bell and people will rush to popular assembly, as they had been accustomed to do for centuries.[89] Later, in exile, Batenkov and Mikhail Bestuzhev gave their rooms historical names from the Novgorod region.[90]

Despite their abject failure as a political movement, the Decembrists' idealism served as an inspiration to subsequent generations of Russian revolutionaries. Russia's preeminent political dissident of the mid-nineteenth century, Alexander Herzen, who had just been born at the time of the Decembrist uprising, wrote eloquently of their impact:

> The revolutionary poems of Ryleev and Pushkin can be found in the hands of young people in the most distant reaches of the empire. There is not a single well-bred young lady who does not know them by heart, not a single officer who does not carry them in his field pouch, not a single priest's son who hasn't made a dozen copies of them . . . an entire generation came under the influence of this fervent youthful propaganda.[91]

The familiar symbol of the veche bell now featured prominently in the poetry of Apollon Grigoryev, Nikolai Yazykov, Dimitri Venevitinov, and, most famously, Mikhail Lermontov and Alexander Pushkin. Although Pushkin never completed the epic poem he intended to write about Novgorod, his sympathies are revealed in a passage from his classic, "The Travels of Eugene Onegin." As Onegin's carriage approaches the city, he imagines that he can see "the shadows of giants" among the ruins of Novgorod.[92]

Lermontov turned to the image of Novgorod in several poems. In "The Last Son of Freedom" (1830) and "Novgorod" (1830), he calls upon Novgorodians to embrace their heritage: "At the name of freedom your heart trembles and churns! . . . There is a poor city; there all nations have seen that to which your spirit soars." A few years later, in "Volkhov" (1832), he is more despairing and asks rhetorically if the Volkhov that winds through this now silent town is really the same river that once flowed through this "holy cradle of warrior Slavs."[93]

During the repressive reign of Nicholas I these images increasingly surfaced in political and revolutionary prose. For Vissarion Belinsky, Nikolai Ogaryov, Mikhail Mikhailov, Nikolai Dobrolyubov, and Gleb Uspensky, Novgorod's history legitimated demands for immediate political change. While Slavophiles such as Alexei Khomyakov and Yuri Samarin still clung to a romantic view of Novgorod, Novgorod's key symbols were by now so overwhelmingly associated with republicanism that it would have been exceedingly difficult for any supporter of the monarchy to embrace them. By the latter half of the nineteenth century, the Novgorod Myth was co-opted by the Westernizers who, as their own ideals drifted toward Marxism, began to fill it with a content quite at odds with medieval Novgorod's republican and mercantile values.[94]

Typical in this regard is Alexander Herzen, who despised contemporary Novgorod and had little knowledge of or attraction for its past but was not above using it to call for revolution.[95] From London, he and Nikolai Ogaryov decided to publish a journal that could respond to current events and influence the thinking of young revolutionaries. When Ogaryov proposed the name *The Bell*, Herzen immediately seized on the familiar image, replying, "Yes, Ogaryov, let us publish a journal and call it *The Bell*. Let us ring the veche bell."[96]

What appealed to Westernizers was the familiarity people would have with the Novgorod Myth, not its message. But try as they might to reforge that message into something different, the core associations stuck. The degree to which the veche bell, Martha the Magistrate, and Vadim the Brave remained evocative images, albeit not for the ideas that Marxist revolutionaries would have liked, can be gleaned from Georgy Plekhanov's plaintive appeal to the Russian intelligentsia to give up its "castle-in-the-air image of the feudal-veche era."[97]

Thus, by the end of the nineteenth century, if not earlier, it is clear that specific images from Novgorod's past had become key symbols in Russian political consciousness. The actual number of such images is surprisingly small. They include the veche itself and the veche bell, the Cathedral of St. Sophia, and the historical figures of Vadim the Brave, Sadko the Merchant, St. Alexander Nevsky, and Martha the Magistrate. As centuries passed and Novgorod's political and cultural distinctiveness dissipated, the symbols and values of the Novgorod Myth retained a surprising potency, eventually becoming a fixture of political reform efforts and the common heritage of the Russian intelligentsia.

THE IMAGE OF NOVGOROD IN THE TWENTIETH CENTURY

At the turn of the twentieth century, as at other times of crisis, the intelligentsia showed a renewed interest in Novgorod. Mamin-Sibiryak wrote a very popular series of tales for children about Novgorod's history.[98] In the first decade, Russia's most widely read illustrated journal, *Niva*, ran a series of articles about the history of medieval Novgorod by P. N. Polevoi and I. F. Timofeev. The journal's editors were inspired by historian Nikolai Kostomarov's view that early medieval Russia had benefited from a highly decentralized and democratic political system.[99] Swept up by patriotic fervor at the outset of the First World War, the young poet Sergei Esenin wrote a poem about Novgorod in which Ivan III sells his soul to the devil to defeat a saintly Martha the Magistrate. Now, Esenin writes, the time has come to restore Novgorod's ancient liberty and return the veche bell.[100]

Political parties found the Novgorod Myth particularly valuable in popularizing alternatives to the autocracy. In 1917 Russia's popular agrarian party, the Socialist Revolutionaries, published a brochure, "The Novgorod Republic," specifically to dispel "the commonplace assertion that republican practices are contrary to Russian tradition."[101] During the Russian Civil War, White Army General Anton Denikin had currency printed with Novgorod's famous monument to the millennium of Russia on it in a blatant, but ultimately unsuccessful, attempt to mobilize public sentiment against the Bolsheviks.[102]

During the Soviet era, as under the most reactionary tsars, Novgorod symbols were again taboo. Because the Novgorod Myth was far too deeply ingrained in Russian culture to eradicate, however, it proved easier to replace politically unacceptable interpretations with politically neutral ones. Acceptable themes included Novgorod's nature and landscape, its heroic resistance to foreign invaders, and the Novgorod proletariat's struggle to overcome the region's backwardness.[103]

After the Nazi invasion, selected historical images were briefly rehabilitated to serve as patriotic rallying points. At the same time, communist propagandists were careful to underscore the benefits Novgorod had gained from unification with Muscovy. This approach, by and large, continued during the postwar reconstruction.[104] V. V. Zhavoronkov, the author of several monographs about the image of Novgorod in Russian literature, has left us the following description, written in 1959:

> Saved in the fifteenth century from the coming foreign invasion and incorporated by the great Moscow into a unified Russian state, Novgorod, together with all Russian lands, shared the fate of the entire country, its common path of historical development and, together with the rest of the country under the leadership of the party of Lenin, achieved complete economic and spiritual freedom. This is why Moscow is so close and so dear to us.[105]

Understandably, Zhavoronkov goes to great lengths to stress Novgorod's love for Moscow, since his entire opus testifies to the opposite.

Despite occasional mention of Novgorod in the writings of the "village prose writers" of the 1960s, it is not until the early 1970s that we see Novgorod again emerge as a literary-political topic, thanks to the determined efforts of one of Russia's most widely read authors, Dmitry Balashov.[106] In 1972 his *Martha the Magistrate*, the first in a series of historical novels on Novgorod themes, was published. Although Balashov concludes that the subjugation of Novgorod did indeed serve the broader national interest, his portrayal of Martha's rebellion, like Karamzin's nearly two centuries earlier, was so sympathetic that communist censors accused him of clinging to a "nostalgic view of Novgorodian freedoms."[107]

With the collapse of communism, an important branch of Russian intellectual life that had been banished in 1917, returned to Russia. Today the writing of these émigrés and their efforts to make sense of the Russian Revolution, exert a considerable fascination for post-Soviet intellectuals. One prominent group of émigrés was directly inspired by the Novgorod Myth. Their journal *Novyi Grad* (The New City) was published in Paris during the 1930s.

Novyi Grad, as philosopher Fyodor Stepun put it, was meant to appeal to those who could feel "the deep sigh of eternity in history."[108] Another frequent collaborator, Harvard historian Michael Karpovich, saw the journal's purpose as trying to find a middle ground between the sociopolitical conservatism of the "right" and the social radicalism of the "left."[109] The "New City," according to its editor, George P. Fedotov, must be built with old stones but use new architectural plans. The key building materials included the saints of Russia, Pushkin, the opponents of Ivan IV, but above all the sociopolitical ideals of Novgorod the Great.

It was Novgorod, Fedotov reminds readers, that had inspired Russia's greatest icon painters and built its most famous monasteries. Even though its republicanism was distinctly theocratic in nature, the Church there had managed to preserve its independence far better than in Moscow.[110] In the Republic of St. Sophia, Fedotov writes, the magistrate, as head of the victorious party, was the "prime minister"; the archbishop, a figure above the political fray, was the president; and St. Sophia was the embodiment of sovereignty, like the Cathedral of St. Mark was for Venice.[111]

Sadly, says Fedotov, this "incomparably richer" cultural and spiritual history has been overshadowed by Moscow's expansion.[112] But whereas for Herzen, Moscow's victory meant only that Russia had become "the most unhappy, the most enslaved country on earth," Fedotov saw a way out in the recovery of Novgorodian ideals.[113] "Novgorod is not some curious upstart in Russian life," he tells readers, "it is its most Russian development. . . . Here the Orthodox supporters of democratic Russia can find their inspiration. . . . within the confines of the Eastern Orthodox world, Novgorod found the best solution to the eternally troubling question of the relationship of Church and State."[114]

As we have seen, both Soviet and tsarist historians regarded Moscow's triumph as inevitable and, hence, historically justified. Post-Soviet efforts to reassess Novgorod as a viable political and cultural alternative to Moscow are, therefore, an effort to construct a new intellectual foundation for the nation's political history. The floodgates were opened in 1998 by the publication in Russia's flagship academic journal, the *Herald of the Russian Academy of Sciences*, of the polemical piece, "What if at the end of the fifteenth century Novgorod had defeated Moscow . . . ?"[115]

The author, a respected specialist in Slavic languages at the University of Vienna, Alexander Issatchenko, dismisses the argument that Moscow was in any way more progressive than Novgorod. Russia's comparative backwardness in science, culture, finances, and law, he says, can be traced directly to the "actively reactionary spirit" that reigned in Muscovy.[116] In Novgorod, by contrast, extensive foreign trade, the absence of threats from marauding steppe peoples, and sophisticated military weaponry and diplomatic strategies developed to deal with the Teutonic Order had created a more pragmatic and flexible political system.

Issatchenko claims that cultural, linguistic, and iconographic elements in Novgorod's culture tie it directly to the Western Slavic cultures of Moravia and Bohemia. Foreshadowing an argument later advanced by archeologist Valentin Yanin, he also finds that Novgorod was more advanced than Kiev in its legal tradition, trade language, and in the secularization of its language. Had Novgorod's development not been cut short, a modern Russian literary language would have arisen much earlier. He concludes:

> Moscow, with its ultrareactionary isolationism, was incapable of transforming a semi-Asiatic state into a European power, but if we consider that the guiding force in Rus in the fifteenth century could have been Novgorod instead of Moscow, then that infamous window [St. Petersburg, Peter the Great's "window to the West"] becomes unnecessary in that, through Novgorod, the door to Europe was already wide open.[117]

Several scholars immediately took issue with the piece's "obvious political agenda," noting that it had originally been published a quarter century earlier in Austria, and that it offended traditional assumptions and sensibilities.[118] Still, as one critic astutely remarked, "When you reflect on what you have read, you understand that this publication is intended for the future."[119]

With the debate now engaged, one of the nation's leading medieval historians, St. Petersburg University's Ruslan Skrynnikov, suggested that while Novgorod had certainly been chaotic and prone to oligarchy, it had also been quite successful in maintaining its citizens' prosperity and, but for Muscovy's aggression, would probably have continued to thrive.[120] Efforts to portray Novgorod as doomed, Skrynnikov concluded, simply do not hold water. He concludes:

> The demise of the Novgorod veche republic was the result not of the exhaustion of its political culture but of naked external violence. . . . It laid

the foundation for the future Russian empire and became a turning point in the development of her political culture. Democratic tendencies yielded to autocratic ones.[121]

This new Novgorod theme has been picked up by many prominent scholars in recent years. The world renowned medievalist and public intellectual Dmitry S. Likhachev wrote that native pride had led the descendants of the former Novgorod lands to think of themselves as part of "Scandoslavia" rather than "Eurasia."[122] Russia's foremost medieval archeologist, Valentin Yanin, has suggested that Novgorod has a stronger claim to being the forerunner of today's democratic Russia than Kiev because, while Muscovy inherited its centralized form of government from Kievan Rus, Novgorod preserved its political pluralism and strong commercial ties with the West.[123] Lest his point be lost on the political elite, Yanin adds: "Our current rulers could learn quite a bit from the history of ancient Novgorod."[124]

Popular writers and essayists have also started highlighting Novgorod's political significance for the present. In a provocative piece titled "Tsar Boris and the Fall of the Golden (Soviet) Horde," popular political commentator Gennady Lisichkin suggests that Russia first lost its way not in 1917 but in 1478 with the fall of Novgorod. Communism's triumph in Russia, he says, was the result rather than the cause of overcentralization.[125] Today, the country's elites remain a significant obstacle to democracy because regardless of ideology, they are united in the belief that Moscow alone can dictate the country's fate. The Mongols have fallen, the communists have fallen, but Muscovite "occupation," he says, still endures. Regional governors continue to profit from submissiveness to Moscow, just as the appointed satraps of the Great Khan once did. The true "Slavic path of development," Lisichkin argues, was Novgorod, with its extensive local pluralism in politics and commerce. Like the Decembrists, he believes that these democratic Slavic practices have been preserved in the nation's "genetic memory" and are now ready to be tapped.[126]

Another popular genre that combines history and political commentary is historically based fiction, or "alternative history." In 1998 the best-selling detective writer Alexander Bushkov tried his hand at historical fiction with the novel *The Russia That Never Was*. A young historian at Krasnoyarsk University named Andrei Burovsky wrote a complimentary afterword to it, which he later followed up with his own sequel, *The Russia That Never Was—2: The Russian Atlantis*. Burovsky's book became a best-seller as well, going through an astronomically high (for Russia) print run of fifty thousand copies and receiving considerable media attention.

In *The Russian Atlantis* Burovsky strives to correct what he calls the one-sided interpretation of Russian history as the history of Muscovy. Many other perfectly viable Russias have been lost to us thanks to the imposition of what Burovsky calls "the great Muscovite myth"—the view that Russia's survival as a nation required that Moscovy absorb all other Russian lands.[127] This myth has been fed to the populace for so long that no other path of development now seems possible, but Burovsky argues that this is not true. Novgorod, he says, was "a variant . . . of Orthodox culture that could have been no less dynamic, no less active, than Catholicism and that might have even spawned a Russian variant of Protestantism."[128]

Like Fedotov, Lisichkin, and the Decembrists, Burovsky finds contemporary political significance in Novgorod's ancient history. While dismissing the notion of any lingering genetic memory, he does find it remarkable that "throughout its entire history Novgorod has stubbornly insisted on being a 'special' city."[129] Moreover, efforts by the city's current political leaders to revive the past, he says, prove that Russians are not condemned to relive their Muscovite past:

> The ideology of restoring Novgorodian liberties is very noticeable in Novgorod the Great. Under certain conditions—specific economic circumstances, the appearance of new political institutions—the process of forming a northwestern ethnos could engulf a significant territory.[130]

The Russian northwest has indeed seen several nativist sociopolitical movements based on the Novgorod Myth in recent years, but because many of them call for a radical decentralization that borders on separatism, they occupy a very marginal place on the political spectrum. Their strident tone is emblazoned in the titles of many of their articles: "Five Hundred Years Ago the Novgorod Republic Was Occupied by Moscow," "Novgorod—An Alternative to the All-Powerful Princes," "Muscovy Is Not Our Homeland!" and "How to Disassemble Russia, or New Tasks for True Patriots."[131] Remarkably, despite these movements having no apparent connections with the regional political establishment, somehow their appeals manage to appear often in St. Petersburg's leading newspapers and even, occasionally, in such national periodicals as *Komsomolskaya pravda*, *Smena*, and *Ogonyok*.

Despite its demise as an independent power in the fifteenth century, Novgorod has endured as a powerful cultural myth. The key symbols of this myth are Martha the Magistrate, the veche bell, and, to a lesser extent, Vadim the Brave. Two other popular Novgorod symbols, the sainted Prince Alexander Nevsky and the Cathedral of St. Sophia, evoke images of popular resistance to foreign invaders and a distinctly Orthodox form of codetermination in civic affairs. Despite subtle differences, all these symbols reinforce one another, linking the image of the city inextricably to an indigenous Russian model of prosperity and independence that was forcibly suppressed but never forgotten. The reemergence of these symbols during the 1990s is therefore hardly surprising, since they have been at the heart of every liberal Russian social movement since the eighteenth century. Today's writers and historians appeal to Novgorod's distant past for the same reasons that their ancestors did—because it brings political debates into sharper focus.[132]

As the source of one of Russia's most enduring alternative cultural myths, it is easy to see why contemporary writers and reformers would turn to Novgorod. The more intriguing question is, why have they not done so more often? With such a prominent symbolic pedigree, one would expect the Novgorod Myth to be tapped by any political group seeking to build quick public recognition. Yet, the Novgorod Myth has been much less of a rallying point for post-Soviet intellectuals than it was for previous generations.[133]

There are several possible reasons for this. First, the Russian intelligentsia today is much more numerous and diverse than it was in the eighteenth century, when Herzen and Ogaryov could single-handedly shape the sentiments of an entire generation. Second, through the Internet, there is an unprecedented variety of information available to today's elites. Combined with a sharp public shift from national to local publications, and the loss of influential national media, the task of crafting and conveying a consistent message to the entire country has become much more difficult.

Third, the nihilistic approach to Russian history officially imposed during most of the Soviet era has certainly taken its toll. Literary critic and historian Alexander Goryanin notes that today's Russian intellectuals, following the lead of their Western colleagues, are apt to see little that is worthwhile in Russia, past or present.[134] Often, even well-educated persons have heard about Novgorod only through the writings of Decembrists, and then only as precursors to the Bolsheviks. The postcommunist collapse of the national curriculum and the proliferation of textbooks espousing a wide variety of viewpoints makes it unlikely that a consensus interpretation of Russia's past will emerge any time soon.

Finally, there is the almost sycophantic regard of many intellectuals for anything coming out of Moscow. As Lisichkin aptly notes, not only are Muscovites utterly convinced of the city's inherent superiority, many in the provinces regard this as a dictum as well.[135] There is one place, however, where the Novgorod Myth is inescapable—the city of Novgorod the Great. Here, in the city that Academician Dmitry S. Likhachev dubbed a living lecture hall, the symbols of the past have always been waiting in the wings to be tapped by the political elite.[136]

As distinctive as Novgorod's history has been, however, one cannot attribute the persistence of its myth to any institutional, historical, or ethnic continuity. Too much has changed in the region over the centuries. Instead, it is more appropriate to say that, with the collapse of communism and the rise of regionalism in post-Soviet Russia, the local symbols most relevant to coping with the new challenges of formlessness and decentralization naturally reasserted themselves. The Novgorod Myth resurfaced, just as it did during the Swedish occupation in the seventeenth century, during Alexander II's Great Reforms, during the collapse of the monarchy in 1917, and even during German occupation of the region in World War II.[137] Now that we understand the meaning of those symbols, we can turn to how they have transformed contemporary Novgorod.

CHAPTER 6

███████████████████████

SYMBOLS AT WORK

"Men possess thoughts, but symbols possess men."
MAX LERNER

The emergence of the Novgorod Myth as an active political resource transformed the pace of Novgorod's social development. It led to the emergence of what observers have termed a "Western" or "liberal" elite consensus in the region at a time when most other regions of Russia were riven by political infighting.[1] The emergence of this myth, as traced through its key symbols, can be broken down into three phases.

During the first phase, which lasted from 1989 to 1993, the symbols of the Soviet era were relentlessly attacked by the Novgorod City Soviet of People's Deputies, setting the stage for more sweeping socioeconomic changes. During the second phase, from roughly 1994 to 1998, civic leaders sought out specific symbols from Novgorod's medieval past to help them define a new, long-term vision for the region. In the third phase, which has lasted from 1999 until today, the government has become acutely conscious of the political utility of Novgorod symbols and adopted them quite overtly to build political support for its policies.

ACTIVATING THE NOVGOROD MYTH

Soviet Symbols under Attack: The City Soviet Searches for a Better Past

During the late 1980s, the heyday of perestroika, many previously suppressed historical and religious symbols resurfaced. In Novgorod two issues galvanized society—the restoration of the Cathedral of St. Sophia and the designation of Novgorod as a free enterprise zone.

In medieval Novgorod the Cathedral of St. Sophia was synonymous with the republic. In Soviet times, however, it became a prime target of the atheist regime and was closed in 1929. The policy of perestroika and the prominence given to the celebration of the millennium of Russian Christianity in 1988 encouraged local religious activists to raise questions about changing the status of Russia's oldest cathedral. When the diocese of Novgorod and Staraya Russa was formally reconstituted in July 1990, these became demands that St. Sophia be reopened as an active church.

Restoring St. Sophia as an active church was soon embraced by nearly all segments of Novgorod society, for various reasons. Russian nationalists saw it as a means of reasserting Russia's cultural sovereignty; local democrats supported it as a way of undermining the CPSU; and reform-minded communists pointed to it as proof of the party's ability to change with the times. The Russian Orthodox Church, which had no formal political constituency, could rely on the active support of a large number of cultural and historical preservation societies, whose thinly disguised purpose was to lobby for church restoration.

After 1988, therefore, St. Sophia began to receive an inordinate amount of local press coverage that stressed its role as the symbolic unifier and protector of Novgorod. The stage had been set the previous year when Novgorod served as the site of the Days of Slavic Writing and Culture, an annual pan-Slavic cultural event. The weeklong cultural festivities gave prominent media coverage to the history of the Orthodox Church in the region and to St. Sophia in particular. The next two years saw a sharp rise in the number of adult baptisms in the region (more than sevenfold in some districts), as well as a dramatic increase in the number of petitions to reopen churches.[2]

In 1989 the Novgorod Writers Union founded a weekly newspaper, *Veche*. Edited by writer Mikhail Petrov and with frequent contributions from local historians, *Veche* regularly published articles on Novgorod traditions, local churches, and even the formerly taboo subjects of the Russian monarchy and emigration. The paper thus became a forum where diverse segments of the local intelligentsia could express their appreciation for key components of the Novgorod Myth and appeal for action.

A typical example is the open letter by "representatives of the Novgorod public" to their "countrymen" in Vologda published in the second issue. Noting that "we have the right to call you that [countrymen], because we were once part of a single republic," the letter calls for the return of the bells taken from the belfry tower of St. Sophia that hang in St. Cyril's monastery outside the city of Vologda. The signatories of this highly emotional appeal were a very diverse group: Oleg Ochin, a university administrator who would soon become chairman of the Novgorod City Soviet; Nikolai Grinyov, who would later head the Novgorod Unified State Museum and History Preserve; and Vladimir Tsalpan, the former secretary of the Regional Committee of the CPSU.[3]

On August 16, 1991, the Cathedral of St. Sophia was restored to the Orthodox Church. To this day it is commemorated annually in the local media not just as a church holiday but as a turning point in the region's history. The significance of this early successful collaboration among civic groups, now regarded in the region as a model for church-state relations, is hard to overestimate.

Although it is now commonplace in Russia for public officials to pay lip service to the Orthodox Church, in Novgorod the local administration goes well beyond official piety. It has cosponsored the construction of a new cathedral, supported religious programs on local television, and even subsidized an "experimental" religious school out of the municipal education budget. More than 110 Orthodox churches have been reopened in the Novgorod region in the past decade. Indeed, says the head of the regional directorate for state property, the only thing preventing restorations from occurring faster is the limited finances of the diocese.[4]

The other local issue that captured public attention during these hectic years was whether Novgorod should become one of three experimental "free enterprise zones" (*svobodnye ekonomicheskie zony* or FEZ) in the USSR. A proposal to this effect was made in 1988 by the heads of local industry, who sought to create a favorable investment climate for joint ventures.[5] Local industry and party leaders saw the zone as a rare window of opportunity that could be used to strengthen the region's industrial ties with the West. Local civic activists, on the other hand, saw it as a chance to create an entirely new model of regional development based on tourism and education.[6] They regarded further industrial development as harmful to the region's distinctive cultural and historical identity. When these activists joined with university experts to redraft the original concept, party and industrial leaders withdrew their support from the original concept and the initiative collapsed.

Like the civic activism around St. Sophia, opposition to the FEZ united groups across the political spectrum. The unusually public debate at the time revealed just how receptive the population still was to the symbols of republican Novgorod. Incongruous bedfellows, such as the United Worker's Front (UWF) and the regional ecological society Ekologiya, jointly organized a letter-writing campaign that used the well-known characters of Novgorod myth and legend to portray the zone as nothing but an attempt by Moscow to foist its will on free-thinking Novgorodians.[7]

Indeed, both opponents and advocates of the FEZ relied on these familiar symbols to carry their message to the public—the former to advocate the right of regions *not* to be forced to accept decisions made in Moscow, the latter to argue for the freedom to pursue radical economic initiatives and openness to the West at the local level.

The intense local media attention focused on this issue may have inadvertently also served to assuage fears about foreign investment, facilitating public acceptance of the far more radical economic initiatives that local government proposed just a few years later. By that time the region's failure to get special status in 1989 was viewed by many as a missed opportunity. An internal memo by the regional CPSU's Department of Social Planning and Analysis candidly acknowledged that young people in the region would much rather work for foreign firms than for state-owned ones, and recommended that foreign capital be allowed to "pour into our economy."[8]

A final important side effect of this debate was to galvanize reformers to run for local office. In September 1989, the independent electoral association Veche sponsored a slate of candidates for the 1990 elections that favored local self-government and political and economic liberalization.[9] Despite having been organized just a few months earlier, Veche candidates captured nearly one-third of the seats in the regional legislative assembly and nearly half of the Novgorod City Soviet.[10] Among the latter there were so many deputies from the Novgorod Polytechnic Institute that locals jokingly began to refer to it as the Communist Party's "second regional committee." The leadership of the new Novgorod City Soviet openly identified itself with the Novgorod Myth and for nearly three-and-a-half years conducted an intense media campaign to educate the populace about the virtues of republican Novgorod.

The main vehicle for this campaign was the newspaper *Novgorod*, which was created in October 1990 to serve as the voice of the new city soviet and is still distributed free of charge to every family in the city. In its premier issue the editors promised to devote significant space to local history and appealed to the intelligentsia to "help us become aware of our historical past and, by connecting it with the present, more clearly see the road ahead."[11]

In his first interview as chairman of the city soviet, Oleg Ochin complains that much had been lost, most important "pride in one's right to call oneself a Novgorodian." Ochin then launches into a panegyric that leaves no doubt about where the new city leaders intended to look for guidance:

> What a sense of pride those Novgorodians must have had in their contacts, not only with their own countrymen but with the foreigners who came here

in large numbers . . . curious about the people who had placed such a rich city among the marshes and decorated it with magnificent cathedrals; who ruled over an expanse larger than most in Europe and were nearly all literate . . . a people who knew the value of free speech and who, unlike the Church obscurantism and court intrigues that held sway in Europe, created a unique democratic construct—the Novgorod state, a republic in the Middle Ages. In my opinion, we have yet to fully appreciate the historical importance of this phenomenon, which can and must serve as an inspiration for the tasks before us.[12]

The city soviet's most critical initiative in this direction was purging the city of all its communist-era street names. Vasily Andreyev, local history professor turned city councilman, cultivated the idea in the public's mind for more than a year. He wrote scores of articles in the local press pointing out how absurd it sounded to walk along "May First" Street to reach the Church of the Savior Transfigured, or to say that the Church of the Holy Spirit stands at the corner of [Commissar Maxim] Litvinov and Proletariat Streets.[13] Calling these communist-era names a "blasphemy, a violent offense against our native history," Andreyev urged his fellow citizens to get rid of these "faceless" names and restore the "true" names of historical Novgorod.[14]

Andreyev's efforts bore fruit on January 4, 1991, when, by a two-thirds majority, the city soviet restored the pre-1917 names of all streets in historical Novgorod. In one fell swoop, the names Lenin, Bolshevik, Komsomol, Proletariat, Soviet, and Worker's were stricken from the city map in what remains to this day the most comprehensive cultural decommunization of any city in Russia.[15]

On this issue, as on many others, the city soviet refused to recognize the supremacy of the more conservative regional soviet. Money, as well as ideology, lay at the heart of this conflict. In the past, the regional soviet had disbursed funds among cities and rural areas as it saw fit, regardless of their contributions to the local budget. Now, however, the Novgorod City Soviet insisted on keeping a portion of the budget for itself. As the largest contributor to the regional budget, this was tantamount to demanding administrative and financial independence.

In a direct challenge to the regional soviet, the Novgorod City Soviet invited all twenty-two district soviets to coordinate their activities and budgets with one another, bypassing the regional soviet.[16] Tensions were exacerbated when the regional soviet took a wait-and-see attitude during the attempted Moscow putsch of August 1991, while the Novgorod City Soviet issued a statement the very first day condemning the coup.

After Yeltsin's triumph, Ochin emerged as the de facto political leader of the city and the region, but he was unknown to Yeltsin's advisors, who chose their own candidate, Mikhail Prusak, to be governor. Prusak asked that the city release Ochin to serve as his deputy in charge of social issues, arguing that this would give the city of Novgorod a stronger voice in financial matters. By "promoting" Ochin, Prusak separated him from his power base and reduced his standing as a political rival. After Yeltsin disbanded all soviets in October 1993, Ochin was again "promoted" to be Novgorod's representative to the state Duma in Moscow, where he has remained.

Although inclined to resist Yeltsin's 1993 decree, Ochin's successor as chairman of the city soviet, Alexander Vasilyev, frankly acknowledges that its defiance met with little public support.[17] Skeptics might well ask: If the Novgorod Myth was so influential, why didn't the Novgorod City Soviet have more support in 1993? The short answer is that while the city soviet had created new reservoirs of political support, in its headlong rush to change it had also generated enormous confusion and resentment among the elderly, who represented more than a quarter of the city's population.

The conclusion of this first phase in Novgorod's post-Soviet history thus reveals a rather typical pattern for rapid symbolic changes—the populace exercising constraint on the speed of changes by withdrawing its support from those segments of the elite that go too far, too fast. It would be unfair, however, to remember the city soviet only as a failure. Its politically risky break with the symbols of the communist past helped to lay the foundation for a new social consensus that lingers to this day.

Oddly enough, the only clear winner in this symbolic conflict between familiar Soviet values and "new" Novgorodian values was the freshly minted governor Mikhail Prusak. Prusak managed to portray himself as someone who understood the need for change but also respected the people's desire to have it implemented gradually. Although he obeyed Yeltsin's decree to disband all soviets, he did not reverse any of the controversial changes already made by the city soviet, though many expected that he would. Instead, Prusak chose to build on the weakening of communist-era symbols and launch a bold set of social and economic reforms that relied, to a great extent, on the symbolic foundation laid by the city soviet.

Alexander Vasilyev, the Novgorod City Soviet's last chairman, has called it one of the most democratic Russia has ever had.[18] In fact, however, similar efforts were commonplace between 1990 and 1992, during the heyday of anticommunist euphoria. What made the Novgorod City Soviet unusual was that local leaders did more than just disavow the past. From the outset, they linked their reforms to a particular image—the Novgorod Myth of a prosperous state of self-governing people.

Although the city soviet did not achieve everything it set out to do, it brought to a decisive end the communist claim to be the sole legitimate interpreters of Russia's past, thereby encouraging people to consider options outside their immediate Soviet-era experience.

The Elite Regroups: Linking Old Symbols to New Policies

The appeal of the Novgorod Myth is perhaps most evident in the fact that it persisted, despite the obvious reluctance of the first Prusak administration to embrace it. Concerned with practical results, and wary of getting caught up in the sort of ideological confrontation that had led to the downfall of the city soviet, Prusak and his advisors assiduously avoided any appearance of creating a new regional ideology, at least during this period.

Prusak's efforts to get the local budget under control, pack the regional duma with heads of local districts, and introduce cost-cutting measures put symbolic resources on the back burner. Although the Novgorod Myth was recognized as valuable in establishing good rapport with foreign investors, it was not yet regarded as a political resource for domestic consumption. Prusak remarked that "our people do not as yet recognize the importance of our past; that is why we created the university to help us."[19] Indeed, the most significant efforts to activate the Novgorod Myth now came from Novgorod State University, established in 1993 and later officially renamed in honor of the eleventh-century prince and lawgiver Yaroslav the Wise.[20]

One the first university-sponsored initiatives to promote the Novgorod Myth is "The Novgorod Project: A Leap into Postindustrial Society." The Novgorod Project is an effort by the local intelligentsia, with the help of the Gorbachev Foundation, to make Novgorod's medieval history the centerpiece of a new strategic regional vision.[21] Novgorod was chosen as the pilot region because, as the final project report says, "Russia's entire history has gone through the lands of Novgorod, and the Novgorod veche was, and remains to this day, a source of inspiration for Russian democrats and republicans."[22]

The report begins by noting that the world is undergoing an information revolution and moving into a "postindustrial" phase that emphasizes cultural and intellectual products. This emphasis could be quite advantageous for Russia because, rather than imitating the developmental path taken by the West, Russia can use its traditions of communitarianism, collective action, and cooperation to "leap" directly into postindustrial development. Only by relying on such traditional cultural values can Russia preserve its core identity and resist the excesses of globalization.[23]

The key to empowering postindustrial values is greater regional autonomy, which will spawn civic initiative in support of local historical preservation. Modernization efforts should therefore be targeted first and foremost at increasing sociocultural diversity and cultural pluralism. Novgorod, the report notes, is already at the forefront of this process and should focus on creating a technology infrastructure that would "incorporate the historical-cultural heritage of the Novgorod Region into the world cultural-educational space."[24]

Creating such an infrastructure involves teaching cultural workers to use the Internet, introducing a humanities component into the university's core curriculum, training civil servants to respond to the demands of a postindustrial society, and setting up an array of regional cultural databases, laboratories, and centers that can assist such training.[25] Novgorod State University and local Novgorod television were to be the main actors in a strategy designed to "incorporate the historical-cultural heritage of the Novgorod lands in intensive cultural, educational, and practical methodological usage, and to broaden the access of diverse groups of actual and potential users to cultural-historical materials."[26] The final report was widely distributed among local elites, and it briefly fed media speculation about a possible political alliance between Gorbachev and Prusak. After the bankruptcy of the project's American sponsor, however, it was shelved and apparently forgotten by all but senior university officials.[27]

At this point, remarkably, the report's recommendations began to take on a life of their own. Tourism, touted as central to postindustrial society, was officially designated as one of the region's key cultural and investment initiatives. Telecommunications also became a priority for the administration, so much so that in 1997 Prusak could boast that Novgorod had the nation's third most highly developed telecommunications infrastructure.[28]

In 1995, the former Institute of Marxism-Leninism was converted into a training center for local civil servants, which places special emphasis on the history and traditions of the Novgorod Region. Each year some twelve hundred public and private managers take short training courses at the center, now known as Dialog. Ultimately, its director hopes to establish a regional school of public administration that looks to Novgorodian traditions, history, and culture to the solve local problems.[29]

Meanwhile the local television station, Slaviya, has made local culture and history a mainstay of its programming. In addition to regular programs such as *Historical Monologues*, it has produced several feature films that focus on Novgorod's cultural and political heritage, including *Lord Novgorod the Great* (2001) and *The First Republic* (2002–2003), a five-part series devoted to the lessons that the "Novgorod model" holds for Russia today.

The station's managing director, Victor Smirnov, a noted historical novelist, is quite unabashed about his own sympathies for republican Novgorod. Once, during a television interview, he was asked which side he would have taken during the legendary fifteenth-century veche debate between the supporters of union with Moscow and the pro-Lithuanian party headed by Martha the Magistrate. Smirnov replied that "as a patriot of Novgorod" he would certainly have sided with Martha. Though history took another path, he added, Novgorod now has a chance for a bit of "historical revenge," by showing that its own traditions provide a better model for Russia today.[30]

Even the report's prescient call for an emphasis on regionally based civic initiatives and for a state partnership with local NGOs seems to have been heard. Studies show that Novgorod NGOs evaluate their interaction with the regional and city administration and their access to the local press far more positively than do NGOs in most other regions.[31]

Despite scarce funding, the university has set up its own Center for the Study of Culture that explores the impact of Novgorod history and traditions on contemporary political and spiritual life.[32] The idea for such a center, according to director Svetlana Kovarskaya, emerged simultaneously from both the university, where scholars wanted a place where information about Novgorod would be readily available, and from the regional administration, which was looking for a place they could turn to for solutions to recurring local problems.

The center's first major undertaking was a conference, organized with the district administration of Kresttsy, on the historical role and cultural traditions of self-government expressed in the Novgorod regional *zemstvo*.[33] Senior administration officials have also turned to the center for guidance as to what role Novgorod might play in the search for a "Russian Idea."[34] Ultimately, Kovarskaya hopes the center becomes a full-fledged institute, with a dedicated staff capable of preparing an *Encyclopedia Novgorodica*. As she puts it, "Everything we gather here will be handed over to our young people, our students, infecting them with these ideas. . . . I tell my students, 'You, today's Novgorodians, have in you all that once was.' "[35]

Fulfilling a part of this dream, in 2001 the university was awarded a multiyear grant from the Russian Ministry of Education and a consortium of U.S.–based foundations to establish a national center that will examine the role that culture plays in the social sciences.[36] The newly formed Novgorod Interregional Institute for the Social Sciences (NovIISS) will organize conferences, seminars, and symposia that focus particular attention on the cultural legacy of Novgorod as it applies to politics, economics, and public administration.[37] According to its mission statement, the culture of Novgorod is key:

Russian statehood originated in a specific region—the Russian Northwest. Elements of social and political democracy first appeared here, in the territory of Novgorod, and they remained alive here despite our checkered historical development. This is reflected in the heritage of the democratic "Veche Republic" and in the European political identity of the local population.[38]

Thus, despite its failure to receive funding, the effort to set up a "Novgorod Project" back in 1995 helped local elites to formulate a long-term development strategy rooted in the Novgorod Myth. The process not only drew attention to the political and economic usefulness of the Novgorod Myth but described in extensive detail exactly how Novgorod's symbolic resources could be used, so that when the opportunity arose, the blueprint was already at hand. The next phase would see that blueprint embraced as avidly by the region's political elite as it had been by its cultural elite.

The Political Utility of Symbols: Prusak's Symbolic Transformation

Winning 56 percent of the popular vote in the 1995 gubernatorial elections could scarcely have been reassuring to Governor Prusak. Despite the impressive successes of his investment strategy, his mandate was lukewarm at best. In his gubernatorial campaign Prusak had portrayed himself as an effective manager. Among foreign audiences, however, he relied just as heavily on the Novgorod Myth to set Novgorod apart from neighboring regions. The former had resulted in a hard-fought victory, while the latter had catapulted him to national prominence. Clearly, there were lessons to be drawn here.

When I interviewed Prusak in 1998, he readily acknowledged that foreigners were more receptive to the Novgorod Myth than his fellow countrymen. It would take at least a generation, he said, before people in Novgorod were again sufficiently familiar with their own history to make good use of it.[39] Less than two years later, however, his views had changed. Whereas earlier he could not explain why a social consensus had emerged in Novgorod ("somehow our political parties, administration, trade unions, and social movement were able to show wisdom. Somehow people came together, though it wasn't easy"), he now knew the answer.[40] The "Novgorod model," he wrote in 1999, is a direct extension of the principles of the Novgorod Republic:

There is no need to invent artificial ideas, no need to mechanically transfer the American Dream onto Russian soil. If we refer to our own past, we see that in Russian history there was a city that combined democracy, free market relations, and other accomplishments of civilization with national traditions. That city was Lord Novgorod the Great, the capital of a once-flourishing civic republic that extended from the White Sea to the Urals.

Academician [Valentin] Yanin, who has devoted his entire life to the study of Novgorod's history, has shown conclusively that Rus originated here. In contrast to the starkly centralized model that Muscovite Rus inherited from Kievan Rus (adding to it absolutist tendencies of its own), the Novgorod model was characterized by greater openness and democracy. All major decisions were taken by the popular assembly—the veche. It elected its own spiritual leader—the archbishop—who was the leading figure in the city, while the prince fulfilled the role of military commander.

The Novgorod model demonstrated its viability, giving the world a unique culture that created enormous spiritual and material wealth. History, however, decreed that the country should take another path. The eastern tradition, represented by the principality of Vladimir-Suzdal, and later Moscow, gained the upper hand. The Novgorod Republic was forcibly destroyed, and yet, over the course of centuries, it has continued to exist in people's memory. Today this model has a new historical opportunity. Our generation can return to the principles of our ancestors, but on a new basis. Self-government, elections, public accountability of authority, private property, individual liberty—the very cornerstones of the Novgorod Republic— are regaining their former significance.

On January 27, 1998, a joint session of the city and regional dumas took a truly symbolic step. The deputies unanimously resolved to restore Novgorod's previous historical name—Novgorod the Great. In taking this decision, the deputies not only rectified a historical injustice but reaffirmed their commitment to the principles our ancient city once lived by. Without foisting our views on anyone, it seems to us that it is precisely in these principles that we must seek the roots of that national idea that the new Russia so desperately needs.[41]

What led to this astonishing turnaround? First, there was the role that the Novgorod Myth had played in attracting foreign investment, the governor's main claim to fame. Novgorod's Hanseatic past may not seem very impressive to Russian investors, but it served as an effective calling card for delegations from Denmark, Sweden, and Germany, who often cited these historical ties.[42] The lesson, clearly, was that the appropriate use of symbols could open doors.

Second, the introduction of a new, locally oriented school curriculum had begun to transform public attitudes toward Novgorod's past more quickly than expected. Since 1996, a regional studies component, known as *kraevedeniye* or Novgorodica, has been a mandatory part of the secondary school curriculum. From the seventh through the eleventh grades, students in the region receive at least one hour a week of Novgorod history. The curriculum is designed to promote "patriotic qualities" among schoolchildren, but now, as distinct from Soviet times, these include "a Novgorodian and Russian self-awareness . . . [and] an ability to compare our own national, European, and regional histories, and discuss different versions of historical events."[43] The ultimate goal is to "Novgorodify" the entire school curriculum. As the principal of School No. 22, Svetlana Matveeva, points out, "Not only the study of history but also literature, geography, and biology here is tied to local materials."[44] The deputy director of the Novgorod City Educational Committee, Svetlana Shubina, argues that "children must be given every opportunity to understand the region they live in, what the value orientations of our region are, and how these can help them in life."[45]

Given the dearth of educational materials on Novgorod in the early 1990s, local educators learned to be creative.[46] Because the city's archeological excavations are prominently featured in the local media, many extracurricular programs, such as "City under the City" build on it. Others, like "I Am a Novgorodian" and "Be a Magistrate [posadnik]," provide civics education by asking students to imagine what their role might have been in the cultural and political life of medieval Novgorod.[47] Recently the Novgorod Region's Committee on Education introduced a preschool component aimed at "resurrecting the national-cultural traditions of the Russian people through a focus on the historical and ethnographic past of the Novgorodian land."[48]

The educational curriculum also involves a vast array of local cultural and volunteer organizations, and the Novgorod practice of organizing local history museums in rural village and district libraries has been touted as a model for other regions.[49] During the school year more than three thousand students each month visit the region's history museums and participate in a wide variety of educational programs designed to promote local civic identity, many with names such as "Voyage to the Past" and "My City."[50]

Prusak's public conversion to the Novgorod Myth has, naturally, also encouraged other government officials to embrace the imagery of Novgorod's past. Historical analogies that would seem far-fetched in other regions are quite common in Novgorod.[51] Thus, in describing how the Novgorod Regional Duma differs from those of other regions, its chairman, Anatoly Boitsev, draws attention to the fact that the final budget hearings are open to the public and broadcast live on television and radio. "If there is a modern veche in Novgorod today," he concludes, "this is it."[52] For the late mayor of Novgorod the Great, Alexander Korsunov, the city's efforts to promote trade and close ties with the West showed that "the spirit of our ancestors has been preserved."[53] In the last interview given before his untimely demise in 2002, he eloquently summarized his personal vision of Novgorod's historical significance:

While people in the capitals spar with each other in search of "high politi-cal ideals" that will satisfy their ambitions, we can wait. With more than eleven centuries of experience, we have no need to rush. Here in Novgorod the Great is the one, true, centuries-old pillar of tradition, of culture, of principles, and government experience that we can all count on. Sooner or later they will come here for the right decisions.

Our task lies not in adopting fleeting goals. Ours is a special trust. We are not closed to contemporary trends but rather follow our ancient Novgorod traditions in being active and entrepreneurial, some might even say excessively so. I recommend to all who feel "lost"—and particularly to those whose decisions affect the lives of millions—come here, feel the real roots and voices of those who came before us. That will be enough.[54]

The fact that "in Novgorod tradition lives," has also had more imme-diate policy implications.[55] Before reviewing the administration's pro-grams in support of small business, for instance, Prusak reviewed sixteenth-century records that showed there had once been more weavers in Novgorod than in Kazan, Tula, Ustyug, and Mozhaisk combined. Because of this tradition he thought it would make sense to fund a regional program to revive local linen weaving.[56] When the research center Dialog was given the task of developing the region's housing reform program, it first conducted a study of living arrangements in the city from the twelfth to the seventeenth centuries, with appendices and charts comparing those eras to the present.[57] At a conference on local self-government cosponsored by the regional administration, the mayor of Novgorod the Great underscored the importance of territorial self-administration by pointing out that it was fully "in keeping with centuries of Novgorod traditions and customs."[58]

Given the elite's predisposition to look to the past for solutions to current problems, it is not surprising to find the head of a district talking about the problems that his predecessor faced in the nineteenth century, or to read an article on the legal and administrative reforms proposed by a nineteenth-century Novgorod governor written by the chairman of the regional duma.[59] The city and regional administrations never miss a chance to link themselves to the glory days of republican Novgorod. In 1999 they celebrated the 1,140th anniversary of Novgorod's founding, and in 2002, the 1,140th anniversary of Russian statehood "with its center in Novgorod the Great."

By binding the region's political and economic success to the Nov-gorod Myth, Prusak has created a strong bond between that myth and his own administration, reaping the political rewards described by Abner Cohen in *Two-Dimensional Man*:

The leadership process . . . involves the mobilization of old and new symbols, and their interpretation and reinterpretation. . . . At any one time, some symbolic forms can provide better solutions to the current problems of the group than others and those members who create, mobilize, or articulate them become potential leaders.[60]

Prusak intuitively understood that more direct use of the Novgorod Myth would generate a reservoir of public trust among elites and the public, and in his second run for governor in 1999 this intuition was rewarded with a phenomenal 91 percent voter approval rating. At the time, we should recall, people's standard of living had fallen sharply as a result of the August 1998 economic collapse; Prusak had recently been engaged in a bitter public feud with Prime Minister Evgeny Primakov; and he was being accused locally of shirking his duties as governor by launching a new political party. The only factor in Prusak's favor going into the 1999 elections was that this time he was campaigning not merely as a competent manager but as a Novgorod patriot.

HOW SYMBOLS PROMOTED DEMOCRATIC CONSOLIDATION IN NOVGOROD

Key cultural symbols play a crucial role in promoting broad public acceptance of rapid social change. When confronted with a bewildering array of new data, individuals seek ways to simplify their responses. Local myths and symbols allow people to reduce the complexity of selecting the values that shape their actions.[61] Those symbolic shortcuts that best fit our cultural self-image are most readily accepted, while those deemed "foreign" are rejected.

Although the cultural environment broadly determines which symbols are the most suitable for the support of a particular policy, it is not a serious constraint on policy options. The cultural patrimony should be viewed as the context from which a wide variety of symbols can emerge; their contemporary meaning, however, is given by the elite. Elite advocacy of new interpretations for old symbols is an essential component of social change because it sets the stage for their further political usage. The greater the degree of elite consensus around the interpretation, the more convincing it will be to the public and the more useful in building support for new policies.

Symbols thus promoted development in Novgorod through their specific ability to change people's perceptions of what is possible. Once explicitly linked to particular policy initiatives, however, they also become measurable markers of social change. A thorough knowledge of their meaning, therefore, allows analysts to be quite explicit about the type of political change being advocated, who is advocating it, and how success-ful that effort has been.

What distinguishes Novgorod from other regions of Russia is not that it had better symbols, or even a better history, for these are politically useless unless coupled with a strategy that illuminates their meaning for the present. Rather, Novgorod benefited from the early emergence of an unusually strong elite consensus around the interpretation that should be given to the key symbols of Novgorod's past. This consensus on the meaning of symbols eased social tensions, built trust, and provided the administration with a strategic vision, even before it consciously adopted the mantle of the Novgorod Republic.

To be successful in creating a new social consensus, however, elite inter-pretations of key symbols must also be accepted by the populace. By its ongoing acceptance or rejection of new interpretations, the populace exercises a powerful constraint on elite mythmaking. Put simply, while elites propose new interpretations for key symbols, the masses dispose of them.

To translate changes in consciousness into changes in political behav-ior, Allison Brysk says, symbols must transform individual perception by "rewriting and reframing elements of identity. . . . Reframing leads to renaming, and renaming leads to reclaiming."[62] Seemingly simple gestures, such as the renaming of street names, are crucial because through them reformers transform the symbols of Novgorod's past into a current identity. It was also critical that the communist-era monopoly on the interpretation of symbols be broken so that alternative voices could legitimately claim to speak on behalf of Novgorod and propose noncommunist political solu-tions. Coincidentally, our analytical focus on symbols also reveals why the abrupt removal of ideological constraints per se does not result in rapid social changes. People rarely, if ever, prefer uncertainty to a dismal reality. Hence, stable social transformations require that elites not only reject old interpretations and symbols but find suitable replacements for them.

The political development of the region in the 1990s suggests that the Novgorod Myth succeeded in altering previous patterns of public behavior. One such pattern was the rather low level of civic activism. Before 1991 civic activism in Novgorod lagged behind the rest of Russia. Between 1987 and 1991, the high level of latent political opposition, indi-cated by the success of anticommunist candidates in regional elections, conspicuously failed to coalesce into voluntary political activity.[63] In subsequent years, however, this pattern was reversed and Novgorod emerged as a region of dramatic NGO growth at a time when national growth stagnated.[64]

Most important, the high level of public trust in local government mirrors the well-defined symbolic consensus established among key

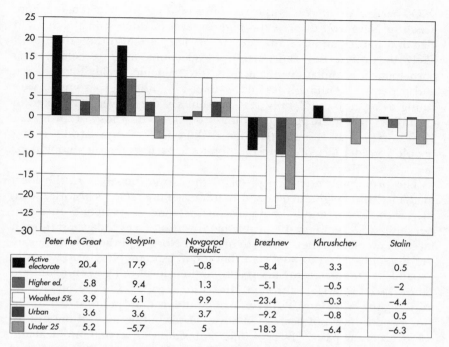

	Peter the Great	Stolypin	Novgorod Republic	Brezhnev	Khrushchev	Stalin
Active electorate	20.4	17.9	−0.8	−8.4	3.3	0.5
Higher ed.	5.8	9.4	1.3	−5.1	−0.5	−2
Wealthest 5%	3.9	6.1	9.9	−23.4	−0.3	−4.4
Urban	3.6	3.6	3.7	−9.2	−0.8	0.5
Under 25	5.2	−5.7	5	−18.3	−6.4	−6.3

Source: "Monitoring—Novgorodskaya oblast, July 1999" (Veliky Novgorod: MNOU Dialog), commissioned by Sberbank of Novgorod. In all 2,586 participants responded from all 22 regions of Novgorod.

FIGURE 6.1 Elite values compared to popular values in the Novgorod Region, July 1999 (Percentage of responses among selected economic and political subgroups answering the question: "What was the best period in Russian history?", compared with the averge percentage responding similarly for the Novgorod Region as a whole.)

segments of the elite. In a comprehensive survey of thirty-four values and concepts among Novgorod residents, "history of one's native region" had the most positive and the fewest negative responses, beating out "history of the country," "Russian culture," "Russian science," and "nature." By contrast, "Moscow structures" evoked the fewest positive responses (less than 10 percent), in the same ballpark as bureaucrats, national-patriots, crime, corruption, and the mafia.[65] A breakdown of these results by elite political and economic subgroups reveals that elites rate "Peter the Great," reformist tsarist Prime Minister [Peter] "Stolypin," and the "Medieval Novgorod Republic" even more positively than the population as a whole (see fig. 6.1).[66]

Of particular interest is the response of the "under 25" age group, which in Novgorod displays the highest level of interest in politics and electoral participation of any age group. They are also the group most likely to protest the cancellation of elections and to believe that participation in philanthropic activity is a "valuable quality for a citizen and a patriot." Although less likely than any other age group to view voting as a "civic duty," only 12.4 percent say they never participate in elections.[67] These surprising findings coincide with those of an earlier 1996 survey that showed that more than half of Novgorod's young people consider lack of interest in politics to be uncommon among their peers.[68]

The prominent attention given to the Novgorod Myth in the local media has also heightened public awareness of the region's historical conflicts with Moscow and led both civic activists and government officials to see similarities between the problems Novgorod faces today and those it faced in medieval times. The late mayor of Novgorod the Great, Alexander Korsunov, liked to point out that today, as then, Novgorod needs to expand its commerce to survive, strengthen local self-government, and "know how to navigate through Muscovite shoals."[69] On the other side, local regime critic Igor B. Alexandrov contends that "political activism in Novgorod is high not because of Soviet ideals but because of the historical ideals of the past."[70] By providing both sides with a common ideal and a common enemy, the Novgorod Myth helped forge a unifying political framework at a time when the rest of the country was in disarray. The result has been an unusually high level of public comity and trust in local media.

Surveys show that local press and television are trusted nearly twice as often as the leading national media outlets, and fewer than 10 percent in Novgorod distrust their local media, compared to 37 percent nationwide.[71] One can only wonder how much of the difference is due to the emphasis on historical coverage in the Novgorod media.

Finally, there has been a dramatic increase in interest in local history and culture, as exemplified by the pattern of visitation and borrowing at the Novgorodica department of the regional library, which specializes in local history and culture (fig. 6.2). While visitors to the library have remained relatively constant over the last two decades, the number of visitors to the Novgorodica department has more than doubled in the last ten years. Although some of this increase can be attributed to the introduction of mandatory courses in Novgorodica in elementary and secondary schools, that particular trend peaked in 1996 and 1997, while overall growth rates continued to rise.

A detailed breakdown of the visitation and usage statistics shows that the most dramatic increases have been among "scientific researchers," a

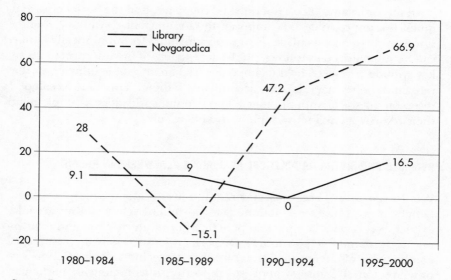

Source: Requests for items from the Novgorod Regional Library and its Novgorodica department. Data received from the library's deputy director, Valentina F. Berezhnova, and from the head of the Novgorodica department of the library, Elizaveta N. Kustova, on February 19, 2002.

FIGURE 6.2 Increased popular interest in Novgorodica 1980–2000 (percentage change in five-year increments)

category that includes university professors; "economists," a category that includes managers, brokers, and accountants; and "civil servants."[72] Only slightly less impressive has been the increase among the "creative intelligentsia" (writers, actors, and artists) and "cultural workers" (librarians, musicians, and local museum staff). These figures suggest that interest in Novgorod's past is more or less evenly spread among the Novgorod elite and has been gathering momentum during the past decade, as the symbols and rhetoric of the Novgorod Myth have become more prominent in the public arena.

Rapid social change took place in Novgorod society thanks to propitious circumstances that favored both the emergence of an elite consensus on new values and their acceptance by the populace. Public familiarity with key Novgorod symbols coincided with an unusual level of elite consensus on how they should be interpreted for the present. This coincidence reduced the number of discordant policy messages and images appearing in the local media, thereby reinforcing a sense of social unity. The result—higher levels of public trust in local media and local government than in the rest of Russia.

In these circumstances, not only did the symbols of the Soviet era seem much less appropriate but, importantly, an alternative symbolic agenda stood ready to take its place. Novgorod's formula for rapid social change can be summarized as follows: public acceptance of the interpretations of key symbols proposed by the elite conferred an aura of legitimacy on the reformist policy agenda that accompanied them. This aura created a reservoir of social support that allowed political leaders to implement their reform agenda more rapidly and effectively.

SYMBOLS AND MYTHS AS POLITICAL RESOURCES ELSEWHERE IN RUSSIA

Was Novgorod's success just a serendipitous accident? Does Novgorod benefit from a history so unique that no other region of Russia could expect to receive a comparable benefit from reinterpreting and managing its own symbolic patrimony? Or perhaps its success is the result of a combination of circumstances so rare that it precludes replication in any other region? Because symbols speak to the subconscious of particular populations, some might argue that Novgorod's distinctive symbolic repertoire can hardly be expected to have the same appeal in other regions. The type of benefits we have seen in Novgorod would then be highly unusual, and the failure of national authorities to pick up on the obvious democratic themes in Novgorod history would be proof of their limited national appeal.

Such critiques fundamentally misunderstand the symbolist approach to politics. The comparative political analysis of symbols is concerned with comparing the social impact and political usage of symbols, not their particular meaning.[73] It would therefore lead us to expect the same positive socioeconomic effects in any region where local symbols serve *functions* similar to those filled by local symbols in Novgorod.

As for Novgorod being unique among Russian regions, the similarities far outweigh the differences. Novgorod has suffered from the same sense of formlessness, absence of civil society, and heavy dependence on outdated industrial technology that characterized the Soviet Union as a whole. True, its environment is unusually rich culturally. This, however, only ensured that the local elite could not help but keep stumbling over Novgorod's historical legacy in their search for political strategies. It is not the existence of such a legacy per se that determines the success or failure of democratic reforms, however, but the symbolic interpretation given to it by elites.

The Search for Russia's "Golden Age"

Since the fall of communism in Russia interest in local life has risen sharply throughout Russia. In the 1960s and early 1970s only 20 percent of Russians read local periodicals. Today, more people read local papers than national ones.[74] Yet, despite the growth of localism, there are very few studies that look at the political implications of the resurgence of local identity.

One valuable exception is the study *Politics and Culture in the Russian Provinces*, which was produced by the University of Bremen in Germany and the Moscow-based Institute for Humanities and Political Studies. According to its authors, patterns of regional development can be traced back to the very earliest period of settlement. Eventually a region reaches a point where it sees itself as a potential capital city. This does not mean the national capital is actually moved there but that the region undergoes a period of such intense political, cultural, and economic activity that it rivals the capital in influence. The authors' term this period a region's "golden age."

The authors look at the golden ages of four Russian regions and find that they form the basis of recurring patterns of development. The golden age for Novgorod was the period between the twelfth and fourteenth centuries. For Voronezh, it was the 1920s and 1930s, when the region served as "Capital of the Central Black-Soil Region." Saratov's golden age was the period of prodigious cultural activity from 1890 to 1923, while the intense cultural and political development that the Sverdlovsk Region is undergoing today indicates that it is currently experiencing its golden age.[75]

Once a region's golden age has been reached, say the authors, specific historical motifs and institutional arrangements from that period become fixed in people's minds as "the best" and serve as local models. In each region, therefore, golden age themes can be found at the heart of political and commercial advertising. Political changes have little impact on these fundamental regional characteristics because they are rooted in a "genetic structural logic."[76] Even if a region's population is entirely replaced, the authors say, its golden age remains the most reliable guide to its subsequent political development.[77]

The contributors to this seminal comparative study have done a great service by applying cultural analysis directly to the regional level. Yet, although I agree with their identification of Novgorod's golden age, I disagree with most of what they say about its present-day impact. Given the weakness of Novgorod's princes, for example, it seems odd to call Novgorod's traditional pattern of government "single-person centralization." It was not until the beginning of the seventeenth century, as the authors themselves note, that new patterns of Muscovite government became settled in the region.[78]

The authors also assert that when a region's current status does not correspond to its golden-age image, the resulting identity crisis leads to a withdrawal from contact with neighbors.[79] In Novgorod, however, the opposite has been true. The region's cultural elite played a key role in establishing the Union of Russian Cities of the Northwest, which was specifically set up to foster horizontal contacts among regional centers.[80] Regional folk groups and festivals have sprung up throughout the northwest, many with the explicit purpose of resurrecting Novgorod's traditions throughout these ancient "Novgorod lands"; and cross-regional television programs such as *Neighbors* and cultural journals such as *Russkaya provintsiya* have arisen to keep people informed about life in neighboring regions.

Nor does the evidence support the authors' contention that Moscow-appointed figures dominate the region and that "there is no evidence of new external influence" in Novgorod.[81] Local surveys rate Moscow-appointed figures as the least influential category of civil servants in the region.[82] As for external influences, it is hard to imagine a more powerful influence than foreign direct investment.

At the root of these misperceptions lies a failure to distinguish between history and myth in the shaping of political attitudes. Myths are seen as somehow less "objective" than history and, hence, derivative of it. This approach results in a vulgar form of path determinism (not to be confused with path dependency) that forces researchers to label as key myths those that correspond to the a priori "objectively defined" pattern of regional development.[83] Thus, in Novgorod the imposition of administrative centralization becomes part of the natural developmental pattern because it is part of "objective history," even though it directly contradicts the local golden age myth and derives from an entirely different time period.

Myth and history exist in close proximity, but they are not the same thing. When history and myth are conflated, the result is a static view of a region's development that, once past its golden age, can never again hope for any better political or economic fate. In Novgorod's case, this would mean that political development can never move beyond the fifteenth century![84] A better approach would be to focus on the way elites have used key myths and symbols throughout history. This would not only provide an empirical base against which to define a region's golden age but give researchers a way to trace the impact of golden age ideas over time.

Despite its flaws, however, this book makes a very compelling case that regional political development is a product of local myths and that there are many myths to choose from.[85] Two general patterns of symbolic usage emerge. On the one hand, there are regions such as Novgorod where elites use local symbols and myths to encourage adaptation to new social and economic conditions. Elites in these regions then propose themselves as the indispensable conduits of change. On the other hand, there are regions where elites use symbols and myths to thwart change and identify the reforms being foisted on the region as the source of the crisis. These regional elites then propose themselves as the indispensable bulwarks against chaos. Yaroslavl, Saratov, and the Russian Far North fall into the first category, while the regions of Orenburg and Pskov fall into the second.

Yaroslavl's "Heritage Industry"

Geographer Beth Mitchneck has aptly dubbed Yaroslavl's use of historical reference points to stabilize the local economy and political institutions a "heritage industry."[86] The key component of institutional identity in this central Russian city has been the revival of the zemstvo tradition, which the local elite regards as "the democratic ideal for Russian local government." In four specific areas—assistance to local industry, assistance to the poor, local food sufficiency, and land management—Mitchneck finds that local government has not only modeled its responsibilities on those of the prerevolutionary zemstvos but even copied previous legislative and budgetary priorities.[87] "The myth of the *Zemstvo*," says Mitchneck, "establishes it as an innovative, populist institution independent of the federal government. By reinventing local government, in part, in the image of the zemstvo, the Yaroslavl local government attempted to link itself to a more popular and legitimate form of government."[88]

Although the actual symbols differ—in Yaroslavl they evoke a prosperous and cosmopolitan nineteenth-century Volga port, in Novgorod a prosperous and cosmopolitan medieval trading port—the myths they support share a common message that each government uses to craft a "post-Soviet identify that is consistent with Russian history and the capitalist world."[89] Thanks to its location on the "Golden Ring"—a distinctive ensemble of cities that preserved portions of their twelfth- to seventeenth-century architecture—Yaroslavl benefits from a cultural environment that, like Novgorod, allowed local elites to tap into local support for historical preservation.[90]

But Yaroslavl's success cannot be attributed to this alone, because other cities on the Golden Ring do not share the same tendency. Vladimir, for example, also on the Golden Ring, is one of only two Russian regions that still retains its Soviet-era regional flag.[91] As with Novgorod, a conducive environment may have made it easier to reference aspects of Yaroslavl's historical myth, but it was the elite's desire to use this particular heritage to support a reform agenda that set the process in motion.

Although the region's politics are considered solidly proreform, the results in Yaroslavl seem less dramatic than those in Novgorod.[92] Without conducting a detailed cultural audit of the region (a process I describe in the final chapter), one can only speculate as to the reasons why. The discrepancy, however, serves as a reminder that symbolic interpretations unattached to clear agendas have little political significance. The political utility of symbols lies in their ability to reduce the intense psychological discomfort people feel with rapid economic and political changes, but if these changes are not carried out the potential benefit is squandered.

Stolypin's Legacy in Saratov

The regional elite of the Saratov Region has also derived considerable political capital from local symbols. When running for election as governor in 1996, Dimitry Ayatskov campaigned on a slogan that would allow people to "know what they are sacrificing for. . . . For us in the Saratov Oblast the idea that unites the inhabitants is 'Saratov—Capital of the Volga Region.' "[93]

As governor, Ayatskov institutionally consolidated the elite by having all local social and political organizations sign an accord for social harmony and join a social chamber attached to the governor's office. As in Novgorod, all social groups were invited to join the chamber, and, just as in Novgorod, the local CPRF and sundry leftist organizations refused. A clear dividing line was thus established in the public's mind between those who wanted social harmony and those who did not. Also, in a manner reminiscent of Novgorod's interpenetration of the branches of government, Ayatskov has encouraged members of the regional legislature to serve in the executive branch, arguing that the advantages of better coordination outweigh those of strict separation. By 1998 more than half of the Saratov Region's senior administration had served in both the legislative and executive branches.[94]

On the heels of the success of his "capital of the Volga region" campaign theme, Ayatskov embraced another prominent symbol of the region's past-prerevolutionary Russian Prime Minister Peter A. Stolypin. Ayatskov restored to the village of Kalinino its historical name of Stolypino and has seized every opportunity to portray himself as following in Stolypin's footsteps, remarking coyly that "the Saratov Region has already given Russia one prime minister."[95]

Each year the region holds public gatherings on Stolypin's birthday at which writers, educators, and government officials commemorate

Stolypin's legacy.[96] During that week, officially known as Stolypin Week, students write essays on "Why We Need a Great Russia," reflecting on Stolypin's famous reply to his critics.[97] In 2002, to commemorate the 140th anniversary of Stolypin's birth, the capital city of Saratov renamed one of its central squares in his honor. It will eventually be the site of a three-meter-tall bronze statue of Stolypin and a museum dedicated to his life.[98] When the Internet Center of Saratov University opened, its first videoconference was devoted to "Peter Stolypin Today: The Continuity of Time."[99]

The combination of these two key symbols—Saratov as capital city of the Volga, and Ayatskov as successor to Stolypin—seems to have been quite effective in shoring up popular support for reform initiatives in a region that, prior to Ayatskov, was seen as solidly procommunist. It hardly seems coincidental, for example, that the two regions that have pioneered commercial land use and the auctioning of state land are Saratov and Novgorod.[100] Even those uncomfortable with the way Ayatskov constantly wraps himself in Stolypin's mantle admit that his proreform policies enjoy broad public support without the heavy handed constraints that local officials often impose on the opposition press.[101] As if by way of explanation, Ayatskov has remarked, "The homeland of Stolypin is not afraid of reforms."[102]

The "Pomor Idea" in the Russian North

A third region where elites have made noticeable use of symbols to promote regional development is the Russian north. Here the myth identifies the local inhabitants, known as Pomors, as the true inheritors of the freedom-loving and entrepreneurial spirit of republican Novgorod. RAND Corporation analyst Theodore W. Karasik, a frequent visitor to the region, offers the following insight:

> Arkhangelsk politics and economics often focused on notions of democracy and identity imported from Western Europe. . . . Citizens claimed that the North was heir to the Novgorodian tradition of political and religious freedom. The northerner [severianin], in this view, was free from the corrupting influences of autocratic, bureaucratic and noble Russia, self-reliant and independent, and uniquely prepared for democratic government and an egalitarian society. . . . Moscow is indeed a "separate country" from the Russian north.[103]

Sociologists Sergei Filatov and Vladimir Lunkin have studied the political symbols and myths of the region and ascribe local attitudes to the prominent role of the Russian Orthodox Church, which has embraced the heritage of medieval Novgorod.[104]

The Novgorod tradition of tolerance for religious diversity that allowed Old Believer communities to thrive in the region also extended to the Evangelical-Reform, Calvinist, and German Lutheran congregations that appeared in Arkhangelsk in the mid-seventeenth century. They may explain why friendly ties with Western churches have persisted in the region, despite the generally frosty attitude of the Moscow Patriarchate.[105] Even the religious persecutions of the Soviet period could not entirely eradicate the region's distinctiveness, say Filatov and Lunkin, and today this heritage is spilling over into the social and political arenas.[106]

Arkhangelsk, Petrozavodsk, and Syktyvkar all display an unusual level of cooperation among cultural/museum workers, university intellectuals, and local clergy.[107] At Pomor University in Arkhangelsk, the Department of Culturology and Religious Studies has been established with the express purpose of creating "a contemporary Orthodox myth of the North."[108] In Novgorod, Petrozavodsk, and Karelia, where there are as yet no religious studies departments at the local university and no theological seminaries, local clergy lecture at the state university, reviving the age-old tradition of public outreach by the local Orthodox clergy.[109]

In Arkhangelsk, the capital city of the Russian north, a distinctive local myth known as the "Pomor Idea" has even spawned a secular ideology with close ties to the religious leaders of the region. Its political movement, Democratic Renaissance of the North, is led by Alexander Ivanov, former chairman of the regional duma's budget committee and candidate for governor. His description of the region and its people is reminiscent of the type of rhetoric one finds among civil servants in Novgorod:

> The Pomor have a special sense of their own dignity and a love of freedom. The reason for this is that that there was no serfdom in the North, and the basic organizational unit of economic life was not the commune but the cooperative. The sense of having enemies is alien to the Pomor. Since there were always enough natural resources for everyone, foreigners were perceived as trading partners, not competitors. From ancient times our contact with Europe (by sea Edinburgh, Oslo, and Bremen are closer to us than Moscow) contributed to a Western European consciousness, an absence of xenophobia and respect for democratic institutions. Throughout their history the Pomor have despised Muscovite rule, whether tsarist, Soviet or post-Soviet. . . . What central and southern Russia calls patriotism—hatred for the West, hatred for freedom and democracy, and hatred for the intelligentsia—from the Pomor point of view is not patriotism at all, but philistinism.[110]

Filatov and Lunkin see the absence of communists in the region's senior political leadership, and the overt anticommunism of many senior Orthodox clergy, as further evidence of this Pomor mentality.[111] For its part, the clergy has shown that it is aware of local traditions and encourages them. When the newly appointed head of the diocese of Arkhangelsk, Bishop Tikhon (Stepanov), an alumnus of St. Vladimir's Orthodox Theological Seminary in Crestwood, New York, arrived to assume his seat, in keeping with local custom he first asked local parishioners whether they would accept him as their archbishop.[112]

The key symbols accessed by the Pomor elite are essentially the same as those in Novgorod. In this instance, however, it is the Orthodox Church that has taken the lead in using symbolic resources to ease society's transition from militant atheism to a Christian social presence. They have done so by referencing the local symbols and myths that present Orthodoxy as an integral part of the region's history and identity, and they have been joined in this effort by the cultural, financial, and political elite. Nowhere else in Russia is political and financial support for the Orthodox Church as strong as in the north, say Filatov and Lunkin, who suggest that the Pomor example might someday serve as a model for the rest of Russia:

> Contemporary, thoughtful northerners talk about the ideals and values of their native region in language that is redolent with the legends and myths of the Medieval North. . . . The northern Russian worldview now has its own ideologists, who can help northerners become more aware of their own history and realize the priorities of social and church life.[113]

Orenburg: Russia's Bulwark against Islam

Although symbols can be a powerful force in promoting social change, they can also be used to thwart reforms. The regions of Orenburg and Pskov provide good examples of how local elites have used local myths and symbols to respond to the challenge of suddenly finding themselves on the border.

According to local mythology, with the collapse of the USSR, Orenburg has become the only authentically Russian region between European Russia and Siberia. Strategically situated at the crossroads of Europe and Asia, it is now up to Orenburg to defend Russian interests in this zone of cultural conflict. While some in the local elite argue that Orenburg should become a crossroads of trade and cultural interaction ("Russia's gateway to Asia"), others warn against welcoming the marauders from the "wilds of the Steppe," as the plains of northern Kazakhstan are known in Russian history and literature.[114]

The local elite has responded by promoting a peculiar form of multicultural "civil community" (*grazhdanskoe soobshchestvo*) that gives ethnic Russians, who form just over three-quarters of the population, a dominant role in local culture and politics. Russian culture, so the myth goes, should be privileged because it is a "stabilizing factor" in the region, capable of uniting all nationalities, thanks to "the well-known traditions of tolerance rooted in the Orthodox religion."[115] A senior member of the regional administration underscores this point with surveys that show "peoples of Muslim culture are three times more prone to conflict than the traditionally Orthodox."[116] By treating the territorial integrity of the region as a defense not only of the state but of Russia's cultural and religious identity, many in the Orenburg elite believe they have found a model appropriate for all of Russia. Intellectuals close to the regional administration speak of having found a "Eurasian socialist tradition" that can transcend national, religious, or ethnic differences and restore peace and prosperity to the entire country.[117]

Critics, however, point to what they call the "openly colonialist aspect" of the Orenburg Myth—the local historians who argue that the region once formed part of a larger East-West "Russian corridor" that has historically included Bashkortostan, most of the Chelyabinsk and Kurgan Regions, and even parts of western Kazakhstan. A "historical commonality" binds the various peoples of the region and brought benefits to all, particularly to the underdeveloped Kazakhs.[118]

By masking nationalism in the garb of cultural pluralism, the Orenburg Myth serves as a convenient tool for defending the privileges of the local elite. The local administration has used it to focus attention on the region's importance to the defense of Russian strategic interests, the resolution of interethnic conflict, and the promotion of a new national idea. This decidedly ethnocentric myth, however, seems more likely to heighten than to reduce tensions in the region. It has not, for example, diminished demands by local Turks and Muslims for more cultural autonomy, and it seems only a matter of time before these demands spread to the political arena.

Pskov: Defending Russia against the West

As we saw in chapter 3, Novgorod and Pskov are so close in demographics, size, and location that there is no simple structural explanation for their very different levels of political and economic development. True, after having a "liberal" governor, Pskov elected a "nationalist" governor in 1996 but this only begs the question of why, and does not explain the significant policy differences that had already begun to emerge between Novgorod and Pskov before 1996. A better explanation can be found in the local myths that dominate politics in Pskov.

Novgorod and Pskov share impressive historical similarities. Each was administratively divided into boroughs (six for Pskov, five for Novgorod), and both had a veche that elected princes and other officials. In both cities the church served as the seat of the republic's legal records and coffers. Initially, the bishop of Pskov was subordinate to the bishop of Novgorod, and this was apparently fairly well tolerated until Moscow gained the upper hand, after which heresies spread throughout both regions.[119] After the subjugation of Pskov to Muscovy in 1510, just as in Novgorod, many prominent Pskov families were exiled.[120]

But there are also significant differences. "As one moves from the chronicles of Novgorod to those of Pskov," historian Vasily Klyuchevsky writes, "one feels a sense of calm, as if moving from a bustling market-place to a quiet street corner. . . . In Pskov there are no agitated scenes of fighting in the veche square in front of the Trinity Cathedral, none of Novgorod's passion with respect to princes, no social antagonisms or party battles."[121] Although one should not make too much of Pskov's relative tranquility, which after all saw a peasant uprising in 1483 that killed the mayor and seized control of the city for nearly three years, it is fair to say that Pskov was more politically centralized than Novgorod. Because its outlying districts were much closer, they were treated as administrative extensions of Pskov proper and not as self-administered colonies, as in Novgorod.[122]

More important, from its earliest founding Pskov was a contested region, and its renown derives from such decisive military engagements as the Battle on the Ice (April 5, 1242), the siege by Polish King Stefan Batory (1581–1582), and the Northern Wars (1700–1721), during which Peter the Great wrested control of the Baltic from Sweden. Unlike Novgorod, which always viewed its princes with suspicion (especially those, like Alexander Nevsky, who were able military commanders) and therefore forbade them to live near the city, in Pskov the prince and his retinue lived in the very heart of the kremlin, the Krom. The popular Pskov Prince Dovmont even set up his own fort directly adjoining the Krom in a district that still bears his name. Whereas Novgorod is known in medieval chronicles as a trading town, Pskov is most often referred to as a fortress, and it seems reasonable to assume that some of its political tranquility was due to the fact that, in the face of so many external threats, domestic dissension seemed an unaffordable luxury.

The enormous sacrifices made by the people of Pskov in defense of their land (and later in defense of all of Russia) have thus become the distinguishing feature of the Pskov Myth.[123] According to this myth, the region's highest calling is to guard against the foreign invaders who are ever ready to plunder Russian territory.

This myth dominates cultural and political discourse in the region to this day. In one popular collection of local legends published in 1993, for example, nearly half are devoted to the defense of Pskov against foreign invaders. The legend of "Mikola and the Cannon called 'Pebble,'" describes Pskov as surrounded by "hungry and pitiless enemies."[124] The legend of "The Prince's Shadow" tells of how the people of Pskov "had to defend themselves almost without respite, sword in hand, from the onslaughts of knights and other hordes, who had set their mind to the unachievable dream of conquering a free people."[125] The rich lands of Pskov, says a legend from the town of Gorodok, "attracted all sorts of evil people from abroad like a magnet."[126]

The Battle on the Ice remains the single most important local symbol, and it is commemorated by a gargantuan bronze statue at the outskirts of the city. In the local legend of the "Raven's Stone," the boulder upon which Alexander Nevsky once stood to direct the battle rises up dramatically out of the lake to defend the city each time it is threatened by the Teutonic knights.[127] Since historically Pskov would occasionally join forces with the Teutonic Order against rival Baltic tribes, it is significant that these contemporary renditions mention them only as bloodthirsty villains, never as potential allies.

Not surprisingly, the Pskov Myth has a strong antiforeign component. One interesting legend tells of the seventeenth-century Pskov merchant Sergei Pogankin, who enjoyed close ties with foreign merchants. His cautionary tale continues:

> Foreigners in those days, if truth be told, were strongly disliked in Pskov and quite unwelcome. Those of foreign faith had brought far too much sorrow and misfortune to Pskov lands with their endless attacks and deceptions. During the Middle Ages foreigners were prohibited from entering the city, and if a foreigner did gain entrance to the heart of Pskov, the Krom, he could expect to be executed. In those days foreigners were known exclusively as "damned" [*pogannye*]. The people of Pskov transferred this dislike to the Pskov merchant who had befriended foreigners, and began to call him Pogankin.[128]

Another legend, from the village of Sinovitse, describes how invading Lithuanian soldiers once roamed the land in search of shelter from a storm. All the local villages were miraculously hidden from their sight. Finally, they came upon a lone church standing on a hill and, as foreigners are wont to do, entered it on horseback. As soon as the last foreigner had entered the church it sank into the ground, being "overfilled with foreigners."[129]

As if echoing the past, the current archbishop of Pskov, Evsevy, has warned ominously of Catholic proselytism in the region: "We should know that Catholics are not our benefactors, they have not brought anything good or useful to any nation. Wherever they came, there was ruin, division, destruction."[130] Although there are also many Pskov legends that tell

of fruitful meetings with foreigners, the high concentration of xenopho-
bic narratives readily available in downtown bookstores and kiosks, sets
a tone for social discourse very different from that of neighboring
Novgorod.

Walking down the streets of Pskov one gets the sense that time stopped
in the early 1980s. All the main streets still bear the names of the heroes
of the Bolshevik Revolution. A statue of Sergei Kirov, head of the
Leningrad party organization until his murder by Stalin in 1934, stands
in front of the entrance to the regional administration facing October
Street. In contrast to Novgorod, where the early transfer of key national
relics to the church helped to forge a link between reformers and clergy,
Pskov's Cathedral of the Holy Trinity and its most famous monasteries
remain in the sharply curtailed legal limbo of "joint administration" with
civil authorities.[131]

After a brief flurry of interest in Pskov's medieval republican heritage
at the outset of perestroika, local elites seems to have turned their
back on this aspect of their symbolic inheritance and chosen to retool
for present-day use the image of Pskov as Russia's defensive perimeter
against the West. Pskov Governor Evgeny Mikhailov's comments about
the historical differences between Novgorod and Pskov are quite
revealing:

> The most important events in ancient and modern Russian history are con-
> nected with Pskov: the concept of "Moscow the Third Rome" was devised
> by a monk of Pskov's Elizarov monastery, Nicholas II's abdication occurred
> in these lands. . . . The territory of Pskov has its own face—there were no
> Mongols here, and Pskov, as opposed to Novgorod, voluntarily joined the
> Muscovite state; that is, unlike Novgorod, [it] did not betray Moscow. [In
> my discussions with Putin] I did not hide my belief that the significance of
> Pskov may have been somewhat diminished in the historical literature com-
> pared with that of Novgorod.[132]

The present-day Pskov Myth, which some analysts have aptly named the
"Fortress Russia Syndrome," has changed little since the end of the Soviet
Union, and its strength seems confirmed by Mikhailov's reelection in
2001.[133]

Should the priorities of local elites change, however, it would not
be difficult to fashion an alternative Pskov Myth that is more friendly to
the outside world. For example, much could be made of the fact that
the region's most revered prince, Dovmont, was a Lithuanian who fled
the dynastic intrigues of his homeland and found a haven in the more
tolerant Pskov. Medieval Pskov's social stability and democratic institutions could be portrayed as having outlasted even those of Novgorod,
and as having surrendered to Moscow only because of treachery and

betrayal.[134] Rather than looking exclusively to its military heroes, the elite could draw attention to the legacy of Pskov's famed governor, Afansii Ordin-Nashchokin, a seventeenth-century diplomat, economist, and political reformer who advocated cooperation with leading Western powers. His efforts have recently received attention among scholars of public administration—albeit in Novgorod—as a model for a new regional self-awareness.[135] There is, in sum, as much raw symbolism that can be used to serve the interest of political and economic reform in Pskov as there is in Novgorod, given the political will to do so.[136]

HOW DIFFERENT IS RUSSIA?

Although Novgorod benefited from auspicious circumstances, we have seen that symbols have also played an important role in the political development of other Russian regions. Readers, however, might be wondering whether Russia's own history and culture make it particularly susceptible to the influence of myths and symbols. Perhaps communism has heightened the psychological impact of symbols? Or, maybe Russians are more receptive than others to myths and symbols during periods of political uncertainty?

Although there is a temptation to view Russia as sui generis, scholarship on political transitions around the world shows that it is quite common for elites to invent traditions and tailor them to fit present-day needs. Such invention typically accompanies the birth of a new nation or a new political system—the United States, the Soviet Union, Germany, Japan, and Israel readily come to mind. In countries such as Wales, where cultural self-awareness was all but lost, Welsh historian Prys Morgan notes that it took "a great deal of invention."[137]

Studies of democratic transition in regions as diverse as Turkey, Taiwan, and Slovakia show that symbols and myths have played a crucial role in the early phases of democratic transition.[138] In her study of post-Franco Spain, Laura Edles shows how, in a very short period of time, Spanish political culture underwent a totally unexpected reorientation—an elite obsessed with Spain's distinctiveness from Europe came to view itself as an integral part of Europe, an elite that once aggressively suppressed all manifestations of regionalism came to take federalism for granted.[139] Behind these startling conversions, she says, lay "an extraordinarily powerful transitional symbolic framework" that provided the ground rules for a new politics of consensus.[140] Significantly, this symbolic framework emerged not in the capital, Madrid, but in Catalonia, where the core symbols of local identity more closely matched the values that were emerging in post-Franco Spain.

Edles's description of Catalonia's heritage is strikingly reminiscent of medieval Novgorod.[141] Catalans, she says, are proud of their medieval democratic institutions, particularly the Usatges, the charter that established the legal equality of free men. In the fifteenth and sixteenth centuries, when Castille and the Catholic Church centralized Spain, Catalonia retained its own currency, customs, and tax system. And, just as the late nineteenth century and early twentieth century cultural revival movements saw the bishop of Novgorod, Arseny (Stadnistsky), founding the Novgorod Archeological Society and actively promoting the region's past, so in the same period the bishop of Vic, Josep Torras i Bagès, studied and promoted the language and lifestyle of the Catalan people.[142] Because the core symbols of Catalan culture overlapped so well with the core symbols of the new Spanish democracy, Catalan elites could embrace the transition without calling into question their commitment to Catalanism.

Edles, however, still sees elites as essentially passive partakers of their cultural heritage. Although she discusses the media's unabashed support of new European values, and points to how the Moncloa Pacts of 1977 between the Spanish government and political parties forced party leaders to create new symbols and rituals to resolve potentially explosive issues, she is reluctant to see this as a *conscious* choice by elites.[143] Instead, she attributes Spain's democratic transition to the good fortune of having "an effervescent system of shared symbols" that combined Catalan nationalism and democracy "in a largely nonrational and unconscious way."[144] One should not expect anything similar to happen in Eastern Europe, she warns, because unlike Spain it is not supported by Western monetary and mentoring relationships.[145]

Political scientist Jan Kubik agrees with Edles about the rarity of successful democratic transitions, except that his successful exception is from Eastern Europe. Reviewing the reasons for the collapse of communism in Poland, he finds that all the traditions revived and invented during the period of transition emerged from the framework of "Catholic mythology." The Solidarity movement arose "from a need to reconsider afresh collective identity and the ethical foundations of society. There is only one language suitable for such considerations: the language of symbols and myths."[146]

The Catholic Church's ability to form a counterculture prepared public consciousness for revolution in Poland. By relying on the rituals of the Catholic Church and the historical symbols of past Polish insurrections, elites forged a new symbolic vision that led to a qualitative change in social relations.[147] Poland has been more successful than its neighbors, says Kubik, precisely because its cultural revival preceded its political revival.[148] Curiously, as in Spain, the key symbols of change emerged first in an outlying region, the port city of Gdansk.[149] Like Edles, however,

Kubik tends to regard elites as subconscious recipients of culture and to find the explanation of rapid social change in the uniqueness of Polish history and culture.[150]

Another intriguing example of how symbols affect the course of rapid political change comes from anthropologist David Kertzer, who illustrates how much politics is a struggle over identity, which is constructed by weaving together the symbols provided by elites. Kertzer looks at how, in the early 1990s, the leadership of the Italian Communist Party (PCI) manipulated the party's political symbols to rapidly transform the PCI into the Democratic Party of the Left (PDS). The strategy chosen by the party's leader, Achille Occhetto, involved "desacralizing" the symbols most resistant to change and replacing them with symbols taken from "the Left" that could be more easily reinterpreted to suit the needs of current party leaders.[151]

Occhetto proposed replacing the Russian Revolution with the French Revolution as the party's new source of intellectual and symbolic inspiration. This would allow the PCI to focus on such issues as democracy and human rights, rather than on the narrower agenda of the working class. In February 1991 the party leadership adopted Occhetto's new vision of the party. A significant minority, however, rejected it and established a new party that took more than a quarter of the communist electorate with it. It had taken less than two years for Occhetto and his supporters to redefine what it meant to be a communist, but at a cost from which the Italian communist movement never recovered.

In studying Occhetto's strategy, Kertzer comes to the conclusion that the key to managing rapid political transition lies in the ability to control ritual. Kertzer agrees with Edmund Leach that myth and ritual are merely different ways of making the same symbolic statements about the social order.[152] Because symbols are by nature ambiguous and difficult to correlate with the evolution of social consensus, however, he prefers to focus on rituals. The greater the divisions in society, the greater the need for compensatory rituals to hold it together, and the greater the comfort that people derive from such rituals. Ritual actions promote social stability by encouraging public support without requiring shared values. "Solidarity," Kertzer says, "is produced by people acting together, not people thinking together."[153]

Positive rituals and symbols reinforce social communion, while negative ones (witch hunts, impeachments) forge solidarity by identifying a common enemy.[154] For rituals to be used for social transformation they must be "wrapped in a web of symbolism."[155] The process, says Kertzer, does not even require new symbols. Old symbols will serve just as well—"the trick is to introduce dramatic variations on these powerful symbols, to change their meaning by changing their context."[156]

Kertzer's emphasis on rituals rather than symbols as the instrument of social consensus, however, is not entirely convincing, for at the heart of every ritual there must be a key symbol that gives it meaning. Attempts by the French parliament in the 1890s to create a national festival commemorating Joan of Arc revealed the deep divide between Catholics and secularists in that country. In Russia, November 7 is still celebrated as the "Great October Socialist Revolution" by some, as the "Day of Sorrow and Irreconcilability" by others, with only a small minority referring to it by its new official name, as the "Day of National Reconciliation." So long as the meaning of symbols remains unresolved, rituals like these will placate some while incensing others. To mitigate conflicts, societies impose overarching thematic boundaries on symbols within which their definition can range without contradicting each other. Although symbolic anthropologists all agree on the arbitrariness of symbols, Sherry Ortner reminds us that "they do insist that the choice of a particular symbolic form among several possible, equally arbitrary symbols for the same conception is not only not arbitrary but has important implications that must be investigated."[157]

Ultimately, Kertzer's view that symbols are meaningless but rituals are meaningful leads to ambiguity on the crucial question of whether elites can consciously use symbols or rituals to promote change. On the one hand, he says, rituals have a "conservative bias" which causes them to change more slowly than other elements of culture. On the other hand, he asserts that rituals are not simply blind products of communal existence but serve certain political interests and undermine others.[158] Although some in the elite consciously manipulate ritual for political ends, he suggests that most do so without even being aware of the ultimate political effect.[159] Thus, while Kertzer prefers rituals to symbols, he shares Edles's and Kubik's reluctance to treat them as constructive instruments for achieving rapid social change.

THE VARIETY AND POWER OF SYMBOLS

The case studies we have discussed reveal several limitations in the ways that analysts see symbols affecting political behavior. One is the tendency to view the success of symbols in a particular case study as unique. Because each instance is viewed as sui generis, the recurring patterns of symbolic transformation—from the destruction of old symbolic attachments, through the creation of new symbolic attachments, to their linkage to new policy agendas—is missed.

Second, elites are often seen as helpless in the face of "objective" social forces, when in fact they are far more likely to manipulate symbols to overcome obstacles and promote their interests. Sometimes they are successful, sometimes not. Either way, however, changing the interpretation of key symbols to match new policy agendas is a sensible strategy for new and untested elites trying to survive.

Third, as a rule, historical reality generally bears little resemblance to the political myth. It is the coherent embrace of this myth by elites, and the willingness of the populace to accept it as a framework for resolving daily dissonances, that are the keys to success. The failure of a new policy agenda is always foreshadowed by the public's rejection of its symbols. During periods of upheaval, when old symbolic certainties come under fire, the elite has a somewhat wider latitude for innovation in the interpretation of symbols. As the crisis recedes, however, dramatic innovations tend to meet with less and less popular approval.

Finally, when thinking about the prospects for democratic development, it is important to remember the extraordinary variety of symbols from which elites can choose. Regions are not destined by their culture to be either progressive or reactionary, for the simple reason that it is symbols, not culture, that give policies cognitive consistency, and the variety of symbols that elites can choose from is staggering. Analysts need to look through the veil of culture to the concrete meaning of symbols and their specific usage. They will then see that "path dependency" is often better understood as the particular set of symbols that elites have chosen to promote particular policies; i.e. a choice not a constraint.

The wide variety of symbolic interpretations available, however, should not be confused with ambiguity. The examples discussed in this chapter all show that ambiguity about the meaning of symbols is removed as elites interpret and link them to specific policy initiatives. A great deal of vagueness can surround the abstract meaning of symbols, but as specific symbols are linked to specific policies they come to define a clear-cut political agenda.

Finally, the manipulation of symbols by local political elites always hints at a broader agenda—the reconstitution of the community on a new moral and cultural foundation. If accepted by the populace, this cultural agenda gradually broadens and deepens the narrow social coalition that reformers relied on at the outset of the transition. If successful locally, it is often touted as having national significance. The many and varied ways in which symbols are used to overcome formlessness and reshape social relations suggests that they can be a valuable resource for promoting rapid acceptance of democratic values and institutions in almost any setting.

CHAPTER 7

CRAFTING DEMOCRACY

We have all witnessed how countries with two- or
three-hundred-year histories have tried to instruct states with
histories of a thousand years. Such ignorance has been the cause of many
woes, and conflicts have arisen because all things were subordinated to
economics. The future, however, rests with those politicians and
those nations who delve into history more deeply.

MIKHAIL PRUSAK

Having reviewed the inadequacies of current theories of democratic development and, through the unlikely example of Novgorod, seen how they are improved by refocusing on regions and their cultural symbols, we are now ready to ask whether the power of symbols can be harnessed to promote democracy more generally.

To date, the primary emphasis of Western assistance to former communist countries has not been on symbols, or even on promoting democracy. It has been on implementing economic reforms. The benefits of a rapid transition to capitalism were considered so obvious that the psychological and social costs involved in so dramatically reorienting individual values were minimized. The resulting development philosophy, known as the Washington Consensus, dominated Western approaches to economic and democratic development through much of the 1990s, the very period when Novgorod was undergoing its remarkable transformation.

The Washington Consensus is a set of beliefs, widely held among senior policy makers at the International Monetary Fund, World Bank, and U.S. Treasury Department, that rapid economic development requires tight fiscal and monetary policies, the loosening of restrictions on international trade and capital flows, and the privatization of government property. These policies need to be implemented as early as possible, so that "economic good sense" begins to dominate the thinking of new regimes.[1]

To smooth the way, formerly communist governments were advised to engage in what the senior chief economist at the World Bank, Joseph Stiglitz, candidly refers to as "institutional blitzkrieg"—the destruction of old regulatory institutions before new ones were fully established.[2] Waiting for new regulatory institutions to emerge, it was argued, risked slowing down the momentum of reform and undermining the focus on economic rationality, which is key to social change. Because the economic reforms would provide all the incentives needed for political and legal reform, paying attention to local traditions, customs, and institutions was often dismissed as a delaying tactic.[3]

In the former Soviet Union, where this approach was known as "shock therapy," attacking the social and economic institutions of the old regime had the added appeal of undermining the very institutions that the communists might use to regain power. Simply put, the Clinton administration, sought to ensure that even if the communists come to power, they would never be able to rule the country effectively. Former Deputy Secretary of State Strobe Talbott aptly dubbed this the "Yeltsin-the-wrecking-ball" strategy.[4]

The appeal of the Washington Consensus to analysts and policy makers rested on two assumptions. First, that economic laws "are like the laws of engineering. One set of laws works everywhere."[5] Second, that imposing economic rationality would automatically remove the major social and cultural obstacles to reform, a point reinforced none-too-subtly by the distribution of assistance. During the 1990s less than 3 percent of U.S. government assistance to Russia was devoted to democracy assistance.[6] This overwhelming emphasis on first building up a new economic system was justified by arguing that, because the same incentives applied to both political and economic choice, free markets and private property were bound to create a demand for pluralistic political institutions, even where none had existed before.[7]

Although there were some critical rumblings about the damage that the Washington Consensus was causing in Latin America and Africa, it was not until the global economic collapse of 1998 that it came under heavy scrutiny.[8] It was revealed that, far from promoting economic stability, the Washington Consensus had resulted in the largest peacetime decline in living standards ever witnessed in Eastern Europe. Stiglitz notes that Russian industrial production between 1990 and 1999 fell by almost 60 percent. By comparison, during the Second World War the USSR's industrial production fell by only 24 percent.[9] In less than ten years the number of Russians living in poverty—a rate of less than $4 a day—had gone from 2 percent to 40 percent.[10] Former proponents like Stiglitz noted with chagrin that the most successful countries during the 1990s had ignored the IMF's advice to implement marketization and had forged a social consensus *before* plunging into economic reforms.[11]

Similar issues plagued the development of democratic institutions. The USAID approach to democracy, as Thomas Carothers describes it, was to break everything down into "quantifiable bits to fit numerically based systems of evaluation."[12] This one-size-fits-all approach led to the imposition of inflexible bureaucratic guidelines, failure to cede control of democracy initiatives to local organizers, and the setting of priorities in Washington without regard to local needs.[13] Not surprisingly, in *every* country of Eastern Europe and the CIS, direct foreign assistance resulted in weaker ties between civic institutions and society and greater dependence on foreign support.[14] The only exceptions were groups whose basic function was to deliver social services.[15] By the end of the 1990s many analysts and politicians were asking who had "lost Russia." While some blamed misguided IMF policies, most assigned the lion's share of the blame to the usual suspect—Russia's lack of democratic traditions.[16]

The ensuing disappointment has led to recommendations that the West rethink its whole assistance strategy and lower its expectations for democracy around the world. Marina Ottaway and Theresa Chung, for example, have argued that democratic institutions may simply be too expensive for many nations.[17] Promoting less costly electoral processes and "bottom up" development can help a bit, they say, but the sad truth is that most nations are not really transitioning to democracy at all. They are stuck in a "gray zone," a sort of democratic purgatory from which they may never emerge.[18]

The critics are right to fault the extravagance and "supply-driven" nature of many democratic assistance programs being peddled today, but they are wrong to conclude that the main obstacles to democracy are either fiscal or cultural. Such pessimism derives from the questionable assumption that all nations must follow a single script for democratic development or else fail, an assumption deeply rooted in the Washington Consensus approach to development.

Novgorod's success during this same decade shows just how unwarranted pessimism is. Instead of *lowering our expectations* about democratic transition, we should be *broadening our understanding* of how localities adopt new democratic values and institutions. The reason so many democratic transitions fail is not because they are too costly but because new regimes rarely spend the time needed to place new institutions and policies into a cultural context that can lower public resistance to reforms.

Indeed, it is a hallmark of the Washington Consensus to claim that the cultural context is irrelevant.[19]

A symbolist approach to political change, however, would argue that Russian democracy remains in the doldrums precisely because national elites have brushed aside Russian history and culture, and thus failed to construct a post-Soviet myth capable of easing the trauma of transition. Novgorod's successful transition reveals the power of democratic myth-making. We can gain even further insight into what makes democratic transitions succeed by contrasting the failure of the nationally touted Russian Idea to the success of such regional ideas as the Novgorod Myth.

THE RUSSIAN IDEA VERSUS REGIONAL MYTHS

Surveys show that Russians are undergoing a severe identity crisis, the result of a sudden loss of faith in the ideals of the Soviet era and a prolonged failure to embrace alternatives to those ideals. People's nostalgia for the past, as sociologist Yuri Levada points out, does not reflect a desire to restore the Soviet system. Rather, it is the direct result of the absence of symbols that would allow people to envision a future different from the past they have known.[20]

Shortly after his reelection in 1996, Russian President Boris Yeltsin suggested that a new ideology, a "Russian Idea," might serve as a guide to that future.[21] His efforts were sharply criticized by those who feared that, however well-intentioned, state sponsorship of any national idea would eventually lead to the suppression of dissident views.

Despite the scorn heaped on the government's efforts, however, public opinion polls showed widespread support for a unifying national idea, as well as considerable agreement on its main components. A 1997 nationwide survey indicated that the top three values people agreed on were: (1) that Russia must be a state that ensures the growing prosperity of its citizens; (2) that Russia must be a state with a market economy where democratic freedoms and human rights are observed; and (3) that Russia must be a multiethnic state where all people enjoy equal rights.[22] This consensus cuts across the political spectrum and is equally strong among highly educated city dwellers as it is among poorly educated villagers. It is as popular among Great Russians as it is among members of other ethnic groups.[23]

These results, which have held up in a number of subsequent national surveys, suggest that the populace is far less polarized about the essential meaning of the Russian Idea than the elites who are constantly debating it. This explains why politicians keep returning to the concept, and why Vladimir Putin wasted no time in giving us his own version of it—"an organic unification of universal general humanitarian values with traditional Russian values that have withstood the test of time"—as soon as he was designated Yeltsin's successor.[24]

Yet, despite prominent government backing and more than two thousand articles written on the subject, state-sponsored efforts to forge a Russian Idea have failed miserably, mired in power struggles or buried under so many qualifications that no strategic choices are ever made.[25] A typical example of such pseudo consensus building is Moscow Mayor Yuri Luzhkov's proposal to simultaneously erect statues of Tsar Alexander II, liberator of the serfs, and Felix Dzerzhinky, the first head of the Soviet secret police.[26]

Frustrated with these repeated failures, local elites have tried their hand at forging regional versions of the Russia Idea, a process that Novosibirsk-based analyst Sergei Moiseyev aptly calls "regional-level nation building."[27] One region that has approached the task of building consensus very systematically is Tomsk. There, a group of scholars, with the support of the local governor and Moscow foundations, is seeking to identify the values that are most conducive to social consensus in today's Russia through an intensive study of the Tomsk Region. They call this ambitious project the "Tomsk Initiative."

The problem with such efforts in the past, say the Tomsk researchers, is that they were based on forcing Russians to adopt preexisting developmental models. Instead, the Tomsk researchers propose studying the behavioral stereotypes, values, myths, and symbols of the new social constituencies that have arisen since 1990 to identify the values and behavioral patterns that are most conducive to the formation of stable group identities and thus ultimately to a new Russian national identity. The Tomsk region, say the scholars, is ideal for this task because it is a cross-section of typical Russian values and behavior.[28]

Politically, this project is noteworthy because it is headed by Professor Nelli S. Krechetova, a political advisor to the governor of Tomsk Region and head of the local liberal party, Union of Right Forces, or the SPS. She makes no secret of the fact that the information derived from their surveys is meant to guide policy choices in Tomsk.[29] But the Tomsk Initiative, while intriguing, suffers from many conceptual flaws. First, it is really a national agenda in regional disguise. The value of the research is said to lie in the degree to which it can help forge a Russian national consensus. As a result, purely local symbols and myths disappear from the radar screen.

Second, the Tomsk Initiative can be more aptly characterized as a nation-building effort rather than part of a democratization process. It attempts to identify the carriers of new social values and, as the researchers have candidly said, to promote a domestic version of the

"Protestant ethic."[30] It is essentially an elitist approach that seeks to identify a new vanguard of society. Significantly, despite noting the "triumph" of liberal myths in Russia, the Tomsk researchers remain highly skeptical about whether Russians actually have the cultural resources to implement these myths.[31]

Finally, while the Tomsk researchers acknowledge the power of myths to shape reality, they interpret this power very narrowly. Myths and symbols are studied to understand how they are formed and how they prevent change, but they are not linked to actual policy in any meaningful way.[32]

The contrast between the Tomsk Initiative, the Russian Idea, and other regional mythmaking efforts discussed in the previous chapter gives us a good idea of what works and what doesn't when crafting a democratic myth. National efforts failed because they were undertaken *ab novo*, as if in a historical vacuum. The most successful regional efforts, by contrast, focused on linking local government policies to key symbols from Russia's past, carefully making the case that that past is more than just the USSR.

Too often national efforts have been shrouded in secrecy and the results announced as if they were a mandate from heaven.[33] Successful regional efforts, however, are more like public relations campaigns. Secrecy defeats the purpose, which is to forge a link in the voter's mind between current policies and popular symbols of the past. By trying to be all things to all people all of the time, national efforts have produced a confusing and uninspiring jumble of images. Successful regional efforts, by contrast, target and promote selected solutions from a limited local repertoire. This creates a clear strategic vision that appeals to voters.

Finally, whereas national efforts have revolved around changing institutions without changing values, successful regional efforts tend to graft new ideas onto traditional institutions. The former creates the semblance of change without its substance; the latter creates a vested interest in reform among both the local elite and populace.

Regional myths allow local elites to manage the process of transition more effectively. They provide a framework within which people can find solutions to the problems of modernization without turning their backs on their own history and traditions. By easing the shock of cultural discontinuity, regional myths broaden the social constituency in favor of reforms and increase the level of confidence in local government.

The Novgorod Myth did this by evoking the specific images of Novgorod's past that provided Russian solutions to the challenges of modernity. It contrasted Novgorod's federalist heritage to Moscow's history of political and economic centralization, to evoke a Russian framework for center-periphery relations that corresponded to modern feder-alism. It emphasized Novgorod's ancient economic and political ties with the West to evoke a pro-Western mindset in the region. In sum, the Novgorod Myth worked because it gave people the opportunity to envi-sion a modern Russian polity that is comfortable with its past, rather than forcing Russians to choose between modernity and tradition. Any region, in any country, can do the same.

WHAT SYMBOLS CAN DO FOR DEMOCRATIC DEVELOPMENT

Tracing the emergence of regional myths has revealed two important things about the relationship of myths and symbols to democratic devel-opment. First, however propitious local myths may be, to realize their political potential they must be linked to a corresponding policy agenda by local elites. Second, it is far easier to achieve such a linkage at the subnational level because elites at that level are more homogeneous and the pool of key symbols is smaller. This suggests that differences in historical tradition, geography, and the quality of political leadership may be less important to the success of early democratic consolidation than the *process* by which elites forge a new social consensus. At the heart of that process lies the effective linkage of key symbols of the past to a new social agenda.

Symbols promote democratic consolidation because they provide a shortcut for emerging from formlessness.[34] The shortcuts that best fit our cultural self-image are the easiest to accept, while those we deem foreign are typically rejected.[35] The fact that the same handful of key symbols keep resurfacing during periods of formlessness suggests that core political legitimacy rests on a fairly small group of symbols that epitomize the myth.

The political struggles of early democratic transitions can thus be said to center around elite efforts to recode key symbols to their political advantage. At the same time, however, it is important to understand that, because key symbols have core meanings that change very little over time, they are *not* infinitely malleable. Their political interpretation and usage must always be plausibly linked to the core meaning. Well-crafted policies build political consensus by relying on appropriate and internally consis-tent symbols *and* by avoiding jarring symbols. Savvy political leaders will test their interpretation of symbols and, if they do not work, abandon them as quickly as possible.

When key symbols match new policies in ways that appear to preserve cultural continuity, they facilitate the acceptance of new realities and new policy solutions by casting them in a familiar light. Sociologist Ann Swidler calls this "cultural recoding." Movements for social change typically use such recoding to undermine existing cultural codes and pave the way for new ones.[36] As a result, what political culture theorists see as highly unlikely—a rapid change of fundamental cultural values—social movement theorists regard as rather commonplace: a reinterpretation of symbols that allows citizens to make sense of new situations.

Part of the confusion over the role that symbols play arises from the apparent contradiction of asserting that symbols are multivalent and ambiguous, allowing individuals to interpret events and images differently, and yet that they also provide a "socially shared coding system" that facilitates cultural and social integration.[37] How can symbols do both?

The contradiction is resolved when one realizes that, to be effective, symbols need to maintain their historical and internal consistency. The meaning of long-standing key symbols can vary little because they are established by generations of consensus. Current interpretations must therefore be linked to this consensus in a plausible way, or they will be rejected. It is this stability and durability that gives key symbols the power to transcend formlessness and reconstitute social consensus. Symbols are thus ambiguous only within the parameters set by cultural tradition and plausibility. As Roger Cobb and Charles Elder put it, symbols "index" cultural premises and prescriptions, creating expectations that limit the possibility of symbolic manipulation.[38]

The coinage of new currency illustrates how this process works. The symbols chosen for currency are meant to convey longevity, reliability, and to reinforce confidence in what are, after all, merely pieces of paper. That is why the U.S. Treasury did considerable research on the appropriate symbols to use on new Iraqi bank notes, considering, among other images, that of Hammurabi.[39]

In Iraq, as in Russia, the inherited culture broadly determines which symbols are available for political use, but because there are so many symbols to choose from, it cannot act as a constraint on policy options. Specific symbols, not culture, are the filters that constrain policy because of the psychological imperative for cognitive consistency among images. In the hands of government leaders aware of their power, therefore, symbols become policy markers capable of identifying the agenda of political leaders and the direction of change.

Understanding how symbols overcome formlessness allows us to overcome a dichotomy that has plagued development studies for more than two generations. Observing development projects during the 1960s, Albert O. Hirschman identified two favored approaches, "trait-taking" and "trait-making."[40] The former takes local cultural attitudes as given and tries to work around them, while the latter works to change those attitudes. No matter which approach one took, however, Hirschman believed there was no escaping the criticism of cultural imperialism, a conundrum that led many to view culture as an impractical tool for development.

The multivalent nature of symbols, however, allows them to reconcile key needs of both. The same symbols can serve to reassure those wary of reforms that changes will be gradual and in keeping with traditional values (trait-takers), while at the same time reassuring those eager for reform that the agenda is indeed one of change (trait-makers). This is why one of the most successful strategies for overcoming formlessness is recasting current challenges as ones the polity has successfully dealt with in the past. The accumulated wisdom of the past is thereby validated, even as it is being reinterpreted to serve a new purpose.

In chapter 4 I asked whether rapid social and political change might ever be possible and found that it was indeed theoretically conceivable. Now I can describe the optimal conditions for it. First, political and social turmoil must be of a sufficient magnitude to break down the symbolic coherence of the reigning ideology and undermine the validity of the symbols associated with existing institutions. This results in formlessness, an uncomfortable condition to which individuals respond by seeking social stability and the reassurance of traditional values.

But this is now also an environment in which old symbolic associations no longer serve and new institutions do not yet have credibility, so the popular demand for stability leads elites to recode old symbols in ways that serve new political agendas. Those elites that can offer the most plausible merger of old symbols and new agendas gain in popularity, while those that cannot lose it. Old institutions, moreover, should never be simply discarded. For transitions to occur quickly and smoothly they must be recoded with "new" cultural archetypes that are no less comforting than the previous ones. This sort of recoding allows institutions to serve new functions while benefiting from established cultural paradigms, thereby significantly reducing the effort that government must expend to legitimize new policies and institutions to the public.

The successful management of change thus depends very largely on how well elites can knit together old symbols and new policies so that they appear to fit together seamlessly. This suggests that development practitioners looking to promote democratic consolidation should do so by trying to identify which symbols in the target culture have the ability to do this. This is known as conducting a cultural audit.

THE CULTURAL AUDIT

Taking symbols into account when planning democratic assistance may sound simple, but it is a radical departure from current practices and training. Instead of emphasizing new democratic institutions that, like beachheads in enemy territory, are meant to overcome the resistance of traditional culture, it would mean treating traditional culture, and even some popular institutions of the old regime, as potential allies of democracy, placing greater value on how symbolic continuities can reduce popular political disorientation.

Introducing symbols into the equation would also force analysts to more clearly differentiate among the various phases of democratization and to apply the appropriate tool to each one. Symbols ought to play the leading role in moving a society from democratic transition to democratic consolidation, because they can most effectively bring to an end the central impediment to a new social consensus—formlessness. Once democratic consolidation is well underway, however, the focus should shift to strengthening institutions. The Washington Consensus approach of focusing on institution building before proper attention is paid to shoring up symbolic support for them puts the cart before the horse.

The key to early democratic consolidation rests, as we have seen, on the ability of elites to provide symbols that allow people to transfer as much legitimacy as possible from old institutions to the new ones. Confidence in a new institution obviously cannot derive from the institution itself, because it has not yet had time to prove itself. The transfer of legitimacy in people's minds, therefore, actually takes place *before* new institutions are fully established and functional. The process of building confidence in new institutions is quintessentially an effort to instill confidence in institutions that have not yet earned that confidence.

This paradox highlights a crucial flaw in development strategies that prioritize institution building as a first step—the failure to recognize that it is not an institution's ability to provide goods and services that assuages people's fears about the future but people's belief in the as yet unfulfilled promise of the institution to do so. At its very earliest stages, democratization is mostly about shoring up that belief, and the best tool for promoting belief is an appropriate symbol rooted in a familiar myth. Unfortunately, while aid agencies and governments spend large sums of money on establishing new institutions, they spend very little to make sure that there is a cultural environment in which they can operate. This is like trying to erect a building without first checking to see if the soil can support it. Rapid democratic development is encouraged by establishing a receptive environment for change *before* building new institutions.

Our earlier discussion of regional myths shows that it is far easier to build a receptive cultural environment for reform regionally than nationally. Regions are therefore where the lion's share of resources for democratic assistance should be going. Democratic assistance strategies that build on local myths and employ key symbols of regional success will not only hasten the formation of a receptive cultural environment but they will also help specific reform initiatives adapt more quickly to local needs.

How might a symbolic approach to democratic development be implemented? Let us assume that the essential elements of democratic transition have occurred. The old regime has been repudiated and a new political leadership, ostensibly committed to democratic rule, has emerged and is seeking domestic and international support. The most urgent task facing such a regime is to transform the popular good will that brought it to power into a stable base of political support that will allow it to pursue new policies. This can be accomplished most rapidly by linking the new regime's agenda to familiar and respected key cultural symbols.

As a first step, senior government officials should clarify the political objectives of the administration, specifying the nature of the transformations they wish to achieve, and what new policies and institutions are needed to achieve them. This task is typically assigned to policy planning (or strategic planning) staffs. Once the strategic objectives and policy priorities are defined, in symbolic development a second group enters the picture, consisting of experts on regional culture—cultural and literary historians, anthropologists, and ethnographers. Their task would be to identify the key democratic myths in the local culture and the symbols that can best frame the policies the government wishes to put forward. In the course of examining different symbolic options, public hearings on the relevance of the past to the present would be a useful way to assess public reaction to the proposed symbolic linkages. Once the appropriate symbols are attached to specific policies and all symbols integrated into a comprehensive political framework, the government has achieved a consistent political message that should be attached to all public initiatives.

Properly conducted, such a "cultural audit" can assist democratization in several ways.[41] First, it would encourage a healthy conservatism in the new political elite, which, given its recent triumph over the old elite, is only too eager to push for radical changes. Ideally, the cultural experts engaged by the government should be in a position to raise red flags about policy initiatives that cannot be framed effectively by any key regional symbol, or when such symbols strike a discordant note within the overall political agenda. Persisting with such policies or symbols, they should point out, is likely to evoke a similarly equivocal public response.

Second, it would help to create a common bond between civil servants and citizens. A certain amount of nativism lies at the heart of both civic pride and civic activism, hence government efforts to promote what has worked in the past simultaneously serve to make civil servants more knowledgeable administrators and local residents better citizens. Tapping into this reservoir of public support would also help newly emerging elites appreciate the social value of the institutions left over from the old regime, which often retain a strong residue of popular support even when the ideals of the old regime do not.

Such institutions can be divided into three categories. First, there are those that reconcile new agendas and old archetypes fairly easily because they are apolitical. This includes many essential service providers, such as the post office and pension administration. Such institutions tend to retain their social standing and usefulness even during the most tumultuous political transformations. It would be wise of governments to expedite the recoding of the symbols associated with such institutions, since it costs little and the gains in political capital are great.

Second, there are those institutions that do more harm than good to democratic consolidation because they resist easy recoding and actively oppose the current social agenda of society (in Russia the Communist Party is an example). Although such institutions are often seen as a convenient target by new regimes which fear the restoration of the past, the massive investment of resources needed to recode them generally makes such efforts not very worthwhile, particularly if recoding is already proceeding in the socially useful areas mentioned above.

Finally, there are the institutions that do not yet exist but which must be created for democracy to thrive. Here, every effort should be made to match cultural archetypes to the new needs of society. A good example of an institution that would benefit from such an approach is the jury trial system currently being introduced throughout Russia. The fact that pre-revolutionary Russia was one the first countries in Europe to have an extensive jury trial system could be used very effectively to support its introduction today. Western development analysts have the most to offer here, because they can identify the Western institutional models that form the best match with regional values.

To sum up, regional government can accelerate the process of social change at the very outset by: (1) consciously linking successful symbols from the past to present-day policies; (2) promoting reinforcing archetypes and symbols in the media, thereby providing a deeper and more receptive cultural context for reforms; and (3) prioritizing support to those institutions that operate along the patterns of recoded archetypes. By consciously linking symbols to policy initiatives, local governments can ensure a degree of control over the content and management of symbols within the limits of popular interpretation. This allows governments to more easily identify sources of tension, and by co-opting or adapting to them, forge greater public support for new policies.

There is one other important benefit to conducting a cultural audit. Instead of providing aid to suit the priorities of Western donors—which, as we have seen, only increases the dependence of elites on foreign support and distances government from the populace—the primary focus would now be on local cultural traditions, thereby strengthening the bond between the new elite and the populace, and providing a more supportive cultural context for government policies.

Given these advantages, I believe most development assistance in the democratic transition period should be shifted from institution building to the recoding of symbols. Harnessing symbols to democratic development will free up resources that governments would otherwise have to devote to easing the shock of cultural discontinuity and enable them to create new institutions more rapidly. It promotes a greater level of comfort with change among the population, and affords an easier acceptance of new values and institutions among the populace. Ultimately, the better the match between local symbols and new policies, the lower the level of public resistance to new policies, and the more cumulative and stable social change will be.

The consequences of not harnessing the power of symbols during the critical, early phase of democratic transition can be dire. Just as political benefits derive from raising people's comfort level with reforms, there are political costs to lowering it. As Stiglitz puts it, "When there is a perception that reforms were imposed from outside, the reforms themselves become the subject of political debate, lessening their sustainability."[42] New governments that fail to frame their policies in a traditional context invariably find themselves devoting more and more resources to defending the changes they seek, rather than to implementing them.

TRAINING FOR A NEW TYPE OF DEVELOPMENT

Some might ask why Western assistance in symbolic development is even needed. Are not local scholars far better suited to identifying and interpreting the key symbols of their own culture? Generally speaking, yes, but there are other reasons, equally important, for involving Western scholars in the process of symbolic recoding.

Because the objective of symbolic development is to encourage popular acceptance of the social and institutional changes needed for democratic consolidation, a logical division of labor emerges. Local scholars are ideally suited to identifying the key symbols of the past that best match the policies needed today, while Western scholars are ideally suited to identifying the features in those symbols that are most compatible with Western institutions and perceptions. Combining these approaches can reveal insights into local behavior and customs that local scholars may have overlooked, while at the same time showing local reformers how their efforts can be placed in a cultural and institutional context that Westerners can understand and support.

The most important thing in this collaboration is that Western experts involved in a cultural audit adhere to the same general rule that guides the entire process of symbolic development—that they work with, rather than against, local cultural traditions. Such a commitment quickly diminishes both concerns of ethnocentrism and fears of cultural imperialism. It has also been my experience that critiques of native cultural traditions voiced within such a constructive framework of dialogue are generally seen as helpful because they imply a respect for local traditions. The very fact that the task of development is no longer defined as making sure "the past is past, irrelevant, and obsolete" makes it far easier to swallow.[43] Last, but not least, encouraging Western experts to look for development solutions that are tailored to specific cultural traditions would restrain the impulse of Western financial and governmental institutions to exert tutelage over the process, and encourage the far healthier view of democratic development as a partnership.

Because such a view is still very far from the norm, the propagation of symbolic development will require a very different sort of training from what development specialists currently receive. Such training would complement the existing focus of public affairs programs on economics and institutions with courses that draw attention to the symbolic resources that cultures have to offer. This might involve a sequence of seminars that examine how symbols and myths have been used to promote social change (as social movement theorists do), and then explore their role as agents of social stability. Through case studies, students could explore the comparable functions of different symbols and myths in a wide variety of settings, highlighting their power to transform social discourse, while also raising critical questions about their transferability to other situations.

The purpose of such training should be to prepare students to recognize the key democratic symbols of a given culture, to describe the benefits of using symbols to build social consensus, and to identify the specific policy areas where they might be applied to promote social change. Finally, students should also be able to discern which conditions lend themselves to the use of symbols for democratic development, and which do not. Preliminary evidence suggests that symbols and myths are most effective in assisting societies to move through democratic transition more rapidly and into the early phases of democratic consolidation. As regimes become more settled, and the anxiety generated by formlessness recedes, people develop greater confidence in their institutions, which then become the primary guarantors of further democratic development.

That is why, in training for democratic development, I would focus a good deal of attention on how symbols and institutions interact. Both are important to democratic development because they represent the different tools appropriate to the different stages of such development. Without symbols to generate a supportive cultural context, institutions can fail to establish the connection with local traditions that generates a sense of legitimacy. Without further institutionalization, however, there is a danger that symbols will be used to confer legitimacy on a particular leader rather than on the democratic process, with the result that a change of leadership will resurrect feelings of insecurity and formlessness. Democratic development analysts and practitioners should be taught to identify the signs that tell us that the focus of assistance should be shifted from symbolic development to institution building.

This ties in directly with another problem noted by development analysts—the proper sequencing of democratic assistance.[44] This problem arises from viewing institutions as the exclusive agents of change, and dismissing culture as merely an impediment to change. Until we integrate cultural and area studies into our development training, so that we can figure out what each sequence should entail, calls for sequencing democratic assistance will yield very little.

What I propose, summarized in table 7.1, is much more than simply training analysts to be more sensitive to culture. Cultural sensitivity was much touted in the 1970s but is widely regarded as a failure today.[45] Some development analysts have even reached the conclusion that past cultural approaches failed because they were overly sensitive and avoided targeting the traditional values that were obstacles to change. As Robert Klitgaard puts it, this only led to a "new and somewhat more sophisticated set of rationalizations for giving up."[46]

One would be hard pressed, however, to argue that there has been a shortage of Third World leaders willing to run roughshod over native traditions in the name of development. At one point or another, nearly all embraced the view, most succinctly expressed by former Mozambican President Samora Machel, that "We must kill the tribe to build the nation."[47] If, as Lawrence E. Harrison argues, the statute of limitations on colonialism as an explanation for underdevelopment has lapsed, then it has just as surely lapsed for the notion that countries can achieve rapid development through a wholesale reconstruction of their values and institutions.[48]

Still, the idea that some cultures are so pathological that their core values simply need to be replaced seems to be the main lesson that some modern-day cultural analysts would have us glean from the failures of

TABLE 7.1
Two development paradigms

Cultural adjustment	Cultural congruence
1. Rapid social change is not possible. Early childhood socialization and the resistance of culture to change makes the re-examination of traditional values too painful;	1. Rapid social change is possible. When symbols are used to provide continuity, traditional values can be recoded and resistance to change is lowered;
2. Modernization therefore involves the rejection of traditional culture;	2. Modernization therefore involves adapting traditional culture to the needs of the present;
3. Highly centralized governments are better suited to modernization because they can use the power of the state to overcome the resistance of traditional cultural enclaves in society;	3. Locally decentralized governments are better suited to modernization because they can adapt more quickly to local needs and customs;
4. Rejecting traditional culture is painful but necessary for modernization. Development should focus on mechanisms and strategies that accomplish the transition from tradition to modernity as quickly as possible.	4. The pain of modernization is the key obstacle to its success. Development should focus on mechanisms and strategies that reduce the pain of the transition from tradition to modernity.
Premise: traditional culture is an enemy *Solution: people-changing and new institutions*	*Premise: traditional culture is an ally* *Solution: building consensus by redefining key symbols*

Third World development. The very survival of nations, they insist, demands replacing local cultural values with Western values of hard work, ethical norms, rule making, and respect for institutions.[49] Unfortunately, the fact that these positive Western values came along with the historical legacies of Western exploitation, colonialism, and racism has created enormous resistance to Western-inspired cultural change. As a result, proposals that sound quite benign, and are no doubt put forward with the best of intentions, become highly contentious when seen as proposals for a Western-style cultural transformation.[50]

Cultures with roots that go back thousands of years have outlasted most efforts to remake them. Such longevity suggests a remarkable level of adaptability to changing circumstances, something development analysts must learn to tap into. To do so, however, we must be willing to accept local culture as an ally of democracy. Rather than struggling against the cultural tide, analysts and practitioners should be looking for the eddies and currents in that tide that will allow political leaders to chart a course for democratic consolidation with minimal opposition. As the example of Novgorod shows, even the seemingly unlikeliest cultural environment holds ample symbolic resources for democratization. All one has to do is look for them.

OPPORTUNITIES AND PITFALLS

The pressing need to overcome formlessness has led Russian scholars to pay particular attention to the developmental potential of myths and culture. Their efforts provide valuable insights into the benefits and dangers posed by a cultural audit.

One of the most prominent of such scholars is Igor Chubais, the estranged older brother of political power broker Anatoly Chubais and a noted critic of government-sponsored efforts to promote a Russian national idea. The true challenge of the Russian Idea, says Chubais, is much larger than any government can imagine—it is to heal the "rift in time" that plagues Russian intellectual life by integrating the Soviet and pre-Soviet past. Only in this way can the continuity of Russia's historical path of development be restored.[51]

To do this the intellectual elite must provide a framework within which all of Russian history, not just its Soviet period, can be evaluated. This would force the different generations living today to engage in the dialogue they have so far assiduously avoided. It would also allow proponents of the Russian Idea, currently hijacked by Russian nationalists, a chance to reassert its liberal strands.[52] Chubais's efforts have resulted in several textbooks and a national curriculum that has been adopted experimentally in the armed forces.[53]

Two things that stand out about Chubais's approach are its positive evaluation of the democratic resources available in Russian culture and its encouragement of the broadest possible public discussion of the meaning of Russian historical values. He spends much of his time traveling around the country making speeches, gauging public response, and proposing regional curriculum reforms.[54] His approach to the Russian Idea, however, is tantamount to social reeducation. While valuable in the long run, it does little to help political leaders deal with the problem of democratic legitimacy today.

Another prominent advocate of the importance of myths and symbols in governance is liberal economist Valery Naishul. Well known as a free market economist and principal author of voucher privatization, Naishul has more recently argued that Russia needs to introduce "microarche-types" from preimperial Russia that provide concrete grassroots examples of sensible economic and political behavior. The search for such arche-types has led Naishul and a team of social scientists gathered around his National Institute for Economic Modeling to catalog and analyze Russian traditions and proverbs. In a manner very reminiscent of Swidler's cul-tural "toolkit" approach, Naishul argues that each person's stored arche-typal modes of behavior and beliefs serves as a cultural inheritance that they tap into during times of crisis. Even modes that have been dormant for centuries are part of that inheritance, and are subconsciously avail-able to us when we need them.[55]

The task before Russia today is therefore preeminently one of cultural enrichment, reactivating those dormant models of social discourse that value individual initiative. Both the Soviet and late tsarist regimes stressed state mobilization at the expense of the individual, says Naishul, but there are earlier periods of Russian history that did not. The language, con-cepts, and archetypes of those periods are what Russia needs today to transform social consciousness.

The lexicon of preimperial Russia differs so drastically from that of the Soviet era, says Naishul, that combining the two results in sharp cognitive dissonance (like the discomfort one might feel from hearing of a "Holy Russia Nuclear Regulatory Commission"). Reintroducing previous arche-types would therefore completely transform political discourse, which makes it an attractive, low-cost solution to the problem of political insta-bility. When resources are scarce, says Naishul, archetypes are like "free gas for the machine of state."[56]

Approaches to mythmaking like those of Naishul, Chubais, or the Tomsk Initiative described earlier all run into problems because they focus primarily on the national rather than the regional level, and because they do not fully appreciate the immediate role that symbols can play in anchoring democratic values in society. Moscow State University philoso-phy professor and political activist Alexei Kara-Murza, however, has devised a promising strategy for the use of symbols that addresses these issues.

Kara-Murza, too, recognizes that the main task facing Russian society is finding an appropriate national identity, but he believes this can be done by getting people to identify with Europe *through* Russia's own dem-ocratic heritage.[57] To accomplish this, he says, regional elites must "create a new gallery of Russian heroes" from local anti-Bolshevik and earlier historical figures. By responding in this way to people's natural desire to learn more about their own past, local elites will be creating the new cultural icons of a democratic Russia.[58]

Such icons, says Kara-Murza, are vitally important to a functioning democracy because they allow people to reconcile their ideals with their actions. While democratic symbols and rhetoric do not guarantee democracy, "there can be no democracy without well-developed democratic symbols" that both the state and society have a vested interest in supporting.[59] Every region, Kara-Murza contends, has some local heroes and legacies that can plausibly fit liberal democratic patterns. That is why, as soon as liberal ideals are matched to local traditions, one begins to see dramatic social changes. He points to regions such as Tver and Perm as proof that the process of reconnecting Russian and European liberalism can quickly lead to the creation of new liberal constituencies and a significant shift in local voting patterns.[60] In the Tver Region the Union of Right Forces claims as members two deputy governors, six members of the district government, and elected representatives to the federal, city, and regional dumas. In Perm, the SPS gathered 15.6 percent of the votes in the 1999 legislative elections, compared to less than 9 percent nationwide, and even in the disastrous December 2003 legislative elections got nearly 8.9 percent of the regional vote, compared to less than 4 percent nationwide.[61]

As a leading member of the SPS, Kara-Murza spends much of his time traveling around the country, combining historical lectures with regional party building. He claims that his approach leads to rapid results even in communist strongholds, and he points to the cities of Bryansk and Smolensk where SPS support has reached more than 12 percent. At an SPS meeting in another predominantly communist region, Kursk, he explained to local party faithful how this strategy works:

> Every region should feel the inspiration of its liberal democratic traditions—these were the explorers, the people who built Russia, the philanthropists, the enthusiasts, the intellectuals, the rural doctors and teachers. These traditions are everywhere, in Kursk as well. If we combine this tradition with the liberal idea, people will follow instantly. I've seen how this works in regions: it was enough to tell people that you are needed, that you are a part of this land (freedom must come from inside, it cannot be imported). It was enough to frame the issue in this way and instantly the whole atmosphere changes and people are drawn to you.[62]

Kara-Murza's approach is successful because it taps into three features that are crucial to the effective use of symbols for democratic development. First, he treats local history and culture as an ally. This allows him to see the symbols in it that are conducive to liberalism. Second, he understands that symbols are the enablers of new myths; they provide a bridge that allows people to link their popular images of the past to present-day policies. Finally, he appreciates that the identification and recoding of symbols is far easier to accomplish at the regional level, where the repertoire of symbols is smaller.

For some analysts, however, the potential of symbols to promote rapid democratization is overshadowed by the fear that they will be abused by elites. They regard symbols as part of the mechanism of deception that elites use to control society and prevent social change. Reliance on myths and symbols, they contend, inevitably leads to the degradation of politics.[63]

Among those who espouse this view in Russia is journalist and regional affairs specialist Ilya Malyakin.[64] Acknowledging that regional mythmaking is now commonplace in Russia, Malyakin worries that it serves only to build unrealistic expectations among the populace. When these expectations remain unfulfilled, as they must because regions do not have the resources to meet them, it leads to an even greater distrust of political authority. In their "deeply traumatized" state, people will then follow any new myth, thus perpetuating the cycle of "political infancy."[65]

Malyakin's dismal view of mythmaking assumes that symbols are just substitutes or filters for things that have "real" meaning, such as politics and history. In fact, however, symbols *are* the way in which we comprehend politics and history. It is not the political use of symbols per se that causes cultural trauma, but the attempt to use symbols in ways that are at odds with their core cultural values. It is therefore important to draw a distinction between symbols and myths that are properly coded and those that are not.

During times of social malaise it becomes especially tricky to argue for change, because the first impact of innovations is to undermine traditional patterns of behavior and increase uncertainty. The more rapid and dramatic the change, the higher the drain on public trust, and the more important it becomes to associate it with popular elements of the "stable past." Conversely, the more that innovation can be associated with elements of the "stable past," the greater the reservoir of trust that the administration can draw on in the implementation of change. Poorly recoded symbols are thus a source of social anxiety that, unresolved, can become a threat to the regime. A central function of a cultural audit should therefore be to alert political leaders to such potential symbolic conflicts. Properly coded symbols and myths can be essential tools for easing social tensions.[66]

Although myths and symbols can certainly be abused by political leaders, even greater dangers await governments that fail to properly channel the potential of cultural symbols and archetypes. When political symbols fail to serve their proper conciliatory function in society, it usually means that a fundamental rift has emerged between the elite and society that does not bode well for the regime. If the government cannot channel the meaning of symbols in ways that foster social stability, sooner or later some other group will begin to channel them to serve its own ambitions.

To avert such a danger, it is vital that the search for relevant cultural symbols be conducted as openly as possible, with public discussion of the findings of a cultural audit and frequent opportunities for outside input. A cultural audit is, at its root, nothing more than a rediscovery of the past put in the service of the present. This makes it fundamentally a process of historical and civic reengagement.

In the long run, a proper civic education rests on teaching every schoolchild how to conduct his or her own cultural audit. In this way, rather than being blown about by every new gust of populism, individuals would have the cultural and historical knowledge they need to determine how well a political candidate's program actually fits the cultural traditions of the region they seek to represent. This is not a bad way to evaluate developmental and democratic assistance programs either.

Without the proper cultural context, it is easy to confuse the unfamiliar with the improbable. What Thomas C. Schelling once wrote about the shortcomings of military planning succinctly captures why most analysts failed to recognize the emergence of democratic consolidation in Novgorod: "The contingency we have not considered seriously looks strange; what looks strange is thought improbable; what is improbable need not be considered seriously."[67]

The current study challenges the conventional wisdom about democratic development and asks us to consider the improbable. It finds that the particular genius of Novgorod's political leadership lay in its ability to recognize early on that a culturally receptive environment offered unique opportunities to pursue policy innovations, and that when key symbols of the past are linked to new policies the result is a deeper and broader level of social support for government policy. Symbols and myths thus hold the key to rapid social transformation, but to realize their potential, significant shifts need to occur in the way analysts think of early democratic development—a shift from national to local politics, a shift from viewing culture as an obstacle to viewing it as an ally, and a shift from the role of teacher to that of partner.

It is quite telling that many have likened development efforts to a doctor-patient relationship. But, just as we would not expect doctors to dispense medication without first making a careful diagnosis of the patient, development analysts should not be dispensing advice about democratization without first undertaking a cultural audit of the region.

Extending this analogy a bit further, not long ago doctors routinely prescribed antibiotics for even simple infections. Today, however, doctors more commonly rely on the natural healing power of the body whenever possible. Developmental studies should adopt a similar paradigm. We need to get beyond the view that hefty doses of Western cultural "antibiotics" are the only cure to underdevelopment and, instead, learn to respect the self-healing powers of culture. Three steps would help:

First, economic and political reforms should be seen as closely tied to a revitalized sense of local identity. Finding the appropriate historical reference point should be seen as the key to creating a framework receptive to change. This means that area and cultural studies must be at the very heart of our development training, to help guide practitioners in their choice of tools. A cultural focus is especially important early on, when the choice of symbols and myths that can best frame political options for the populace can make all the difference.

Second, we should recognize that, even in the absence of a national consensus, local governments and elites can forge common values and priorities for their communities. The key to success is minimizing the disruption of old institutions when they continue to serve public needs, while simultaneously embracing new institutions and values. This can be done by placing new institutions within the context of traditional cultural values, with the help of appropriate symbols.

Third, just as working within the context of local culture promotes democratization, ignoring local culture seriously undermines the prospects for democratic consolidation. Efforts to introduce democratic institutions and new economic incentives without first establishing a receptive cultural framework for them increases social tensions and diminishes political stability.

The Novgorod model of development suggests that even societies with little or no democratic tradition have the potential for rapid democratization. This potential can be unlocked by the astute use of key cultural symbols. Novgorod's success in an environment widely regarded as hostile to democracy and free markets provides a clear blueprint for how to transform the "burden of the past" into an ally for change—a guide to crafting democracy.

NOTES

INTRODUCTION

[1] On January 27, 1998, the city and regional dumas passed a resolution restoring Novgorod's previous historical name—Novgorod the Great.

[2] W. W. Lewis, "Russia's Survival of the Weakest," *Asian Wall Street Journal*, November 5, 1999.

[3] Andrei Lazarev, "Novgorodtsev zastavlyayut zhit po moskovskim pravilam," *Ekonomika i vremya*, July 15, 2002; Olga Kolotnecha, "Novgorodchina mozhet i budet sama sebya kormit," *Novgorodskie vedomosti*, June 14, 2000. The Novgorod regional administration maintains an archive of local newspapers, along with an extensive collection of Russian wire service, newspaper, and journal articles about the Novgorod region, on the Internet at http://niac.natm.ru. Unless otherwise noted, this site was my source for all Russian language publications and regional press releases.

[4] "O sotsialno-ekonomicheskom razvitii oblasti v 2001 godu" (January 29, 2002), and "O sotsialno-ekonomicheskoi situatsii oblasti v 2002 godu (po operativnym dannym)," January 30, 2003.

[5] "Gorodskaya Duma," *Novgorod*, April 4, 2002.

[6] Kira Kononovich and E. Yu. Naumova, *Informatsionnyi spravochnik NKO, obshchestvennye obedineniya, i nekommercheskie organizatsii: Veliky Novgorod i Novgorodskaya oblast* (Veliky Novgorod: Severo-zapadnyi tsentr obshchestvennogo razvitiya, 2001); Ludmilla Alekseyeva, "Tendentsii razvitiya nekommercheskogo sektora i budushchee resursnykh tsentrov," a paper presented at a national meeting of NGOs in Moscow (October 29, 1998), personal copy.

[7] Olga Kuznetsova, "Novgorodskaya i Pskovskaya oblasti: Ekonomicheskoe polozhenie i faktory razvitiya," *Voprosy ekonomiki* 10 (1998): 145.

CHAPTER 1. DEFINING DEMOCRACY

[1] Aristotle, *The Politics*, translated by T. A. Sinclair (Baltimore: Penguin, 1962), bk. iv, chap. 4; bk. vi, chaps. 1–4.

[2] Cited in Ian Shapiro, "Democratic Innovation," *World Politics* 46 (October 1993): 122.

[3] Seymour Martin Lipset, *Political Man: The Social Bases of Politics* (Baltimore: Johns Hopkins University Press, 1981), 27.

[4] Seymour Martin Lipset, "Some Social Requisites of Democracy," *American Political Science Review* 53 (March 1959): 56.

[5] Gary Marks, Larry Diamond, Adam Przeworski, and Samuel Huntington have all argued that a significant correlation exists between successful democratic transition and higher living standards. Gary Marks and Larry Diamond, in *Reexamining Democracy: Essays in Honor of Seymour Martin Lipset* (Newbury Park, Calif.: Sage, 1992), 6; Huntington cites Przeworski in Samuel Huntington, *The Third Wave* (Norman: University of Oklahoma Press, 1991), 61–66. Those who disagree include Robert Dahl, Dankart Rustow, and Max Weber. Robert Dahl, "Development and Democratic Culture," in *Consolidating the Third Wave Democracies*, ed. Larry Diamond et al. (Baltimore: Johns Hopkins University Press, 1997), 35; Dankart Rustow, "Transitions to Democracy: Toward a Dynamic Model," *Comparative Politics* 2 (1970): 337–64; and Max Weber in *Capitalist Development and Democracy*, ed. Dietrich Rueschemeyer et al. (Chicago: University of Chicago Press, 1992), 21.

[6] Robert Dahl, *Polyarchy: Participation and Opposition* (New Haven: Yale University Press, 1971); Robert D. Dahl, *A Preface to Democratic Theory* (Chicago: University of Chicago Press, 1956).

[7] Francis Fukuyama, "The End of History?" *National Interest* (Summer 1989): 3–35.

[8] David Collier and Steven Levitsky, "Democracy with Adjectives: Conceptual Innovation in Comparative Research," *World Politics* 49 (1997): 430–51.

[9] Richard Gunther et al., eds., *The Politics of Democratic Consolidation: Southern Europe in Comparative Perspective* (Baltimore: Johns Hopkins University Press, 1995), xii.

[10] Doh Chull Shin, "On the Third Wave of Democratization: A Synthesis and Evaluation of Recent Theory and Research," *World Politics* 47 (1994): 144.

[11] Scott Mainwaring et al., eds., *Issues in Democratic Consolidation: The New South American Democracies in Comparative Perspective* (Notre Dame, Ind.: University of Notre Dame Press, 1992), 3.

[12] Giuseppe Di Palma, *To Craft Democracies: An Essay on Democratic Transitions* (Berkeley: University of California Press, 1990), 109.

[13] Juan J. Linz and Alfred C. Stepan, *Problems of Democratic Transition and Consolidation: Southern Europe, South America, and Post-communist Europe* (Baltimore: Johns Hopkins University Press, 1996), 3.

[14] Larry J. Diamond, "Is the Third Wave Over?" *Journal of Democracy* 7, no. 3 (1996): 33; Michael McFaul, "The Perils of a Protracted Transition," *Journal of Democracy* 10, no. 2 (April 1999): 4–19.

[15] Guillermo O'Donnell, "On the State, Democratization, and Some Conceptual Problems: A Latin American View with Glances at Some Postcommunist Countries," *World Development* 21, no. 8 (1993): 1356.

[16] Guillermo O'Donnell, "Illusions about Consolidation," in *Consolidating the Third Wave Democracies*, ed. Diamond et al., 46.

[17] Viviane Brachet-Marquez, "Democratic Transition and Consolidation in Latin America: Steps toward a New Theory of Democratization," *Current Sociology* 45, no. 1 (1997): 32.

[18] Juan J. Linz, "Transitions to Democracy," *Washington Quarterly*, 13 (1990): 156.

[19] Diamond et al., *Consolidating the Third Wave Democracies*, xvii.

[20] Gunther et al., *Politics of Democratic Consolidation*, 79; Juan J. Linz and Alfred Stepan, "Toward Consolidated Democracies," *Journal of Democracy* 7, no. 2 (1996): 14–33.

[21] Philippe Schmitter, "Civil Society East and West," in *Consolidating the Third Wave Democracies*, ed. Diamond et al., 240–41. Robert Dahl cited by Diamond, *Consolidating the Third Wave Democracies*, xvii.

[22] Gunther et al., *Politics of Democratic Consolidation*, 15.

[23] Mark J. Gasiorowski and Timothy J. Power, "The Structural Determinants of Democratic Consolidation: Evidence from the Third World," *Comparative Political Studies* 31, no. 6 (December 1998): 745–46. In footnote 9 Gasiorowski cites Philippe Schmitter as finding that three legislative sessions may be considered an appropriate time frame for consolidation.

[24] Diamond, "Is the Third Wave Over?" 23.

[25] David G. Becker, "Latin America: Beyond 'Democratic Consolidation,'" *Journal of Democracy* 10, no. 2 (1999): 140.

[26] Gunther et al., *Politics of Democratic Consolidation*, 12–13.

[27] Samuel J. Valenzuela, "Democratic Consolidation in Post-transitional Settings: Notion, Process, and Facilitating Conditions," in *Issues in Democratic Consolidation*, ed. Mainwaring et al., 69.

[28] O'Donnell, "Illusions about Consolidation," 56.

[29] Gunther et al., *Politics of Democratic Consolidation*, 77, 259.

[30] Shapiro cited in M. Steven Fish, "Postcommunist Subversion," *Slavic Review* 58, no. 4 (1999): 815; John Higley and Richard Gunther, *Elites and Democratic Consolidation in Latin America and Southern Europe* (New York: Cambridge University Press, 1992), 339. See also Michael G. Burton and Jai P. Ryu, "South Korea's Elite Settlement and Democratic Consolidation," in *Classes and Elites in Democracy and Democratization*, ed. Eva Etzioni-Halevy (New York: Garland, 1997), 194.

[31] Gunther et al., *Politics of Democratic Consolidation*, 8.

[32] Richard Gunther et al., "O'Donnell's 'Illusions': A Rejoinder," *Journal of Democracy* 7, no. 4 (1996): 154–56.

[33] Andreas Schedler, "What Is Democratic Consolidation?" *Journal of Democracy* 9, no. 2 (1998): 101.

[34] John Mueller, "Democracy, Capitalism, and the End of Transition," in *Postcommunism: Four Perspectives*, ed. Michael Mandelbaum (New York: Council on Foreign Relations, 1996), 110.

[35] Di Palma, *To Craft Democracies*, 141.

[36] Walter A. McDougall, "On Creative Corruption," *FPRI Night Thoughts* 1, no. 6 (October 1999); Michael Scammell, "What's Good for the Mafia Is Good for Russia," *New York Times* (December 26, 1993), II-E; Mueller, "Democracy, Capitalism, and the End of Transition," 111.

[37] Fish, "Postcommunist Subversion," 816.

[38] Mueller, "Democracy, Capitalism, and the End of Transition," 112. William Reisinger discusses the wide range of findings for Russia in "Survey Research and Authority Patterns in Contemporary Russia," in *Can Democracy Take Root in Post-Soviet Russia? Explorations in State-Society Relations*, ed. Harry Eckstein et al. (Lanham, Md.: Rowman and Littlefield, 1998), 163–76.

[39] Robert J. Shiller, Maxim Boychko, and Vladimir Korobov, "Popular Attitudes toward Free Markets: The Soviet Union and the United States Compared," *American Economic Review* 81, no. 3 (June 1991): 385–400.

[40] Timothy J. Colton and Michael McFaul, "Are Russians Undemocratic?" *Post-Soviet Affairs* 18, no. 2 (April–June 2002): 91–121. An extensive, long-term monitoring study concluded in 2002 by the Institute of Philosophy found that "a new social order is taking root, in which Western liberal values are combined with the values traditional for a particular ethnic group—a kind of Russian liberalism of the East European type, markedly influenced by Orthodox culture and the personification of power." "Poll Reveals New Optimistic, Assertive Outlook among Russians," *Rossiyskaya gazeta*, January 9, 2003, cited in *Johnson's Russia List*, no. 7014, http://www.cdi.org/russia/johnson/.

[41] See Donna Bahry et al., "Tolerance, Transition, and Support for Civil Liberties in Russia," *Comparative Political Studies* 20 (August 1997): 484–510; and Donna Bahry, "Comrades into Citizens?" *Slavic Review* (Winter 1999): 846.

[42] A. I. Kolganov, "Russia: Consolidation of the National Consciousness," *Jamestown Foundation Prism* 6, no. 9, pt. 2 (September 2000), http://www.jamestown.org/pubs/view/pri_006_009_004.htm.

[43] Mueller, "Democracy, Capitalism, and the End of Transition," 116.

[44] Frederick D. Weil, "The Sources and Structure of Legitimation in Western Democracies: A Consolidated Model Tested with Time-Series Data in Six Countries since World War II," *American Sociological Review*, 54 (1989): 691; Mueller, "Democracy, Capitalism, and the End of Transition," 117.

[45] Dahl, "Development and Democratic Culture," 35; Max Weber in *Capitalist Development and Democracy*, ed. Rueschemeyer et al., 21.

[46] M. Steven Fish, "Democratization's Requisites: The Postcommunist Experience," *Post-Soviet Affairs* 14, no. 3: 232–33.

[47] Lipset, "Some Social Requisites of Democracy," 56; Adam Przeworski et al., "What Makes Democracies Endure?" in *Consolidating the Third Wave Democracies*, ed. Diamond et al., 297.

[48] Lawrence E. Harrison, "The Rich-Poor Gap: If Brazil Can Address It, U.S. Can and Should," *Christian Science Monitor*, January 13, 2003. In France, Israel, and Portugal the level of public discontent with income inequality rivals and sometimes exceeds that of many post-communist countries, including Russia. Marc Suhrcke, "Preference for Inequality: East vs. West" *Innocenti Working Paper* no. 89 (Florence: UNICEF Innocenti Research Center, 2001), http://www.unicef-icdc.org.

[49] Linz and Stepan, "Toward Consolidated Democracies," 19.

[50] While Linz and Stepan categorically reject the notion that their definitions of democratic consolidation are teleological, Schedler embraces it. Andreas Schedler, "What Is Democratic Consolidation?" *Journal of Democracy* 9, no. 2 (1998): 104.

[51] Terry D. Clark, *Beyond Post-Communist Studies: Political Science and the New Democracies of Europe* (Armonk, N.Y.: M. E. Sharpe, 2002), 55–57. James Manor points out alongside democratization, "Leaders in less developed countries, and especially in the development agencies that provided them with advisors . . . encouraged regimes to persist in the belief that they were better informed than ever before, and that they need not listen to or yield decision making power to local communities." James Manor, *The Political Economy of Democratic Decentralization: Directions in Development* (Washington, D.C.: World Bank, 1999), 25.

[52] Dahl, "Development and Democratic Culture," 36; Brachet-Marquez, "Democratic Transition and Consolidation in Latin America."

[53] Mainwaring et al., eds., *Issues in Democratic Consolidation*, 60.

[54] Lawrence Harrison and Samuel P. Huntington, eds., *Culture Matters: How Values Shape Human Progress* (New York: Basic Books, 2000).

[55] John Lloyd, "Who Lost Russia? The Russian Devolution," *New York Times Magazine* (August 18, 1999), 34–41, 52, 61, 64; the conventional wisdom is aptly summed up in the title of Jeffrey Tayler's article, "Russia Is Finished: The Unstoppable Descent of a Once Great Power into Social Catastrophe and Strategic Irrelevance." *Atlantic Monthly*, May 2001, http://www.theatlantic.com/issues/2001/05/tayler-p1.htm. This nihilistic attitude is appropriately skewered by Anatole Lieven, "Against Russophobia," *World Policy Journal* 17, no. 4 (Winter 2000/2001), cited in *Johnson's Russia List* #5109, http://www.cdi.org/russia/johnson/.

[56] Sergei Pletnev, "Regiony reshili udvoit VVP svoimi silami," *Strana.Ru* (October 16, 2003), http://www.strana.ru/text.stories/01/09/19/1588/196715.html; Vitaly Golovachev, "25 Russian Regions Extricate Themselves from Poverty," *Trud* (December 23, 2000), cited in *Johnson's Russia List* No. 5005, http://www.cdi.org/russia/johnson/; "Regional Data Depict Broad Russian Economic Expansion," *Jamestown Foundation Monitor* (February 27, 2001), cited in Johnson's Russia List No. 5123; "Mer Velikogo Novgoroda Aleksandr Korsunov: Lyudei ne obmanesh," *Pravda.Ru* (July 30, 2002), http://www.pravda.ru.

[57] Robert Dahl, for example, is lukewarm in his praise of decentralization to privately owned firms, fearing that it would diminish the public sphere. Cited in *Classes and Elites*, ed. Etzioni-Halevy, 272.

[58] Cited in Vladimir Shlapentokh et al., *From Submission to Rebellion: The Provinces versus the Center in Russia* (Boulder, Colo.: Westview Press, 1997), 10.

[59] Michael Keating, *State and Regional Nationalism: Territorial Politics and the European State* (London: Harvester Wheatsheaf, 1988), 22.

[60] Kevin Morgan, "Regional Regeneration in Britain: the Territorial Imperative and the Conservative State," *Political Studies* 33 (1985): 565. Apparently, none of the major works on democratic consolidation even mention decentralization or subsidiarity as criteria or conditions of liberal democracy (Becker, "Latin America," 142).

[61] A case in point is Harald Baldersheim et al., eds., *Local Democracy and the Processes of Transformation in East-Central Europe* (Boulder, Colo.: Westview, 1996).

[62] Robert Cottrell, "Central Planning," *Financial Times*, June 10, 2002.

[63] John Loewenhardt and Stephen White, "Beyond the Garden Ring: A Bibliography," mimeo, University of Glasgow (1999); Neil J. Melvin and Rosaria Puglisi in collaboration with the Institute for Humanities and Political Research (IGPI) in Moscow maintain

an excellent electronic bibliography on Russian regions at the website of the Leeds University Centre for Russian, Eurasian and Central European Studies at http://www.leeds.ac.uk/lucreces/.

[64] Clark, *Beyond Post-Communist Studies*, 56–57; Mary McAuley, "Politics, Economics, and Elite Realignment in Russia," *Soviet Economy* 8, no. 1 (January–March 1992): 76.

[65] Stephen Holmes, "Cultural Legacies or State Collapse? Probing the Postcommunist Dilemma," in *Postcommunism*, ed. Mandelbaum, 22–76.

[66] Aaron Wildavsky, "What Other Theory Would Be Expected to Answer Such Profound Questions? A Reply to Per Selle's Critique of Cultural Theory," *Scandinavian Political Studies* 14, no. 4 (1991): 358.

[67] Harry Eckstein, "A Culturalist Theory of Political Change," *American Political Science Review* 82, no. 3 (1988): 798.

[68] Ibid. Eckstein's remarks coincide with Becker's finding that in Latin America "by protecting certain liberties and sheltering democratic modes of social interaction, they [local governments] have helped keep alive the demand for liberal democracy at the center and preserve the social habits required to make it work. We need comparative research to learn why some systems of local government, despite their limited authority and straitened fiscal circumstances, are better able than others to retain a measure of autonomy and to continue to serve as training grounds for democracy." Becker, "Latin America," 148.

[69] Harry Eckstein, "Case Study and Theory in Political Science," in *Handbook of Political Science*, vol. 7, *Strategies of Inquiry*, ed. Fred I. Greenstein and Nelson W. Polsby (Reading, Mass.: Addison-Wesley, 1975).

[70] Ibid.

[71] Rueschemeyer et al., eds., *Capitalist Development and Democracy*, 35.

[72] "Even a few comparisons have a dramatic effect on disciplining explanatory accounts," says Rueschemeyer in ibid., 32–33.

[73] Margaret Levi, "A Model, A Method, and a Map: Rational Choice in Comparative and Historical Analysis," in *Comparative Politics: Rationality, Culture, and Structure*, ed. Mark I. Lichbach and Alan S. Zuckerman (Cambridge: Cambridge University Press, 1997), 29–31; Edgar Kiser and Margaret Levi, "Using Counterfactuals in Historical Analysis: Theories of Revolution," in *Counterfactual Thought Experiments in World Politics*, ed. Philip E. Tetlock and Aaron Belkin (Princeton, N.J.: Princeton University Press, 1996), 187–210.

[74] Laurence Whitehead, "The Drama of Democratization," *Journal of Democracy* 10, no. 4 (1999): 95.

[75] Eckstein, "Case Study and Theory," 113–23.

CHAPTER 2. DEMOCRATIC DEVELOPMENT IN RUSSIA

Epigraph source: Alexander Herzen. *Povesti. Byloe i Dumy. Stati* (Moscow: Olimp, 1999), 362.

[1] Harry Eckstein, "Russia and the Conditions of Democracy," in *Can Democracy Take Root in Post-Soviet Russia? Explorations in State-Society Relations*, eds. Harry Eckstein et al. (New York: Rowman and Littlefield, 1998), 349.

[2] Eckstein, "Russia and the Conditions of Democracy," 362.

[3] Ibid.

[4] Eckstein, "Russia and the Conditions of Democracy," 355–56; James March and Johan Olsen, "The New Institutionalism: Organizational Factors in Political Life," *American Political Science Review* 82, no. 3 (September 1984): 853–74.

[5] Eckstein, "Russia and the Conditions of Democracy," 362.

[6] Ibid., 363.

[7] Ibid.

[8] Richard Gunther et al., eds., *The Politics of Democratic Consolidation: Southern Europe in Comparative Perspective* (Baltimore: Johns Hopkins University Press, 1995), 79; Juan J. Linz and Alfred Stepan, "Toward Consolidated Democracies," *Journal of Democracy* 7, no. 2 (1996): 14–33.

[9] John Thornhill, "Investors Drawn to Local Dynamo," *Financial Times*, April 15, 1998, 9; Blair Ruble and Nancy Popson, "The Westernization of a Russian Province: The Case of Novgorod," *Post-Soviet Geography and Economics* 9, no. 8 (1998): 433–46; Merja Tekoniemi and Laura Solanko, "Novgorod and Pskov: Examples of How Economic Policy Can Influence Economic Development," *Review of Economies in Transition* (June 1998): 64–76.

[10] "Ustav Novgorodskoi oblasti," sec. 6, art. 45, pars. "g" and "d" in *Novgorodskaya oblastnaya Duma*, ed. Sergei Ivanov (Novgorod: Kirillitsa, 1995), 27.

[11] A. Chernakov, "Kto k nam s meshkom pridet, zdes ego i ostavit," *Ekspert* (May 17, 1997), 28–33.

[12] Ibid., 29.

[13] A. G. Voronin, "O sostoyanii i osnovnykh tendentsiyakh stanovleniya i razvitiya mestnogo samoupravlemiya v Rossiiskoi Federatsii," in *Mestnoe samoupravlenie v Rossii: Istoriya i sovremennost*, ed. B. N. Kovalyov (Novgorod: Novgorodskii gosudarstvennyi universitet im. Yaroslava Mudrogo i Administratsiya Goroda Novgoroda, 1997), 5.

[14] Ivanov, *Novgorodskaya oblastnaya Duma*, 65. Under Putin, Andreyeva notes, the Novgorod Duma has sent amendments to preserve what has already been accomplished. R. I. Gainutdinov and L. A. Gainutdinova, *Munitsipalnaya sluzhba: Sovremennoe sostoyanie i perspektivy* (St. Petersburg: VSR Ltd., 2001), 12.

[15] Gainutdinov and Gainutdinova, *Munitsipalnaya sluzhba*, 11.

[16] Chernakov, "Kto k nam s meshkom pridet," 28.

[17] Ivanov, *Novgorodskaya oblastnaya Duma*, 58, 168.

[18] Mikhail M. Prusak, "Mestnoe samoupravlenie v Novgorodskoi oblasti: Sostoyanie i perspektivy," paper delivered in St. Petersburg, Russia (February 12, 2002), personal copy, 12. Reported in *Kommersant*, February 22, 2002. My home state of Rhode Island, for example, is one of ten with no separation of powers clause in its constitution. L. Anderson, "Why the Struggle for Separation of Powers?" *Providence Journal*, January 26, 2003.

[19] When elites shift from clientelism to concertation, redistricting is often one of the mechanisms whereby this is accomplished. Simona Piattoni, "Can Politics Create Communities? Evidence from the Italian South," paper delivered at the annual meeting of the American Political Science Association, Boston, September 3–6, 1998.

[20] Interview with Anatoly Boitsev, chairman of Novgorod Regional Duma, Novgorod the Great, Russia, May 5, 2000; Vitaly Eryomin, "Kadry snova reshayut vse," in a special edition of *Rossiiskaya Federatsiya segodnya* "Molodost drevnego Novgoroda" (January 2002): 25–26.

[21] "O vremennom polozhenii i territorialno obshchestvennom samoupravlenii v gorode Novgorode," *Novgorod*, April 3, 1997, 8–9.

[22] Vladimir Shaikovsky, "Vperedi eshche dva goda," *Novgorod*, October 15, 1998, 3.

[23] Vasily Dubovsky, "Zhilye so znakom kachestva," *Novgorod*, March 14, 2002, 3.

[24] Vladimir Shaikovsky, "U menya 23 tysyach nachalnikov," *Novgorod*, August 12, 1999; Olga Paritskaya, "Ushedshii poezd ne vernut," *Novgorod*, August 30, 2001; Shaikovsky, "Vperedi eshche dva goda," 3.

[25] Vitaly Eryomin, "Obsuzhdenie budzheta—vkhod svobodnyi," in a special edition of *Rossiiskaya Federatsiya segodnya* "Molodost drevnego Novgoroda" (January 2002), 13.

[26] Alexander V. Korsunov, "Reforma mestnogo samoupravleniya: Shag k pravovomu gosudarstvu," in *Mestnoe samoupravlenie v Rossii*, ed. Kovalyov, 10.

[27] *Informatsionno-analiticheskie materialy po itogam raboty Novgorodskoi oblastnoi Dumy pervogo sozyva: S aprelya 1994 goda po oktyabr 1997 goda* (Novgorod: Novgorodskaya oblastnaya Duma, 1997), 65.

[28] Ivanov, *Novgorodskaya oblastnaya Duma*, 168.

[29] *Informatsionno-analiticheskie materialy*, 66.

[30] Evgeny Malkov, "Veto deputatov," *Novgorodskie vedomosti*, September 10, 2002.

[31] Sergei Fabrichnyi, "Razvitie mestnogo samoupravlenie na territorii Novgorodskoi oblasti," in *Zemstvo i vozrozhdenie ego kulturno-khozyaistvennykh traditsii*, ed. V. I. Romashova (Novgorod: Novgorodskaya oblastnaya nauchnaya biblioteka, 1996), 39.

[32] Prusak, "Mestnoe samoupravlenie," 14–15, 12; Ivan Generozov, "Novgorod ne khochet zaviset ot rossiiskogo budgeta," *Ekspert: Severo-Zapad*, October 1, 2001; Vitaly Eryomin, "Finansirovanie dolzhno byt podushevym in normativnym," in a special edition of *Rossiiskaya Federatsiya segodnya*, "Molodost drevnego Novgoroda" (January 2002), 15.

[33] Thus, even though the regional budget received only 69.6 percent of what it was owed by federal authorities in 1998, it transferred 81.4 percent of its resources to the districts. Olga Senatova and Andrei Yakurin, "Ekonomicheskoe i politicheskoe razvitie Novgorodskoi oblasti" (1999), a report commissioned by the Federal Institute for East European and International Studies (BIOst) in Germany, personal copy, p. 28.

[34] Prusak, "Mestnoe samoupravlenie," 5.

[35] The fund was distributed according to this formula: district revenues plus fund support equals mandatory budget articles. Elena Soldatova, "Nagruzka bolshe-muskulatura krepche?" *Munitsipalnaya vlast,* October 1, 1997, 38–39.

[36] Evgeny Malkov, "V interesakh vsekh Novgorodtsev," *Novgorodskie vedomosti,* January 10, 2004; Miles A. Pomper, "Economic Aid Goes Local: U.S. Puts Hope in Provincial Russian Governments Led by Market-Oriented Pragmatists," *Congressional Quarterly,* July 9, 1999.

[37] Fabrichnyi, "Razvitie mestnogo samoupravlenie," 38–40; "K voprosu o voprosakh," Novgorod news digest prepared by Vladimir Rusakov, February 18–24, 1998, http://www.novgorod.ru.

[38] Interview with Igor V. Verkhodanov, then chief aide to the chairman of the Novgorod Regional Duma, Novgorod the Great, Russia, May 24, 1999; Fabrichnyi, "Razvitie mestnogo samoupravlenie," p. 40.

[39] Eryomin, "Obsuzhdenie budzheta," 13.

[40] *Informatsionno-analiticheskie materialy,* 69.

[41] Eryomin, "Obsuzhdenie budzheta," 13; *Informatsionno-analiticheskie materialy,* 66.

[42] "Polozhenie o Novgorodskoi trekhstoronnei komissi po regulirovaniyu sotsialno-trudovykh otnoshenii" (October 20, 1995), personal copy received from the chairman of the Novgorod branch of the Federation of Trade Unions, Vladimir Fishin.

[43] Point No. 7, "Reglament raboty Novgorodskoi trekhstoronnei Kommissii po regulirovaniyu sotsialno-trudovykh otnoshenii," addendum to the "Polozhenie."

[44] Laura D. Edles, "Rethinking Democratic Transition: A Culturalist Critique of the Spanish Case," *Theory and Society* 24, no. 3 (1995): 357–58.

[45] Evgeny Malkov, "Samoe dorogoe-eto zhizn," *Novgorodskie vedomosti,* September 12, 2001; Ludmila Mitrofanova, "Sporili no soglasilis," *Novgorodskie vedomosti,* December 18, 2001.

[46] Laura D. Edles, *Symbol and Ritual in the New Spain: The Transition to Democracy after Franco* (Cambridge: Cambridge University Press, 1998), 101; Edles, "Rethinking Democratic Transition," 363.

[47] Vladimir Sokolov, "Radi sotsialnykh garantii," *Novgorod,* September 14, 2000.

[48] "Kto luchshe rabotaet, tot dolzhen luchshe zhit," *Novgorodskie vedomosti,* December 28, 2001; Vladimir Shaikovsky, "Sobranie Soyuza gorodov Sever-Zapada Rossii," *Novgorod,* March 4, 1999; Ludmila Mitrofanova, "Alexander Korsunov: 'Dlya normalnoi zhizni gorodu ne khvataet deneg, a regionu—polnomochii,'" *Novgorodskie vedomosti,* July 24, 2001; Vasily Krutikov, "Aleksandr Korsunov: Mestnaya vlast mezhdu molotom i nakovalnei," *Novgorod,* March 8, 2001.

[49] "Kakaya vlast," *Novgorod,* October 30, 1990, 2.

[50] Vasily Dubovsky, "Munitsipalitety: Za dialog s tsentrom," *Novgorod,* February 28, 2002, 3.

[51] Ibid.

[52] "Analiticheskaya zapiska ob itogakh sotsiologicheskogo issledovaniya sotsialno-ekonomicheskoi situatsii v Novgorodskoi oblasti v avguste–sentyabre 1998 goda," tables 2.7–2.9 (Veliky Novgorod: MNOU Dialog, 1998), personal copy.

[53] "Zhdem peremen k luchshemu," *Novgorod,* October 25, 2001, 1. There is also the election of Nikolai Bindyukov to a seat in the federal Duma, but this is based on his ranking in the CPRF national party list.

[54] On Prusak's ratings see "Izmenenie reiting doveriya k politicheskim deyatelyam zhitelei Novgorodskoi oblasti, iun 1995–yanvar 2000" (Veliky Novgorod: MNOU Dialog, 2000), personal copy. For other governors see "Svezhie reitingi: 'Edinaya Rossiya' padaet, SPS rastet," VTsIOM, April 26, 2002, http://www.polit.ru/documents/483733.html.

[55] "Regionalnye indeksy korruptsii," Transparency International–Russia and INDEM Fund, tables 6.1 and 7.1, October 9, 2002, http://www.anti-corr.ru/rating_regions.

[56] "Monitoring Novgorodskaya oblast, July 1997," commissioned by Sberbank of Novgorod (Veliky Novgorod: MNOU Dialog); "Monitoring Novgorodskaya oblast, July 1999" (Veliky Novgorod: MNOU Dialog), diagram 2.1; "Analiticheskaya zapiska ob itogakh," table 2.1.

[57] Results of a survey of 445 people (74 homeowners) in Novgorod the Great conducted by the Center for the Analysis of Realty Markets in Moscow. Vladimir Sokolov, "Rubl v eksperimente," *Novgorod*, September 16, 1999.

[58] Among the top ten regions in which support for Yeltsin in 1996 and for Putin in 2000 exceeded category expectations, Novgorod made the highest jump, from eighth place to fourth. Matthew Wyman, Stephen White, Ian McAllister, and Stephen Oates, "Regional Voting Patterns in Postcommunist Russia," paper presented at the Centre for Russian and East European Studies (CREES) annual conference, Cumberland Lodge, U.K., June 16–18, 2000.

[59] V. Izmailov, "Kurs: Na razvitie," *Novgorod*, February 13, 1997; Vitaly Eryomin, "Zontik dlya investora," in a special edition of *Rossiiskaya Federatsiya segodnya*, "Molodost drevnego Novgoroda," January 2002, 7–8.

[60] "Pervyi chudovsky 'inostranets,'" *Novgorodskie vedomosti*, October 30, 1999; A. Andreasyan, "Desyat let uspeshnoi raboty rossiisko-finskogo predpriyatiya 'Chudovo RVS,'" radio Golos Rossii, November 16, 2000.

[61] Andrei Chernakov citing Vasily Semyonov, head of the region's economic committee, "Kto k nam s meshkom pridet," 30. Semyonov prophetically noted that so far the Ministry of Finance had not paid attention to Novgorod because it was small, but "when the secretaries sitting in Ministry of Finance departments finally figure out what's going on here, they will arrange some sort of snag for us." In 2001 the ministry ruled that several innovative portions of the Novgorod tax vacation programs were illegal. Ibid., 33.

[62] Eryomin, "Obsuzhdenie budzheta," 13.

[63] L. Alieva and M. Omarov, "Nekotorye aspekty vneshneekonomicheskoi deyatelnosti Novgorodskogo regiona," *Upravlencheskoe konsultirovanie* (Veliky Novgorod: MNOU Dialog) 1 (1999): 10. Mikhail Skibar, "Ekonomicheskie reformy v Novgorodskoi oblasti," in *Promyshlennost Novgorodskoi oblasti, 2002* (Veliky Novgorod: Information Resources Fund "Kompass Nord-West," 2002), 44.

[64] Svetlana Kudryashova, "Arnold Shalmuev: 'Dobitsya uspekha mozhno tolko komandoi,'" *Novgorodskie vedomosti*, December 4, 2002.

[65] Ya. Rochkus and N. M. Zolin, "Razvitie mekhanizmov funktsionirovaniya zony ekonomicheskogo blagopriyatstvovaniya v Marevskom rayone," in *Osobennosti budzhetnogo upravleniya Novgorodskoi oblasti* (Novgorod: RAN, otdelenie ekonomiki, NovGU, administratsiya Novgorodskoi oblasti, 1998), 88.

[66] "V novyi god s novymi zakonami," *Novgorodskie vedomosti*, December 20, 2002.

[67] Lyudmila Timofeyeva, "Chto russkomu khorosho, to nemtsu khorosho tozhe," *Vremya-MN*, February 20, 2003.

[68] Senatova and Yakurin, "Ekonomicheskoe i politicheskoe razvitie Novgorodskoi oblasti," 18.

[69] Looking at data for 1996, Anders Aslund found that regional governments received over 60 percent of local taxes in such money surrogates. For local and district governments that figure was 43 percent. Anders Aslund, "Russia's Virtual Economy: A Comment," *Post-Soviet Geography and Economics* 40, no. 2 (1999): 100. In Novgorod, however, the picture for 1996 was quite different. Money revenues constituted 74.9 percent of taxes, while money surrogates constituted only 25.1 percent. Eighty percent of the local tax base is generated by enterprises that have received foreign investment. Data received from Igor V. Verkhodanov, then chief aide to the chairman of the Novgorod Regional Duma, Novgorod the Great, Russia, May 24, 1999.

[70] Interview with Valery I. Trofimov, then first deputy governor of the Novgorod Region, Novgorod the Great, Russia, April 10, 1997; Gainutdinov and Gainutdinova, *Munitsipalnaya sluzhba*, 14.

[71] To attract FDI to depressed districts, Novgorod offered guaranteed deferments not only on local taxes but also on the federal portion of the "extrabudgetary funds." These were compensated from a regional Investment Insurance Fund. Rochkus and Zolin, "Razvitie

mekhanizmov," 87; "Kontseptsiya sotsialno-ekonomicheskogo razvitiya oblasti na 2002 god," approved as regional law no. 13–03 (December 27, 2001).

[72] Olga Kolotnecha, "Novgorodchina mozhet i budet sama sebya kormit," *Novgorodskie vedomosti*, June 14, 2000; Generozov, "Novgorod ne khochet zaviset."

[73] Irina Kibina, "Federalism in the Russian Federation," report prepared for the law firm Steptoe & Johnson in Washington, D.C. (Summer 1999), 24–26, personal copy.

[74] Eryomin, "Kadry snova reshayut vse," 25–26.

[75] Eryomin, "Zontik dlya investora," 8.

[76] Valery Fadeev, "V Rossii nikogda ne otnimali dengi—otnimali zhizn," *Ekspert*, November 1, 1999. At the height of public anger at NATO over the bombing of Yugoslavia, Prusak remarked that "the communist slogan 'Today Yugoslavia—tomorrow Russia' doesn't attract followers here. People think to themselves: Why would NATO aim its rockets at the Novgorod Region when there is so much foreign capital invested here? Economics is more convincing than anti-Western propaganda." Mikhail Prusak, "Vkhodite—ser, gerr, mesye, sinyor!" *Novgorodskie vedomosti*, May 25, 1999.

[77] As Governor Prusak puts it, "When the issue concerns them, I can introduce economic proposals to the regional duma only if it is approved by the regional association of producers or the association of small businessmen . . . business is directly involved in both the preparation and adoption of decisions." Vladimir Zhovannik, "Nenuzhnyi progress: Unikalnyi opyt Novgoroda federalnuyu vlast ne interesuyet," *Ekspert* 29, no. 22 (December 25, 2000).

[78] "Nightly News" on the Novgorod public television station TVS, Veliky Novgorod (April 9, 2002); "Soobshechnie press-tsentra Novgorodskoi administratsii za 28.01.2004 v 13:09."

[79] "Soobshechnie press-tsentra Novgorodskoi administratsii za 12.03.2002 v 10:59."

[80] Prusak, "Mestnoe samoupravlenie," 11–12.

[81] "Soobshchenie press-tsentra Novgorodskoi administratsii za 16.10.2002"; "Kontseptsiya sotsialno-ekonomicheskogo razvitiya oblasti na 2002 god."

[82] Svetlana Shevlyagina and Marina Marinina, "Veter peremen na nive professii," *Novgorod*, June 7, 2001.

[83] Olga Kuznetsova, "Novgorodskaya i Pskovskaya oblasti: Ekonomicheskoe polozhenie i faktory razvitiya," *Voprosy ekonomiki* 10 (1998): 151–52.

[84] "Novgorod rasprodaet sobstvennost," *Delovoi Peterburg*, July 20, 2001.

[85] Ivan Generozov, "Platnye dorogi i besplatnye napravleniya," *Ekspert: Severo-Zapad*, November 5, 2001.

[86] Ivanov, *Novgorodskaya oblastnaya Duma*, 69.

[87] Evgeny Malkov, "Strategiya razvitiya," *Novgorodskie vedomosti*, December 29, 2000; Yuri Krasavin, "Mikhail Prusak: Rynok vsem dast shans,'" *Zemlya novgorodskaya*, June 12, 1992; Olga Kolotnecha, "Budzhetu vazhen kazhdyi rubl," *Novgorodskie vedomosti*, December 1, 2001; Valery Tagansky, "Malyi biznes dorogogo stoit," *Novgorod*, June 15, 2000.

[88] "Anvar Shamuzafarov o reforme zhilishchno-kommunalnogo khozyaistva," interviewed by Nikita Kirichenko on the Russian national television channel RTR for the program *Natsionalnyi dokhod*, May 26, 2001.

[89] Sergei Vetkin, "Pozvolte vam vyiti von!" *Novgorodskie vedomosti*, January 24, 2001; "Eto novoe slovo—'ipoteka,'" *Novgorod*, July 6, 2000.

[90] Viktor Troyanovsky, "Reforma ZhKKh po-Novgorodskii," *Itar-Tass*, July 12, 2001. Communal housing expenditures in the region are still substantial (22 percent of the consolidated budget for 2000), but this seems to be less the result of spiraling costs than of the administration's decision to provide more subsidies and to spend twice as much in preparation for winter. "Dopolnitelnye uslugi v ZhKKh," *Novgorod*, July 18, 2000. This is a very different situation from regions that have not yet seriously begun to address communal housing reform. For a comparison see "Stoimost ZhKU i ikh oplata naseleniem (na okt.)," *Ekonomika i zhizn*, December 18, 2000.

[91] Viktor Troyanovsky, "Novgorodskaya oblast stala 'pilotnym' regionom v strane po realizatsii novoi modeli priemnoi semyi," *Itar-Tass*, October 7, 2000; "Sankt-Peterburg: V Novgorodskoi obl. zavershilsya pervyi etap rossiisko-datskogo eksperimentalnogo proekta po sboru i pererabotke bytovogo i promyshlennogo musora," *RIA RosBiznesKonsalting*, August 29, 2000; Yulia Generozova, "NEFCO profinansiruet modernizatsiyu ZhKKh

Novgoroda," *Delovoi Peterburg*, November 2, 2001; "Operatisya 'Chistyi vozdukh.'" *Akkumulyator novostei*, April 28, 2001; Evgeny Malkov, "Molodym vezde u nas doroga," *Novgorodskie vedomosti*, February 19, 2002; Alexander Sergounin, "The External Relations of the Novgorod Region of the Russian Federation," *Kiel Peace Research Series (SCHIFF)* no. 60 (1999). Published by the Kiel Peace Research Institute, Kiel, Germany, 17–19.

[92] Christa Capozolla, "Assessment of Regional Investment Initiative in Russia: Summary Report—March 1999," prepared for the U.S. Department of State, personal copy.

[93] "Gorodskaya Duma," *Novgorod*, April 4, 2002.

[94] Eryomin, "Kadry snova reshayut vse," 25–26.

[95] "Mer Velikogo Novgoroda Aleksandr Korsunov: Lyudei ne obmanesh" *Pravda.ru* (July 30, 2002), http://www.pravda.ru.

[96] Kibina, "Federalism in the Russian Federation," 5.

[97] Andrew Jack, "The Power behind Russia's Top 100: Korkunov's Sweet Success," *Financial Times* (U.K.), April 2, 2003; Vlada Melkova, "Russian Middle Class Hits 25 Percent," *Russia Journal* (February 3–9, 2001), cited in *Johnson's Russia List* no. 5072, http://www.cdi.org/russia/johnson/.

[98] "Gorodskaya Duma," April 4, 2002; Vitaly Eryomin, "Stolp oblastnogo budzheta," in a special edition of *Rossiiskaya Federatsiya segodnya*, "Molodost drevnego Novgoroda," January 2002, 9; Antonina Smirnova, "Vremya otchityvatsya o dokhodakh," *Novgorod*, January 23, 2003.

[99] Yulia Generozova, "Plastik osvaivaet platezhi za elektroenergiyu," *Delovoi Peterburg*, May 26, 2003. The automobile figure for Novgorod comes from Mayor Nikolai Grazhdankin, quoted in Evgeny Malkov, "Mikhail Prusak: My slishkom dolgo shli na kompromis," *Novgorodskie vedomosti*, February 14, 2003. The figure for Russia comes from Maya Kulikova, "Byt neschastlivym nekrasivo," *Ogonyok* no. 26 (June 2002), http://www.ropnet.ru/ogonyok/win/200226/26-14-16.html.

[100] Olga Semyonova, "Ekonomika Novgoroda—stolitsa 'Mersedesov'?" *Novgorodskie vedomosti*, August 16, 2000.

[101] "Short Justification of the Novgorod Environmental Financing Strategy: Submitted to the Novgorod Oblast Administration," 9–10. A report prepared by the Danish Environmental Protection Agency and Danish Cooperation for Environment in Eastern Europe (2000), http://www.mst.dk/inter/pdf/Short%20justification%20of%20the%20Novgorod%20environmental%20financi_uk.pdf; Kudryashova, "Arnold Shalmuev," December 4, 2002.

[102] "Personal Savings Rise Quickly and without Risk," *RosBusinessConsulting*, August 20, 2003, cited in *Johnson's Russia List* no. 7297, http://www.cdi.org/russia/johnson/.

[103] Robert Cottrell, "The Mega-Mall Comes to Moscow," *Financial Times*, April 26, 2002.

[104] Vasily Dubovsky, "God finansovykh zabot," *Novgorod*, April 25, 2002, 3.

[105] From 3,613 in 1999 to 1,552 in 2001. "Naselenie Velikogo Novgoroda v tsifrakh i faktakh (zdravookhranenie i sotsialnaya zashchita)," a regional conference on social and medical services for the population, Novgorod the Great (March 6, 2002), personal copy.

[106] "Kto luchshe rabotaet," *Novgorodskie vedomosti*, December 28, 2001.

[107] According to the former mayor of Novgorod the Great, Alexander Korsunov, in 2002 the city handed over 82 percent of its revenues to the federal government. The chair of the region's finance committee, Elena Soldatova, contends that if the Ministry of Finance had not changed the rules midway through the game, Novgorod would have had a budget surplus of nearly 18 percent in 2002, instead of a looming budget deficit of 15 percent. Igor Svintsov, "Budzhetu prisvaivaetsya zvanie 'narodnyi,'" *Novgorodskie vedomosti*, April 19, 2002.

[108] Mikhail Prusak interviewed by Nikolai Svanidze on Russian national television channel RTR for the program *Pered zerkalom*, February 27, 2000.

[109] Robert D. Putnam, *Making Democracy Work* (Princeton, NJ: Princeton University Press, 1993), 175.

[110] Zhovannik, "Nenuzhnyi progress," http://wwwexpert.ru.

[111] Article 2.1, "Polozhenie ob oblastnoi obshchestvennoi palate," (August 29, 1994), received from Igor Verkhodanov, then aide to chairman of the Novgorod Regional Duma, personal copy.

[112] Roman Berger, "Das Wirtschaftswunder von Nowgorod," *Tages-Anzeiger* (Zurich), July 17, 2000, http://tages-anzeiger.ch/ta/genArtikel?ArtId=21899.

[113] Points 4, 4.7, and 7 amended *Reglament* pertaining to the social chamber, received from Igor Verkhodanov, aide to chairman of the Novgorod Regional Duma, personal copy.

[114] Evgeny Malkov, "Korotko obo vsem, no seryezno," *Novgorodskie vedomosti*, November 17, 1999. Ludmila Mitrofanova, "Predvybornaya khronika: O kompromatakh, publikatsiyakh, provokatsiyakh," *Novgorodskie vedomosti*, December 17, 1999. In another incident, Prusak was accused of publishing campaign materials in the local press. The electoral commission found, however, that he was doing so in his capacity as local head of the political party Nash Dom Rossiya [Our Home Is Russia], not as governor.

[115] In November 1999, for example, he was taken to task for allegedly having supported a third term for Yeltsin (Prusak claims he was misquoted). Another time, the governor was asked whether he would support a law on private land ownership like the one recently passed by the governor of Saratov (yes, but it would be meaningless in the absence of national legislation). Malkov, "Korotko obo vsem"; Ludmila Mitrofanova, "Partii ne dolzhny brat dengi u gosudarstva," *Novgorodskie vedomosti*, February 28, 2001.

[116] Irina Vinitskaya, "Negosudarstvennye organizatsii v politicheskom protsesse v Novgorodskoi oblasti," *CDC North-West*, April 8, 2001, http://www.ngosnews.ru/djst_pgs/002.htm; Igor B. Alexandrov, "Russia's 'Road Less Traveled': Novgorod Oblast Today," *Jamestown Foundation Prism* 3, no. 12, July 25, 1997, http://www.jamestown.org/pubs/view/pri_003_012_004.htm.

[117] Eryomin, "Zontik dlya investora," 7.

[118] Alexandrov, "Russia's 'Road Less Traveled.'"

[119] Aleksei Komarov, "My—instituty budushchei vlasti," *Novgorod*, November 4, 1999.

[120] "Oblastnoi zakon o sotsialnom partnerstve," #36-OD (January 27, 1998), personal copy; pt. 2, par. 3 "Polozhenie of Novgorodskoi trekhstoronnei kommisii."

[121] Roman Zolin, "Dengi gde-to est, ikh prosto ne mozhet ne byt," *Metsenat: Novye resursy*, no. 1 (February 1998): 3.

[122] Tatyana Shchipanova, "Na igle u zapadnykh fondov," *Nogorodskie vedomosti Plus*, February 5, 1999. Another twenty-nine thousand dollars were received from USIA under the "Linkages Program" between the city of Rochester and Novgorod the Great in 1998. Sergounin, "The External Relations of the Novgorod Region," 23.

[123] Shchipanova, "Na igle u zapadnykh fondov."

[124] Ibid.

[125] Natalya Dinello, "What's So Great about Novgorod-the-Great: Trisectoral Cooperation and Symbolic Management," (June 3, 2001), contract no. 814–25 by the National Council for Eurasian and East European Research (NCEEER), Washington, D.C., p. 24.

[126] Prusak, "Mestnoe samoupravlenie," 15.

[127] Roman Kononovich and E. Yu. Naumova, *Informatsionnyi spravochnik NKO, obshchestvennye obedineniya, i nekommercheskie organizatsii: Veliky Novgorod i Novgorodskaya oblast* (Veliky Novgorod: Severo-zapadnyi tsentr obshchestvennogo razvitiya, 2001), 5.

[128] Marina Liborakina, Mikhail Flyamer, and Vladimir Yakimets, "Sotsialnoe partnerstvo," *Dengi i blagotvoritelnost* 1, no. 13 (February 1997), http://www.ngosneews.ru. The first sector of society refers to the government, the second sector to business, the third sector to nongovernmental organizations that are "apolitical, not trade union, and not religious organizations." Kononovich and Naumova, *Informatsionnyi spravochnik NKO*, 5.

[129] Irina Urtayeva, "Vzaimotnosheniya NKO i vlasti," *Zhenskii Parlament* 7, no. 10 (August 2001); Vladimir Yakimets defines a social mandate as "an assignment given by the authorities (or their representative) to realize an important social task; or for a project in the framework of a social program." V. Yakimets, "Tretii sektor v regionakh Rossii: Osobennosti razvitiya i vzaimodeitsviya s mestnoi vlastyu i biznesom," in *Regiony Rossii: Vzaimodeitsvie i razvitie*, ed. E. Alekseyeva (Moscow: Insait Poligrafic, 2001), 130.

[130] Yakimets, "Tretii sektor v regionakh Rossii," 128–30; Fridrikh Borodkin, "Stroitsya li iz sozvuchii edinaya melodiya?" *Munitsipalnaya vlast* 2 (March–April 1998), 9. In a series of in-depth surveys of top government officials, businesspeople, and leaders of civic associations in both Novgorod and Pskov, Dinello found that 69 percent of the NGO leaders she

interviewed in Novgorod (as compared with 27 percent in Pskov) expressed their trust in government officials. Dinello, "What's So Great about Novgorod-the-Great," 22.

[131] Dinello, "What's So Great about Novgorod-the-Great," 10.

[132] Sarah E. Mendelson and John K. Glenn, "Introduction: Transnational Networks and NGOS in Postcommunist Societies," in *The Power and Limits of NGOs*, ed. Sarah E. Mendelson and John K. Glenn (New York: Columbia University Press, 2002), 3; Vasily Dubovsky, "Bolshoe delo malogo granta," *Novgorod*, April 3, 2003.

[133] The first step in this direction was a citywide conference of all NGOs sponsored by the Novgorod city government in March 2001 to overcome mutual stereotypes and establish common priorities. Marina Marinina, "Politika podderzhki i sotrudnichestva," *Novgorod*, March 1, 2001.

[134] V. I. Aksenov, "Zapiska ideologicheskogo otdela obkoma KPSS 'O deyatelnosti i napravlennosti samodeyatelnykh formirovanii v oblasti,' " no. 02–8 (February 28, 1989) for internal use, p. 7. Available at the State Archives of the Contemporary Political History of the Novgorod Region, ul. Desyatinnaya 6, Novgorod the Great; T. N. Yarysh, "Svyaz s obshch-estvennostyu: Vosmidesyatye gody—nachalo dialoga," *Upravlencheskoe konsultirovanie* (Veliky Novgorod: MNOU Dialog), vol. 1 (1998): 42.

[135] Svetlana Petrova, "Tendentsii razvitiya 'tretyego sektora' v regione (na primere Nov-gorodskoi oblasti)," *Upravlencheskoe konsultirovanie* (Veliky Novgorod: MNOU Dialog), vol. 2 (1999), 18–29.

[136] Alla Putii, "Community Involvement and NGO Support Program, Partnership for Freedom: Quarterly Report for the Period July 12, 1997–October 1997," personal copy received from Alla Putii, Eurasia Fund regional director in Novgorod, 12.

[137] Ludmilla Alekseyeva, "Tendentsii razvitiya nekommercheskogo sektora i budushchee resursnykh tsentrov," a paper presented at a national meeting of NGOs in Moscow (October 29, 1998), personal copy.

[138] Valentina Fyodorova, "Zhizn davat i po zhizni vesti," *Novgorodskie vedomosti*, April 26, 2000; "Plan raboty Parlamenta v 2001 godu," *Zhenskii Parlament* 6, no. 9 (July 2001). A list of current activities is available at the Women's Parliament website at http://www.natm.ru/womenpar.

[139] Fyodorova, "Zhizn davat." With this much social and political support, it is not sur-prising to find many prominent women in the business community. In 2003 the "Woman Director of the Year" chosen by the National Association of Women Entrepreneurs of Russia from among forty regions was from Novgorod, "Soobshchenie press-tsentra Novgorodskoi administratsii za 05.03.2003."

[140] Although the administration attempted to distribute funding itself, the Eurasia Fund rebuffed this effort and was adamant about keeping control of both the grant competition and funds independent of the administration. "Community Involvement and NGO Support Program," 8.

[141] Vinitskaya, "Negosudarstvennye organizatsii."

[142] Dinello, "What's So Great about Novgorod-the-Great," 10.

[143] Urtayeva, "Vzaimotnosheniya NKO i vlasti."

[144] "Novoe grazhdanskoe obshchestvennoe dvizhenie . . . ," Rosbalt information agency, June 18, 2001.

[145] Kononovich and E. Yu. Naumova, *Informatsionnyi spravochnik NKO*, 5.

[146] Darya Ivanova, "Spisok politicheskikh obshchestvennykh obedinenii, zaregistrirovan-nykh Upravleniem Ministerstva Iustitsii RF po Novgorodskoi oblasti," *Regions.ru*, February 6, 2001, http://www.regions.ru/article/comments/id/418041.html; "State Duma Makes Progress on Local Election Law," EastWest Institute's *Russian Regional Report* 7, no. 16 (May 8, 2002), http://www.iews.com.

[147] Harry Eckstein, "Congruency Theory Explained," in *Can Democracy Take Root in Post-Soviet Russia?*, ed. Eckstein et al., 25–34.

[148] Interestingly, some researchers have found that local NGO success correlates most strongly with the internal political stability of a region. Larry Dershem and Valeri Patsiorkovski, "Needs and Capacity Assessment of the Third Sector in Central Russia: Kaluga, Yaroslavl, Smolensk, Tula, Tver, Vladimir, Ryazan, and Moscow Oblasts," a report prepared for Save the Children (August 19, 1997), 1–39, personal copy.

CHAPTER 3. HOW WE MISSED NOVGOROD'S DEMOCRATIC CONSOLIDATION

[1] Nicolai N. Petro, "Novgorod's Governor Prusak: A Young Turk to Watch," *St. Petersburg Times*, April 7–13, 1997; Robert Cottrell, "Russia: An Old-fashioned, Modern Look," *Economist*, June 14–20, 1997; Elizabeth Williamson, "Russian Area Returns to Its Former Ways: Free Thinking, Trading Help Boost Novgorod," *Chicago Tribune*, August 20, 1997, 11; Peter Ford, "Medieval City Holds Key to 'Russian Idea,'" *Christian Science Monitor*, June 5, 1997; John Thornhill, "Investors Drawn to Local Dynamo," *Financial Times*, April 15, 1998; Miles A. Pomper, "Economic Aid Goes Local," *Congressional* Quarterly, July 9, 1999; Barbara Kerneck, "Von Steuern und Offizierspastete," *taz, die tageszeitung*, July 25, 2000; Roman Berger, "Das Wirtschaftswunder von Nowgorod," *Tages-Anzeiger* (Zurich), July 17, 2000; Kathy Lally, "A Russian Journey," *Baltimore Sun*, September 20, 2000; Richard Threlkeld, "Pieces of the Bell," in his *Dispatches from the Former Evil Empire* (Amherst, N.Y.: Prometheus Books, 2001), 277–87; Andrew Meier, "The Once and Future Road," *Time* (Europe) 157, no. 22 (June 4, 2001).

[2] Adam Przeworski et al., "What Makes Democracies Endure?" *Journal of Democracy* 7, no. 1 (1996): 39–53; Seymour Martin Lipset, "The Indispensability of Political Parties," *Journal of Democracy* 11, no. 1 (2000): 48–55; Samuel Huntington, *Political Order in Changing Societies* (New Haven: Yale University Press, 1968), 1–92; Larry Diamond and Marc F. Plattner, *The Global Resurgence of Democracy* (Baltimore: Johns Hopkins University Press, 1996), 238.

[3] As Diamond puts it, "Only political parties can fashion diverse identities, interests, preferences and passions into laws." Larry Diamond, "Introduction," in *Nationalism, Ethnic Conflict, and Democracy*, ed. Larry Diamond and Marc F. Plattner (Baltimore: Johns Hopkins University Press, 1994), 15.

[4] Jack Bielasiak, "The Structuring of Party Systems in Post-communism," in *The Experience of Democratization in Eastern Europe*, ed. Richard Sakwa (New York: Macmillan, 1999), 138–67.

[5] Dietrich Rueschemeyer et al., *Capitalist Development and Democracy* (Chicago: University of Chicago Press, 1992), 8. Morlino cited in *Classes and Elites in Democracy and Democratization*, ed. Eva Etzioni-Halevy (New York: Garland, 1997), 205.

[6] Gunther calls cynicism a "general characteristic of political culture in Southern Europe." Richard Gunther et al., eds., *The Politics of Democratic Consolidation: Southern Europe in Comparative Perspective* (Baltimore: Johns Hopkins University Press, 1995), 24. The same has been said about Latin America; see Larry J. Diamond, "Rethinking Civil Society," *Journal of Democracy* 5, no. 3 (July 1994): 15.

[7] Gabor Toka, "Political Parties in East Central Europe," in *Consolidating the Third Wave Democracies*, ed. Larry Diamond et al. (Baltimore: Johns Hopkins University Press, 1997), 116.

[8] Suzanna N. Pshizova, "Kakuyu partiinuyu model vosprimet nashe obshchestvo?" *Polis*, no. 4 (1998): 101–13; Klaus von Beyme, "Leadership and Change in Party Systems: Towards a Postmodern Party State?" *Government and Opposition* 31, no. 2 (1996): 147.

[9] Russell Dalton and Martin P. Wattenberg, eds., *Parties without Partisans: Political Change in Advanced Industrial Democracies* (New York: Oxford University Press, 2000); David Broder, *The Party's Over: The Failure of Politics in America* (New York: Harper and Row, 1972); and Kay Lawson and Peter Merkl, eds., *When Parties Fail: Emerging Alternative Organizations* (Princeton, N.J.: Princeton University Press, 1988).

[10] H. R. Lloyd and C. V. R. Wait, "Nongovernmental Organizations in Regional and Provincial Economic Development," *South African Journal of Economics* 64 (June 1996): 28–29.

[11] Philippe Schmitter, "Civil Society East and West," in *Consolidating the Third Wave*, ed. Diamond et al., 260, citing Tracy Fitzsimmons, "Paradoxes of Participation: Organizations and Democratization in Latin America," Ph.D. diss., Stanford University, 1995.

[12] Schmitter, "Civil Society East and West," 246–47.

[13] Philippe Schmitter, "Interest Systems and the Consolidation of Democracies," in *Reexamining Democracy: Essays in Honor of Seymour Martin Lipset*, ed. Gary Marks and Larry Diamond (Newbury Park, Calif.: Sage, 1992), 160.

[14] Terry Lynn Karl, "Dilemmas of Democratization in Latin America," *Comparative Politics* 23 (1990): 1–21. National conferences have been successful in many central African countries, because they are rooted in "traditional consensus building system in Africa." By

contrast, multiparty systems are seen as part of the colonial heritage. Mamadou Dia, "Indigenous Management Practices: Lessons for Africa's Management," in *Culture and Development in Africa*, ed. Ismail Serageldin and June Taboroff (Washington, D.C.: The International Bank for Reconstruction and Development/The World Bank, 1994), 180–82.

[15] Jerry F. Hough, "The Failure of Party Formation and the Future of Russian Democracy," in *Growing Pains: Russian Democracy and the Election of 1993*, ed. Timothy J. Colton and Jerry F. Hough (Washington, D.C.: Brookings Institution Press, 1998), 669–701; Kathryn Stoner-Weiss, *Local Heroes: The Political Economy of Russian Regional Governance* (Princeton, N.J.: Princeton University Press, 1997).

[16] John Higley and Richard Gunther, eds., *Elites and Democratic Consolidation in Latin America and Southern Europe* (Cambridge: Cambridge University Press, 1992), 11, 34.

[17] Vaclav Havel, *Disturbing the Peace* (New York: Alfred Knopf, 1990); Petruska Sustrova, "The End of Nonpolitical Parties," *Uncaptive Minds* 4, no. 2 (1991): 16; Aviezer Tucker et al. "From Republican Virtue to Technology of Political Power: Three Episodes of Czech Nonpolitical Politics," *Political Science Quarterly* 115, no. 3 (2000): 421–45.

[18] Larry Diamond, *Promoting Democracy in the 1990s: Actors and Instruments, Issues, and Imperatives* (New York: Carnegie Corporation of New York, 1995), 41.

[19] Toka, "Political Parties in East Central Europe," 118, 115–16.

[20] Kathryn Stoner-Weiss, "The Limited Reach of Russia's Party System: Under-institutionalization in the Provinces," Program on New Approaches to Russian Security Policy Memo Series (PONARS) Memo No. 122 (April 2000), http://www.fas.harvard.edu/~ponars/POLICY%20MEMOS/Stoner-Weiss122.html.

[21] Gabor Toka, *Inventory of Political Attitude and Behavior Surveys in East Central Europe and the Former Soviet Union, 1989–1997* (Bergisch Gladbach, Germany: Erwin Ferger, 2000); and Harald Baldersheim et al., eds., *Local Democracy and the Processes of Transformation in East-Central Europe* (Boulder, Colo.: Westview, 1996), 140.

[22] Olga Bobrovskaya, "Raikov prodal Rogozina 'Edinoi Rossii' za 60 odnomandatnikov?" *Strana.ru* (February 20, 2003), http://www.strana.ru.

[23] Novgorod ranked 28th out of 31 regions in legislative influence. Neil J. Melvin, "Federalism and Democracy in the Russian Federation," University of Leeds, Leeds, U.K. (July 8, 2000), 8, 11, personal copy.

[24] Sergei Ivanov, ed., *Novgorodskaya oblastnaya Duma* (Novgorod: Kirillitsa, 1995), 10.

[25] Ludmla Mitrofanova, "Davaite zhit druzhno!" *Novgorodskie vedomosti*, December 8, 1998.

[26] Stuart N. Eisenstadt and Luis Roniger, *Patrons, Clients, and Friends: Interpersonal Relations and the Structure of Trust in Society* (Cambridge: Cambridge University Press, 1984); Christopher Clapham, ed., *Private Patronage and Public Power* (London: Frances Pinter, 1982).

[27] Some recent examples include popular opposition to the proposal for a high-speed rail line cutting through the Valdai National Park; the defeat of the administration's candidate for mayor of Staraya Russa, the region's third largest city, in 1999; the failure of Gennady Burbulis to defeat incumbent Evgeny Zelenov in the 2000 election for a seat in the federal Duma; popular opposition to the renaming of one of the city's major thoroughfares in honor of the deceased mayor of Novgorod the Great, Alexander Korsunov; the election of Valery Gaidym in 2001, the first Communist Party candidate elected to a seat in the regional duma since 1991; the controversy in spring 2003 surrounding the construction of a metal smelting plant near Novgorod the Great; and the rejection of Anatoly Boitsev, the governor's choice, to lead the Novgorod section of the United Russia Party in May 2003.

[28] Olga Kryshtanovskaya, "Vybory otmenit, Dumu raspustit," *Argumenty i Fakty* 15, no. 912 (1998).

[29] Simona Piattoni, "Can Politics Create Communities? Evidence from the Italian South," paper delivered at the annual meeting of the American Political Science Association, Boston (September 3–6, 1998), 13. The writings of Lee Komito on Ireland include "Irish Clientelism: A Reappraisal," *Economic and Social Review* 15, no. 3 (1984): 173–94; "Dublin Politics: Symbolic Dimensions of Clientelism," in *Ireland from Below: Social Change and Local Communities*, ed. Chris Curtin and Thomas Wilson (Galway: Galway University Press, 1989), 240–59; and "Personalism and Brokerage in Irish Politics," in *Irish Urban Cultures*, ed. Chris Curtin, Donnan Hastings, and Thomas M. Wilson (Belfast: Institute of Irish Studies, Queen's University of Belfast, 1993), 79–98.

[30] Piattoni, "Can Politics Create Communities?" 13.

[31] Vladimir Zhovannik, "Nenuzhnyi progress: Unikalnyi opyt Novgoroda federalnuyu vlast ne interesuyet," *Ekspert* 29, no. 22 (2000).

[32] Schmitter, "Civil Society East and West," 246.

[33] Phillipe Schmitter, "Reflections on Where . . . ," in *Patterns of Corporatist Policymaking*, ed. Gerhard Lehmbruch and Phillipe Schmitter (Beverly Hills: Sage, 1982), 250.

[34] Joyce M. Mushaben, "Die Lehrjahre Sind Vorbei! Re-forming Democratic Interest Groups in the East German Länder," sixth triennial congress of the East German Studies Group, "After the GDR," in Montreal, Canada, 1998; Elena Iankova, "Transformative Corporatism of Eastern Europe," *Eastern European Politics and Society* 12, no. 2 (Spring 1998): 222–57; Graeme Gill, *The Dynamics of Democratization* (New York: St. Martin's, 2000), 228–30; I. Luksic, "Corporatism Packaged in Pluralist Ideology: The Case of Slovenia," *Communist and Post-Communist Studies* 36, no. 4 (December 2003), 509–25.

[35] Iankova, "Transformative Corporatism," 226.

[36] Ibid., p. 232.

[37] Ibid.

[38] See the project description by Igor Yakovenko, "Public Expertise: What Is It and Why Is It Needed?" *Russia Journal,* http://www.freepress.ru/eng/text/II.htm.

[39] Interview with Igor V. Verkhodanov, chief aide to the head of the Novgorod Regional Duma, Novgorod the Great, Russia (May 24, 1999).

[40] Yulia Generozova, "Boris Giller zavoevyvaet provintsiyu," *Delovoi Peterburg,* August 28, 2002. Statistics on circulation for major Novgorod periodicals also come from http://www.novgorod.net/~dolgomer/Russian/Media/media2_1.html and from http://www.reklamka.ru/reg/pr_1042.php.

[41] Interview with Aleksandr Zhukovsky, director of the municipal research center Dialog, Novgorod the Great, Russia (June 4, 2002).

[42] The list of new periodicals that have sprung up since the beginning of 2000 is very long, but among the most prominent are *Novaya Novgorodskaya gazeta,* a venture of local publishing entrepreneur Sergei Brutman who also publishes the local commercial paper *Vechevoi tsentr,* the newspaper *Zvezda,* the weeklies *Volkhov* and *Argumenty i Fakty (Novgorod)* (the latter two both local ventures of larger national or regional media conglomerates); *Vremya Novgorodskoe,* supported by Isaak Slutsker, leader of the Union of Novgorod Industrialists and Entrepreneurs; and *Novgorodskii obyvatel,* supported by the chairman of the board of directors of the Akron fertilizer plant, Vyacheslav Kantor.

[43] Generozova, "Boris Giller zavoevyvaet provintsiyu," August 28, 2002.

[44] "Reiting upominaemosti gubernatorov . . ." for the period from October 7 through November 17, 2002, come from *Regions.ru,* http://www.regions.ru.

[45] "Soobshchenie press-tsentra Novgorodskoi administratsii za 16.10.2002," October 16, 2002.

[46] See http://www.novgorod.net/~dolgomer/Russian/Media/media2_4.html.

[47] Generozova, "Boris Giller zavoevyvaet provintsiyu," August 28, 2002. The independent press became a force to be reckoned with during the highly contested elections for mayor of Novgorod the Great in December 2002. For the first time, leading members of the business community openly challenged the governor and used their media influence to garner almost 20 percent of the vote for an alternative candidate. For the first time since 1990, the region's fabled political unity split. "Veliky Novgorod: Obzor mestnoi pressy za 11–12 December 2002 o vyborakh mera goroda," *IA-Regnum* wire service, December 14, 2002.

[48] See Allen C. Lynch, "Roots of Russia's Economic Dilemmas: Liberal Economics and Illiberal Geography," *Europe-Asia Studies* 54, no. 1 (January 2002): 31; Herbert Kitschelt, "Postcommunist Economic Reform: Causal Mechanisms and Concomitant Processes," paper delivered at the annual meeting of the American Political Science Association, San Francisco, August 30–September 2, 2001.

[49] Bert van Selm, "Economic Performance in Russia's Regions," *Europe-Asia Studies* 50, no. 4 (June 1998): 618–19.

[50] Cynthia Buckley and Regina Smyth, "The Ties That Bind: The Importance of Region in the Construction of Social and Political Citizenship," in *Fragmented Space: Center and Region in the Russian Federation,* ed. Blair Ruble, Nancy Popson, and Jodi Koehn

(Washington, D.C.: Woodrow Wilson Center Press; Baltimore: Johns Hopkins University Press, 2001), 81–122.

[51] Peter J. Stavrakis, "Understanding Russian Regionalism: What Remains to Be Done," *IEWS Russian Regional Report* 2, no. 22 (June 19, 1997); Philip Roeder, "Soviet Federalism and Ethnic Mobilization," *World Politics* 43, no. 2 (January 1991): 196–232; Philip Roeder, "Transitions from Communism" in *Can Democracy Take Root in Post-Soviet Russia? Explorations in State-Society Relations,* ed. Harry Eckstein et al. (New York: Rowman and Littlefield, 1998), 201–28.

[52] Kathleen M. Dowley, "Striking the Federal Bargain in Russia: Comparative Regional Government Strategies," *Communist and Post-Communist Studies* 31, no. 4 (December 1998): 363.

[53] It has been argued, for example, that regions that have negotiated the greatest autonomy from the center have also tended to be the most internally repressive. See Ruslan R. Galliyamov, "Politicheskie elity rossiiskikh respublik: Osobennosti transformatsii v postsovetskii period," *Polis,* no. 2 (1998): 108–15. Lidia Reznichenko has noted the high percentage of ethnic republics—including Tatarstan, Bashkortostan, Adygeyia, and Sakha-Yakutiya—that, in violation of the Russian Constitution, have replaced local self-government with direct rule by the regional center. L. B. Reznichenko, "Zakonodatelnoe obespechenie mestnogo samoupravlenie, *Polis,* no. 4 (1998): 166.

[54] Svetlana Sukhova, "Prognoz na osen: Vo vlasti oblachno," *Itogi,* April 30, 2001.

[55] Dmitri A. Zimine and Michael J. Bradshaw, "Regional Adaptation to Economic Crisis in Russia: The Case of Novgorod Oblast," *Post-Soviet Geography and Economics* 40, no. 5 (1999): 343.

[56] Mikhail M. Prusak, *Reformy v provintsii* (Moscow: Veche, 1999); Sergei Yu. Fabrichnyi, "Razvitie mestnogo samoupravleniya na territorii Novgorodskoi oblasti," in *Zemstvo i vozrozhdenie ego kulturno-khozyaistvennykh traditsii,* ed. V. I. Romashova (Novgorod: Novgorod Regional Scientific Library, 1996), 39.

[57] This point was made by Mark Urnov at a conference on "Societal Change and the Role of Social Capital in Russia's Regions," at the Federal Institute for East European and International Studies (BIOst), Cologne, Germany, May 26–28, 1999. At the time Urnov was head of Boris Yeltsin's Presidential Analytical Center.

[58] Zimine and Bradshaw, "Regional Adaptation," 341.

[59] Mitrofanova, "Davaite zhit druzhno!" (December 8, 1998). In fact, the Novgorod Duma does have a professional staff that reviews legislation, drafts amendments, and sends proposed legislation back for review to the originating body. It is, however, attached to the duma as a whole rather than to individual deputies. Interview with Anatoly Boitsev, chairman of the Novgorod Regional Duma, Novgorod the Great, Russia (May 5, 2000).

[60] Zimine and Bradshaw, "Regional Adaptation," 341.

[61] Interview with Anatoly Boitsev, May 5, 2000.

[62] Ibid. In his interview with me, Boitsev gave the higher figure for 1999. Olga Kuznetsova, an expert at the Russian government's Working Center for Economic Reforms, gives the figure of 20 percent for 1997. "Novgorodskaya i Pskovskaya oblasti: Ekonomicheskie polozhenie i factory razvitiya," *Voprosy Ekonomiki* 10 (1998): 148.

[63] Irina Kibina, "Federalism in the Russian Federation," report prepared for the law firm Steptoe & Johnson in Washington, D.C. (Summer 1999), 24–26, personal copy.

[64] Joel C. Moses, "Rethinking Political Typologies of Russian Regions," paper delivered at the annual convention of the American Association for the Advancement of Slavic Studies (September 1999), 9, personal copy.

[65] Ibid., 16. Moses's most recent study confirms his earlier assessment that regional democratization is still quite tentative. See Joel Moses, "Political-Economic Elites and Russian Regional Elections, 1999–2000: Democratic Tendencies in Kaliningrad, Perm, and Volgograd," *Europe-Asia Studies* 54, no. 6 (September 2002): 905–32.

[66] Driven by the inexorable logic of their own model, regional analysts can come up with truly bizarre findings. Thus, Nikolai Petrov finds Pskov much more democratic than Novgorod, and Ulyanovsk more so than Samara. "Press conference with Nikolai Petrov, Moscow Carnegie Center Official, Regarding the Democracy Standards in Russian Regions," Federal News Service (October 15, 2002), cited in *Johnson's Russia List* no. 6498, http://www.cdi.org/russia/johnson/.

[67] Kathryn Stoner-Weiss, "Why Are Some Regions Doing Better than Others?" *IEWS Russian Regional Report* 2, no. 19 (May 29, 1997).

[68] Yuri Golub, Vladimir Dines, and Dmitry Konnychev, "Saratovskaya oblast: Konsolidatsiya vlasti," *Vlast* 5 (1998): 37–45.

[69] Blair Ruble and Nancy Popson, "The Westernization of a Russian Province: The Case of Novgorod," *Post-Soviet Geography and Economics* 39, no. 8 (1998): 433–46.

[70] See Joel C. Moses, "Saratov and Volgograd, 1990–1992: A Tale of Two Russian Provinces," in *Local Power and Post-Soviet Politics*, ed. Theodore H. Friedgut and Jeffrey W. Hahn (Armonk, N.Y.: M. E. Sharpe, 1994), 96–137.

[71] Natalya Dinello, "What's So Great about Novgorod-the-Great: Trisectoral Cooperation and Symbolic Management," (June 3, 2001), contract no. 814–25 by the National Council for Eurasian and East European Research (NCEEER), Washington, D.C., 19.

[72] Ibid, 12.

[73] Ibid., 12–13.

[74] Vladimir Gelman and Sergei Ryzhenkov, "Politichskaya regionalistika v sovremennoi Rossii: Ot obshchestvennogo interesa—k nauchnoi distsipline?" (August 1996), 28, personal copy. A comprehensive listing of Gelman's writings can be found at his website, http://www.eu.spb.ru/socio/staff/socio4.htm.

[75] Vladimir Gelman, "Transformatsiya politicheskogo rezhima i vykhody iz neopredelennosti," paper prepared for the "Regional Russia" workshop at the Kennan Institute for Advanced Russia Studies, Washington, D.C. (May 8–9, 1998), 13, personal copy. Later translated and published in English as "Regime Transition, Uncertainty, and Prospects for Democratization: The Politics of Russia's Regions in a Comparative Perspective," *Europe-Asia Studies* 51, no. 6 (1999): 939–56.

[76] Ibid., 18–20.

[77] Ibid., 19.

[78] Prusak, *Reformy*, 5. Interview with Mikhail M. Prusak, governor of the Novgorod region, Novgorod the Great, Russia (November 5, 1998).

[79] A valuable biography prepared by Elena Nachkebia on December 8, 1995 for the National News Service in Moscow (currently the Integrum Information Agency) is available at http://www.nns.ru/ssi/persons.cgi.

[80] From Prusak's electoral program as a candidate for the Federation Council, "Pomozhem sebe sami," *Provintsial: Ezhenedelnaya gazeta Severo-Zapada Rossii* (December 19, 1993), 3.

[81] Natalya Arkhangelskaya, "Kak podelit stranu," *Ekspert*, October 29, 2001; Natella Boltyanskaya, "V pryamom efire radiostantsii 'Ekho Moskvy' gubernator Novgorodskoi oblasti . . . ," June 7, 2000.

[82] Boltyanskaya, "V pryamom efire. . . ." When Prusak talks about clear accountability and "strong state authority" he is referring only to the executive branch. The legislative branch, he says, must reflect the diversity of local Russian traditions and customs. A. Orlov, "Nastupilo vremya stroit," *Posev* 50, no. 4 (April 1994): 58–59.

[83] Yuri Krasavin, "Rynok vsem dast shans," *Zemlya novgorodskaya* (June 12, 1992), 3.

[84] Mikhail Prusak, Evgeny Savchenko, and Oleg Bogomolov, "I vlast, i ekonomika, i prezident na 7 let," *Nezavisimaya gazeta*, February 25, 2000.

[85] "M. Prusak: Reformy v Rossii provodyatsya ne na doverii, a na protivostoyanii," *RIA Ros-Bizness Consulting*, June 28, 2000. Kim Holmes has called Prusak's proposal "a wholesale copy of James Madison's Constitution," but it owes far more to his own experience with the Novgorod Social Chamber and other regional concertation arrangements. Kim R. Holmes, Caspar W. Weinberger, James Woolsey, and Ariel Cohen, "Who Lost Russia?" *Heritage Lecture* no. 629 (January 8, 1999), http://www.heritage.org/Research/RussiaandEurasia/HL629.cfm.

[86] Prusak, the principal author, published his program in coauthorship with the governors of Belgorod and Kurgan. See Prusak, Savchenko, and Bogomolov, "I vlast, i ekonomika, i president." Although both Prusak and Putin have called for restoring the government's vertical chain of command (the "vertical of power") Prusak actually first used the term in 1991. "Mikhail Prusak: Budu sovetovatsya s novgorodtsami," *Novgorodskie vedomosti* (November 2, 1991), 1.

[87] "Titov preduprezhdaet o gotovyashchemsya putche," *APN* News Service, March 2, 2000. Actually, under Prusak's arrangement, while the presidency would be marginally stronger, the power of local legislatures would remain unchanged. The only person weakened in this arrangement, paradoxically, is the governor. Although the governor appoints local district heads, he can do so only with the consent of district assemblies, and he can be removed at the request of the regional representative assembly if he upsets too many local interests. Should a conflict arise between the legislature and the governor, the regional representative assembly would emerge as the arbiter because it could potentially call for the governor's removal.

[88] Elena Tokareva, "Generalnaya linea stala generalskoi," *Obshchaya gazeta*, October 12, 2000.

[89] Ludmila Mitrofanova, "Mikhail Prusak: Ya khochu bit trevogu," *Novgorodskie vedomosti*, October 3, 2000.

[90] M. M. Prusak, "Podkhody k formirovaniyu grazhdanskogo obshchestva v Rossii—Novgorodsky aspect," personal copy. This speech is cited in Olga Dramaretskaya, "V Peterburge nachalos formirovanie grazhdanskogo obshchestva," *Kommersant*, February 22, 2002.

[91] Stanislav Stremidlovsky, "Gubernator Novgorodskoi oblasti Mikhail Prusak," *Vek*, August 9, 2002; Olga Boguslavskaya, "Zachem gubernatoru kroliki?" *Moskovskii komsomolets*, July 15, 2002.

[92] Vladimir Gelman, "Regime Transition, Outcome of Uncertainty, and Prospects for Democratization: The Politics of Russia's Regions in a Comparative Perspective," paper prepared for a conference of the same name organized by the Federal Institute for East European and International Studies (BIOst), Cologne, Germany (May 26–28, 1999), personal copy, 15.

[93] Prusak has long called for a constitutional convention that would balance the various branches of government. Viktor Troyanovsky, "Tolko izmenenie konstitutsii obespechit stabilnost v Rossii . . . ," *Itar-Tass*, August 9, 1999.

[94] Gelman, "Transformatsiya politicheskogo rezhima," 16. Prusak specifically identifies the arbitrariness of the present governmental system as reason to call a constitutional convention. Troyanovsky, "Tolko izmenenie konstitutsii."

[95] Andrei Tsygankov, "Manifestations of Delegative Democracy in Russian Local Politics: What Does It Mean for the Future of Russia?" *Communist and Post-Communist Studies* 31, no. 4 (1998): 335. This definition is very close to that used in Juan J. Linz and Alfred Stepan, "Towards Consolidated Democracies, " *Journal of Democracy* 7, no. 2 (1996): 14–33; and in Guillermo O'Donnell's "On the State, Democratization and Some Conceptual Problems: A Latin American View with Glances at Some Postcommunist Countries," *World Development* 21, no. 8 (1993): 1366.

[96] Interview with Archbishop Lev of Novgorod and Staraya Russa at his residence at Khutyn Monastery, Russia, January 27, 1998.

[97] Merja Tekoniemi and Laura Solanko, "Novgorod and Pskov—Examples of How Economic Policy Can Influence Economic Development," *Review of Economics in Transition* (June 1998): 68; Olga Kuznetsova, "Novgorodskaya i Pskovskaya oblasti: Ekonomischeskoe polozhenie i faktory razvitiya," *Voprosy ekonomiki* 10 (1998): 143. For 2002, Novgorod's per capita gross regional product exceeded Pskov's by almost 30 percent. Yulia Generozova, "Defitsit budzgeta Novgorodskoi oblasti," *Delovoi Peterburg*, November, 28, 2003.

[98] Tekoniemi and Solanko, "Novgorod and Pskov," 66.

[99] Aleksei Zhuravlev, "Pskovskaya oblast: Ekonomika, partii, lidery," *Vlast* (April 1996): 48–49.

[100] M. Makfol [Michael McFaul] and Nikolai Petrov, *Politicheskii almanakh Rossii 1997* (Moscow: Tsentr Karnegie, 1998), 786.

[101] Zhuravlev, "Pskovskaya oblast," 48.

[102] According to Andrei Manakov, communists have never beaten a "patriotic" candidate in local elections, "Gubernatorskie vybory 2000 g. v Pskovskoi oblasti: Preemstvennost elektorata i geografiya golosovaniya," *Carnegie Moscow Center Working Papers* no. 5 (Moscow: Carnegie Endowment for International Peace, 2001), 55.

[103] Tekoniemi and Solanko, "Novgorod and Pskov," 71.

[104] Ibid., 72. Vladimir V. Vagin, *"Visokosnyi" politicheskii god v Pskovskoi oblasti: Oktyabr 1995–noyabr 1996 gg.* (Pskov: izd Tsentr "Vozrozhdenie", 1998), 93.

[105] Yuri A. Shmatov, "Predstavitelnyi organ vlasti pskovskoi oblasti kak faktor ee razvitiya," in *Upravlenie regionom na urovne subekta Federatsii,* ed. Zh. T. Toshchenko et al. (Pskov: Rossiiskaya akademiya gosudarstvennoi sluzhby pri prezidente RF, Severo–Zapadnaya Akademiya gosudarstvenoi sluzhby, filial v g. Pskove, 1998), 18–22.

[106] Kuznetsova, "Novgorodskaya i Pskovskaya oblasti."

[107] Andrei Shcherkin, "Protsessy zarozhdeniya, razvitiya i stanovleniya politicheskikh partii i massovykh obshchestvennykh dvizhenii v Pskovskoi oblasti v 1988–94 g." Personal copy received November 20, 2000.

[108] Makfol and Petrov, *Politicheskii almanakh Rossii 1997,* 790.

[109] Shmatov, "Predstavitelnyi organ vlasti," 19–20.

[110] "Stavlennik 'Edinstva' ot LDPR poluchil eshche chetyre goda," *National News Service,* Russia, November 13, 2000, http://www.nns.ru/chronicle/index.html; Andrei Morozov, "Izbiratelnye tekhnologii i administrativnyi resurs: Pskovskii retsept sokhranenie vlasti," *Working Papers* no. 5 (Moscow: Carnegie Endowment for International Peace, 2001), 63–64; Fyodor Gavrilov, "Pskovskaya satyagrakha," *Ekspert, Severo-Zapad* 31, no. 2 (February 5, 2001), http://www.expert.ru/sever/current/edit.shtml.

[111] Vagin, *"Visokosnyi" politicheskii god,* 61.

[112] Krasavin, "Rynok vsem dast shans," 3.

[113] Prusak interviewed for the television program *Politicheskii olimp,* December 23, 1998.

[114] Tekoniemi and Solanko, "Novgorod and Pskov," 70. This dependence is heightened by the fact that nearly half of the electorate are pensioners, two-thirds of the working population are state employees, and one in ten serve in the military. Morozov estimates that no more than 12 percent of the population are not somehow dependent on the government budget. Morozov, "Izbiratelnye tekhnologii," 60.

[115] Kelly McMann and Nikolai Petrov, "A Survey of Democracy in Russia's Regions," *Post-Soviet Geography and Economics* 41, no. 3 (2000): 160.

[116] Makfol and Petrov, *Politicheskii almanakh Rossii 1997,* 789.

[117] Shcherkin, "Protsessy zarozhdeniya," 2–3.

[118] Ibid., 16–21.

[119] During his electoral campaign, Vladislav Tumanov, the Democratic Party of Russia candidate, opposed any attempt to weaken the military's presence in the region and condemned Moscow's weak opposition to Latvian and Estonian territorial claims. Mikhail A. Alexseev and Vladimir Vagin, "Russian Regions in Expanding Europe: The Pskov Connection," *Europe-Asia Studies* 51, no. 1 (1999): 44.

[120] One noted incident involved the closing of a local television program, *Perspektiva,* because of a commentary that local activist Lev Shlosberg wanted to run that described the USSR as an "empire." Vladimir V. Vagin, *"Visokosnyi" politicheskii god,* 83–84.

[121] Svetlana S. Mintz, "Some Remarks on 'Provincial Culture' in Contemporary Russian Studies," *CSEES Newsletter,* University of California at Berkeley, vol. 13, no. 2 (Summer 1996): 11–12.

CHAPTER 4. THREE KEYS TO UNDERSTANDING RAPID SOCIAL CHANGE

[1] Philippe C. Schmitter and Terry Lynn Karl, "From an Iron Curtain to a Paper Curtain: Grounding Transitologists or Students of Postcommunism?" *Slavic Review* 54, no. 4 (1995): 978.

[2] Valerie Bunce, "The Political Economy of Postsocialism," *Slavic Review* 58, no. 4 (1999): 756–93; Valerie Bunce, "Should Transitologists Be Grounded?" *Slavic Review* 54, no. 1 (1995): 111–27.

[3] M. Steven Fish, "Postcommunist Subversion," *Slavic Review* 58, no. 4 (1999): 802.

[4] Valerie Bunce, "Comparing East and South," *Journal of Democracy* 6, no. 3 (1995): 97; Bunce, "Political Economy of Postsocialism," 790; Valerie Bunce, "Regional Differences in Democratization: The East versus the South," *Post-Soviet Affairs* 14, no. 3 (1998): 200. In "From an Iron Curtain to a Paper Curtain," Schmitter and Karl argue that an excessive preoccupation with the past among area specialists has limited their receptiveness to change.

[5] In the wake of the turmoil wrought by Oliver Cromwell's Glorious Revolution, for example, Scottish Enlightenment philosopher David Hume remarked that too rapid a process of social change had damaged the structures of authority needed to stabilize a liberal order and eroded the basic units of social cooperation. Laurence Whitehead, "Introduction: Some Insights from Western Social Theory," *World Development* 21, no. 8 (1993): 1246–48. While calling for a sharp break with the institutional past, Bunce simultaneously calls for a strong state that is "rule-bound and that can extract compliance." Bunce, "Political Economy of Postsocialism," 791.

[6] Marc Howard Ross, "Culture and Identity in Comparative Political Analysis," in *Comparative Politics: Rationality, Culture, and Structure*, ed. Mark I. Lichbach and Alan S. Zuckerman (Cambridge: Cambridge University Press, 1997), 43.

[7] Ibid., 46.

[8] Cited in Chalmers Johnson and E. B. Keehn, "A Disaster in the Making: Rational Choice and Asian Studies," *National Interest* (Summer 1994): 18; Harry Eckstein, "Culture as a Foundation Concept for the Social Sciences," *Journal of Theoretical Politics* 8, no. 4 (1996): 471–97.

[9] Aaron Wildavsky, "Choosing Preferences by Constructing Institutions: A Cultural Theory of Preference Formation," *American Political Science Review* 81, no. 1 (1987): 4.

[10] Aaron Wildavsky, *Culture and Social Theory* (New Brunswick, N.J.: Transaction Publishers, 1998), 252.

[11] Some cross-cultural studies suggest that firmly entrenched psychological principles and hypotheses can be discordant with the way cultural groups think and act. Joseph E. Trimble, "Considering the Cultures Within," *Radcliffe Quarterly* (2000): 12–13.

[12] Peter C. Ordeshook, "Institutions and Incentives," *Journal of Democracy* 6, no. 2 (1995): 48. Bates et al. argue that choices result both from rational conjecture and from fear of the unlikely. Every rational actor thus faces a set of rational and irrational choices he can make. The former profit him, the latter do not. But what Bates and other rational choice theorists see as distinctive paths are in fact paths that often overlap. Moreover, judging the impact of the irrational in this way is suspect because analysts can easily argue post facto that if fears prove correct then the choice made was rational; if not, then the choice made was irrational, as they do in their example of Zambia. Robert H. Bates, J. P. Rui De Figueiredo Jr., and Barry R. Weingast, "The Politics of Interpretation: Rationality, Culture, and Transition," *Politics and Society* 26, no. 4 (1998): 619, 628.

[13] Bates et al., "Politics of Interpretation," 628.

[14] Ibid., 605, 632.

[15] Ibid., 605.

[16] Wildavsky, *Culture and Social Theory*, 218.

[17] Wildavsky's notion of rationality, like Eckstein's, is not an absolute standard. In fact, he speaks of "plural rationalities . . . that vary with the preferences or objectives to be realized." Ibid., 229.

[18] Reid Cushman, "Rational Fears: Political Science's Ascendant Methodology," *Lingua Franca* (November/December 1994): 51.

[19] Ross, "Culture and Identity," 45.

[20] Ibid.

[21] Ibid., 46–47.

[22] Harry Eckstein, "A Culturalist Theory of Political Change," *American Political Science Review* 82, no. 3 (1988): 796.

[23] Some deem Russia a perfect test case of whether culturalist or rational choice approaches have been better at predicting the pace of change. Harry Eckstein, "Russia and the Conditions of Democracy," in *Can Democracy Take Root in Post-Soviet Russia? Explorations in State-Society Relations*, ed. Harry Eckstein et al. (New York: Rowman and Littlefield, 1998): 349–82; Johnson and Keehn, "A Disaster in the Making," 19.

[24] Gabriel Almond, "Comparative Political Systems," *Journal of Politics* 18 (1956): 391.

[25] Gabriel Almond and Sidney Verba, *The Civic Culture: Political Attitudes and Democracy in Five Nations* (Princeton, N.J.: Princeton University Press, 1963), 25–29.

[26] Nicolai N. Petro, *The Rebirth of Russian Democracy: An Interpretation of Political Culture* (Cambridge: Harvard University Press, 1995), 4–9; Ross, "Culture and Identity," 56.

[27] Harry Eckstein, "Social Science as Cultural Science, Rational Choice as Metaphysics," in *Culture Matters: Essays in Honor of Aaron Wildavsky*, ed. Richard J. Ellis and Michael Thompson (Boulder, Colo.: Westview, 1997), 30–31.

[28] Frederic L. Fleron, "Post-Soviet Political Culture in Russia: An Assessment of Recent Empirical Investigations," *Europe-Asia Studies* 48, no. 2 (1996): 231.

[29] Robert D. Putnam, *Making Democracy Work* (Princeton, N.J.: Princeton University Press, 1993), 169; Eric M. Uslaner, "Democracy and Social Capital" in *Trust and Government*, ed. Mark Warren (New York: Cambridge University Press, 1999), 121.

[30] Francis Fukuyama, *Trust: The Social Virtues and the Creation of Prosperity* (New York: Free Press, 1995).

[31] M. Foley and B. Edwards, "Civil Society and Social Capital Beyond Putnam," *American Behavioral Scientist* 42, no. 1 (1998): 133; C. J. Paraskevopoulos, "Social Capital and the Public-Private Divide in Greek Regions," *West European Politics* 21, no. 2 (1998): 154–77; J. Fox, "How Does Civil Society Thicken? The Political Construction of Social Capital in Rural Mexico," *World Development* 24, no. 6 (1998): 1089–1103.

[32] Richard Rose, "Uses of Social Capital in Russia: Modern, Pre-modern, and Anti-modern," *Post-Soviet Affairs* 16, no. 1 (2000): 33–57; Thomas M. Nichols, "Russian Democracy and Social Capital," *Social Science Information* 35, no. 4 (1996): 631; Francis Fukuyama, "The Primacy of Culture," *Journal of Democracy* 6, no. 1 (1995): 7–14; M. Aberg, "Putnam's Social Capital Theory Goes East: A Case Study of Western Ukraine and L'viv," *Europe-Asia Studies* 52, no. 2 (2000): 295–317.

[33] Rose, "Uses of Social Capital in Russia," 36.

[34] David Stark, "The Great Transformation? Social Change in Eastern Europe," *Contemporary Sociology* 21 (1992): 300.

[35] Joyce M. Mushaben, "Die Lehrjahre Sind Vorbei! Re-forming Democratic Interest Groups in the East German Länder," sixth triennial congress of the East German Studies Group, "After the GDR," in Montreal, Canada (1998), later published in *Democratization* 8, no. 4 (Winter 2001): 95–133; Christopher Marsh, "Civic Community, Communist Support, and Democratization: The View from Smolensk," *Demokratizatsiya* 8, no. 3 (Fall 2000): 447–60; Christopher Marsh, "Social Capital and Democracy in Russia," *Communist and Post-Communist Studies* 33, no. 2 (June 2000): 183–99.

[36] Aberg, "Putnam's Social Capital Theory Goes East"; Alena V. Ledeneva, *Russia's Economy of Favors: Blat, Networking, and Informal Exchanges* (New York: Cambridge University Press, 1998): 313–14.

[37] Mushaben, "Die Lehrjahre Sind Vorbei!" 96.

[38] Eckstein, "Congruence Theory Explained," in *Can Democracy Take Root*, ed. Eckstein et al., 5.

[39] Ibid., 12–14, 37; Eckstein, "Russia and the Conditions of Democracy," 360.

[40] Harry Eckstein, *Division and Cohesion in Democracy: A Study of Norway* (Princeton, N.J.: Princeton University Press, 1966); Harry Eckstein, *The Evaluation of Political Performance: Problems and Dimensions* (Beverly Hills, Calif.: Sage, 1971).

[41] William M. Reisinger, "Congruence Theory as a Perspective on Russian Politics," 153, and Eckstein, "Russia and the Conditions of Democracy," 379, both in *Can Democracy Take Root*, ed. Eckstein et al.

[42] Eckstein, "Congruence Theory Explained," 23.

[43] Ibid., 28.

[44] Ibid., 24, 28.

[45] Eckstein, "A Culturalist Theory of Political Change," 799; Lucian W. Pye, *Asian Power and Politics: The Cultural Dimensions of Authority* (Cambridge, Mass.: Belknap Press, 1985), 12–25; Charles Lockhart, "Political Culture and Political Change," in *Culture Matters*, ed. Ellis and Thompson, 91.

[46] Eckstein, "Congruence Theory Explained," 6.

[47] Russell Bova, "Political Culture, Authority Patterns, and the Architecture of the New Russian Democracy," in *Can Democracy Take Root in Post-Soviet Russia? Explorations in State-Society Relations*, ed. Harry Eckstein et al. (New York: Rowman and Littlefield, 1998), 178.

[48] Cited in Clifford Geertz, *Available Light: Anthropological Reflections on Philosophical Topics* (Princeton, N.J.: Princeton University Press, 2000), 131–32.

[49] Wildavsky, "Choosing Preferences," 5.

[50] Ibid., 5.

[51] Fukuyama, "Primacy of Culture," 7–9.

[52] Rogowski cited by Lockhart, "Political Culture and Political Change," 91–95.

[53] Charles Lockhart, "Cultural Contributions to Explaining Institutional Form, Political Change, and Rational Decisions," *Comparative Political Studies* 32, no. 7 (1999): 871–72.

[54] Thomas R. Rochon, *Culture Moves: Ideas, Activism, and Changing Values* (Princeton, N.J: Princeton University Press, 1998), 12.

[55] Ibid., 16–25, 54.

[56] Ibid., 89.

[57] Richard Gunther et al., "Introduction," in *The Politics of Democratic Consolidation: Southern Europe in Comparative Perspective*, ed. Richard Gunther et al. (Baltimore: Johns Hopkins University Press, 1995), 18. The range is from five years for Spain to thirty for Italy, according to Juan Linz, Alfred Stepan, and Richard Gunther, in "Democratic Transition and Consolidation in Southern Europe, with Reflections on Latin America and Eastern Europe," in *Politics of Democratic Consolidation*, ed. Gunther et al., 119. Ralf Dahrendorf has argued that it takes one year to establish a democracy, six years to create a free market economy, but sixty years to create a civil society. See his remarks on the website of the Templeton Foundation at: http://www.templeton.org/archives/freedomrussia.asp. Most scholars, however, simply treat it as a matter of generational change. Harry Eckstein, "Lessons from the Third Wave," in *Can Democracy Take Root*, ed. Eckstein et al., 276.

[58] "Although formal rules may change overnight as a result of political or judicial decision, informal constraints embodied in customs, traditions, and codes of conduct are much more impervious to deliberate policies. These cultural constraints not only connect the past with the present and future but provide us with a key to explaining the path of historical change." Douglas North, *Institutions, Institutional Change, and Economic Performance* (Cambridge: Cambridge University Press, 1990), 6.

[59] Path dependency has also been used to categorize countries as more or less susceptible to rapid cultural change. Thus, Michael Mandelbaum divides European countries into regions with three distinct histories. The "West" controlled by the House of Habsburg, the "East" by the Romanovs, and the "South" by the Ottomans, which he claims corresponds neatly to the historical impact of the liberal tradition in each region. Alas, this correspondence is so neat only because of the odd inclusion of Bulgaria, Estonia, Latvia, Lithuania, and Poland into the Habsburg Empire. "Introduction," in *Postcommunism: Four Perspectives*, ed. Michael Mandelbaum (New York: Council on Foreign Relations, 1996), 14–15.

[60] Thus, it is common to find Russians endowed with "a deeply held cultural fear of innovation" and "suspiciousness of outsiders, envy, parochialism, intolerance, and above all, unthinking, blind patriotism." Carol Barner-Barry and Cynthia A. Hody, *The Politics of Change: The Transformation of the Former Soviet Union* (New York: St. Martin's, 1995, 31); Edward Allworth, ed., *Ethnic Russia in the USSR: The Dilemma of Dominance* (New York: Pergamon, 1980), 34. A useful antidote that puts such views in historical and political context is Anatole Lieven's "Against Russophobia," *World Policy Journal* 17, no. 4 (Winter 2000/2001), 25–32.

[61] John Mueller, "Democracy, Capitalism, and the End of Transition," in *Postcommunism*, ed. Mandelbaum, 137.

[62] Wildavsky, *Culture and Social Theory*, 197.

[63] Geertz, *Available Light*, 226.

[64] Eckstein, "Culturalist Theory," 794.

[65] Ibid., 4. On the two faces of culture see David D. Laitin, *Hegemony and Culture: Politics and Religious Change among the Yoruba* (Chicago: University of Chicago Press, 1986).

[66] Ross, "Culture and Identity," 45.

[67] Wildavsky, *Culture and Social Theory*, 196.

[68] William G. Doty, *Mythography: The Study of Myths and Rituals* (University, Ala.: University of Alabama Press, 1986), 133–34.

[69] David Bidney, "Myth, Symbolism and Truth," in *Myth: A Symposium*, ed. T. A. Sebeok (Bloomington: Indiana University Press, 1965), 14.

[70] Vladimir Tismaneanu, *Fantasies of Salvation: Democracy, Nationalism, and Myth in Post-Communist Europe* (Princeton, N.J.: Princeton University Press, 1998), 9–10; Giuseppe Di Palma, *To Craft Democracies: An Essay on Democratic Transitions* (Berkeley: University of California Press, 1990), 182, 231; Stephen Holmes, "Cultural Legacies or State Collapse?" 51–69, and Mandelbaum, "Introduction," *Postcommunism*, 26.

[71] Haralds Biezais, ed., *The Myth of the State* (Stockholm: Almqvist and Wiksell, 1972).

[72] Ibid., 149–50.

[73] Erik Erikson cited in Doty, *Mythography*, 136.

[74] Doty, *Mythography*, 131.

[75] Ernst Cassirer, *The Philosophy of Symbolic Forms* (New Haven: Yale University Press, 1953), 65.

[76] Ibid., 53. Cassirer even suggests that fundamental concepts of mechanics, such as mass and force, are "fictions" created by the logic of the natural sciences. Ibid., 75–76.

[77] William K. Wimsatt Jr. and Cleanth Brooks, *Literary Criticism: A Short History* (New York: Knopf, 1957), 699–708; Suzanne K. Langer, *Philosophy in a New Key: A study in the Symbolism of Reason, Rite, and Art* (Cambridge: Harvard University Press, 1967).

[78] Ernst Cassirer, *The Myth of the State* (New Haven: Yale University Press, 1946), 4.

[79] Cassirer, *Philosophy of Symbolic Forms*, 86.

[80] Cited in Michael Brint, *A Genealogy of Political Culture* (Boulder, Colo.: Westview, 1991), 89–90.

[81] Sherry B. Ortner, "Theory in Anthropology since the Sixties," in *Culture/Power/History: A Reader in Contemporary Social Theory*, ed. Nicholas B. Dirks et al. (Princeton, N.J.: Princeton University Press, 1994), 374–75.

[82] Clifford Geertz, "Ideology as a Cultural System," in *Ideology and Discontent*, ed. David F. Apter (London: The Free Press of Glencoe, 1964) 61. This is very similar to Eckstein, who points out that the touchstone of culturalist theory is the belief that actors do not respond directly to situations but to "orientations" that allow them to properly interpret each situation. Harry Eckstein, "A Culturalist Theory of Political Change," *American Political Science Review* 82, no. 3 (1988): 790.

[83] Clifford Geertz, " 'From the Native's Point of View': On the Nature of Anthropological Understanding," in *Symbolic Anthropology: A Reader in the Study of Symbols and Meanings*, ed. Janet L. Dolgin et al. (New York: Columbia University Press, 1977), 481.

[84] Geertz, "Ideology as a Cultural System," 64.

[85] Clifford Geertz, *After the Fact: Two Countries, Four Decades, One Anthropologist* (Cambridge: Harvard University Press, 1995), 100. Despite their many similarities, Eckstein and Geertz part company here. Eckstein believes that Geertz's approach to culture ultimately repudiates positive social science and Comte's attempt to design a "social physics," a project that Eckstein hoped to salvage. Harry Eckstein, "Culture as a Foundation Concept for the Social Sciences," *Journal of Theoretical Politics* 8, no. 4 (1996): 476, 495.

[86] Cited in Kenneth Burke, *On Symbols and Society* (Chicago: University of Chicago Press, 1989), 27.

[87] Geertz, *After the Fact*, 26.

[88] Ibid., 27.

[89] Geertz, " 'From the Native's Point of View,' " 486, 492.

[90] Geertz, *Available Light*, 198.

[91] Ibid., 226–27.

[92] Ann Swidler, "Cultural Power and Social Movements," in *Social Movements and Culture*, ed. Hank Johnston and Bert Klandermans (Minneapolis: University of Minnesota Press, 1995), 28.

[93] Cited in Robert C. Tucker, "Culture, Political Culture, and Communist Society," *Political Science Quarterly* 88, no. 2 (June 1973): 177.

[94] David I. Kertzer, *Ritual, Politics, and Power* (New Haven : Yale University Press, 1988), 40.

[95] Victor Turner, *Dramas, Fields, and Metaphors: Symbolic Action in Human Society* (Ithaca: Cornell University Press, 1974), 64; Victor Turner, "Liminality and the Performative Genres," in *Studies in Symbolism and Cultural Communication*, ed. F. Allan Hanson (Lawrence: University of Kansas, 1982), 27.

[96] Ortner, "Theory in Anthropology," 374–75.

[97] Victor Turner, *The Forest of Symbols* (Ithaca: Cornell University Press, 1967), 36.

[98] Abner Cohen, *Two-Dimensional Man* (Berkeley: University of California Press, 1974), 132.

[99] Abner Cohen, *The Politics of Elite Culture* (Berkeley: University of California Press, 1981), 210.

[100] Karl Lamb made much the same point in his classic study of voters in Orange County, California: "An appeal for meaningful political change which involves . . . voters must be couched in terms of the national values and traditions they accept. Political leaders must be dedicated to the restoration of presumed past grandeurs. These voters will not follow those who tell them they have accepted a misinterpretation of history or claim that the promises of America were always fraudulent." Karl A. Lamb, *As Orange Goes: Twelve California Families and the Future of American Politics* (New York: Norton, 1974), 302.

[101] Abner Cohen, *The Symbolic Construction of Community* (London: Routledge, 1985), 102.

[102] Cohen, *Politics of Elite Culture*, 155.

[103] Abner Cohen, *The Management of Myths* (Manchester, U.K.: Manchester University Press, 1974), 12.

[104] Roy Wagner, *The Invention of Culture* (Chicago: University of Chicago Press, 1981), 158.

[105] Ibid., 51, 104–6.

[106] Cited in Burke, *On Symbols and Society*, 5.

[107] Richard Jenkins, *Pierre Bourdieu* (London: Routledge, 1992), 39.

[108] Ibid., 37.

[109] David Swartz, "Bridging the Study of Culture and Religion: Pierre Bourdieu's Political Economy of Symbolic Power," *Sociology of Religion* 57, no. 1 (1996): 74–75.

[110] Swartz, "Bridging the Study of Culture and Religion," 71.

[111] Ibid., 76.

[112] Nicholas Garnham, "Bourdieu, the Cultural Arbitrary, and Television," in *Bourdieu: Critical Perspectives*, ed. Craig Calhoun et al. (Chicago: University of Chicago Press, 1993), 180.

[113] Swartz, "Bridging the Study of Culture and Religion," 80–81.

[114] Harold Blumer, *Symbolic Interactionism: Perspective and Method* (Berkeley: University of California Press, 1969), 26–27.

[115] Ibid., 80.

[116] Ralph H. Turner and Lewis M. Killian, *Collective Behavior* (Englewood Cliffs, N.J.: Prentice-Hall, 1957); Neil J. Smelser, *Theory of Collective Behavior* (New York: Free Press, 1962).

[117] Ann Swidler, "Culture in Action: Symbols and Strategies," *American Sociological Review* 51 (1986): 277.

[118] Ibid., 273.

[119] Ibid., 281.

[120] Ibid., 282–83.

[121] Ibid., 283.

[122] Mayer N. Zald, "Culture, Ideology, and Strategic Framing," in *Comparative Perspectives on Social Movements: Political Opportunities, Mobilizing Structures, and Cultural Framings*, ed. Doug McAdam et al. (Cambridge: Cambridge University Press, 1996), 268.

[123] Ibid., 270–71.

[124] I call these "alternative political cultures" in my book *The Rebirth of Russian Democracy: An Interpretation of Political Culture* (Cambridge: Harvard University Press, 1995).

[125] Stephen Hart, "The Cultural Dimension of Social Movements: A Theoretical Reassessment and Literature Review," *Sociology of Religion* 57, no. 1 (1996): 91, 96.

[126] Cited in Carol Mueller, "Conflict Networks and the Origins of Women's Liberation," in *New Social Movements: From Ideology to Identity*, ed. Enrique Larana et al. (Philadelphia: Temple University Press, 1994), 236.

[127] Ibid., 239.

[128] "Of the four dimensions of opposition movement emergence, grievances, ideology, capacity to organize, and political opportunity, the first three were set already in late 1988 and early 1989, and probably even earlier." Anthony Oberschall, "Opportunities and Framing in the 1989 Revolts," in *Comparative Perspectives*, ed. McAdam et al., 121.

[129] Richard J. Ellis and Michael Thompson, eds., *Culture Matters: Essays in Honor of Aaron Wildavsky* (Boulder, Colo.: Westview, 1997), 1.

[130] Murray Edelman, *Constructing the Political Spectacle* (Chicago: University of Chicago Press, 1988).

[131] Ibid., 7.

[132] Murray Edelman, "Language, Myths, and Rhetoric," *Society* 35, no. 2 (January/February 1998): 132.

[133] Ibid., 103.

[134] Ibid., 46–47.

[135] Edelman, *Constructing the Political Spectacle*, 22.

[136] Murray Edelman, *From Art to Politics: How Artistic Creations Shape Political Conceptions* (Chicago: University of Chicago Press, 1995).

[137] W. Lance Bennett, "Myth, Ritual, and Political Control," *Journal of Communication* 30, no. 4 (1980): 171.

[138] W. Lance Bennett, "Constructing Publics and Their Opinions," *Political Communication* 10 (April 1993): 108, 117.

[139] Ibid., 173.

[140] "The assumption that people are generally uneducable in a mass communication context (or, more basically, that they tune out and turn off 'highbrow' media in favor of more shallow and sensational alternatives) is the founding assumption that keeps this constructed world reproducing itself . . . most journalists and news watchers would agree that it makes little sense to introduce the views of uneducable publics into representations of politics that are believed to be beyond them." W. Lance Bennett and John D. Klockner, "The Psychology of Mass-Mediated Publics," in *The Psychology of Political Communication*, ed. Ann N. Crigler (Ann Arbor: University of Michigan Press, 1996), 93.

[141] Richard M. Merelman, "Introduction," in *Language, Symbolism, and Politics*, ed. Richard M. Merelman (Boulder, Colo.: Westview, 1992), 4.

[142] James Scott, "False-Consciousness, or Laying It On Thick," in *Language, Symbolism, and Politics*, ed. Merelman, 209.

[143] Ibid., 221.

[144] Ibid., 216.

[145] Ibid., 235–36.

[146] Charles D. Elder and Roger W. Cobb, *The Political Uses of Symbols* (New York: Longman, 1983), 23–26.

[147] David O. Sears, "Symbolic Politics: A Socio-Psychological Theory," in *Explorations in Political Psychology*, ed. Shanto Iyengar and William J. McGuire (Durham, N.C.: Duke University Press, 1993), 143.

[148] Ibid., 131, 136.

[149] Lowell Dittmer, "Political Culture and Political Symbolism: Toward a Theoretical Synthesis," *World Politics* 29, no. 4 (July 1977): 561.

[150] Ibid., 570.

[151] Ibid., 578–79.

[152] Ibid., 562.

[153] Ibid., 583.

[154] Alison Brysk, "Hearts and Minds: Bringing Symbolic Politics Back In," *Polity* 27 (1995): 567.

[155] Ibid., 561–62.

[156] Ibid., 576.

[157] Ibid., 579–81.

[158] Ibid., 582.

[159] Eckstein, "A Culturalist Theory," 795.

[160] Eric Hobsbawm and Terence Ranger, *The Invention of Tradition* (Cambridge: Cambridge University Press, 1983), 11.

[161] "When mythical themes and myth-related language are stripped away from public discourse," W. Lance Bennett writes, "very little of substance remains." Cited in Kertzer, *Ritual, Politics, and Power*, 13.

[162] Cohen, *Symbolic Construction of Community*, 8.

[163] Eric Hobsbawm, *On History* (New York: New Press, 1997), 16.

[164] D. Fahrni, *An Outline History of Switzerland* (Zurich: Pro Helvetia, 1987); U. Im Hof, *Mythos Schweiz* (Zurich: Neue Zurcher Zeitung, 1991).

CHAPTER 5. NOVGOROD IN RUSSIA'S MEMORY

Epigraph source: Henry Tudor, *Political Myth* (New York: Praeger Publishers, 1972), 132

[1] Available online from the website of *Russkaya mysl* (Paris), http://www.rusmysl.ru/1999III/4284/428435.html.

[2] Robert D. Blackwill, former national security adviser to President George Bush, cited by David S. Broder, "A 'Success Story' Gone Sour," *Washington Post*, December 19, 1993, p. C-8.

[3] I. Y. Froyanov, *Myatezhnyi Novgorod: Ocherki istorii gosudarstvennosti, sotsialnoi, i politicheskoi borby kontsa IX–nachala XIII stoletiya* (St. Petersburg: S-Peterburgskii universitet, 1992), 69; O. V. Martyshin, *Volnyi Novgorod: Obshchestvenno-politicheskii stroi i pravo feodalnoi respubliki* (Moscow: Rossiiskoe pravo, 1992), 59.

[4] M. V. Popelkhov, "Sotsialno-politicheskii kontekst prisutstviya varyagov v severo-zapadnoi Rusi v 850–860-kh godakh," in *Proshloe Novgoroda i Novgorodskoi zemli: Materialy nauchnoi konferentsii 11–13 noyabrya 1998 goda*, ed. Vasily Andreyev (Novgorod: Novgorodskii gosudarstvennyi universitet im. Yaroslava Mudrogo, 1998), 25–26. They were allocated a household five kilometers outside the city and granted a lot on which to graze their horses. This limitation applied to the prince and his direct family. Valentin Yanin, "Na zemlyakh drevnego Novgoroda u istokov Rossiiskoi gosudarstvennosti," *Novgorod* (October 22, 1998), 8.

[5] Historian Vladimir Bernadsky terms the corpus of these accords "Novgorod's written constitution." Vladimir N. Bernadsky, *Novgorod i Novgorodskaya zemlya v XV veke* (Moscow and Leningrad: Akademiya Nauk SSSR, 1961), 22.

[6] Galina Luchterhandt, Sergej Ryshenkow, and Alexej Kusmin, *Politik und Kultur in der Russischen Provinz: Nowgorod, Woronesh, Saratow, Jekaterinburg* (Bremen, Germany: Edition Temmen, 1999), 27.

[7] Dmitry Likhachev, *Razdumya o Rossii* (St. Petersburg: Logos, 2001), 146.

[8] Ibid., Svetlana Sukhova, "Ryurik zhil na odnu zarplatu," *Itogi*, November 26, 2002.

[9] Likhachev, *Razdumya*, 146.

[10] Ibid., 197, 198; Henrik Birnbaum, *Novgorod in Focus: Selected Essays* (Columbus, Ohio: Slavica Publishers, 1996), 21.

[11] Theodor Schilling, "Subsidiarity as a Rule and a Principle, or: Taking Subsidiarity Seriously," *Jean Monnet Working Papers* no. 10 (1995) at: http://www.jeanmonnetprogram.org/papers/95/9510ind.html.

[12] Martyshin, *Volnyi Novgorod*, 259.

[13] Historian A. V. Petrov believes that the attempt by princes to assert greater authority in the late eighth century encouraged the emergence of a decentralized federal system and a stronger magistrate. A. V. Petrov, "K izucheniyu otnoshenii s knyazyami i vnutrennei borby v Novgorode vtoroi poloviny XIII v.," in *Problemy istorii Severo-zapada Rusi*, ed. Igor V. Dubov and Igor Ya. Froyanov (St. Petersburg: Izdatelstvo S.-Peterburgskogo universiteta, 1995), 135.

[14] The word "veche" stems from the word *veshchat*, which means to speak with authority.

[15] Ruslan G. Skrynnikov, *Tragediya Novgoroda* (Moscow: Izd. im. Sabashnikovykh, 1994), 16; Martyshin, *Volnyi Novgorod*, 185–87.

[16] Martyshin, *Volnyi Novgorod*, 179.

[17] A. Ya. Efimenko, *Elementarnyi uchebnik Russkoi istorii dlya sredne-uchebnykh i vysshikh nachalnykh uchilishch* (Petrograd: Ya. Bashmakov & Co., 1916), 4–5; Martyshin, *Volnyi Novgorod*, 243.

[18] Klyuchevsky speculated that several *ulitsy* formed a *sotnya*, and two *sotni* a *konets*. Martyshin, *Volnyi Novgorod*, 253–54.

[19] Maria Yu. Melchakova, "K probleme sushchestvovaniya drevnerusskoi demokratii," in *Novgorodskaya Rus: Istoricheskoe prostranstvo i kulturnoe nasledie*, ed. A. T. Shashkov et al. (Ekaterinburg: Uralskii gosudarstvennyi universitet im A. M. Gorkogo, 2000), 203.

[20] Ibid., 204.

[21] Martyshin, *Volnyi Novgorod*, 175–76.

[22] Ibid., 88, 191.

[23] Ibid., 189.

[24] Efimenko, *Elementarnyi uchebnik Russkoi istorii*, 3–4.

[25] Martyshin, *Volnyi Novgorod*, 210. The distinctive Novgorod tradition of its bishops wearing a white cowl emerges as a statement of opposition to the dominance of secular rulers. Serge Zenkovsky, *Medieval Russia's Epics* (New York: E. P. Dalton, 1974), 328–29.

[26] Martyshin, *Volnyi Novgorod*, 162.

[27] T. A. Mikhailova, "Veliky Novgorod," in *Pamyatniki istorii i kultury Novgorodskoi oblasti–katalog*, ed. S. P. Guryev (Veliky Novgorod: Ministerstvo kultury Rossiiskoi Fedratsii, 1999), 35.

[28] Martyshin, *Volnyi Novgorod*, 182.

[29] Mikhailova, "Veliky Novgorod," 42.

[30] Sergei Filatov and Roman Lunkin, "Drugaya Svyataya Rus," *Druzhba narodov* 5 (2001): 2–19.

[31] It has been estimated that during the latter half of the fifteenth century the church owned 21.7 percent of all arable land, nearly a third of it administered directly by the archbishop. Martyshin, *Volnyi Novgorod*, 161.

[32] E. A. Gordienko, *Novgorod v XVI veke i ego dukhovnaya zhizn* (St. Petersburg: Rossiiskaya akademiya nauk, 2001), 294.

[33] Stavr and his friends apparently received their comeuppance, but this did not in the least diminish the region's reputation for rebelliousness. Stanislav Desyatskov, "Boyarstvo i dvoryanstvo na novgorodskoi zemle," *Novgorod*, October 14, 1999. A rich compilation of foreign visitor's accounts of Novgorod can be found in *Veliky Novgorod v inostrannykh sochineniyakh XV–nach. XX veka*, comp. G. M. Kovalenko (Veliky Novgorod: NovGU im. Yaroslava Mudrogo, 2002).

[34] V. A. Varentsov and G. M. Kovalenko, *V sostave Moskovskogo gosudarstva: Ocherki istorii velikogo Novgoroda kontsa XV–nachala XVIII vv.* (St. Petersburg: Russko-Baltiisky informatsionnyi tsentr "BLITs," 1999), 157–59.

[35] Evgeny Shmurlo, *Kurs russkoi istorii* (Prague, 1931–1935), vol. 1, 9–11; Likhachev, *Razdumya*, 142.

[36] Elena A. Rybina, *Torgovlya srednevekovogo Novgoroda: Istoriko-arkheologicheskie ocherki* (Veliky Novgorod: Novgorodskii gosudarstvennyi universitet imeni Yaroslava Mudrogo, 2001), 98.

[37] Ibid., 178, 209.

[38] Ibid., 224.

[39] Ibid.

[40] Zoya Sogrina, "Simvol sily, simvol slavy . . . ," *Novgorod* (May 27, 1999), 9.

[41] Birnbaum, *Novgorod in Focus*, 72.

[42] Rybina argues that Novgorod's republican political system predated that of the cities it traded with and that they were not strongly affected by the West. Rybina, *Torgovlya srednevekovogo Novgoroda*, 195. Historian Marc Szeftel, on the other hand, argues that Novgorod's political institutions were the indirect result of contact with Hanseatic institutions. Szeftel, *Russian Institutions and Culture up to Peter the Great* (London: Variorum Reprints, 1975), 375–430.

[43] Rybina, *Torgovlya srednevekovogo Novgoroda*, 94.

[44] Martyshin, *Volnyi Novgorod*, 267–68.

[45] Cited in David B. Miller, "The Luebeckers Bartholomaeus Ghotan and Nicolaus Buelow in Novgorod and Moscow and the Problem of Early Western Influences on Russian Culture," *Viator: Medieval and Renaissance Studies* 9 (1978): 409.

[46] Svetlana A. Kovarskaya, "Dukhovno-obrazovatelnye traditsii v sotsiodinamike kultury Velikogo Novgoroda," *Vestnik Novgorodskogo gosudarstvennogo universiteta: Seriya "Gumanitarnye*

nauki" 16 (November 2000): 13; Birnbaum, *Novgorod in Focus,* 101, 103; Gordienko, *Novgorod v XVI veke,* 34.

[47] Varentsov and Kovalenko, *V sostave Moskovskogo gosudarstva,* 124.

[48] Birnbaum, *Novgorod in Focus,* 36–37.

[49] L. Grigoreva, "Iz istorii idei Rennessanskogo gumanizma v Novgorodskoi kulture XVI–XVIII vv.," in *Proshloe Novgoroda,* ed. Andreyev, 68.

[50] Kovarskaya, "Dukhovno-obrazovatelnye traditsii," 9.

[51] Ibid., 12.

[52] Birnbaum, *Novgorod in Focus,* 165.

[53] During the decisive battle at the Shelon River (July 14, 1471), the archbishop's troops refused to fight against the Muscovites. Nikolai Grinev, "Otsyuda poshla zemlya Russkaya . . . ," *Novgorod* (June 10, 1999), 9.

[54] Casimir was given the same terms that every other prince in Novgorod had had: he and his representatives could not reside in the city; he could have no more than fifty persons in his retinue including servants; he could not own land; and he was forbidden to build Catholic churches or to involve himself in any way in the election of the archbishop or the veche. Skrynnikov, *Tragediya Novgoroda,* 11.

[55] Andrei Burovsky, *Rossiya, kotoroy ne bylo–2: Russkaya Atlantida* (Krasnoyarsk: Bonus, 2000), 390.

[56] In 1200 Prince Vsevolod III of Suzdal defeated Novgorod's army, but a decade later he was forced to confirm their right to select their own prince.

[57] Gordienko, *Novgorod v XVI veke,* 107. Desyatskov, "Boyarstvo i dvoryanstvo," October 14, 1999.

[58] Skrynnikov, *Tragediya Novgoroda,* 105; Varentsov and Kovalenko, *V sostave Moskovskogo gosudarstva,* 23; Gordienko, *Novgorod v XVI veke,* 362.

[59] Varentsov and Kovalenko, *V sostave Moskovskogo gosudarstva,* 9; Birnbaum, *Novgorod in Focus,* 180; Gordienko, *Novgorod v XVI veke,* 301.

[60] V. A. Varentsov, "Struktura upraveleniya Novgorodom v XVI veke," *Vestnik Novgorodskogo gosudarstvennogo universiteta: Seriya "Gumanitarnye nauki"* 4 (May 1996): 41–42.

[61] Cited in Varentsov and Kovalenko, *V sostave Moskovskogo gosudarstva,* 8, 108.

[62] Ibid., 89.

[63] Ibid., 11.

[64] Ibid., 42.

[65] Svetlana A. Kovarskaya, "Novgorodskoe zemstvo v dorevolutsionnoi istoriografii," in *Proshloe Novgoroda,* ed. Andreyev, 128–29.

[66] A. S. Turgaev, "Pozemelnaya arenda i sobstvennye zemli pakhotnykh soldat Novgorodskoi gubernii v seredine XIX v.," *Novgorodskii istoricheskii sbornik* 14, no. 4 (1993): 152.

[67] E. K. Rozov, "Puti resheniya agrarnogo voprosa v Novgorodskoi gubernii s 1861 po 1917 g.," in *Proshloe Novgoroda,* ed. Andreyev, 135–36.

[68] Several *byliny* (epic tales) hinted at widespread literacy, but it was not until the 1970s that archeological expeditions confirmed the extensive use of written documents in the early Middle Ages in Novgorod. See Likhachev, *Razdumya,* 166; and V. L. Yanin, "The Archaeology of Novgorod," *Scientific American* 262, no. 2 (February 1990): 84–92. With the establishment of the central Moscow printing house in 1650, it became possible to order printed books in major Russian cities. For the latter half of that year, records indicate that among thirty-two Russian cities with subscriptions to the code of laws (*sobornoe ulozhenie*), Novgorod ordered the most copies—forty-five. Varentsov and Kovalenko, *V sostave Moskovskogo gosudarstva,* 144.

[69] Skrynnikov, *Tragediya Novgoroda,* 153; Martyshin, *Volnyi Novgorod,* 72, 248; Aleksei Gippius, "Novgorodskie berestyanye gramoty prodolzhayut prepodnesti syurprizy," *Itogi,* April 13, 1999.

[70] Martyshin, *Volnyi Novgorod,* 13, 19, 34.

[71] Stalin tried to rehabilitate the image of Ivan IV and apparently personally ordered historians to seek justifications for Ivan IV's decimation of Novgorod. He even got the Central Committee of the CPSU to pass a resolution on Eisenstein's film *Ivan the Terrible* stating that the famous filmmaker had not given sufficient attention to the "progressive" nature of Ivan's rule and the "reactionary" nature of the princes and boyars. Vladmir V. Tyurin, "Drevnii

Novgorod v Russkoi literature XX veka," *Chelo* 3, no. 2 (1998): 26; Burovsky, *Rossiya, kotoroy ne bylo–2*, 357; Martyshin, *Volnyi Novgorod*, 20, 29.

[72] Filatov and Lunkin, "Drugaya Svyataya Rus," 3.

[73] Ibid., 8.

[74] "Vechevoi Novgorodskii Kolokol," available online at the site of the bell museum of Valdai at: http://www.novgorod.ru/city/history/kolokola/txt/veche.htm. I first heard this legend from my neighbor one week after first arriving in Novgorod in August 1996.

[75] This coincides with a Muscovite chronicler's version that, on coming to Moscow, the Novgorod bell was put in a place of honor in the Uspensky Cathedral to sing along with others, after setting aside its pride.

[76] Vladimir V. Tyurin, *Na zemle Sadko* (Leningrad: Lenizdat, 1986), 178.

[77] This inquiry was apparently passed along to the Archeological Society of Moscow, which replied that the veche bell from Novgorod had been recast by Ivan Motorin in the eighteenth century and now sits in the Kremlin Armory. "Vechevoi Novgorodskii kolokol."

[78] A. Z. Zhavoronkov, comp., *Novgorod v russkoi literature XVIII–XX vv.* (Novgorod: Novgorodskaya pravda, 1959), 8–9.

[79] Ibid., 7.

[80] Sergei N. Travnikov, "Tema drevnego Novgoroda v proizvedeniyakh A. N. Radishcheva," *Literatura drevnei Rusi* 2 (1975): 109; E. F. Tikhonov et al., eds., *Pisateli na Novgorodskoi zemle* (Novgorod: Novgorodskaya pravda, 1960), 9.

[81] Tyurin, *Na zemle Sadko*, 13.

[82] Travnikov, "Tema drevnego Novgoroda," 106, 110.

[83] Tyurin, *Na zemle Sadko*, 49.

[84] Zhavoronkov, *Novgorod v russkoi literature*, 15, 18–19.

[85] Tikhonov et al., eds., *Pisateli na Novgorodskoi zemle*, 23.

[86] Zhavoronkov, *Novgorod v russkoi literature*, 99.

[87] S. S. Volk, *Istoricheskie vzglyady dekabristov* (Moscow and Leningrad: Izd. Akademii Nauk SSSR, 1958), 329–46.

[88] Volk, *Istoricheskie vzglyady dekabristov*, 326.

[89] Ibid., 344.

[90] Ibid., 328.

[91] Alexander I. Herzen, *Povesti. Byloe i Dumy. Stati* (Moscow: Olimp, 1999), 363.

[92] Zhavoronkov, *Novgorod v russkoi literature*, 108.

[93] Ibid., 21.

[94] Martyshin, *Volnyi Novgorod*, 14–15.

[95] Alexander Herzen, "Novgorod Velikii i Vladimir na Klyazme," in Zhavoronkov, *Novgorod v russkoi literature*, 135–36. Later in life, when he reached the conclusion that Russia's salvation lay in its peasant communes, the *obschina*, and he had convinced himself that in Novgorod the obshchina had a higher status than the prince, Herzen warmed a bit to Novgorod. Ibid., 25.

[96] Ibid., 26.

[97] Volk, *Istoricheskie vzglyady dekabristov*, 347.

[98] Tikhonov et al., eds., *Pisateli na novgorodskoi zemle*, 30, 61.

[99] M. P. Mokhnacheva, "Istoriya Novgoroda Velikogo v osveshchenii zhurnala 'Niva,' " in *Proshloe Novgoroda*, ed. Andreyev, 109.

[100] Zhavoronkov, *Novgorod v russkoi literature*, 200–201.

[101] Martyshin, *Volnyi Novgorod*, 12.

[102] Victor G. Smirnov, *Rossiya v bronze* (Moscow: Veche, 2002), 59.

[103] Among the former, one could mention *Gospodin Veliky Novgorod* and *Marfa posadnitsa*, both by Dmitry Balashov; Boris Izyumsky's *Timofei s kholopei ulitsy*, and P. Gubanov's *Nabatnoe utro*. The latter include A. Yugov's *Rotobortsy*, V. Kargalov's *Russkii shchit*, V. Usov's *Tsari i skitaltsy*, E. Zorin's *Bolshoe gnezdo*, V. Chivilikhin's *Pamyat*, and V. Yazvitsky's *Ivan III*.

[104] Tikhonov et al., eds., *Pisateli na Novgorodskoi zemle*, 36–37.

[105] Zhavoronkov, *Novgorod v russkoi literature*, 38.

[106] See, for example, Vladimir Soloukhin's *Vladimirskie prosyolki* and *Chernaya doska*, in which the heavy hand of communist (read Muscovite) rule is contrasted to the rich spiritual heritage of the Russian north (that is, the lands of Novgorod).

[107] Martyshin, *Volnyi Novgorod*, 47.

[108] N. A. Omelchenko, *V poiskakh Rossii* (St. Petersburg: Russkii khristianskii gumanitarnyi institut, 1996), 441.

[109] Ibid., 443.

[110] George P. Fedotov, "Respublika svyatoi Sofii," *Narodnaya pravda* (New York) no. 11–12 (November 1950), 23.

[111] Ibid., 22. Curiously, archeologists have recently discovered evidence of a direct intellectual link between Venice and Novgorod—an early coin showing St. Sophia bestowing the symbols of authority on the magistrate appears to be a copy of a Venetian coin that shows St. Mark doing the same to the doge. Svetlana Sukhova, "Ryurik zhil na odnu zarplatu," *Itogi*, November 26, 2002.

[112] Fedotov, "Respublika svyatoi Sofii," 21.

[113] Zhavoronkov, *Novgorod v russkoi literature*, 147.

[114] Fedotov, "Respublika svyatoi Sofii," 21, 23.

[115] For a similar argument juxtaposing positive Novgorod patterns of economic and political development against poor Muscovite ones, see Thomas C. Owen, "Novgorod and Muscovy as Models of Russian Economic Development," *Harvard Ukrainian Studies* 19 (1995): 497–512.

[116] Alexander V. Isachenko, "Esli by v kontse XV veka Novgorod oderzhal pobedu nad Moskvoi," *Vestnik Rossiiskoi akademii nauk* 68, no. 11 (1998) at: http://www.ibmh.msk.su/vivovoco/vv/journal/vran/novgorod.htm. Originally published in *Wiener Slawistisches Jahrbuch* 18 (1973): 48–55.

[117] Ibid.

[118] V. B. Krysko, "Bez gneva i pristrastiya . . . ," *Vestnik Rossiiskoi akademii nauk* 69, no. 12 (1999) at: http://www.ibmh.msk.su/vivovoco/vv/journal/vran/novgorod.htm#first; V. I. Suprun, "Smelyi eksperiment," *Vestnik Rossiiskoi akademii nauk* 69, no. 12 (1999), http://www.ibmh.msk.su/vivovoco/vv/journal/vran/novgorod.htm#scnd.

[119] Suprun, "Smelyi eksperiment."

[120] Varentsov and Kovalenko, *V sostave Moskovskogo gosudarstva*, 7.

[121] Skrynnikov, *Tragediya Novgoroda*, 19.

[122] Dmitry S. Likhachev, "Nelzya uyti ot samikh sebia . . . ," *Novyi mir* (June 1994): 113–14.

[123] Peter Ford, "Medieval City Holds Key to 'Russian Idea,'" *Christian Science Monitor*, June 5, 1997; "Historian Champions Medieval Novgorod as Model for Russia's Democratic Development," *Jamestown Foundation Monitor*, May 7, 1997.

[124] Aleksandr Ivanov, "Veche zamolchalo," *Expert: Severo-zapad* 20, no. 27 (November 27, 2000).

[125] Gennady Lisichkin, *Est li budushchee u Rossii* (Moscow: Kultura, 1996), 164.

[126] Ibid., 171, 180.

[127] Burovsky, *Rossiya, kotoroy ne bylo-2*, 183.

[128] Ibid., 394.

[129] Andrei M. Burovsky, "Veliky Novgorod: Problema istoricheskoi sudby," *Vestnik Novgorodskogo gosudartsvennogo universiteta: Seriya "Gumanitarnye nauki"* 12 (August 1999): 4.

[130] Burovsky, *Rossiya, kotoroy ne bylo-2*, 246.

[131] More than a dozen articles each in *Nevskoe vremya* and *Pereburgskii Chas pik*, two dozen more in *Delo, Severo-Zapadnyi Zelenyi Krest, Smena, Komsomolskaya Pravda, Ogonyok, Pulse-Sankt-Peterburg, Petrovsky kuryer* (Vyborg region), *Liga izbiratelnits, Andreyevski Fond, Tribuna-Delovoi vtornik, Severnyi Kuryer,* and *Posev*, http://ingermanland.narod.ru/Inger06.htm.

[132] Moris Simashko, "Pyatyi Rim," *Oktyabr* no. 7 (2001); Sergei Filatov, "Kareliya: Pravoslavno-lyuteransoe pogranichya," *Druzhba narodov* no. 5 (2000); Igor Chubais, "Razgadannaya Rossiya," *Russkiy zhurnal* (July 3, 2001), http://www.russ.ru/politics/meta/20010703-chub.html.

[133] Thus, in May 1999, Vladimir Ryzhkov, the head of the Our Home Is Russia faction in the Russian Duma, proposed moving Russia's capital to Novgorod because it was "the birth-

place of Russian republicanism." "Vopros: kuda by stolitsu perenesti?" *Kommersant-vlast*, May 5, 1999.

[134] Alexander Goryanin, *Mify o Rossii i dukh natsii* (Moscow: Pentagraphic, 2002).

[135] Lisichkin, *Est li budushchee*, 184.

[136] Likhachev, *Razdumya*, 148.

[137] Local archives have revealed interesting new details about the population's response to German occupation, including that the pro-German local administration regarded appeals to Novgorod's Hanseatic past as a good way to build popular support. Boris N. Kovalyov, "Funktsii i deyatelnost Novgorodskoi politsii v usloviyakh natsistskogo okkupatsionnogo rezhima (1941–1943gg.)," in *Proshloe Novgoroda*, ed. Andreyev, 184–85. Interestingly, in 2002 a debate raged in the Novgorod press over whether the Soviet characterization of these individuals as traitors should be revised, since some of these wartime collaborators acted to preserve local historical and religious monuments. Yana Vilena, "Spasti, chtoby ukrast," *Novaya novgorodskaya gazeta* (April 24, 2002); Roman Konev, "Sledy ischeznuvshikh," *Vremya novgorodskoe* (May 9, 2002), and replies by historian Boris Kovalyov, who was interviewed by Maksim Vladimirov, "Tsennye lyudi tretyego reikha," *Novgorodskie vedomosti* (May 18 and May 25, 2002).

CHAPTER 6. SYMBOLS AT WORK

Epigraph source: Max Lerner, *Ideas for the Ice Age* (New York: Viking, 1941), 235

[1] Mikhail M. Prusak, "Nastupilo vremya stroit," *Posev*, no. 4 (July–August 1994): 56–59; Blair Ruble and Nancy Popson, "The Westernization of a Russian Province: The Case of Novgorod," *Post-Soviet Geography and Economics* 39, no. 8 (1998): 433–46; Olga Senatova and Andrei Yakurin, "Ekonomicheskoe i politicheskoe razvitie Novgorodskoi oblasti" (1999), a report commissioned by the Federal German Institute for East European Studies (BIOst), personal copy.

[2] Irina D. Savinova, *Likholetie: Novgorodskaya eparkhiya i sovetskaya vlast, 1917–1991* (Novgorod the Great: Chelo, 1998), 102. In December 1987 such an appeal garnered only eighty signatures. By early 1988, however, that number had risen to 1,462.

[3] "Otkrytoe pismo," *Veche* 1, no. 2 (1989), 1.

[4] Yulia Generozova, "Za poslednie 9 let v Novgorodskoi oblasti tserkvi bylo peredano okolo 100 tserkvei," *Delovoi Peterburg*, October 3, 2001. Deputy governor Galina Matveeva meets regularly with representatives of different regional confessions to discuss their needs. Dmitry Zlaerov, "Bogoiskateli s ulitsy Kochetova," available on the *Pravda.ru* website (November 12, 2003), http://society.pravda.ru/society/2003/8/26/81/14726_baptist.html.

[5] V. Sochilin, head of the socioeconomic section of the regional committee (*obkom*) CPSU, "O prorabotke novogo varianta kontseptsii Novgorodskogo otkrytogo sektora," October 2, 1989. A memo prepared for the members of the obkom, available at the State Archives of the Contemporary Political History of the Novgorod Region, ul. Desyatinnaya 6, Novgorod the Great, Russia.

[6] Interview with Igor B. Alexandrov, former chief architect for the city of Novgorod and member of the working group established to examine the FEZ, Novgorod the Great, Russia (May 1, 2000).

[7] Galina Makeeva, "Novgorod s molotka . . . ," *Literaturnaya Rossiya* (November 11, 1989), 2. Unknown to many no doubt sincere activists, local communist authorities had set up the UWF to discredit the FEZ and prevent it from turning the oblast "into a hotbed of speculators, prostitutes, and carriers of AIDS." V. I. Aksyonov, "Zapiska ideologicheskogo otdela obkoma KPSS 'O deyatelnosti i napravlennosti samodeyatelnykh formirovanii v oblasti,'" no. 02–8 (February 28, 1989). Available at the State Archives of the Contemporary Political History of the Novgorod Region, ul. Desyatinnaya 6, Novgorod the Great, Russia.

[8] A. Afanasyev, head of the department for social analysis and planning, ideological section of the obkom CPSU, "Otchet o resultatakh sotsiologicheskogo issledovaniya 'Vzglyady i otsenki sovremennoi molodezhi,'" February 13, 1991. Available at the State

Archives of the Contemporary Political History of the Novgorod Region, ul. Desyatinnaya 6, Novgorod the Great, Russia.

[9] Aksyonov, "Zapiska ideologicheskogo otdela obkoma."

[10] Senatova and Yakurin, "Ekonomicheskoe i politicheskoe razvitie," 7.

[11] "Zdravstvuyte!" *Novgorod* (October 30, 1990), 1. The editorial stance of *Novgorod* was fairly typical at the time. The newspaper *Zemlya Novgorodskaya* played a similar function for rural readers, and its editor recalls that some 20 percent of the content dealt specifically with reintroducing historical themes from local Novgorod history; 30 percent dealt with the reorganization of collective farms and new concepts such as private farming; and the rest was regional news, national news, and biographies of new political leaders. At its height the paper had a circulation of over ten thousand. Interview with Valery N. Stovba, former editor of *Zemlya Novgorodskaya* and press secretary to Governor Prusak from 1990 to 1993, Novgorod the Great, Russia (April 16, 2002).

[12] "Kakaya vlast na dvore," *Novgorod* (October 30, 1990), 1.

[13] Mikhail Petrov, "Imeni Pervogo Sekretarya obkoma," *Novgorod* (January 25, 1991), 3.

[14] Vasily Andreyev, "Chto v imeni tebe moem . . . ?" *Novgorod* (January 4, 1991), 3.

[15] A few Soviet-era names still appear in the newer regions of the city that were built after World War II.

[16] "Zanimalis i politikoi," *Nezavisimaya gazeta* (October 16, 1993), 1.

[17] Alexander Vasilyev, "Sobitiya nedeli," *Novgorod* (October 22–29, 1993), 1–2.

[18] Ibid., 1.

[19] Mikhail Prusak, opening remarks to the eightieth anniversary of the founding of the Communist Youth League, Novgorod, Novgorod Political Archives Fund (October 29, 1998), personal notes.

[20] Although he never stood for public office, the university's first rector, Vladimir Soroka, actively encouraged his aides to enter local politics. Until his untimely death in 1998, he promoted a vision of a classical university in which, unlike typical Soviet institutions of higher learning, regional concerns and the humanities would play a primary role. Vladimir V. Soroka, *Vysshee obrazovanie v Novgorode* (Novgorod: Novgorodskii gosudarstevennyi universitet, 1996).

[21] Petr Shchedrovitsky and Valentin Tolstykh, "Novgorodskii Proekt: Proryv v postindustrialnoe obshechestvo" (Moscow: Gorbachev Foundation, 1995), personal copy. Among the participants from Novgorod were Vladimir Averkin, head of the region's educational administration; Anatoly Gavrikov, then vice-rector and now president of Novgorod State University; Nikolai Grinev, head of the Novgorod State Unified Museum-Preserve; Viktor Smirnov, head of the local television studio Slaviya and local historian; Oleg Ochin, then deputy to the federal Duma deputy from the Novgorod Region; Andrei Masalov, head of the region's economic committee; and Vladislav Alekseev, head of the department for development and support of entrepreneurs in the Novgorod region.

[22] Ibid., 5.

[23] Ibid., 11–14.

[24] Ibid., 39.

[25] Ibid., 28, 37–38.

[26] Ibid., 45–46.

[27] Novgorod State University President Vladimir Soroka wrote in 1997 that the university would continue to "formulate and realize" this program as part of its efforts to help improve local self-government. Vladimir V. Soroka, "Mesto i rol sistemy obrazovaniya v mestnom samoupravlenii Novgorodchiny," in *Mestnoe samoupravlenie v Rossii: Istoriya i sovremennost*, ed. B. N. Kovalyov (Novgorod: Novgorodskii gosudarstvennyi universitet im. Yarolsava Mudrogo i Administratsiya Goroda Novgoroda, 1997), 17.

[28] *Novosti* for November 28–December 3, 1997, citing a Mikhail Prusak speech of November 14, 1997, http://www.novgorod.ru.

[29] Interview with Alexander I. Zhukovsky, director of the regional municipal research center Dialog, Novgorod the Great, Russia (April 9, 2002).

[30] Viktor Smirnov interviewed for the program *Sophia* on Novgorod television (rebroadcast July 27, 2003). Smirnov was also the ghost writer for Prusak's 1999 political autobiography, *Reform in the Provinces* [*Reformy v provintsii*].

[31] Igor B. Alexandrov, "Russia's 'Road Less Traveled': Novgorod Oblast Today," *Jamestown Foundation Prism* 3, no. 12 (July 25, 1997) at: http://www.jamestown.org/pubs/view/pri_003_012_004.htm; Sergei Fabrichnyi, "Razvitie mestnogo samoupravlenie na territorii Novgorodskoi oblasti," in *Zemstvo i vozrozhdenieego kulturno-khozyaistvennykh traditsii*, ed. V. I. Romashova (Novgorod: Novgorodskaya oblastnaya nauchnaya biblioteka, 1996), 33–41; V. Yakimets, "Tretii sektor v regionakh Rossii: Osobennosti razvitiya i vzaimodeitsviya s mestnoi vlastyu i biznesom," in *Regiony Rossii: Vzaimodeitsvie i razvitie*, ed. E. Alekseyeva (Moscow: Insait Poligrafic, 2001), 125–43.

[32] Svetlana Kovarskaya, director of the Center for the Study of Culture at Novgorod State University, personal correspondence (May 17, 2002).

[33] "Programma nauchno-prakticheskoi konferentsii 'Zemstvo i vozrozhdenie ego kulturnykh traditsii" (Kresttsy, 1996), personal copy.

[34] Interview with Svetlana Kovarskaya, Novgorod the Great, Russia (October 28, 1998).

[35] Ibid.

[36] These include the ISE Center (Information, Science, Education), the Russian Ministry of Education, the Kennan Institute (United States), the Carnegie Corporation of New York, the John D. and Catherine T. MacArthur Foundation (United States), and the Open Society Institute. Although I participated in early discussions on this project with the project director, Valery P. Bolshakov, and the present book helped inspire one of its four original research programs, I had no input in the final submission or in the awarding of the grant.

[37] Sergey Devyatkin, "Novgorod Interregional Institute for the Social Sciences (NovIISS)," personal copy.

[38] Ibid.

[39] Interview with Mikhail M. Prusak, governor of the Novgorod Region, Novgorod the Great, Russia (November 5, 1998).

[40] Prusak, "Nastupilo vremya stroit," 56–57.

[41] Mikhail M. Prusak, *Reformy v provintsii* (Moscow: Veche, 1999), 94–96.

[42] Interview with Igor V. Verkhodanov (May 24, 1999); interview with Valery Trofimov, former first deputy governor of the Novgorod Region, Novgorod the Great, Russia (October 30, 1998). One of the region's first major investors, the Danish chewing gum company Stimorol, reportedly brought up Novgorod's Hanseatic legacy during negotiations and subsequently named their two local factories Ryurik-1 and Ryurik-2.

[43] *Programma kursa "Novgordika"*, facsimile copy obtained at the Novgorod Regional Library, no date or author.

[44] Gennady Naryshkin, "Obrazovanie i patriotism," *Novgorod*, May 29, 1997.

[45] Ibid.

[46] Dmitry Likhachev, *Razdumya o Rossii* (St. Petersburg: Logos, 2001), 148.

[47] Dasha Galkina, "Shkola 'Veche,'" *Novgorodskie vedomosti*, December 26, 2000.

[48] Fr. Alexei Moroz, "O problemakh sovremennogo doshkolnogo i shkolnogo vospitaniya," *Novgorodskie eparkhalnye vedomosti*, no. 5 (May 1999), 3.

[49] "Novgorodskii opyt organizatsii bibliotek prodemonstriruyut uraltsam," *Novgorodskie vedomosti*, August 9, 2000.

[50] Ibid. With the financial support of the Open Society Institute (Soros Foundation), the regional ministry of education has set up the website "Novgorodskii krai," with detailed information about the regionalization of local education, http://novkray.home.nov.ru/.

[51] Igor Verkhodanov, who has held a variety of senior political appointments, likes to point out, for example, how closely Prusak's view of the "party of power" resembles medieval Novgorod's Council of Lords. Interview with Igor V. Verkhodanov, chief aide to the chairman of the Novgorod Regional Duma, Novgorod the Great, Russia (May 24, 1999).

[52] Vitaly Eryomin, "Obsuzhdenie budzheta—Vkhod svobodnyi," *Rossiiskaya Federatsiya segodnya* special edition, "'Molodost drevnego Novgoroda" (January 2002), 13.

[53] Kathy Lally, "A Russian Journal," *Baltimore Sun*, September 20, 2000.

[54] "Mer Velikogo Novgoroda Aleksandr Korsunov: Lyudei ne obmanesh,'" *Pravda.ru*, July 30, 2002.

[55] Mikhail Prusak interviewed by Nikolai Svanidze on the Russian national television channel RTR for the program *Pered zerkalom* (February 27, 2000), http://niac.natm.ru.

[56] Mikhail Prusak, "Vidnye ekonomisty, gosudarstvennye i obshchestvennye deyateli o sobytiyakh poslednikh let," in *Rossiiskoe predprinimatelstvo: Istoriya i vozrozhdenie* (Moscow: Russkoe delovoe agentstvo, 1997), 1.

[57] A. N. Panov and S. G. Ovcharov, *Stanovlenie kommunalnogo khozyaistva Novgoroda Velikogo v XII–XVI vekakh* (Novgorod: Severo-zapadnaya akademiya gosudarstvennoi sluzhby, 1997).

[58] Aleksandr V. Korsunov, "Reforma Mestnogo samoupravleniya—shag k pravovomu gosudarstvu," in *Mestnoe samoupravlenie v Rossii*, ed. Kovalyov, 12.

[59] Romashova, ed., *Zemstvo i vozrozhdenie*; S. V. Moiseev, *1917: Metamorfozy revolutsionnoi idei i politicheskaya praktika ikh voploshcheniya* (Novgorod: Arkhivnoe upravlenie Novgorodskoi oblasti, 1998); Aleksandr A. Boitsev, "Novgorodskii gubernator E. V. Lerkhe i ego deyatel-nost," *Zapiski filiala RGGU v g. Veliky Novgorod* 1, no. 1 (2001): 7–13; Nikolai Renkas in "Programma nauchno-prakticheskoi konferentsii Zemstvo i vozrozhdenie ego kulturnykh traditsii" (Kresttsy 1996), personal copy.

[60] Abner Cohen, *Two-Dimensional Man* (Berkeley: University of California Press, 1974), 132.

[61] Aaron Wildavsky, "Choosing Preferences by Constructing Institutions: A Cultural Theory of Preference Formation," *American Political Science Review* 81, no. 1 (1987): 16.

[62] Alison Brysk, "Hearts and Minds: Bringing Symbolic Politics Back In," *Polity* 27 (1995): 574.

[63] T. N. Yarysh, "Svyaz s obshchestvennostyu: Vosmidesyatye gody—nachalo dialoga," *Upravlencheskoe konsultirovanie* (Veliky Novgorod: MNOU Dialog), vol. 1, no. 1 (1998): 40–42; Senatova and Yakurin, "Ekonomicheskoe i politicheskoe razvitie."

[64] Ludmilla Alekseyeva, "Tendentsii razvitiya nekommercheskogo sektora i budushchee resursnykh tsentrov," a paper presented at a national meeting of NGOs in Moscow (October 29, 1998), personal copy. During the same period, the number of civic associations in Novgorod increased *sixteen-fold*. Nicolai N. Petro, "The Novgorod Region: A Russian Success Story," *Post-Soviet Affairs* 15, no. 3 (September 1999): 235–61.

[65] "Otnoshenie k ponyatiyam i opredeleniyam," commissioned by Sberbank of Novgorod, survey conducted by MNOU Dialog, Novgorod the Great (July 1999); "Regionalnye indeksy korruptsii," Transparency International–Russia and INDEM Fund, tables 6-1 and 7-1, October 9, 2002, http://www.anti-corr.ru/rating_regions.

[66] "Otnoshenie k ponyatiyam i opredeleniyam."

[67] Ibid.

[68] "Molodezhnaya anketa," *Novgorod*, November 15, 1996.

[69] Viktor Krutikov, "Dela gosudarstvennye, a zaboty-gorodskie," *Novgorod*, March 28, 2002.

[70] Interview with Igor B. Alexandrov, chairman of the United Democratic Center, Novgorod the Great, Russia (November 1, 1998).

[71] "Russia: Poll Shows Level of Trust in Russian Media," *Interfax*, November 24, 1999; Zhukovsky, "Monitoring—Novgorodskaya oblast," and "Otnoshenie k ponyatiyam"; "Osobennosti elektoralnoi situatsii v Velikom Novgorode," table 9, a report prepared for the Novgorod foundation "Sfera Soglasiya" in 2001, http://www.ngosnews/ru/djst_pgs/006.htm.

[72] This category is entered in the registry as *sluzhashchie*, or civil servant. In the accompanying guidelines, however, "SL" is supposed to refer more narrowly to a category of paramilitary service known in Russian as *siloviki*. Because the category is misidentified as "civil servant," it is likely that the figures reflect usage by people identifying themselves as civil servants.

[73] Abner Cohen, *The Politics of Elite Culture* (Berkeley: University of California Press, 1981).

[74] Vladimir Shlapentokh et al., eds., *From Submission to Rebellion* (Boulder, Colo.: Westview, 1997), 216.

[75] Sergei I. Ryzhenkov, "The Golden Age of 'Provincial Humanity' and Patterns of Regional Development," in *Regions: A Prism to View the Slavic-Eurasian World*, ed. Kimitaka Matsuzato (Sapporo, Japan: Slavic Research Center, Hokkaido University, 2000), 128, 130, 134.

[76] Galina Luchterhandt, Sergej Ryshenkow, and Alexej Kusmin, *Politik und Kultur in Der*

Russischen Provinz: Nowgorod, Woronesch, Saratow, Jekaterinburg (Bremen, Germany: Edition Temmen, 1999), 199.

[77] Ibid., 193.

[78] Ibid., 53.

[79] Ibid., 198.

[80] "Idei proveryayutsya praktikoi," *Novgorod*, February 13, 1997, 4; Vasily Dubovsky, "Munit-sipalitety—za dialog s tsentrom," *Novgorod* (February 28, 2002), 3.

[81] Luchterhandt et al., *Politik und Kultur*, 141.

[82] "Vliyatelnye persony Novgorodskoi oblasti," *Upravlencheskoe konsuitirovanie* (Veliky Novgorod: MNOU Dialog), vol. 8, no. 2 (January 2002): 85–86.

[83] Nicolai N. Petro, *The Rebirth of Russian Democracy: An Interpretation of Political Culture* (Cambridge: Harvard University Press, 1995), 14–15.

[84] Even the authors concede that such severity is implausible and, in the case of Voronezh, suggest "a sort of second golden age." Unfortunately, this only makes the criteria by which regional development is being measured murkier. Luchterhandt et al., *Politik und Kultur*, 130.

[85] Another valuable study that highlights the value of the "golden age" foundation myth for understanding contemporary political developments in Eastern Europe is by Chantal Delsol, Michel Maslowski, and Joanna Nowicki, eds., *Mythes et symboles politiques en Europe centrale* (Paris: Presses Universitaires de France, 2002).

[86] Beth Mitchneck, "The Heritage Industry Russian Style: The Case of Yaroslavl," *Urban Affairs Review* 34, no. 1 (1998): 2, 6. Literary critic Evgeny Ermolin, has written that in the seventeenth century Yaroslavl was a "natural cultural successor to Lord Novgorod the Great," but that its greater political pragmatism led it to compromise with Muscovy. Evgeny Ermolin, "V Yaroslavle literatury net," *Znamya*, no. 6 (2001).

[87] Mitchneck, "Heritage Industry," 19–20.

[88] Ibid., 23–24.

[89] Ibid., 18–19.

[90] Mitchneck cites a survey that found that 71.2 percent of the Yaroslavl population considered historic preservation to be one of the most important problems facing the city. Ibid., 14.

[91] "Regionalnaya simvolika: v poiskakh ideologii" (April 17, 2001), http://www.rocich.ru/other/regsymb.php.

[92] Mitchneck, "Heritage Industry," 24.

[93] Yuri Golub, Vladimir Dines, and Dmitry Konnychev, "Saratovskaya oblast: Konsolidatsiya vlasti," *Vlast* 5 (1998): 43–44.

[94] Ibid., 44–45.

[95] Ilya V. Malyakin, "Russkaya regionalnaya mifologiya: Tri vozrasta," *Pro et Contra* 5, no. 4 (Winter 2000): 113. Available at the website of the Carnegie Endowment in Russia, http://pubs.carnegie.ru/briefings/2001/default.asp?n=issue01-01.asp.

[96] A. Knor, "Mif o zemle," *Volzhskaya kommuna*, no. 49 (March 18, 1998).

[97] *Volga inform* (July 19, 1999), http://www.volgainform.ru/allnews/10099/. "The opponents of state authority would choose the path of radicalism, the path of liberation from Russia's historical past, of liberation from cultural traditions. They need great upheavals, we need a great Russia!" from Stolypin's speech before the State Duma, April 10, 1907, http://borzoi.dvo.ru/elib/stolp000/00000002.htm#a5.

[98] "V voskresenye ispolnyaetsya 140 let so dnya rozhdeniya Petra Stolypina." Available at website of NTV News, http://www.ntvru.com/russia/14Apr2002/stolipin.html.

[99] V. Suvorkov, *Saratovskii universitet* (August 1998), http://www.sgu.ru/win/paper/8_98/u8.html. In 2001, on the ninetieth anniversary of Stolypin's assassination, Ayatskov urged that his remains be moved from Kiev to Saratov. Anna Volodina, "Komu dostanetsya prakh," *Vesti.ru*, http://www.vesti.ru/2001/08/27/998864031.html. One can read about the many events surrounding this commemoration on the official website of the Saratov government at http://www.saratov.gov.ru/events/stolypin/.

[100] Golub, Dines, and Konnychev, "Saratovskaya oblast," 45. See also Martha de Melo and Gur Ofer, "The Russian City in Transition: The First Six Years in 10 Volga Capitals," a study prepared by the Development Research Group of the World Bank, Washington, D.C.,

http://www.worldbank.org/html/dec/Publications/Workpapers/wps2000series/wps2165/wps2165.pdf.

[101] Golub, Dines, and Konnychev, "Saratovskaya oblast," 45; Aleksandr Kakotkin, "Dmitry Volzhsky: Mylnyi puzyr nad Saratovom," *Vechernyaya Kazan,* September 30, 1998, http://www.compromat.ru/main/ayatskov/a.htm.

[102] Dmitry Ayatskov interviewed by the newspaper *Rossiiskie vesti* (October 28, 1997), http://www.akdi.ru/sf/smi/5.htm.

[103] Theodore Karasik, "Russia's Northern Cities," *Johnson's Russia List,* no. 4029 (January 12, 2000), http://www.cdi.org/russia/johnson/. Vladimir Shlapentokh has also noted the region's special character in *From Submission to Rebellion,* 186–87.

[104] Sergei Filatov and Roman Lunkin, "Drugaya Svyataya Rus," *Druzhba narodov,* no. 5 (2001): 26.

[105] In Petrozavodsk the Orthodox Church has supported Finnish Lutherans and Baptists in their efforts to translate the Scripture into Karelian. The diocese of Arkhangelsk cooperates with the government of Norway in a formal interchurch cooperation program, while in Novgorod, Archbishop Lev, a graduate of the Pontifical Gregorian University in Rome, maintains excellent relations with local Catholics, Evangelicals, Baptists, and Old Believers, even giving sermons in their churches. Ibid., 25–26, 28–31. "Revnitetli 'drevlego blagochestiya,' " *Novgorod* (February 28, 2002), 6; Zlaerov, "Bogoiskateli."

[106] Filatov and Lunkin, "Drugaya Svyataya Rus," 27.

[107] Ibid., 28.

[108] Ibid., 17.

[109] Sergei Filatov and Vladimir Lunkin, "Traditions of Lay Orthodoxy in the Russian North," *Religion, State, and Society* 28, no. 1 (2000): 28–29.

[110] Ibid., 34–35.

[111] Filatov and Lunkin, "Drugaya Svyataya Rus," 10–12.

[112] Ibid., 12.

[113] Ibid., 19. Asked by the authors to comment on the article, Father Alexander Ranne, chairman of the section for spiritual education and catechism for the Novgorod diocese, chastised Filatov and Lunkin for exaggerating the significance of what were only the "first sprouts" of change, but added "in about twenty years, if things continue as they are now going, your article will probably correspond to reality." Filatov and Lunkin, "Drugaya Svyataya Rus," 20.

[114] Grigory Kosach, "Orenburg: Regionalnaya mifologiya kak faktor vzaimootnoshenii s sosedyami," in *Chto khotyat regiony Rossii?* ed. A. Malashenko (Moscow: Carnegie Endowment for World Peace, 1999), 78.

[115] Ibid.

[116] Ibid.

[117] Ibid., 81–82.

[118] Ibid., 85–86.

[119] N. Olgina and S. A. Bulanov, *Pskovskaya oblast: Putevoditel* (Moscow: Simon-Press, 2000), 33.

[120] Ibid., 34.

[121] Klyuchevsky cited in *Pskovskie khroniki: Istoriya kraya v dokumentakh i issledovazniyakh,* ed. A. A. Aleksandrov (Pskov: Izd. Dom Strekh, 2001), 7.

[122] Ibid.

[123] For two centuries, from 1500 to 1700, Pskov served as the leading military garrison of northwestern Russia. In the early eighteenth century Peter the Great allegedly put so many men, women, priests, and monks to work in the construction of defensive fortresses and bastions that church services were suspended for lack of people to serve. Inga K. Labutina, *Pskov: Istroicheskaya spravka* (Pskov: Pskovskoe vozrozhdenie, 2001), 22, 34.

[124] Yuri Stepanov, *Legendy i predaniya Pskovshchiny* (Pskov: Pskov-infopress, 1993), 15.

[125] Ibid., 26.

[126] Ibid., 41.

[127] Ibid., 11.

[128] Ibid., 40. The Burgundian traveler Gilbert de Lennoi confirms that the main fortress of the city was closed to any but "true Christians" on penalty of death. Labutina, *Pskov,* 18.

129 Vyacheslav Vasilyev, *Legedny i predaniya Sebezhskogo kraya* (Pskov: Pskovskaya organizatsiya Soyuza zhurnalistov Rossii, 1992), 42.

130 Liam Pleven, "Orthodox, Catholic Church Tensions Mirrors Rift in Russia," *Newsday* (June 9, 2002), available at the website of *Johnson's Russia List,* no. 6298 (June 9, 2002), http://www.cdi.org/russia/johnson/. In March 2002 local authorities sanctioned a protest against the construction of the region's first Catholic church. About eighty people, including two monks blessed by Archbishop Evsevy to carry on a vigil prayer, carried placards reading "He who comes to us with a sword, will die by the sword" (a phrase from the concluding scene of Eisenstein's patriotic film, *Alexander Nevsky*) and "Holy Rus, guard the True Faith!" "Pravoslavnoe dukhovenstvo Pskova protiv stroitelstvsa katolicheskoi tserkvi," *NTV.ru* (March 26, 2002), http://www.ntvru.com/religy/25Mar2002/pskov_cath.html.

131 E. P. Ivanov, *Pskovskii krai v istorii Rossii: Regionalnyi komponent soderzhaniya obrazovaniya* (Pskov: Pskovski oblastnoi institut povysheniya kvalifikatsii rabotnikov obrazovaniya, 2001), 271.

132 Aleksandr Utkin, "Sravnitelnoe kraevedenie," *Versiya v Pitere* (St. Petersburg), January 8, 2002.

133 Mikhail A. Alexseev and Vladimir Vagin, "Russian Regions in Expanding Europe: The Pskov Connection," *Europe-Asia Studies* 51, no. 1 (1999): 44. In 2001, the Pskov television company produced a film about the history of the 104th Regiment of the 76th Airborne Division quartered near Pskov. The film, called *The Heavenly Company* (*Nebesnaya rota*), is shown several times a year on local Pskov television. It recounts the tragic story of those who lost their lives in Chechnya and reminds viewers that now, as always in Russian history, Pskov's sons are fighting to preserve the peace and quiet of Russian homes.

134 Basil III lured Pskov's posadniki and boyars to Novgorod (a day's ride from Pskov), and held them captive until they agreed to accept his terms. Meanwhile, he sent word to the townspeople of Pskov that if they did not agree to his terms he would lead an army to attack the city. Without its military and political leaders, the veche quickly capitulated. Within twenty-four hours the remaining nobility had been rounded up and the entire central portion of town, known as Middle Town, cleared of its population. When, on January 24, 1510, Basil III entered the city in triumph, the local bishop sarcastically congratulated him on "the capture of Pskov." Ivanov, *Pskovksii krai,* 24.

135 Andrei A. Smirnov and Valery M. Tishukov, "Rossiiskii opyt reformiriovaniya i problemy formirovaniya regionalnogo soznaniya novogo tipa," *Vestnik Novgorodskogo gosudarstvennogo universiteta: Seriya "Gumanitarnye nauki,"* no. 4 (May 1996): 32–37.

136 There are signs that some segments of the Pskov elite may be preparing to launch just such a "counter-myth." The celebration of the city's 1,100th anniversary in July 2003 provided them with a convenient vehicle. The director of the regional history museum appeared several times on national television to discuss not the region's military past but a special exhibit devoted to Pskov's medieval civic assembly, the veche. Both times she pointedly used a phrase that has been also picked up by the governor, and seems likely to serve as a new motto for the region: "Pskov—the first Slavic democracy." With the help of local business leaders, the museum has also undertaken to recreate the site of the city's fabled veche. "Pskov otmechayet 1,100-letie" broadcast July 23, 2003, on the NTV television channel on the program *Strana i mir.* "Zhitelyam Pskovskoi oblasti," *Pskovskaya guberniya,* July 23–29, 2003, http://gubernia.pskovregion.org/number_148/2.php#anons. "Proekt Vechevoi stepeni dlya Pskovskogo kremlya" (August 13, 2003). Available at the website of the Pskov Regional Museum, http://museum.pskov.ru/docs/news/index.php?i=305.

137 Eric Hobsbawm and Terence Ranger, *The Invention of Tradition* (Cambridge: Cambridge University Press, 1983), 98.

138 Stéphane Corcuff, ed., *Memories of the Future: National Identity Issues and the Search for a New Taiwan* (Armonk, N.Y.: M. E. Sharpe, 2002); James Meyer, "Memory and Political Symbolism in Post-September 12 Turkey," master's thesis, Princeton University, June 2001; Judy Batt, *The New Slovakia: National Identity, Political Integration, and the Return to Europe* (London: Royal Institute of International Affairs, 1996); Alan Smith, *The Return to Europe: The Reintegration of Eastern Europe into the European Economy* (Basingstoke, Eng.: Macmillan, 2000); and Ilja Srubar, *Eliten, Politische Kultur, und Privatisierung in Ostdeutschland, Tschechien, und Mittelosteuropa* (Konstanz, Germany: UVK Universitätsverlag Konstanz, 1998).

[139] Laura Desfor Edles, *Symbol and Ritual in the New Spain: The Transition to Democracy after Franco* (Cambridge: Cambridge University Press, 1998), 56.

[140] Ibid., 375.

[141] "Democracy and western Europeanism have been central Catalan nationalist symbols for centuries . . . Catalonia has long celebrated her early liberal democratic institutions. The Catalan parliament (Corts) was inaugurated at the time of the Magna Carta, and the constitutional system of the Crown of Aragon . . . is said to have been the most advanced constitutional system in fourteenth-century Europe. Moreover, Catalans are known for their modernism, pragmatism, rationality, and business acumen, which is negatively stereotyped as stinginess and coldness." Ibid., 117.

[142] Ibid., 319. A later piece by Edles suggests several more interesting comparisons with Novgorod. Laura Desfor Edles, "A Culturalist Approach to Ethnic Nationalist Movements," *Social Science History* 23, no. 3 (1999): 317.

[143] Edles, *Symbol and Ritual*, 22, 83–84, 101.

[144] Edles, "A Culturalist Approach," 139, 321.

[145] Edles, *Symbol and Ritual*, 6–7.

[146] Jan Kubik, *The Power of Symbols against the Symbols of Power: The Rise of Solidarity and the Fall of State Socialism in Poland* (University Park: Pennsylvania State University Press, 1994), 228, 256.

[147] Ibid., 243, 252–54.

[148] Ibid., 256.

[149] Ibid., 258.

[150] Ibid., 229, 242. Influenced by the work of David Laitin, Kubik has since come to view elites more as conscious manipulators of culture. Personal discussion.

[151] David I. Kertzer, *Politics and Symbols: The Italian Communist Party and the Fall of Communism* (New Haven: Yale University Press, 1996), 116.

[152] Ibid., 67.

[153] Ibid., 76.

[154] Ibid., 64.

[155] Ibid., 9.

[156] David I. Kertzer, *Ritual, Politics, and Power* (New Haven: Yale University Press, 1988), 92.

[157] Sherry B. Ortner, "Theory in Anthropology since the Sixties," in *Culture/Power/History: A Reader in Contemporaray Social Theory*, ed. Nicholas B. Dirks et al. (Princeton, N.J.: Princeton University Press, 1994), 404.

[158] Kertzer, *Politics and Symbols*, 12, 82, 125.

[159] Ibid., 42.

CHAPTER 7. CRAFTING DEMOCRACY

[1] John Williamson, "Democracy and the 'Washington Consensus,'" *World Development* 21, no. 8 (1993): 1330.

[2] Brendan Martin, "New Leaf or Fig Leaf? The Challenge of the New Washington Consensus," 7. A report prepared for the Bretton Woods Project (2000) at: http://www.brettonwoodsproject.org/topic/knowledgebank/ newleaf/newleaf_or_figleaf.pdf.

[3] Ibid., 9; Peter Reddaway and Dmitri Glinski, *The Tragedy of Russia's Reforms: Market Bolshevism against Democracy* (Washington, D.C.: United States Institute of Peace Press, 2001), especially chapter 5; Joseph Stiglitz, "What I Learned at the World Economic Crisis," *New Republic* 222, issue 16/17 (April 17, 2000). 56–60.

[4] Strobe Talbott, "But Russia Is a Special Case," *slate.com* (June 2002), reprinted in *Johnson's Russia List*, no. 6304 (June 12, 2002) at: http://www.cdi.org/russia/johnson/.

[5] Reddaway and Glinski, *Tragedy of Russia's Reforms*, 56.

[6] Sarah E. Mendelson and John K. Glenn, "Introduction: Transnational Networks and NGOS in Postcommunist Societies," in *The Power and Limits of NGOs*, ed. Sarah E. Mendelson and John K. Glenn (New York: Columbia University Press, 2002), 5.

[7] Andrei Shleifer cited in Joseph E. Stiglitz, *Globalization and Its Discontents* (New York: W. W. Norton, 2002), 163–64.

[8] James M. Cypher, "The Slow Death of the Washington Consensus on Latin America," *Latin American Perspectives* 25, no. 6 (November 1998): 47–51; Peter Stavrakis, "Bull in a China Shop: US AID's Post-Soviet Mission," *Demokratizatsiya* 3, no. 3 (Fall 1995); Janine R. Wedel, *Collision and Collusion: The Strange Case of Western Aid to Eastern Europe, 1989–1998* (New York: St. Martin's, 1998).

[9] Stiglitz, *Globalization and Its Discontents*, 143.

[10] Ibid., 153. Although recent evidence suggests that the economic collapse of the Soviet economy may not have been as great as initially believed, the point remains that advisors subscribing to the Washington Consensus were perfectly willing to accept such a collapse as part of the price for introducing new, "rational" economic policies. Anders Aslund, "The Myth of Output Collapse after Communism," *Working Papers* no. 18 (March 2001), the Carnegie Endowment for International Peace, Washington, D.C.; Anders Aslund, "Think Again," *Foreign Policy* (July/August 2001), at: http://www.foreignolicy.com/issue_julyaug_2001/Tajulyaug.htm; Roland Goetz, "Russlands Wirtschaftlicher Rueckstand Geringer Als Angenommen: Neue Sozialproduktberechnung der Weltbank," *Aktuelle Analysen* of the German Federal Institute for Eastern and International Studies (BIOst), no. 30 (June 8, 2000).

[11] Martin, "New Leaf or Fig Leaf?" 9.

[12] Thomas Carothers, "Democracy, State, and AID: A Tale of Two Cultures," *Foreign Service Journal* (February 2001), at: http://www.ceip.org/files/Publications/FSarticle.asp?p=1.

[13] Marina Ottaway and Thomas Carothers, "Toward Civil Society Realism," in *Funding Virtue*, ed. Marina Ottaway and Thomas Carothers (Washington, D.C.: Carnegie Endowment for International Peace, 2000), 305–6.

[14] Mendelson and Glenn, "Introduction," 3.

[15] Ottaway and Carothers, "Toward Civil Society Realism," 300.

[16] Reddaway and Glinski, *Tragedy of Russia's Reforms*, 297–99.

[17] Marina Ottaway and Theresa Chung, "Toward a New Paradigm," *Journal of Democracy* 10, no. 4 (1999): 100.

[18] Ibid., 109–10.

[19] Stiglitz, "What I Learned at the World Economic Crisis," 56–60.

[20] Yuri Levada, " 'Chelovek nostalgicheskii': Realii i problemy," *Polit.ru*, December 17, 2002. Available at the website of the Russian Center for the Study of Public Opinion (VTsIOM) at: http://www.wciom.ru/vciom/magazine/archiv/N6(62).htm#1.

[21] "In Russian history of the twentieth century, there were various periods: monarchism, totalitarianism, perestroika, and finally a democratic path of development. Each stage had its ideology. We have none." Cited in George W. Breslauer and Catherine Dale, "Boris Yel'tsin and the Invention of a Russian Nation-State," *Post-Soviet Affairs* 13, no. 4 (1997): 303.

[22] Richard Boudreaux, "Russians Sift Past to Find Selves," *Los Angeles Times*, March 7, 1997.

[23] "When we in our survey asked whether Russia needed a state ideology, a clear majority of the respondents, 72 percent, answered affirmatively. Against the background of their experiences with state ideology in the Communist period this, in our view, was a remarkably high figure. The support was particularly strong among those who defined themselves as left-leaning politically (90.1 percent) but, somewhat surprisingly, also among people with higher education (82.7 percent)." Pål Kolstø, "Epilogue: Values and State Ideology in Post-Communist Russia," in *Nation-Building and Common Values in Russia*, ed. Pàél Kolstø and Helge Blakkisrud (New York: Rowman and Littlefield, 2004), 330.

[24] Vladimir V. Putin, "Russia at the Turn of the Millennium," originally on the website of the Russian government at: http://www.pravitelstvo.gov.ru/government/minister/articlevvp1_txt.html.

[25] Andrei Karypov, "Stanet li Tomsk ideinym 'Eldorado' Rossii?" *Tomskii vestnik*, July 25, 2001, at: http://www.tomin.ru/eldorado.html.

[26] Considering that Luzhkov once boasted of personally allocating the municipal cranes that toppled Dzerzhinsky from his pedestal in 1991, it is easy to see why his policies would

be disorienting to the public. Unlike the firestorm of criticism that has accompanied the suggestion that the monument to Dzerzhinsky be restored, Alexander II's statue has aroused little comment. Gregory Feifer, "Russia: What Makes Yurii Run? Moscow Mayor Proposes Resurrecting Soviet Statue," *RFE/RL* (October 1, 2002), reprinted in *Johnson's Russia List*, no. 6467 (September 1, 2002), at: http://www.cdi.org/russia/johnson/.

[27] Sergei Moiseev, "'The Lonely Heart of the World': Nation-Building and Common Values in Novosibirsk Oblast," in *Nation-Building*, ed. Kolstø and Blakkisrud, 160.

[28] Vladimir Pogudin, "Sovsem ne seryi kardinal," *MK Tomsk*, August 4, 2001.

[29] Svetalana Syrova, "Uchenye khotyat uznat, chem my 'dyshim,'" *Argumenty i fakty: Tomsk*, July 10, 2001.

[30] Tatyana D. Solovei, "Russkie mify v sovremennom kontekste," 10, at: http://www.tomin.ru/new.html; Mikhail Remizov, "K ideologii cherez sotsiologiyu?" *Russkii zhurnal*, October 24, 2001, at: http://www.russ.ru/politics/20011024.html.

[31] According to lead researcher Tatyana Solovei, "The transfer of liberal myths to Russian soil has been accomplished, but the resulting synthesis has been largely negative; it probably could not be otherwise given the fundamental illiberality of the Russian soil." Solovei, "Russkie mify v sovremennom kontekste," 8.

[32] Pogudin, "Sovsem ne seryi kardinal."

[33] For Chubais's critique of the efforts of Satarov et al., see "Pochemu tsentr strategicheskikh razrabotok ne mozhet razrabotat strategiyu strany . . . ," April 11, 2000. Available at the website of the National Press Institute in Moscow at: http://www.npi.ru/pcenter/pconf/11_04_2000_1st.htm.

[34] Aaron Wildavsky, "Choosing Preferences by Constructing Institutions: A Cultural Theory of Preference Formation," *American Political Science Review* 81, no. 1 (1987): 16.

[35] Roger M. Keesing, "Models, 'Folk' and 'Cultural,'" in *Cultural Models in Language and Thought*, ed. Dorothy Holland and Naomi Quinn (New York: Cambridge University Press, 1987), 380. On why people reject mismatched metaphors, see Naomi Quinn and Dorothy Holland, "Culture and Cognition," in *Cultural Models*, ed. Holland and Quinn, 30.

[36] Ann Swidler, "Cultural Power and Social Movements," in *Social Movements and Culture*, ed. Hank Johnston and Bert Klandermans (Minneapolis: University of Minnesota Press, 1995), 25–40.

[37] Charles D. Elder and Roger W. Cobb, *The Political Uses of Symbols* (New York: Longman, 1983), 28–56.

[38] Cobb and Elder, 111–12.

[39] Anna Jannello, "Dopo Saddam, Hammurabi," *Panorama*, March 28, 2003, at: http://www.panorama.it/mondo/medioriente/articolo/ix1-A020001018345.

[40] Albert O. Hirschman, *Development Projects Observed* (Washington, D.C.: Brookings Institution, 1967), chapter 4.

[41] I borrow the term "cultural audit" from Aaron Wildavsky, who argued that there are four essential cultural frameworks that people rely on—hierarchist, individualist, egalitarian, and fatalist. Because the values associated with each of these cultural frameworks lead to particular ways of life and serve particular economic strategies, they must all be considered when devising a strategy of development. Several ways of life coexist in a single culture, and it is the balance among them that makes democracy work. A "cultural audit" should be used by development analysts to ascertain which elements in a culture are in short supply and which are overstocked. Aaron Wildavsky, "How Cultural Theory Can Contribute to Understanding and Promoting Democracy, Science, and Development," in *Culture and Development in Africa*, ed. Ismail Serageldin and June Taboroff (Washington, D.C.: International Bank for Reconstruction and Development/The World Bank, 1994), 154–56.

[42] Martin, "New Leaf or Fig Leaf?" 9.

[43] Giuseppe Di Palma, *To Craft Democracies: An Essay on Democratic Transitions* (Berkeley: University of California Press, 1990), 120. Igor B. Chubais makes this very point about the usefulness of foreign analysts in "Kakaya Rossiya vstupaet v XXI vek," *Mezhdunarodnaya poli-*

tika, no. 3 (2000), available online at the website of the German embassy in Moscow, http://germany.org.ru/ru/library/international-politik/2000-03/article11.html.

⁴⁴ Sarah E. Mendelson, "Conclusion: The Power and Limits of Transnational Democracy—Networks in Postcommunist Societies," in *Power and Limits of NGOs*, ed. Mendelson and Glenn, 245; Ottaway and Chung, "Toward A New Paradigm," 109–10.

⁴⁵ Lawrence E. Harrison, "Why Culture Matters," in *Culture Matters: How Values Shape Human Progress*, ed. Lawrence E. Harrison and Samuel P. Huntington (New York: Basic Books, 2000), xx.

⁴⁶ Robert Klitgaard, "Applying Cultural Theories to Practical Problems," in *Culture Matters: Essays in Honor of Aaron Wildavsky*, ed. Richard J. Ellis and Michael Thompson (Boulder, Colo.: Westview, 1997), 201.

⁴⁷ John Gerhart, "Discussant Remarks," in *Culture and Development*, ed. Serageldin and Taboroff, 511.

⁴⁸ Harrison, "Why Culture Matters," xx.

⁴⁹ Harrison and Huntington, *Culture Matters*, xxxi, 44–45, 71, 75.

⁵⁰ Harrison notes that the issue of whether cultural change should be part of the planning for political and economic development became "highly controversial when the initiative for such changes comes from the West, as was the case with this symposium." Harrison, "Why Culture Matters," xxx.

⁵¹ Igor Chubais, "Zhivet Parizh, a zhivet i Kurmysh," *Rossiiskaya gazeta*, January 16, 2002, http://www.rg.ru.

⁵² Chubais, "Kakaya Rossiya"; Ksenya Larina, "Vystuplenie v pryamom efire radiostantsii Ekho Moskvy istorika Igorya Chubaisa . . ." (September 29, 1997), http://www.data.ru/echo/2909chub.html.

⁵³ Marina Uvarova, "Brat za brata ne otvetchik," *Ogonyok*, no. 39 (September 2001), http://www.ropnet.ru/ogonyok/win/200139/39-27-29.html.

⁵⁴ Chubais, "Zhivet Parizh."

⁵⁵ Vitaly Naishul, "Rubezh dvukh epokh," *Vremya MN*, March 6, 2000, http://old.polit.ru/documents/190991.html.

⁵⁶ Ibid.

⁵⁷ Aleksei Kara-Murza, "Stavku nado delat na molodezh i na regionalnyi proekt," presentation at a roundtable titled "Liberal Values Tested in the Elections of 2003," February 19, 2003. Available at the website of *Otkrytyi forum*, http://www.open-forum.ru/meeting/28.html.

⁵⁸ Aleksei Kara-Murza, " 'Ne nado pridumyvat novogo! My vozvrashchaemsya k samim sebe . . . ,' " *Posev* 5 (May 2002), 17.

⁵⁹ Aleksei Kara-Murza, "Nuzhny li demokratii simvoly?" *Nezavisimaya gazeta*, August 19, 2002, http://www.ng.ru/politics/2002-08-19/2_symbol.html.

⁶⁰ Ibid.

⁶¹ Boris Vesnin, "SPS na pervom meste," October 25, 2002. Available at the website of the Union of Right Forces, http://www.sps.ru/text/perm/id/26627.html. The 2003 State Duma elections results can be downloads from the website of the Russian Federal Election Commission, http://gd2003.cikrf.ru/etc/vestnik2.xls.

⁶² "Vezde est traditisii liberalno-demokraticheskoi kultury," Aleksei Kara-Murza interviewed at the SPS congress (May 26, 2001), available online at the website of the Kursk regional SPS party organization, http://sps.kurskcity.ru/posit1.shtml (accessed May 1, 2003).

⁶³ Vladimir Tismaneanu, *Fantasies of Salvation: Democracy, Nationalism, and Myth in Post-Communist Europe* (Princeton: Princeton University Press, 1998); Di Palma, *To Craft Democracies*, 182, 231; Stephen Holmes, "Cultural Legacies or State Collapse?" 51–69; and Michael Mandelbaum, "Introduction," both in *Postcommunism: Four Perspectives*, ed. Michael Mandelbaum (New York: Council on Foreign Relations, 1996), 26. Murray Edelman, while critical of myth, concludes that societies also need myths to overcome social contradictions. The use of myths is thus a Faustian bargain. Murray Edelman, "Language, Myths, and Rhetoric," *Society* 35, no. 2 (January–February 1998): 131–39.

⁶⁴ Ilya V. Malyakin, "Lokalnye mifologii v Rossii kak razobshchayushchii factor," available

online at the website of the Russian State Humanities University (RGGU), http://conference.rsuh.ru/malak.htm (accessed March 15, 2002); Ilya V. Malyakin, "Russkaya regionalnaya mifologiya: Tri vozrasta," *Pro et Contra* 5, no. 4 (Winter 2000), available online at the website of the Carnegie Endowment in Russia, http://pubs.carnegie.ru/briefings/2001/default.asp?n=issue01-01.asp.

[65] Malyakin, "Russkaya regionalnaya mifologiya," 121–22.

[66] Edelman, "Language, Myths, and Rhetoric," 133.

[67] Thomas C. Schelling, "Foreword," in Roberta Wohlstetter, *Pearl Harbor: Warning and Decision* (Stanford: Stanford University Press, 1962), vii.

INDEX

accountability, 29–32, 77–78, 219n82
Adygeyia, 218n53
Alexander II (tsar of Russia), 133, 145, 185, 242n26
Alfred Moser Foundation (Netherlands), 41
Andreyeva, Lyubov, 25, 51–52, 62, 71
anticommunism, 87–88, 151, 170
antisystem actors, 11, 32, 47, 192
area studies, 96, 202
Argumenty i fakty, 67, 217n42
Arkhangelsk, 170, 238n105
associational life. *See* civic participation; voluntary associations
authoritarianism, 9; gubernatorial, 76–81, 87–90
authority patterns, 102, 103
Ayatskov, Dmitry, 74, 168–69

Baptists, 238n105
Bashkortostan, 69–70, 172, 218n53
Basil III, 239n134
Bates, Robert H., 97, 222n12
Battle on the Ice (1242), 173, 174
Becker, David, 12, 13, 206n60
Belarus, 105
Bell, The (journal), 138
Bennett, W. Lance, 118–19, 227n140
Blumer, Harold, 114, 115
Boitsev, Anatoly, 25, 30, 157
Bolsheviks, 175

Boretskaya, Martha, 136. *See also* Martha the Magistrate
Borovichi, 35
Bryansk, 199
Brysk, Alison, 121–22, 160
budgetary planning, 31, 37–38
Burbulis, Gennady, 47, 62, 77
businesses, small, 40
businessmen, 38–39, 211n77
Buslayev, Vasily (legendary figure), 135
byliny (epic tales), 135, 230n68

Calvinists, 170
Can Democracy Take Root in Post-Soviet Russia (Eckstein), 22
Carl Philip (crown prince of Sweden), 133
car ownership, in Novgorod the Great, 43
"Case Study and Theory in Political Science" (Eckstein), 19
case study method, 19–20
Casimir IV (Polish-Lithuanian prince), 131–32, 230n54
Catalonia, 176–77, 240n141
Catherine II (empress of Russia), 135–36
Catholicism, 177, 238n105, 239n130
Caucasus, 77
censorship, 65, 66, 221n120
Chechnya, 76, 239n133
Chelyabinsk, 49, 172
Chernomyrdin, Viktor, 70
child homelessness, 41

245

Christmas charity drives, 39
Chubais, Igor, 197, 198
Chudovo—RWS (plywood factory), 35
Chudovo district, 29, 37
civic culture model, 99–100
civic participation: constitutional order
    and, 34; democracy and, 7; democratic
    consolidation and, 21; historical origins
    of, 126–28; Novgorod Myth and, 160–64;
    in Novgorod republic, 133–34; Novgorod
    vs. Pskov, 88–89, 221n120; Novgorod vs.
    Russia, 2; open doors policy and, 45–47;
    Orthodox Church and, 144; popular
    support for, 51–54; social partnership
    and NGOs, 48–51, 52–54; voluntary
    associations as alternative to political
    parties, 59–61
civil society: Novgorod reforms and, 64;
    Prusak on, 79; social capital theory and,
    101; time frame for establishing, 224n57
clergy, in Novgorod history, 129
clientelism, 61–65, 208n19
Clinton administration, 182
cognitive dissonance, 109
Cohen, Abner, 112–13, 123, 158–59
colonialism, 195–96, 215–16n14
commercialism, 65
communism: collapse of, 21, 145; identity
    struggle within, 178; myths/symbols
    manipulated by, 123, 139;
    overcentralization and, 142
Communist Party of the Russian
    Federation: and cultural recoding, 192;
    electoral standings of, 32, 58; elite
    departure from, 75; and open doors
    policy, 45, 47
Communist Party of the Soviet Union, 60,
    230–31n71
concertation, 64, 208n19
congruence theory, 102–5
consensus, political/social: in Africa,
    215–16n14; democratic consolidation
    and, 21; elite theory and, 73–75; and
    local cultural tradition, 80–81; regional
    myths and broadening of, 186–87;
    structural impact of, 85. See also
    Novgorod elite consensus
constitutional order: mature democracy and,
    2, 22–23. See also Novgorod Constitution
corporate philanthropy, 39
corporatism, 64–65
corruption, mature democracy and, 14
credit, 40
credit cards, 42–43
cultural adjustment vs. cultural
    congruence, as paradigms of
    development, 196

cultural analysis: congruence theory,
    102–5; democratic transition and, 98–99;
    political culture, 99–100, 103–4; and
    rapid social change, 3, 107–8, 201–2;
    rational choice theory and, 118;
    shortcomings of, 105–8; social capital
    theories, 100–102, 103; and Third World
    development failures, 195–96
cultural audit, 191–93, 201, 242n41;
    training for, 193–97
cultural continuity, 103, 187–88, 197
cultural extension, 112–13
cultural identity, shifts in, 106
cultural imperialism, 188–89, 194
cultural invention, 113
cultural legitimacy, 102–3, 113
cultural recoding, 187–88, 189, 200–201
cultural revolutions, 112
cultural sensitivity, 195
cultural sociology, 114–16
cultural substitution, 112
culture: as agent of change, 116–17,
    196–97; elites as subconscious recipients
    of, 177–78; political functions of, 98–99,
    103–5; and rapid social change, 105–8;
    rational choice theory and, 96–98.
    See also myths/symbols
currency, symbols in, 188
Czech Republic, 60, 64

Dahl, Robert, 8, 10, 15, 20
Days of Slavic Writing and Culture, 147
Decembrists, 136–37
decentralization, 145, 206n60
democracy: definitions of, 7–9; delegative,
    10, 80; liberal, 12; mature, 13–16, 22;
    political parties in, 57–58; as process,
    9–16; public support for, 14; regional,
    16–20; representative, 80; time frame for
    establishing, 224n57; Western, 10–11,
    15–16, 99
democratic assistance, Western, 189–91;
    cultural audit of, 189–91; cultural audit
    training for, 193–97; impact of, 182–83;
    limitations of, 202; need for culturally-
    based approach to, 4; and party
    institutionalization, 60–61; resistance to,
    195–96; sequencing of, 195; symbolic
    approach to, 189–93; Washington
    Consensus and, 181–84, 190
democratic consolidation: definition of, 21;
    democratic transition vs., 9–13, 23;
    mature democracy vs., 13–16;
    myths/symbols and, 187; in Novgorod,
    2–3; and rapid social change, 106,
    224n57; regional, 18. See also Novgorod
    as democratic model

democratic institutions: congruence theory and, 102–5; democracy and, 8, 9–11, 12–13; impact of foreign assistance on, 181–84, 190; informal, 10; myths/symbols and legitimacy of, 189–91, 192–93, 194–95; popular acceptance of, 23

Democratic Party of Russia (DPR), 79, 86, 88, 221n119

Democratic Party of the Left (PDS), 178

Democratic Renaissance of the North, 170

democratic transition: authoritarianism vs., 9; democratic consolidation vs., 9–13, 23; failure of, reasons for, 183–84; myths/symbols and, 176–79, 184–87; party development during, 61; rapid social change and, 95–96; symbolic approach to, 189–93

democratization theory, weaknesses of, 2; assumptions of, 10; and cultural differences, 90–91; and democratic consolidation, pace of, 12–13; elite theory, 72–75, 85–87; gubernatorial authoritarianism theory, 76–81, 87–90; lack of universal standards, 20–21; minimalism, 8, 16, 20, 21; structuralism, 69–72, 81–85

Dialog (training center), 153, 158

Diamond, Larry, 12, 13, 58

Di Palma, Giuseppe, 10, 14

district heads, 25–26, 39, 77

Dittmer, Lowell, 120–21, 123

diversity: in Novgorod, 170, 219n82; in Russia, 16–17, 127; tolerance of, and mature democracy, 14

Dovmont (Pskov prince), 173, 175

duma. *See* Novgorod City Duma; Novgorod Regional Duma; Russian State Duma

Dzerzhinsky, Felix, 185, 241–42n26

Eastern Europe: corporatism in, 64–65; democratic transition in, 95, 177–78; impact of Washington Consensus on, 182; political culture in, 117, 226n128; social networks in, 101; voting patterns in, 58

East Germany, 101

Eckstein, Harry, 20; and cognitive dissonance, 109; and congruence theory, 102–3; and cultural adaptation, 106; on democratic maturity, 22–23; and formlessness, 98; Geertz and, 225n82, 225n85; on regional democratic development, 19, 206n60

economic development: democratic consolidation and, 21; FDI and, 34–38; mature democracy and, 2, 22, 23;

Novgorod vs. Russia, 1–2; Washington Consensus and, 181–82

Edinaya Rossiya Party, 32

Edles, Laura, 31, 176–77

education, Novgorod Myth and, 156–57, 162–63

Ekologiya, 148

Ekonomika i zhizn (magazine), 67

Ekspert (magazine), 2

elections: democracy and, 7; media and, 217n47; in Novgorod, 25–26, 29, 32, 159; Novgorod Myth and, 149; in Novgorod republic, 132–33; Novgorod vs. Russia, 2; open doors policy and, 47

elites/elite behavior: cultural audit and, 191–92; democracy and, 3, 23–24; as obstacle to democracy, 142; regional, theories of, 72–75, 85–87; and Russian Idea, 184–85; and Russian symbolic development, 197–201; as subconscious recipients of culture, 177–78; systems of meaning constructed by, 107. *See also* consensus, political/social; myths/symbols, elite manipulation of; Novgorod elite; Novgorod elite consensus

employment fund, 36–37

essential service providers, 192

Estonia, 83, 221n119

Estonian Popular Front, 87

ethnic diversity, 127

ethnic republics, 69–70, 218n53

ethnocentrism, 171–72, 194

Eurasia Foundation, 48, 51, 52, 214n140

European Union (EU), 60

Evangelical-Reform Church, 170, 238n105

Evsevy (archbishop of Pskov), 174, 239n130

exploitation, Western, 196

Federation of Trade Unions, 30

Fedotov, George P., 129, 140

Filatov, Sergei, 169–71, 238n113

Finance, Ministry of, 210n61, 212n107

First Republic, The (TV series), 153

fiscal devolution, 34

Focaltown (Newfoundland, Canada), 112–13

foreign direct investment (FDI): impact of, 24, 41–42, 68; Novgorod Myth and, 156, 235n42; Novgorod vs. Pskov, 89; Novgorod vs. Russia, 2; popular adaptation to, and economic reform, 42–45; Prusak on, 211n76; and regional identity, 166; structural impact of, 34–38; structuralist view of, 70. *See also* Novgorod Region, FDI in

formlessness: causes of, 98, 113;
congruence theory and, 102–3, 104;
cultural analysis and, 107–8; as lack of
stable symbolic forms, 109;
myths/symbols and overcoming of, 145,
187, 188–89, 190; and political
significance of culture, 98–99
Fortress Russia Syndrome, 175
foster families, 41
free enterprise zone (FEZ), Novgorod
proposed as, 148–49, 233n7
French Revolution, 178
Freud, Sigmund, 108–9, 123
Fukuyama, Francis, 8, 100, 105

Gaidar, Yegor, 62, 77, 79
Gdansk (Poland), 177
Geertz, Clifford, 106, 107, 110–12, 113,
225n85
Gelman, Vladimir, 76, 80
Gilbert de Lennoi, 130, 238–39n128
Glorious Revolution (Great Britain),
222n5
golden ages, and regional development
patterns, 165–67
Golden Ring, 167
Gonzov, Gennady (archbishop of
Novgorod), 131
Gorbachev Foundation, 152
Gorbachev, Mikhail, 9, 153
government: accountability of, 29–30; as
agent of change, 117; and cultural
recoding, 200–201; myths/symbols
manipulated by, 118, 123; structural
changes in, 3, 23–24
governor: Novgorod vs. Pskov, 87–90; role
of, in regional development, 76–81,
219n82, 220n87. See also Mikhailov,
Evgeny; Prusak, Mikhail
Great Reforms of 1864, 133, 145
greenfield investors, 40
Grinyov, Nikolai, 148, 234n21
Gunther, Richard, 10, 12, 13, 106,
224n57
Gustavus Adolphus (king of Sweden),
133

habitus, 114
Hanseatic League, 130, 156, 233n137,
235n42
Harrison, Lawrence E., 195, 206n48
Havel, Vaclav, 59
Heavenly Company, The (film), 239n133
Herald of the Russian Academy of Sciences,
140–41
heresies, 131
heritage industry, 167–68

Herzen, Alexander: on Decembrists, 137;
on impact of Moscow expansion, 140;
and Novgorod Myth, 138, 144, 231n95;
on Russian revolutions, 22
Hirschman, Albert O., 188–89
Historical Images from the Life of Ryurik
(Catherine II), 135–36
Historical Monologues (TV program),
153
historic preservation, 237n90
Hobbes, Thomas, 126
Holy Trinity Cathedral (Pskov), 175
home ownership, 33
horizontal cooperation, 31–32
housing fellowships (TSZh), 26–27
housing management, 40–41, 211n90
Hungary, 60, 64

identity: myths/symbols and, 160, 178;
Russian, symbolic development and,
197–201; shifts in, 106
identity, regional: cultural analysis and, 3,
99; and golden-age image, 165–66;
Novgorod vs. Pskov, 3; in Russia, 16–17
ideology, 110–11, 241n23
income, 2, 37, 42–43, 83
Index of Mass Media Freedom in Russia, 65
industrial production, 1–2, 85
information, access to, 29, 65
Institute for Humanities and Political
Studies, 165
Institute of Marxism-Leninism, 153
Institute of Philosophy, 205n40
institution building. See Washington
Consensus
integrated interest organizations, 64
interest aggregation, 59–61
International Monetary Fund (IMF),
181–82, 183
Internet, 144, 169
interpretive theory, 110
investment, foreign. See foreign direct
investment
Investment Insurance Fund, 210–11n71
IREX (International Research &
Exchanges Board), 48
Islam, Orenburg Myth and, 172
Issatchenko, Alexander, 141
Italian Communist Party (PCI), 178
Italy, 62, 178, 224n57
Itar-TASS, 67
Ivan III (grand prince of Muscovy),
131–32, 138–39
Ivan IV (tsar of Russia), 132, 134, 140,
230–31n71
Ivanov, Alexander, 170
Ivan the Terrible (film), 230–31n71

joint ventures, in Novgorod Region, 35
"Journey from St. Petersburg to Moscow, A" (Radishchev), 136
Judaizer heresy, 131
Jung, Carl, 108, 109
jury trial system, 192

Kalinino, 168
Kalmykia, 76
Kara-Murza, Alexei, 198–200
Karamzin, Nikolai, 136
Karelia, 170
Kasyanov, Mikhail, 70, 80
Kazakhstan, 171, 172
Khabarovsk, 41
Kibina, Irina, 38, 52, 71–72
Kiev, 141
Kiev, Prince of, 129
Kirov, Sergei, 175
Komsomolskaya pravda, 143
Konets (Novgorod borough), 128
Korsunov, Alexander: autonomy of, 72; and Novgorod, Inc., 38, 42; and Novgorod Myth, 157–58, 162; on Novgorod's fiscal autonomy, 212n107
Kostomarov, Nikolai, 134, 138
kraevedeniye (regional studies), 156–57
Kuban, Cossack circles in, 77
Kubik, Jan, 177–78
Kulotino, 67
Kurgan Region, 172
Kursk, 199

land ownership, 133, 229n31
land sales, 40
"Last Son of Freedom, The" (Lermontov), 137
Latin America: democracies in, 8, 10; democratic transition in, 95; impact of Washington Consensus on, 182; local government and democracy in, 206n60; Russia compared to, 80
Latvia, 83, 221n119
Lev (archbishop of Novgorod and Staraya Russa), 80–81, 238n105
Liberal-Democratic Party of Russia (LDPR), 32
Likhachev, Dmitry S., 142, 145
Linz, Juan, 10, 11, 15, 224n57
Lipset, Seymour Martin, 7–8, 15
Lisichkin, Gennady, 142, 144
lobbying, 70, 73–74
local cultural traditions: and civic participation, 88–89; elite consensus and, 80–81; elite theory and, 75; stability and, 3; and Western democratic assistance, 4

local financing, 28–29
localism, 165
local knowledge, 111
local self-government, 24–29; dual appointments in, 25–28; elections, 25–26; ethnic republics and, 218n53; FDI and, 37–38; historical origins of, 126–28; home ownership and, 33; and local financing, 28–29; media downplaying of, 57; in Novgorod republic, 130–31, 132–34; Novgorod vs. Russia, 2; Prusak and, 77; public trust in, 160–61; TOS/TSZh, 26–27
longevity, as criterion for democracy, 20
Lord Novgorod the Great (TV film), 153
Luchterhandt, Galina, 228n6. *See also* golden ages, and regional development patterns
Lunkin, Vladimir, 169–71, 238n113
Lutheran Church, 170, 238n105
Luzhkov, Yuri, 185, 241–42n26

Madisonian democracy, 8
magistrates, in Novgorod history, 127, 128, 132–33
Mamin-Sibiryak, Dmitry, 135, 138
market economy, 15, 224n57
Martha the Magistrate, 138, 143, 154
Martha the Magistrate (Balashov), 139–40
Martha the Magistrate (Karamzin), 136
Marxism, 138
Marxism-Leninism, 21
Marx, Karl, 114, 124
Matveeva, Galina, 52, 233n4
media: elite manipulation of, 227n140; freedom of, 65–67, 213nn114, 115, 217n42; independent, 66; influence of, 217n47; and neighboring regions, 166; NGO relations with, 49; and Novgorod Myth, 149, 153–54, 162, 234n11; open doors policy and, 46–47; St. Sophia restoration and, 147–48
medical insurance fund, 36–37
microcredit, 40
middle class, 42–43, 45
Mikhailov, Evgeny, 82–83, 86, 175
"Mikola and Cannon Called 'Pebble'" (Pskov legend), 174
minimalism, 8, 16, 20, 21
Moncloa Accords (Spain), 59, 177
monetization, 37, 210n69
Moscow: Novgorod as alternative political model to, 140–42; Novgorod Myth and, 148–49, 162; Novgorod Myth manipulated by, 135; pseudo consensus building in, 185, 241–42n26; Pskov reliance on, 88–89, 221n119; and

Moscow *(continued)*
    regional identity, 165–66; subjugation of
    Novgorod, 131–32; subjugation of Pskov,
    173, 175–76; toll highway in, 40; as
    "winner takes all" regime, 76
Muscovy. *See* Moscow
museums, local history, 157
Myth of the State, The (Cassirer), 110
myths/symbols: anthropological
    significance of, 110–13, 123, 225n82;
    and democratic assistance programs,
    189–93; and democratic consolidation,
    187–89; and democratic transition,
    176–79, 189–93; elite consensus and,
    159–60; history vs., 166, 180; national vs.
    regional, 184–87, 241n23, 242n31; in
    Orenburg, 171–72; in political science,
    118–22, 123; political significance of,
    114–17, 121–22, 123, 226n100; popular
    acceptance of, 160; in Pskov, 173–76;
    psychological significance of, 108–10,
    123; and rapid social change, 108, 113,
    123–25, 159–60, 201–2; recoding of,
    200–201; and regional political
    development, 165–67; in Russian north,
    169–71; in Yaroslavl, 167–68, 237n86,
    237n90. *See also* Novgorod Myth;
    symbolic development
myths/symbols, elite manipulation of:
    cultural extension vs. cultural
    substitution, 112–13; and cultural
    recoding, 189; media and, 227n140; and
    rapid social change, 111, 116, 118–22,
    159, 179–80

National Association of Women
    Entrepreneurs of Russia, 214n139
National Institute for Economic Modeling,
    198
nationalism, 109, 171–72
nation building, 185–86
nativism, 143, 191–92
NATO, 211n76
Nazism, and symbols, 123
N-Buro (TV program), 67
neighborhood associations, 26–27, 47
Neighbors (TV show), 166
Nemtsov, Boris, 68, 74
neomodernization, 16
Nevsky, Alexander, 138, 143–44, 173,
    174
Nezavisimaya gazeta (newspaper), 67
Nicholas II (tsar of Russia), 175
Nicholas I (tsar of Russia), 137
Nigeria, 106
Niva (journal), 138
Nizhny Novgorod, 68, 74, 76

nobility, in Novgorod history, 126–27, 128,
    129, 228n5
nongovernmental organizations (NGOs):
    as alternative to political parties, 58;
    Novgorod Myth and, 160; Novgorod vs.
    Pskov, 88–89, 213–14n130; Novgorod vs.
    Russia, 2; social partnership and, 48–51,
    52–54, 213–14n130; success of, and
    regional stability, 214n148; third sector
    vs. political, 53–54, 213n128
Northern Wars (1700-1721), 173
Northwest Center for Social Development,
    48, 52–53, 214n140
Novaya Novgorodskaya gazeta, 217n42
"Novgorod" (Lermontov), 137
Novgorod (newspaper), 66, 149, 234n11
Novgorod as democratic model: as
    blueprint for change, 202; challenges
    facing, 67–69; and civic participation,
    45–54; and clientelism, 61–65; and
    constitutional order, 24–34; criticisms of,
    57–67; democratization theory and,
    55–56; and economic development,
    34–45; and federal subsidies, 70–71;
    historical origins of, 126–28; and media
    freedom, 65–67, 217n42; and Novgorod
    Myth, 155–56, 159–64; and political
    parties, lack of, 57–61; progress
    measurements for, 2–3, 54–55; and
    structural limitations, 69–72
Novgorod Center for NGO Support.
    See Northwest Center for Social
    Development
Novgorod City Duma: open doors policy
    and, 47; and TOS/TSZh, 26–27; and
    Union of Russian Cities, 31–32
Novgorod City Soviet of People's Deputies,
    146, 149–52
Novgorod Constitution, 24–34; and elite
    accountability, 29–32; historical origins
    of, 228n5; and local self-government,
    24–29; popular support for, 32–34;
    separation of powers in, 61–62
Novgorod elite: accountability of, 29–32;
    and horizontal cooperation, 31–32; and
    local myths/symbols, 3, 57, 80–81; and
    NGO funding, 48–51; and Novgorod
    Myth, 158–59, 160–64; open doors policy
    and, 47; participation in duma, 30;
    reform redefined by, 3; and regional
    identity, 75
Novgorod elite consensus: constitutional
    order and, 34; disinterest in party
    politics, 64; and Novgorod, Inc., 39–42;
    origins of, 45; Prusak and, 80–81; and
    social partnership, 48–51; structural
    impact of, 85; and Trilateral

Commission, 30–31; unexplained by elite theory, 74–75
Novgorodica, in school curriculum, 156–57, 162–63
Novgorod, Inc., 38–42
Novgorod Interregional Institute for the Social Sciences (NovIISS), 154–55
Novgorod Metropolitan Isidore, 133
Novgorod Myth: FDI and, 156, 235n42; formation/preservation of, 134–38; historical origins of, 126–34, 228n5, 228n13; media and, 149, 153–54, 162, 234n11; Novgorod Project and, 152–55; popular support for, 159–64; in postcommunist era, 140–45; in precommunist era, 138–39; Prusak and, 152, 155–59; during Soviet era, 139–40; Soviet symbolism vs., 147–52; success of, reasons for, 186–87; as "unique," 164
Novgorod Polytechnic Institute, 149. *See also* Novgorod State University
Novgorod Project, 152–55, 234n21
Novgorod Region: cultural extension in, 112–13; democratic development in, 23–24; demographics of, 34–35; economic development of, 1–2, 34–45; elections in, 25–26, 29, 32, 159; FDI in, 34–38, 41–42, 70–71, 210n61, 210–11n71, 211n76; fiscal autonomy in, 28–29, 70–71, 209n33; golden age of, 165; middle class in, 42–43; Nazi occupation of, 145, 233n137; NGO funding and social partnership in, 48–51; political development patterns in, 165–66; popular support for political institutions in, 32–34; poverty statistics for, 43–45; religious diversity in, 170; run as business, 38–42, 211n90; social capital in, 101–2; subsidy cut in, 44–45; tax revenues in, 37, 210n69; "uniqueness" of, 164; voting patterns in, 33–34, 210n58; as "winner takes all" regime, 76. *See also* Novgorod as democratic model; Novgorod Region and Pskov, compared
Novgorod Regional Duma: businessmen in, 38–39, 211n77; debate in, 27–28; deputy participation in, 30; district heads in, 25, 39; elections for, 32; FDI and, 42; legislation initiated by, 25, 71, 85; as modern veche, 157; open doors policy and, 46; proinvestor legislation of, 37–38; and regional diversity, 219n82; and separation of powers, 28, 61–62, 71–72; structuralist view of, 71
Novgorod regional identity, elite and, 75
Novgorod Region and Pskov, compared, 81–90; economic indicators, 81–82; elite

behavior, 82–85; factory ownership, 86–87; FDI, 89; federal subsidies, 87, 88, 221n114; gubernatorial authoritarianism, 87–90; history, 172–73, 175, 238n123; industrial production, 85; monetary income, 83; NGO trust in government officials, 213–14n130; structuralist view of, 81–85; voting patterns, 82–85
Novgorod Region Committee on Education, 157
Novgorod republic: age of, 229n42; Church and, 129, 131–32, 140; impact of foreign trade on, 129–31; literacy in, 230n68; Muscovy invasion of, 131–33; in Novgorod Myth, 134–38; origins of, 126–29; Pomors as inheritors of, 169; and Swedish invasion, 133. *See also* Novgorod Myth
Novgorodskie vedomosti (newspaper), 30, 66
Novgorodskii obyvatel (newspaper), 217n42
Novgorod Social Chamber: FDI and, 42; NGO participation in, 53, 60; and open doors policy, 46–47
Novgorod State University, 152–55, 234n27
Novgorod the Great: community political authority in, 126–27; elections in, 217n47; fiscal autonomy in, 212n107; government run as business in, 40, 41; mayor of, as deputy governor, 71–72; middle class in, 42–43; Novgorod Myth in, 144–45; population of, 35; pre-1917 street names restored in, 150; proposed as capital, 232–33n133; stabilization fund in, 29; transportation links in, 82; trilateral approach to budget planning in, 31. *See also* Novgorod republic
Novosibirsk, 49
Novyi Grad (journal), 140

obshchina (peasant communes), 231n95
Ochin, Oleg, 148, 149–51, 234n21
Ogaryov, Nikolai, 137–38, 144
Ogonyok, 67, 143
Old Believers, 238n105
Omsk, 76
open doors policy, 45–47
Open Society Institute, 48
oral tradition, 135
Ordin-Nashchokin, Afanasy, 176
Orenburg/Orenburg Myth, 167, 171–72
Orthodox Church: and Catholicism, 239n130; and civic participation, 144; and interchurch cooperation, 170, 238n105; land ownership of, 229n31; myths/symbols of, 169–71; Novgorod republic and, 129, 131–32, 140; Pskov and, 175; St. Sophia restored to, 147–48

Parsons, Talcott, 17, 111
Partnership for Peace, 48, 51
paternalism, 70
path dependency, 106–7, 224n59
path determinism, 166
Pechory District (Pskov Region), 83
pension fund, 36–37
people's tribunes, in Novgorod history, 127, 128, 130
perestroika, 87, 134, 146–47
Perm Region, 128, 199
Perspektiva (TV program), 221n120
Peter the Great (tsar of Russia), 173, 238n123
Petrozavodsk, 170, 238n105
Piattoni, Simona, 62–64, 208n19
Pinochet, Augusto, 9, 58
Plekhanov, Georgy, 136, 138
Poland, 9, 60, 64, 177–78
Poland-Lithuania, 131–32
political culture, 99–100, 103–4, 117, 120, 226n124
political parties: disillusionment with, 58–59, 61, 215–16n14; increase in numbers of, 54; institutionalization of, 67–68; lack of, and Novgorod Model, 57–61, 73; in mature democracies, 57–58; and Novgorod Myth, 139; Novgorod vs. Pskov, 86; voluntary associations as alternative to, 59–61, 78
political trust: mature democracy and, 14–15; in Novgorod, 32–34
Politics and Culture in the Russian Provinces, 165–66
polyarchal democracy, 8
Pomors/"Pomor Idea," 169–71
Pomor University, 170
populace, attitudinal changes in, 3, 23–24
populism, 8, 62, 70
posadnik. See magistrates, in Novgorod history
poverty, 2, 43–45, 182–83
press distribution, 66
prigorody (outlying districts), 128
Primakov, Evgeny, 70, 80, 159
princes, in Novgorod history, 126–27, 228n5
"Prince's Shadow, The" (Pskov legend), 174
Protestant ethic, 185–86
Provintsiya (media consortium), 66
Prusak, Mikhail, 181; antipopulist stances of, 62, 63; approval ratings of, 32; and economic proposals in regional duma, 211n77; on FDI in Novgorod, 211n76; Gorbachev and, 153; as governor, 76–81, 151, 219n82, 220n87; lobbying efforts of,

70; on local self-government and civil society, 49; media coverage of, 57, 66–67, 213nn114, 115; NGO criticism of, 53; and Novgorod, Inc., 38; and Novgorod Myth, 152, 155–59; and open doors policy, 45, 47; political setbacks of, 216n27; and separation of powers, 25; and social partnership, 59; transition following rule of, 68
Pskov Myth, 167, 173–76, 238–39n128, 239nn133, 134, 136
Pskov Popular Front, 87
Pskov region: LDPR and, 32; political/economic stagnation in, 3; subsidization of, 44. *See also* Novgorod Region and Pskov, compared; Pskov Myth
Pskov Regional Duma, 85
public ceremonies, 30–31
Public Expertise Project, 65
public-private partnerships, 39–40
Pushkin, Alexander, 137, 140
Putin, Vladimir: and centralization, 17, 68; dominant role of, 76; Prusak and, 62, 78–79; public support for, 210n58; on Russian Idea, 184–85
Pytalovsky District (Pskov Region), 83

racism, 196
rational choice theory, 96–98, 118, 222n12
"Raven's Stone, The" (Pskov legend), 174
Regional Credit Cooperative (Gubernskoe Kreditnoe Sodruzhestvo), 40
regional democratic development, 16–20, 206n60; and authoritarian governor theory, 76–81; and elite theory, 72–73; and local cultural tradition, 90; and regional autonomy, 69–70, 218n53. *See also* Novgorod Region and Pskov, compared
Regional Electoral Commission, 47
Regional Investment Initiative, 41, 48–49, 60
regionalism, 17
Regions.ru, 66–67
rent-seeking, 73–74
representative assemblies, 78
resource mobilization, 69–70
rituals, 112, 178–79. *See also* myths/symbols
Rossiiskaya gazeta (newspaper), 67
Rossiya (radio station), 67
Russia: authoritarian/centralizing tendencies in, 68, 99–100, 136; civic culture, lack of, 99–100, 105; congruence theory and, 102–5; cultural/ethnic diversity of, 16–17; democratic transition in, 9, 96; economy

of, 1–2; "Great Man" in politics of, 76; impact of Washington Consensus on, 182–83, 241n10; myths/symbols in, 176, 178–79; northern regions of, symbols in, 167, 169–72; pacts in, 59; path dependency in, 224n59; political culture in, 117, 226n128; political parties in, 58; public discontent with income inequality in, 206n48; public support for democracy in, 14, 205n40; regional democratic development in, 16–20, 69–70, 218n53; regional development patterns in, 165–67; regional voting patterns in, 210n58; Soviet structural limitations inherited in, 69–70; Swedish invasion of, 133, 145; symbolic development and national identity in, 197–201; U.S. aid to, 182

Russian Atlantis, The (Burovsky), 142–43

Russian Civil War, 139

Russian Constitution, 32, 218n53

Russian Idea, 184–87, 197, 241n23

Russian Ministry of Education, 154

Russian Revolution, 178

Russian saints, as symbol, 140

Russian State Duma, 25, 105

Russian Union of Journalists, 65

Russia That Never Was, The (Bushkov), 142

Russkaya provintsiya (journal), 166

Ryurik (Norse tribal leader), 126, 135–36

Sadko the Merchant (legendary figure), 135, 138

St. Cyril's monastery (Vologda), 147–48

St. Petersburg: conflict in duma of, 62; foundation of, 132; and nativist sociopolitical movements, 143; NGO survey in, 49; Novgorodians employed in, 35; toll highway in, 40

St. Sophia Cathedral (Novgorod), 129; in Novgorod Myth, 138, 143–44, 147; restoration of, as symbol, 147–48

Sakhalin, 41

Sakha-Yakutiya, 218n53

Samara, 41

Samarin, Yuri, 137

Saratov, 74, 165, 167, 168–69

Saratov University, 169

Schmitter, Philippe, 10, 58–59, 64

schra (negotiated agreements), 130, 131

Schumpeter, Joseph, 7, 20

Scott, James, 119–20

Segodnya (newspaper), 67

Semyonov, Vasily, 210n61

separation of powers: historical origins of, 127–28; mature democracy and, 14;

Prusak and, 78–80; violation of, in Novgorod, 25, 61–62, 71–72

Siar Bossard (accounting firm), 35

Siberia, tribal councils in, 77

"Sinav and Truvor" (Sumarokov), 135

Skibar, Mikhail, 38, 47

Skrynnikov, Ruslan, 141–42

Slavic Writing and Culture, Days of, 147

Slaviya (Novgorod TV station), 66, 153–54

Slovakia, 60, 64

Smena, 143

Smirnov, Viktor, 154, 231n102, 234nn21, 30

Smolensk, 199

social apathy, 53–54

social capital theories, 100–102, 103

social change: congruence theory and, 102–5; cultural analysis and study of, 98–105, 201–2; cultural symbols and popular acceptance of, 159–60; democratic consolidation and, 106, 224n57; democratic transition and, 95–96; elite manipulation of myths/symbols and, 111, 116, 118–22, 179–80; myths/symbols and, 108, 113, 123–25, 166–67, 192–93, 201–2; optimal conditions for, 189; political culture and, 99–100, 103–4; rational choice theory and, 96–98; rituals and, 178–79; social capital theory and, 100–102, 103; and state legitimacy, 96, 222n5; symbolic politics and, 122–25. *See also* democratic transition

social conflict, 119–20

social councils, 47

social equity, democracy and, 7, 15, 206n48

socialist networks, 100–102

Socialist Revolutionaries, 139

social movement theory, 116–17, 121–22, 123, 226n128

social networks, 107

social partnership: media downplaying of, 57; and NGOs, 48–51, 53, 213–14n130; political function of, 59

Soldatova, Elena, 52, 212n107

Solidarity movement, 177

Soroka, Vladimir, 234nn20, 27

Sotnya (Novgorod city subdivision), 128

Soviet Union. *See* USSR

Spain, 59, 176–77, 224n57, 240n141

SPS. *See* Union of Right Forces

stability, 3, 20, 34, 214n148

stabilization fund, 29

Stadnistsky, Arseny (bishop of Novgorod), 177

Stalin, Joseph, 230–31n71

Staraya Russa, 35

starosty (village elders), 29
Stavrakis, Peter, 69
Stefan Batory (king of Poland), 173
Stepan, Alfred, 10, 15, 224n57
Stepanov, Tikhon (bishop of Arkhangelsk), 171
Stiglitz, Joseph, 182–83, 193
Stimorol (Danish company), 235n42
Stolypino, 168
Stolypin, Peter A., as symbol, 168–69
Stoner-Weiss, Kathryn, 73–74
Strigolnik heresy, 131
subsidiarity, 127, 206n60
subsidies, federal: and decline in FDI, 68; decreases in, 28, 38, 43–44, 70–71, 209n33; to media, 66; Novgorod vs. Pskov, 87, 88, 221n114
Suzdal, conflict with Novgorod, 132
Sverdlovsk, 62, 76; golden age of, 165
svodobodnye ekonomicheskie zony (free enterprise zone), 148–49
Sweden, 133, 145, 156, 173
Swidler, Ann, 115–16, 120, 187–88
Syktyvkar, 170
symbolic development, 187–89; cultural audit and, 191–93; democratic assistance programs and, 189–93; implementation of, 191; paradigm for, 196; in Russia, 197–201; training for, 193–97, 202
symbolic politics, 122–25
symbolic processing, 120
symbols. *See* myths/symbols

TACIS (EU democratic assistance program), 60
Talbott, Strobe, 182
Tallinn, 88
tariff system, five-tiered, 40
Tatarstan, 69–70, 76, 218n53
tax credits, 66
taxes, 33, 37
tax incentives, 35–36, 57, 210n61, 210–11n71
telecommunications, 153
television: censored in Pskov, 221n120; and media freedom, 66, 67; and neighboring regions, 166; and Novgorod Myth, 153–54; Orthodox Church and, 148. *See also* media
Teutonic Order, 174
Third Wave, 8
Third World development, failures of, 195–96
Toka, Gabor, 58, 60
Tomsk, 76, 185
Tomsk Initiative, 185–86, 198, 242n31
Torres i Bagès, Josep (bishop of Vic), 177

TOS (*territorialno obshchestevennoe samoupravlenie*; neighborhood associations), 26–27, 47
tourism, 153
town meetings, 29, 132–33
trait-taking vs. trait-making, 188–89
transitologists, 95–96
"Travels of Eugene Onegin, The" (Pushkin), 137
Treasury Department, U. S., 181–82, 188
Trilateral Accords, 59
Trilateral Commission, 30–31, 48
"Tsar Boris and the Fall of the Golden (Soviet) Horde" (Lisichkin), 142
TSZh (*tovarishchestvo sobstvennikov zhilya; housing fellowships*), 26–27
Tumanov, Vladislav, 83, 85–86, 88, 221n119
Tver region, 199
Two-Dimensional Man (Cohen), 158–59
tysiatski. See people's tribunes, in Novgorod history

Udmurtiya, 76
Ukraine, 105
Union of Industrialists and Employers, 30
Union of Pskov Electors, 87–88
Union of Right Forces (SPS), 185, 199
Union of Russian Cities of Northwest and Central Russia, 31–32, 166
United States, democratic assistance to Russia, 182. *See also* Regional Investment Initiative; Washington Consensus
United Worker's Front (UWF), 148, 233n7
USAID, 183. *See also* Regional Investment Initiative
Usatges (Catalan charter of liberties), 177
USSR: apathy as legacy of, 54; collapse of, 16–17; Novgorod Myth in, 139–40; opposition to symbolism of, 147–52; political culture in, 117; political/economic centralization in, 17; social capital theory applied to, 100; WWII industrial production, 182

Vadim of Novgorod (Knyazhnin), 136
Vadim the Brave (legendary figure), 135–36, 138
Valenzuela, Arturo, 12
value formation, 105
Vasilyev, Alexander, 31–32, 151
Veche (electoral coalition), 51, 87–88, 149
veche (medieval popular assembly): historical origins/functions of, 127–28; in Novgorod Myth, 138; Novgorod vs. Pskov, 172–73, 239n136; regional duma compared to, 157
Veche (newspaper), 147

veche bell: historical function of, 127; in Novgorod Myth, 134–35, 136–37, 138, 143

Vechevoi tsentr (periodical), 217n42

Venevitinov, Dimitri, 137

Venice, Novgorod linked to, 232n111

Verkhodanov, Igor, 209n38, 210n69, 212n111, 217n39, 235nn42, 51

village prose writers, 139

Vladimir (grand prince), 127

Vladimir Region, 167

Volga, Saratov as capital of, 168–69

Volgograd, 49

"Volkhov" (Lermontov), 137

Volkhov (newspaper), 66, 217n42

Vologda, 147–48

voluntary associations: as alternative to political parties, 59–61, 78; institutionalization of government relations with, 45–47; mature democracy and, 2, 22, 23; NGOs, social partnership and, 48–51; open doors policy and, 45–47; popular involvement in, 51–54; registration procedures for, 54; and social capital theory, 101–2, 103

Voronezh, golden age of, 165

voting patterns, Novgorod vs. Pskov, 82–85

Vremya-MN (newspaper), 67

Vremya Novgorodskoe (newspaper), 217n42

Vyatka, 127, 128

Wales, 176

Walesa, Lech, 9

Washington Consensus, 181–84, 190, 241n10

weaving tradition, 158

Weber, Max, 15

Western Europe, 65

Whitehead, Laurence, 20

Wildavksy, Aaron: and cultural analysis, 104, 106, 108; on cultural audit, 242n41; on plural rationalities, 222n17; and rational choice theory, 97; and regional development, 19

women, in business, 214n139

Women's Parliament, 51–52, 53

World Bank, 181–82

World War I, 138

World War II, 145, 182, 233n137

xenophobia, in Pskov Myth, 174–75, 238–39n128

Yabloko Party, 32, 34

Yakutiya, 69–70

Yanin, Valentin, 141, 142, 156

Yaroslavl, 167–68, 237n86, 237n90

Yeltsin, Boris: dominant role of, 76; Prusak and, 62, 77, 213n115; public support for, 210n58; and Russian authoritarianism, 68; and Russian Idea, 184; and Social Chamber, 46; soviets disbanded by, 29, 88, 150–51; transfer of Novgorod factory ownership, 86

Youth Parliament, 47

Yurga, 128

zemskaya izba (town meetings), 132–33

zemstvo, 154, 167

Zimine, Dimitri A., 70–71, 133

Zvezda (newspaper), 217n42